# WORKING CINEMA

**TOOTSIE** (U.S.A., 1982) DIRECTED BY SIDNEY POLLACK

# WORKING CINEMA
## Learning from the Masters

Roy Paul Madsen

Wadsworth Publishing Company
Belmont, California
A Division of Wadsworth, Inc.

*To The American Film Industry –
Creator of this nation's premiere
art form*

*Senior Editor: Rebecca Hayden*
*Production Editor: Leland Moss*
*Designer: Donna Davis*
*Makeup Artist: Cynthia Bassett*
*Permissions Editor: Bob Kauser*
*Print Buyer: Barbara Britton*
*Compositor: Thompson Type*
*Copy Editor: Jennifer Gordon*
*Editorial Assistant: Tamiko Verkler*
*Cover: Donna Davis*
*Signing Representative: Sue Lasbury*

Printed in the United States of America   85

1  2  3  4  5  6  7  8  9  10
94  93  92  91  90

**Library of Congress Cataloging-in-Publication Data**

Madsen, Roy P. (Roy Paul)
  Working cinema: learning from the masters/
  Roy Paul Madsen.
    p.   cm.
  Bibliography: p.
  Includes index.
  ISBN 0-534-11880-1
  1. Motion pictures.   I. Title.
PN1994.M3226   1990                 89-34502
086—dc20                            CIP

# CONTENTS

*Twelve*

# ANIMATION

*with Art Scott of Hanna-Barbera    350*

# PREFACE

*Working Cinema* may be the first book to be written almost entirely from within the big-budget Hollywood feature film industry—in all craft areas. It offers fresh information and insights to those who already "know it all" as well as instructing those who yearn to become part of that world. This work deals with creation, rather than criticism, written in association with those who are masters of the arts and crafts of making narrative motion pictures.

Each chapter presents the major aesthetic concerns within a given craft, written with the professional input and criticism of a luminary of the film industry—"The Player, with Paul Newman," "Cinematography, with Vilmos Zsigmond," "Comedy, with Jack Lemmon," "Visual Effects, with the Artists of Lucasfilm," to name only a few. Some contributors are stars, some are legendary within the industry, most have received Academy Awards or nominations, and all are masters of what they do.

I have synthesized their input with my own knowledge of production aesthetics to assure that each chapter may be read out of context and understood by people both in and out of the industry. Each working professional reviewed the completed chapter to make corrections and emendations to assure every nuance of authenticity. Many chapters were revised repeatedly until they met the exacting standards of the film industry.

In an overall sense, the chapters sequentially follow the general evolution of a feature film, enabling the reader to follow the conceptual and artistic processes involved. With the exception of the chapters on animation and visual effects, the book skirts the technical side of filmmaking to concentrate on purely cinematic aspects.

Contemporaneously, every chapter clearly presents the working relationship of each craftsperson to every other craftsperson in each succeeding phase of production so the reader may understand how the system works. There is a degree of overlap, as, for example: the producer, the director, the player, and the cinematographer present their points of view regarding who is responsible for doing what during principal cinematography. Sometimes professionals disagree on issues, but all are absolutely correct from the perspectives of their own crafts. All this should convey a between-the-lines sense of how films are made in the world of working cinema.

This work is written for all those who have a passionate interest in knowing how films are actually made in the American feature film industry. I owe much in the preparation of this manuscript to the rigorous editorial criticism of Richard M. Blumenberg, Lewis Jacobs, Arthur Knight, and Donald J. Zirpola. Chapters were added, deleted, and modified at their suggestion, and although I was not always euphoric about making the changes at the time, they were usually right. My thanks to these fine professionals.

R. P. M.

ix

# ABOUT THE AUTHOR

ROY PAUL MADSEN is a professor in Telecommunications and Film at San Diego State University. He has been a writer, director, editor, and animator in films for advertising and education. He has also produced and taught at Syracuse University and at the University of Southern California, where he received his doctorate.

His previous books include *Animated Film* and *The Impact of Film*. The latter was selected by the United States Information Agency as a "significant American book." This recognition led to a USIA-sponsored speaking tour for seven months, during which he lectured on six film topics in twenty-four countries in Europe, the Middle East, and Asia.

Madsen has served as a media expert for the United States Department of State, United States Information Agency, United States Department of Justice, United States Navy, and for nine District Attorney's Offices and many corporations. He has been listed in *Who's Who in the West*, the *Dictionary of International Biography* and *Contemporary Authors*.

A recognized artist, Madsen's work has been written about in *American Artist Magazine* and other publications. His spiritual home is the Sierra Nevada Mountains.

# ACKNOWLEDGMENTS

THE PROFESSIONALS WORKING in the American film industry have been truly kind and helpful in assisting me with interviews, illustrations, releases, and contracts during the writing of this book. Everywhere I turned, it seemed, there were friendly people and open doors and patience to a fault.

George Lucas is the most generous of men. He has my thanks for making available the resources of Lucasfilm and Industrial Light and Magic for several chapters in the book.

Many creative wizards at Industrial Light and Magic contributed their time, expertise, and careful criticism to the manuscript. These include Dennis Muren and Ken Ralston with their talented colleagues Craig Barron, Dave Carson, Michael Pangrazio, Nilo Rodis-Jamero, and Tom St. Amand. My thanks to Debbie Fine for her help in the matter of releases and illustrations.

Robert Watts, Vice President for European Productions at Lucasfilm, went far beyond his commitment to the chapter on The Producer to assist me in every way he could by obtaining needed materials and contacts for other chapters, and in proving himself a friend.

At Amblin Entertainment I wish to thank Steven Spielberg for his good will and cooperation in everything. Frank Marshall and Kathleen Kennedy were generous with their time and input, and careful in the perusal of content. I would like to thank Mary Radford for her help when it was most needed.

Paul Newman went to great pains to give careful insights into the role of The Player, and to great lengths to obtain illustrations and releases, for which I am grateful.

Jack Lemmon has my sincere thanks for drawing on his long experience in film comedy-drama to add what I could not otherwise know, and for his incisive but kindly criticism of the chapter on The Comedy.

Vilmos Zsigmond fitted me into the interstices of his busy schedule, took me onto the sets of principal cinematography, and made everything crystalline for the chapter on The Cinematographer, as well as obtaining stills that would otherwise be impossible to find.

I wish to thank Peter Zinner for working me into the tightest of schedules for the chapter on The Editor, and for his extraordinary dexterity in cutting a film while explaining the ramifications of his work.

Dean Tavoularis shared his remarkable career for the chapter on The Production Designer, and I appreciate the hospitality shown by him and his colleagues in Rome.

Francis Ford Coppola and John Peters, of Zoetrope Studio, have my sincere appreciation for their open-handedness in giving me whatever I needed, and for using their influence with others in the matter of releases.

I wish to thank Mark Rydell for his valuable additions and insights on the role of the film director.

Norman Corwin has my sincere appreciation for his contributions to the chapter on The Screenwriter.

Craig Noel was generous as always in taking time from The Old Globe Theatre to contribute to the chapter on Adaptation.

Walter Murch proved himself a friend as well as The Sound Designer in assisting me with illustrations, releases, and contacts with others.

At Hanna-Barbera, Art Scott, always

generous and cooperative, took time to explain the latest innovations in computer-assisted and computer-generated graphics and animation.

The people at the Margaret Herrick Library of the Academy of Motion Picture Arts and Sciences were unfailingly helpful.

Don Shay of *Cinefex Magazine* came through in the crunch with important and hard-to-get illustrations, and I appreciate his help.

Last to be singled out for thanks, but never less than primary in importance, is the work done by my wife, Barbara. Without her perseverance in locating actors in their peregrinations from agency to agency, diligence in running down picture copyrights in the wake of repeated turnovers and takeovers, and gentle persistence in doing everything logistical that needed to be done, the business aspects of this book could not have been accomplished. Moreover, I wish to thank the artist in her for having done those fine line drawings, and for her editorial insights.

I should like to thank the distinguished actors who agreed to the use of their images in this book: Rudolfo Alejandre, Woody Allen, Bibi Andersson, Margaret Avery, Cathryn Balk for Fairuza Balk, Joe E. Barton, Warren Beatty, Robby Benson, Humphrey Bogart Estate, Charlotte Eagle for Marlon Brando, James Caan, Nicholas Cage, Karen Carlson, John Carradine, Sr., Cher, Julie Christie, Mary Cobb for Lee J. Cobb, Dabney Coleman, Tom Cruise, Tony Curtis, Jane Darwell Estate, Ruby Dee, Robert De Niro, Kirk Douglas, Melvyn Douglas, Jane Fonda, Shirlee Fonda for Henry Fonda, Harrison Ford, Teri Garr, Chief Dan George Estate, Danny Glover, Mel Gibson, Whoopi Goldberg, Barbara Grant for Cary Grant, Sir Alec Guinness, Zaide Silvia Gutierrez, Gene Hackman, Mark Hamill, Daryl Hannah, Michele Henry for Justin Henry, Audrey Hepburn, Katharine Hepburn, Dustin Hoffman, Berdee S. Holt for Tim Holt, Bob Hoskins, Katharine Houghton, Jeremy Irons, Desreta Jackson, Raul Julia, George Kennedy, Kevin Kline, Jessica Lange, Vivien Leigh Estate, Jerry Lewis, Christopher Lloyd, Sophia Loren, Karl Malden, Sean Marshall, Marx Brothers Estate, James Mason Estate, Marsha Mason, Mary Elizabeth Mastrantonio, Walter Matthau, Steve McQueen Estate, Bette Midler, Sal Mineo Estate, Marilyn Monroe Estate, Jack Nicholson, Matt Ogden, Edward James Olmos for Micos Olmos, Lupe Ontiveros, Gregory Peck, Sidney Poitier, Willard Pugh, Randy Quaid, Jessica Rains for Claude Rains, Robert Redford, Eva Marie Saint, John Savage, Michael Sarrazin, Hanna Schygulla, George C. Scott, Wallace Shawn, Talia Shire, Russell Simpson Estate, Sissy Spacek, Kim Stanley, Jimmy Stewart, Eric Stoltz, Rod Steiger, Meryl Streep, Susie Tracy for Spencer Tracy, Liv Ullman, David Villalpando, Jon Voight, David Warner, Ruth Warrick, Orson Welles Estate, O. Z. Whitehead, Oprah Winfrey, Debra Winger, Joanne Woodward, Morgan Woodward, Susannah York, David F. Zarella, and Laura Zimmett.

I should also like to thank those I was unable to locate, despite exhaustive efforts, to obtain written permission: Isabelle Adjani, Doris Bowden, Malick Bowens, Rupert Crosse, Frank Darien, Peter Nicole, John Qualen, Shane Serwin, and Eddie Waller. My thanks also to the two teenagers that appeared in the dance scene of *American Graffiti*, who could not be identified.

I should like to thank the many talent representatives, attorneys, and other executives who took time from their busy schedules to assist me in obtaining the necessary information, illustrations, and permissions: *Abrams Artists Associates; ABC Press Relations; Academy of Motion*

*Picture Arts and Sciences*: all those in the Margaret Herrick Library; *Almi Pictures*: Morris Goldschlager; *Amblin Entertainment*: Julie Moskowitz and Kate Barker; *American Broadcasting Company*: Gloria Nappi; *American International Pictures*: Ralph Bakshi; *Armstrong, Hirsch and Levine*: Geoffrey W. Oblath, Barry Tyerman; *The Artists Group; Associated Talent International*: Rob Kenneally; *AVCO Embassy*: Ed Russell; *Larry Bloom Associates*: Larry Bloom; *Bresler Kelley Associates*: Sandy Bresler; *Brillstein Company*: Gigi Givertz; *Chasin-Park-Citron Agency*: Herman Citron; *Charter Management; Cinefex Magazine*: Don Shay; *Creative Artists Agency*: Martin Baum, Marcia Franklin, Robert Hoffman, Bryan Lourd, Ron Meyer, Catherine Olim, Nick Ricita, Mike Ovitz, Fred Specktor; *Cinecom International*: Ira Deutchman; *Curtis Management Group*: Stephanie Johnson; *Richard Donner Productions*: Terry Depaolo; *David, Hunter, Kimble, Parseghian, Rifken, Inc.*: Arlene Dayton; *Elstree Studios*: Norman Reynolds; *Film Artists Associates*: Richard Heckenkamp; *Forbes and Roth*: John B. Forbes, Bill Sammeth; *The Gersh Agency*: Rebecca Diamond, Bob Gersh, Bernard and Suzanne Larx; *Harry Gold Talent Agency; Gores Field Agency*: Dee Dee Davidson; *Greg Garrison Productions, Inc.*: Greg Garrison; *Harbottle and Lewis, Solicitors; Harris and Goldberg; Janus Films*: Judith Schram, Jonathan B. Turell; *Encore*: James Beaton, Gregory Nava, Anna Thomas; Glen Shimada; *The Greenvine Agency; Guttman and Pam; Hanna-Barbera Productions*: Ginger Otto; Helen Mueller; *International Creative Management*: Sam Cohn, Joe Funicello, Ed Limato, Pat Lynch, Victoria Traube; *Jack Rollins and Joffe*: Norma Lee Clark, Jack Rollins; *Jalem Productions*: Connie McCauley; *Jane Deacy*: Jane Deacy; *Janus Films*: Judith Schram; *Jerry Lewis Films, Inc.*: Jerry Lewis; *Jayne Development Corporation*: Jane Fonda, Debi Karolewski; *Joe Jordan Talent Agency*: Regina Berg; *Lantz Office*: Marion Rosenberg; *Lucasfilm*: Debbie Fine, Anita Gross, Karen Dube, Kerry Nordquist, Terri Tafreshi; *Merrill Lynch Pierce Fenner and Smith*: Patrick Curtis; *National Black Talent Directory*: Clarke Kevin; *National Film Board of Canada*: Ronald Jones; *New Yorker Films*: Suzanne Fedak; *North Texas State University*: Don Staples; *Old Globe Theatre*: Bill Eaton; *Olga Horstig-Primuz; Paul Kohner*: Paul Kohner; *Pierre Marmieusse Associates*: Pierre Marmieusse; *Pyramid Films and Video; PMK Management*: Pat Kingsley; *Robert Sandstrom Productions*: Robert and Karlene Sandstrom; *Robinson Madden Management*: Delores Robinson; *The Roger Richman Agency*: Roger Richman; *Romulus Films; San Diego State University*: Thomas Meador and Joe Renteria; *Screen Actors' Guild Beneficiary Department*: Beth Medway; *Security Pacific Trust; Smith-Gosnell*: Debbie Haeusler; *Susan Smith & Associates*: Philip Carlson; *Jay Stein, Attorney at Law; Svensk Filmindustri; The Taft Entertainment Company*: Sarah Baisley and John Michaeli; *Triad Artists*: Nicole David, Jeff Hunter, Susan Streitfeld; *Tucker, Morgan, Martindale; University of Southern California*: Dean Russell MacGregor; *University Film and Video Association*: Patricia Erens, Richard M. Blumenberg, Michael Selig; *William Morris Agency*: Alan Badiner, Brad Fuller, Lenny Hirshan, Joan Hyler, Tom Ilius, Ed Limato, Helene Shaw, Michael Zimring; *Wildwood Enterprises*: Robert Redford, Teresa Skinner.

I should like to acknowledge the good offices of those copyright holders who arranged to grant reproduction rights for this book: *Horizon Management, Inc.*: Albert Heit; *American Artists*: Frederick F. Roessler; *Canadian National Film Board*: Ronald Jones; *Capitol Cities: ABC, Inc.*: Karen Mohr; *CBS Theatrical Films*: Carol

Morgan; *Columbia Pictures Corporation*: Ivy Orta, Terry Saevig; *Cinecom International Films*: Gregory Nava, Anna Thomas; *De Laurentis Entertainment: Wade De Croce; Englander Communications Group*: Ira Englander; *Republic Pictures Corporation*: Stuart Kleiner; *Steve Krantz Productions*: Steve Krantz; *Lucasfilm, Ltd.*: Debbie Fine, Anita Gross; *MGM/UA*: Joan Pierce, Nancy S. Niederma; *Paramount Pictures Corporation*: Diane Isaacs, David Rosenbaum; *Turner Entertainment Co.*: Diane Brown; *20th Century Fox Film Corporation*: Shary Klamer; *Universal City Studios*: Nancy Cushing-Jones, Debra L. Summers; *Viacom Enterprises*: Lynn Fero; *Nepenthe Productions*: Martin Rosen; *Walt Disney Productions*: Myriam Estany, Helena Quiroz, Wayne Morris; *Warner Bros. Inc.*: Laura Gillen, Judith Singer; *Zoetrope Studios*: Jon Peters.

Among those I wish to thank for their help in research, and for other good offices, are Don Cary, Jan Caswell, Delsey Chenelle, Cheryl Harrington, Michael Kitchen, Marie Coons Lyons, Peggi Murray, Ted and Chris Pastras, Alex Tavoularis, Gerry Williams, and Stephanie Zinner.

It does not seem possible that I could have missed anyone, but if I did, please accept my regrets and know that I appreciate your contribution.

Roy Madsen

*"There is only one reason for a screenplay to be written or an actor to play a role or a director to direct a film: to move the emotions of an audience."*

JACK LEMMON

*Robert Watts, a line producer of feature films, adds his knowledge and expertise to this chapter. Watts comes with a spectrum of credentials: production supervisor of* Star Wars; *associate producer of* The Empire Strikes Back *and* Raiders of the Lost Ark; *co-producer of* Return of the Jedi; *producer of* Indiana Jones and the Temple of Doom; *producer of* Who Framed Roger Rabbit, *and producer of* Indiana Jones *and the* Last Crusade. *He serves as Vice President for European Productions: Lucasfilm.*

NORMAN REYNOLDS, ELSTREE STUDIOS

# One

# THE PRODUCER

*with Robert Watts*

CERTAIN PRODUCTION ASPECTS OF cinema, and the context in which a film is conceived and developed, seriously affect the creative, interpretive, and artistic merits of what appears on the screen. By learning this process, we may better understand how and why film takes form today (Figure 1.1).

## Studios: Then and Now

Filmmaking in America has changed since the halcyon days of the great studios when everyone associated with production was part of a vast factory system that controlled film development from script to screen to distribution. The old reservoir of talent maintained by the studio factory system—writers, directors, producers, cinematographers, actors, all under contract and subject to assignment—has given way to a network of freelancing: Each form of talent is hired for the production of a given film and released afterward. In the glory days the best interests of the studio were generally given higher consideration than any film produced within it. Now, with independent productions the rule rather than the exception, producing a successful film usually is the primary concern.

Moreover, where high-handed studio executives often abused their power over contract-bound producers and other talent, the situation of control is now reversed. An independent producer who develops a viable film package can take it to any of several studios for financing and rental of facilities, and a studio that alienates a producer with a successful track record may find that producer moving elsewhere to produce those box office revenues.

Has the studio then abandoned its original creative function? In part, yes, because today's projects are seldom initiated within the studios but are brought to them by agents, directors, and producers. Nevertheless, studio executives have creative input from the earliest submission of an idea through the screening of unedited footage to the final composite form of the film. Ideally, responsible producers and directors seek out the opinions of respected studio executives at every phase of production; these executives of course have the obligation to protect the studio's vital interests. If a director brings in a film that is a tedious four-and-a-half hours long because he or she cannot bear to give up another precious frame of film, the studio executive not only has the creative option but also the responsibility to insist that the film be edited to a marketable length. The studio's power to exert its will upon the director through the producer is essentially the power it has always had: money.

## The Producers: Who's Who

To judge from the credits that roll across the screen before a film begins, the term *producer* apparently means all things to all people (Figure 1.2). We see such credits as "executive producer," "producer," "associate producer," "production manager," "produced in association with —" and "a film by —." It would be gratifying to assert that these terms each have specific meanings, but, like the word *love*, they tend to mean only what the spokesperson says they do. Although guild regulations

> "The job of everyone associated with a film production has only one primary function—to support the work of the director in telling a story—and all other considerations are subordinated to that end. And the line producer must see to it that every person, every set, every piece of equipment, every artifact, and every bit of costume is there in place to be used by the director when needed in every phase of production—within the framework of the budget."
> —*Robert Watts*

3

FIGURE 1.1   *Steven Spielberg (center), with Frank Marshall (left) and Kathleen Kennedy. Film history was made with the artistic and technical achievements engendered in the production of* Who Framed Roger Rabbit, *and with Robert Watts, these three served as producers of this innovative film. Frank Marshall said, "We had no previous knowledge to draw from because no one had ever attempted this before. For example, if a person walked from bright warm light into a dark shadow, a "Toon" would follow and maintain the same lighting characteristics. Shadows cast on the cartoon characters and by these characters into the live environment rooted the animated characters in each scene. We ended up with over 1,000 optical shots and over 10,000 elements. I am sure this is a Guinness world record. In general, we created new techniques to deal with each new problem as it occurred. I think we can all say that it was the greatest challenge we have ever faced on a movie and equally as satisfying."*

FIGURE 1.2 *Producing a feature film requires the closest possible teamwork. Here director Steven Spielberg (center) is discussing storyboards on location with his colleagues (left to right): David Tomblin, assistant director; Elliot Scott, production designer; Frank Marshall, executive co-producer; and Robert Watts, line producer.*

*"For me," Watts admits, "the worst moment comes about two months before production is actually underway. That's when I do a lot of soul searching and the same question recurs: 'Have I made all the right decisions?' After then the commitment has been made and it is a matter of seeing everything through."*

5

THE PRODUCERS: WHO'S WHO

stipulate meaningful credits in relation to screenwriters, directors, players, editors, and most others associated with production, the one professional purview for which there are no guild ground rules are credits for the producer. The term *producer* is not apocryphal, however; it is significant that the producer often has the power within limits to assign credits to others who work before and behind the camera in various aspects of production.

Robert Watts, a distinguished producer working in Britain and the United States, defines the roles and responsibilities of various grades of producers as follows.

The term *producer*, in the truest sense of the term, without adjectives, should mean the person who found the subject, commissioned the script, secured financing, picked the director, selected the cast, found the production crew, and logistically made the motion picture. Given the complexities of production of a modern feature film, however, the word *producer* has assumed such protean forms and functions as these: *executive producer, line producer, associate producer,* and *production support personnel.*

### Executive Producer

Watts explained, the executive producer is frequently the person who obtained one or more elements of the components necessary to begin the film: control of a literary property or screenplay; financing; the commitment of a bankable star. This person made the project possible and may subsequently have nothing to do with the production of the film, although the credits may read "presented by."

The executive producer may also be someone in a unique position who insisted upon arrogating the credit or giving the credit to someone else. It may be the talent representative who provided the star and who did little more than sign a check. Or it may be the person who brought the property to the company and insisted upon the credit as a condition of sale. Or it may be the magnetic investor, known to have a Midas touch, whose presence as executive producer persuaded others to invest in the motion picture.

### Line Producer

The term *line producer* is generally given to the actual producer of the film, although the word *line* has only recently appeared in the credits. The line producer is the overall manager of the filmmaking process who arranges to have every element of production in place and ready for cinematography when the director and

FIGURE 1.3 *Location cinematography requires that the producer have crew and cameras in place when needed by the director, as in this setup with cinematographers Tim Wade (left) and Glen Shimada.*

players appear on the set (Figure 1.3). He or she is the boss of every logistical aspect of production that transforms words on paper to images and sounds on the screen; the line producer knows how a film is made and how to make the film. Moreover, this honcho supervises day-to-day production efforts to ensure that the film is on schedule and within budget; expedites whatever is needed for a given set and sequence on a given day; makes hard final decisions when the choice is between artistic effect and production costs; and mediates on those rare occasions when differences arise on the set.

Robert Watts observed, "The line producer does not normally come in at the beginning; somebody else—usually the executive producer—found the idea or subject, raised the money, commissioned the script, and then hired the line producer to implement the production. The executive producer is the employer, the line producer the employee. There is frequent discrepancy between job titles held during production and jobs as credited, a reality that sometimes leads to negotiations and even arbitration. The line producer is, however, the senior production officer."

He continued, "Reputation is the basis for selecting a line producer: experience and success in realizing films of varying degrees of difficulty on schedule, within budget, with good box office appeal. Someone who garners production experience may climb from one rank to the next until reaching the capacity of producer.

"Because line producers are no longer employees of a studio but are retained to do specific films, they have become a handsomely paid group of migrant workers who follow the crop of film projects as they ripen from one studio to the next. Producers often surround themselves with

a retinue of skilled technicians and professionals who, because they are employed repeatedly by the same person, tend to be loyal to the line producer and to the film being produced, as well as to the director and the studio. This system offers stable continuing relationships with professionals who not only know filmmaking but also have become an organic cooperative unit."

### Associate Producer

Watts said, "The term *associate producer*, another thing altogether, goes along with the little known title 'associate director.' In the early days of filmmaking some directors were also the film's producers, but because their directorial responsibilities were so demanding, they were not able to perform all of the functions of the producer. Hence, an associate producer was brought in to assist. (It is difficult for one individual to be truly a director while wearing two hats, although the two tend to complement each other.)

"The meaning of the term *associate producer* has since become diluted. 'Associate producer' has become a courtesy title given for special reasons: A writer may receive it because it was part of the deal that he or she should receive an associate producer's credit. An editor may receive it for having performed miracles with the film footage. 'Associate producer' may also be a title assumed by an officer other than the president or CEO of the production legal entity (the studio or film production company). An apprentice producer gaining experience on the job may receive credit for work done in the original sense of the term. And other technical grades may receive it for special services rendered."

Some associate producers, however, are necessary and functional in the implemen-

FIGURE 1.4 *Director Steven Spielberg is making on-the-spot creative decisions to be implemented by associate producer Kathleen Kennedy (left), line producer Robert Watts (second from right), and first assistant director David Tomblin (right). Watts observes, "If there are any additional unanticipated expenses associated with changes, it is the job of the line producer to find the needed funds in some account where reduction will not affect the quality of the film."*

tation of a motion picture (Figure 1.4). In those films with many visual effects, for example, or miniatures that need to be matched to live-action footage during principal cinematography, the liaison work done by the associate producer may be vital to the success of the film. The credit of associate producer is no longer simply a courtesy title but one that is fully earned.

According to Kathleen Kennedy of Amblin Entertainment, all aspects of the role of associate producer are defined in form and function by the characteristics of the film being produced. She defines the position as the expediter for the line producer, as the person who sees to it that principal cinematography does not bog down in a problem somewhere, and as the person who deals with others in a cooperative spirit but gets things done. Common sense is a vital element. Her solid performance in dealing with special effects for *Raiders of the Lost Ark* (Figure 1.5), in collaboration with Frank Marshall and Robert Watts, brought her the role of producer for Steven Spielberg's film *E.T. The Extra-Terrestrial*.

### Production Support Personnel

Robert Watts defined various production support personnel:

The *production manager* works under the line producer and is delegated to carry

FIGURE 1.5 *Visual effects are a major concern of the line producer and associate producer when making a fantasy adventure film. Here the giant boulder hurtling toward Harrison Ford is an illusion created in two parts—the* *actor running on a set, and a boulder tumbling toward the camera—with the images optically printed together to create a drama of excitement and danger for the entertainment of the viewer.*

**RAIDERS OF THE LOST ARK** (U.S.A., 1981) DIRECTED BY STEVEN SPIELBERG.

out whatever tasks the producer assigns. Sometimes a studio executive production manager, not part of the crew, acts as liaison with the studio during principal cinematography. The titles "production manager" and "line producer" may be switched in the line of command, or titles are modified to meet the managerial requirements of a particular film production.

The *production accountant*, who often receives friendly visits from the line producer and the studio production manager, records every dollar spent on a daily basis. Given the rapid expenditure of funds during principal cinematography, there is a premium on keeping records current with production, and on projecting the completion costs of the film.

The *production assistants* are primarily "go-fors" whose essential function is to get something needed for production that was overlooked in planning. A production assistant may serve secretarial functions and be the telephone contact with the world when shooting on remote locations.

## Origins of a Film

Robert Watts adds the insight born of experience to the following discussion of the evolution of a film idea. The beginning may come from any of several sources. A recognized director or producer may be the initiator of a film. A novel picked off a bookrack, an event in the news, or a suggestion by an agent may trigger the creative process and lead to the purchase of an option from the author and the commissioning of a writer to develop a treatment or screenplay for submission to the studios.

The agent, who has been the traditional representative of talent in most of its forms, has served two essential functions for the industry: (1) to find talented writers, players, directors, and producers and to submit them for consideration to the studios; (2) to screen out the untalented and unwanted who lack ability—or who write scripts with blunt crayons on brown wrapping paper.

The agent of today is, however, far more than the representative of a given writer or player. The agent is now often a kind of executive producer who packages several creative elements and submits them as a unit to a studio or a group of investors for funding consideration. These elements may include, for example, a script, a star, and a director to be considered as a film project entity. If the studio, or some other group of investors, considers the story, the talent, and the director a viable commercial project, it may invest in the film; the agent then draws his or her commission from all three.

Studio literary departments are the second line of defense against bad scripts and unpromising ideas. Agents submit their properties or packages to literary departments for consideration by studio readers who do nothing but scan new materials for promising film projects and pass them along in synopsis form to the head of the studio literary department. If the concept seems viable to the department head, it is then passed on to the vice presidents of the studio.

Agents also submit their properties to private production companies that are contracted to a studio. Private production or development companies not connected to a studio may also have significant financing as well as packaging capabilities. Financing feature films has changed in many respects in recent years as a consequence of networking among companies and companies' connections to banks or producers who finance feature films.

The studio vice presidents who review worthy projects consist of the vice presi-

FIGURE 1.6 *Harrison Ford (right) takes time out with Frank Marshall (far left), Kathleen Kennedy (second from left), and Robert Watts (second from right) during the shooting of the famous swordsman scene from* Raiders of the Lost Ark.

dent of production, the vice president of marketing, and every other vice president concerned with the commercial success or failure of a film. Of all the opinions, two vice presidents wield the greatest influence: the head of production who views the proposal in terms of its story, budget, and production values; and the head of marketing who views it in terms of its demographic appeal. An industry axiom states, "If you don't get the under-thirty crowd, the film may be at financial risk."

A film will receive quickest consideration if it comes from an agent known to have good judgment or is submitted by a line producer with a successful track record. The more prestige or clout an agent or a producer has, the higher up the studio chain the project may enter the review process. Those having the highest levels of prestige may bypass the studio literary department and submit an idea to a vice president or even to the president (Figure 1.6).

The studio president is the top of the line. This exalted figure will give a project the most careful consideration in every dimension before saying yes or no. With a film involving high-priced talent or expensive visual effects, the president will request a careful budget and consider the projected target audience thoroughly to be reasonably sure the film will turn a profit. *Reasonably sure* is a meaningful term because it is a truism of the industry that nobody really knows what makes a hit film. *Rocky* was turned down for years because conventional wisdom held that the public was not interested in sports films. That kind of biased mentality still affects decision making at the highest level.

Status is an important passkey to opportunity in the movie industry. In Europe, if a person creates a single important film, book, stage play, or musical composition, that artist is thereafter addressed as *maître* or master. However, a person's status in the United States is dependent upon recent successes. Two or three flops may terminate a career, and the declining artist may encounter treatment more appropriate to a bum than to a master. American filmmakers sometimes have a hard row to hoe in their lifetime careers.

## The Budget

Money is the lifeblood of the enormously expensive art form of motion pictures. Many a brilliant script has been regretfully stored in a filing cabinet because of the consensus that it would cost too much to produce.

A total film budget is often referred to as its *negative cost*—the de facto cost of all elements required to produce a motion picture up to the stage when the negative is complete and ready to reproduce as a print for distribution. The negative cost of

FIGURE 1.7 *"For a film as complex as* Return of the Jedi," *George Lucas says, "one hundred thousand dollars a day is standing-still money."*

*Co-producer Robert Watts observes, "*Star Wars *had a reasonable quota of monsters;* Empire, *less so. This film is* the *monster movie. They are terribly difficult because you are breaking ground each time on each new creature. You never know when they are going to be ready—and if they are ready, will they work?"*

feature films may vary enormously—from a low-budget movie priced under a million dollars to one requiring over fifty million dollars—for movies of approximately the same length. The reasons for the disparity derive from the reality that each film is unique in its requirements; no two films are exactly alike. To dig deeper, the mercurial differences in cost relate primarily to what are *above-the-line* costs and *below-the-line* costs, industry jargon that translates essentially as follows:

*Above-the-line* costs relate to those creative aspects of filmmaking that are subject to negotiations: buying the option for a novel; writing the screenplay; signing the stars for the lead roles; the fee of a good director; the fee and percentage of a skilled line producer; the price of visual effects. All of these are highly variable expenses subject to negotiations with the creative people involved.

*Below-the-line* costs relate to known quantities of physical production: salaries of union crews; cost of film stock and processing; price of building sets and props; employment of large numbers of players and extras; and such mundane services as the cost of electricity, plumbing, and janitorial functions. These below-the-line costs are carefully collated by the heads of various studio departments, people with experience in analyzing cost factors.

A thorough budget estimate is then prepared. The production accountant assembles the finalized costs with estimates submitted by the studio departments of cinematography, set and prop construction, visual effects, electrical engineering, post-production, and so forth. Each department head reads the script and turns in an estimate of what it will cost to produce the film within that purview of expertise. If an expert is unavailable in a given area, an estimate will be obtained elsewhere. The assembled final budget is then sent by the head of operations to the president—usually before a project receives approval for production.

When the estimated budget is completed, it is reviewed by the president of the studio (and by the key investors) for a final decision. Many a film has died aborning because the costs above and below the line were higher than could be risked with the given target audience. Sometimes a sleeper—a low-budget film that makes enormous sums of money—comes along, such as *Rocky*. Sometimes a film that seemingly has everything going for it—stars, story, extravagant production values—bombs, such as *Heaven's Gate*. The potential returns are so lucrative, however, that plenty of high rollers are always willing to risk money on a promising film project.

The initial budgets are subject to pruning sessions in which the studio executives and the line producer try to persuade the director that a cast of hundreds may be as convincing as a cast of thousands if cleverly photographed. The writer may be asked to eliminate costly dramatic sequences that are not critical to the story. Or perhaps the shooting schedule may be reduced by a few days, with fewer expensive sets and locations. The final budget must be balanced against projected revenues, or the studio will walk away from financing the film. Once the final budget has been hammered out, it is eventually signed by a representative of the studio, the director, and the producer; this prevents later nonsense about a mistaken impression that millions more were available to produce the film.

Financing is a contemporaneous concern. Funding to produce feature films comes essentially from three sources: banks, outside groups of investors, and the revenues accrued by the studio in the production of previous films. The larger the budget of the film, the greater the likelihood that the risk will be spread out by drawing funds from many sources. Once

**RETURN OF THE JEDI** (U.S.A., 1983) DIRECTED BY RICHARD MARQUAND.

funding is assured, the line producer begins to logistically produce the film under the eagle eye of the studio production manager, who is in turn watched by the president, who is similarly answerable to the investors. After a commitment has been made in terms of financing and talent, a film may then be given the green light (Figure 1.7).

## Making the Film

Film production falls into three major phases: *pre-production planning*, *principal cinematography*, and *post-production*. (Post-production will be addressed in Chapters 9 and 10.) Although this chapter deals primarily with the work of the line producer, who runs the logistical show for the duration of production, remember that the dominant force in creative decision making in every phase of production is the will of the director.

### Pre-Production Planning

The writer is of course the first to state the concept of the motion picture. *Writer* should be stated in plural, however, because more often than not the single writer's name credited on the screen may be only the last of many to labor over the

13

script. There is often a series of writers on a given film, with the brains of each carefully picked before finalizing a script that may itself be changed during principal cinematography or in editing. Screen credit for the story usually goes to the first writer, and credit for the screenplay goes to the last.

The production designer, in conjunction with other members of the production department, then searches for locations for principal cinematography. After absorbing a visual sense of the locations, the designer imagines the look of the film in paintings and drawings that correspond to the vision of the director. Once approved, sets are made and the costume designer begins work to dress the cast.

The assistant director then breaks down the script and groups those scenes and sequences to be photographed at each location. Films are not produced in the chronological order in which we see them on the screen; all the scenes from a given location are filmed at the same time for logistical convenience and financial advantage, regardless of where they are edited to appear in the final form of the film.

Meanwhile, the director takes the script and casts the lead parts, sets the visual style, plans the camera positions in collaboration with the cinematographer, blocks the movements and dramatic actions of the talent, and rehearses the actors to tell the story. The director and the executive producer typically cast the stars and the supporting players, in conjunction with the casting director.

Other technicians are also engaged in the pre-production phase. Set designers take the drawings of the production designer and transmute them into working blueprints, which are then made tangible by carpenters, painters, and other artisans. The costume designer frequently works from the concepts of the art director to find or make costumes, sometimes from original designs, for the characters. The set decorator is responsible for securing items stipulated by the script: figurines, cocktail glasses, samovar and serving set, and so forth. The property master then sees to it that these items are present when needed for principal cinematography. The makeup and hairdressing technicians prepare the talent for their moments before the camera and stand ready to do frequent retouching jobs between the takes (Figure 1.8).

## Production

Watts said, "It all comes together now. The phase of principal cinematography brings the director, the talent, and the technicians together on the set, or the location, for the maximum effort required to render a story in images and sounds. The needs of the director and the cinematographer dominate at this time, assuming adequate rehearsal and preparation by the actors. The line producer is responsible for the presence of every person, set, and piece of equipment needed by the director."

The director has an entourage of support professionals and technicians during a shooting schedule that normally, for a feature film, lasts anywhere from ten to twenty-six weeks depending upon the scope of the production. The director's supporting team consists of the first and second assistant director, second unit director (if required), script supervisor, and dialogue coach.

The first assistant director can be thought of as a traffic director with the responsibilities of organizing and moving a cast of thousands (if needed) before the camera and ensuring that cast and crew are present where they are needed when they

FIGURE 1.8 *Worldwide adoration came to the most charming space alien ever to emerge from the outer reaches of a filmmaker's imagination and waddle across the screen, munching Reese's Pieces. This enormously successful film was administratively realized by producer Kathleen Kennedy under the creative direction of Steven Spielberg.*

**ET—THE EXTRA-TERRESTRIAL** (U.S.A., 1982) DIRECTED BY STEVEN SPIELBERG.

FIGURE 1.9 *Steven Spielberg and Whoopi Goldberg (the character Celie) are working on The Color Purple. Spielberg remarks, "The Color Purple was a departure for me in that it deals with emotional crisis and tremendous emotional growth, spanning almost forty years, in the lives of eight characters. But I was really drawn to the heroic growth of the central character Celie as she goes from being a contemporary slave in the twentieth century to being a complete—and a completed—person. I want the audience to feel every color in the rainbow," he adds, "the rainbow she makes for herself and dives into headfirst."*

**THE COLOR PURPLE** (U.S.A., 1985) DIRECTED BY STEVEN SPIELBERG.

are needed (Figure 1.9). The second assistant director is the liaison between the first assistant director and the cast, and manages having them present when needed.

The second unit director, if required, heads up the filming crews responsible for photographing special sequences that can be separated in time and location from the main dramatic event. This often involves action sequences photographed before principal cinematography so that footage of the players may be edited into a dramatic sequence rendered later—for instance, staging and filming stunts, battle scenes, or events occurring at a distant location, often using stunt doubles.

The script supervisor stands next to the director during the shooting of every scene, noting on the script everything that has been photographed: dramatic actions, dialogue, camera angles and movements, positions of actors, locations of props—all so that an actor in the edited film will not enter a building wearing a striped tie and sit down in the office with a spotted tie. The script supervisor is the reference person from one take to the next. The dialogue coach, if required, works with players to articulate clear diction and to refine dialects.

Cinematography is the responsibility of the director of photography (D.P.) in association with a group of technicians and support personnel, and this includes lighting. The D.P. directs the *gaffer*, who sets up the lights where indicated to render the subject's forms, masses, lines, and colors on film. The gaffer in turn is assisted in illumination by the *best boy*, followed by an electrician who moves the lamps, trims the arc lights, and maintains the electrical power. Knowing how to light a set to enhance the mood as well as render the subject is analogous to knowing the ropes on a sailing ship: Beautiful things happen when the action begins.

The camera operator, the manual cinematographer, peers through the viewfinder and photographs the images and movements the director and director of photography have asked for. Although union rules specifically forbid directors of photography from operating the camera, some D.P.'s occasionally take control for mobile shots requiring special sensitivity.

The sound crew may consist of the sound recordist (and sometimes an assistant sound recordist), the boom and microphone operator, and the sound designer. The *grips* are responsible for moving things about from scene to scene and for building structures and tracks (on location), and for emplacements of camera and sound recording equipment.

## Post-Production

After cinematography has been finished, the sound recorded, and the quality of both approved following screenings in the projection room, film editors, music composers, and sound mixers complete the movie; then the film laboratory will print the film for final distribution.

The editor assembles the picture and sound tracks into a coherent story. The editor may follow the script or the dictates of a director in recounting the film story; or, if trusted as someone creative in the language of cinema, the editor may interpret characters and story by manipulating who and what are shown and heard. The editor creates only by permission, however, and not by right. His or her version may be superseded by the director's vision, who may in turn be overruled by the studio (Figure 1.10).

Music is thematically sketched by the composer once the cut is locked. After the

**THE COLOR PURPLE** DIRECTED BY STEVEN SPIELBERG.

FIGURE 1.10  *Whoopi Goldberg made her film debut starring as Celie, whose loving spirit and unshakable bond with her sister sustain her through hardships and mistreatment by Mister, the man to whom she has been given as wife and slave. Although the film deals with great brutality, it is a motion picture of enormous beauty and power.*

film is edited, each scene is timed and the music is composed and played to complement the visuals on the screen.

Sound mixers work in rerecording studios to synthesize all the recorded sound tracks into a single sound track. Dialogue, narration, music, and sound effects are synchronized with the edited pictorial footage into a single sound track and given the optimum volume, balance, and timbre. The composite sound track will be transmuted to the release prints sent out for distribution.

At the film laboratories the negatives are cut into continuity order and used to make prints of the film. The director and cinematographer make many artistic decisions at this stage, such as altering colors, creating optical effects, and so forth. Once a trial composite print is aesthetically and technically satisfactory, release prints are made for distribution.

## A Producer: A Production

The line producer is actively involved in nearly every aspect of every phase of pre-production, production, and post-production of a film. Robert Watts gives us an illuminating account of the problems faced and resolved by him as the line producer of a major feature film.

*Indiana Jones and the Temple of Doom* is an action film that simulates the adventure genres of the 1930s; these films often placed dashing heroes in dire straits in exotic faraway lands. Indiana Jones's adventures take him from Shanghai to India, where fictional cultists tear out human hearts, lower captives into boiling oil, turn people into zombies, and try zealously to do the same to Indiana Jones and the heroine. After his abrupt arrival in India, Jones is taken to a village that has fallen on hard times since the theft of its

sacred stone. Good times cannot return to the impoverished villagers until Indiana Jones terminates the fiendish cultists and returns the stone. This light-hearted entertainment required high cinematic standards to make the fantasy credible within the premises of the film. However action-oriented the content, making this film was serious business with great logistical problems and difficult visual effects.

This film production required principal cinematography on three continents, interior sets on sound stages, and a broad range of visual effects. Many of the major problems that may beset a line producer, including injury to a lead actor, were encountered and then resolved during this production.

Watts begins the production of a feature film by breaking down the script according to location and production needs (normally the responsibility of the assistant director) so that every detail of production requirements will be fixed in his memory. Each film is unique in its needs and demands made by the story. Set and location requirements are noted immediately, travel plans are made to possible locations to determine suitability, and set construction arrangements are made for interior scenes to be photographed on rented sound stages. Whatever requires lead time for creation is initiated first so that everything will be completed and in place at the time of principal cinematography.

Because the script indicated that the story would begin in Shanghai and end in India, the producer decided to deal first with overseas locations that would meet the settings requirements of the film. Locations are sought out before interior set production is begun because the locale often reveals something not previously anticipated, something that is of intrinsic interest for inclusion in the film. The interior sets subsequently produced may thereby include color and content elements of whatever was found on location. Seeing the location first also provides insights into light qualities and weather conditions for matching interior scenes with exterior scenes. Moreover, a setting may be found that is ideal for filming a scene originally intended to be photographed in the studio. If done on location, the cost of constructing a set is saved.

Before going abroad to search for locations, it was necessary to determine where to build the interior sets. Shopping for sound stages is a spot market effort involving currently available considerations of access, cost, and competent personnel. A series of calls to the studios around Los Angeles revealed that so many sound stages were committed to television series and feature films that there were not enough sound stages available to accommodate all the sets required for *Indiana Jones*. A telephone call to Elstree Studios in London confirmed that the required sound stages were available there during the needed parameter of time. Moreover, the British pound sterling had dipped in value and the dollar had soared, making set construction somewhat less expensive in Britain.

Finding the best locale for the Shanghai and India sequences was the first concern. Watts therefore approached, in turn, the governments of the People's Republic of China and India. After an initial meeting with the Chinese, it was decided that six days of cinematography was not worth the paperwork and time required for permission to shoot in that country.

The producer decided to consider Hong Kong as a credible alternative with a Chinese context. He found that city supporting an active motion picture industry with good equipment and qualified technicians. Watts then searched for a nearby setting to simulate Shanghai with suitable streets for the chase sequences. This he found in Macao, less than an hour away from Hong Kong by hydrofoil. By employing local film technicians and sending only key personnel to Macao for cinematography, the producer thereby saved the cost of transporting a full U.S. production crew to that location. Moreover, the local crew, accustomed to working in that area, was able to give assistance in finding settings, set items, and extras. And, because Macao is a free enterprise zone, permits were readily obtained.

The locations of the Shanghai sequences confirmed, Watts then turned to India. Watts submitted his script to the Indian government officials, who require government approval (and censorship) of any film production being photographed in that nation. His request made, he began to travel throughout India to find locations for this film. The Amber Palace in Jaipur was ideal for exterior palace sequences. What he also realized, however, was that the locations were extremely far apart and would engender enormous costs in transporting cast, crew, and equipment from place to place, with much expensive time invested in setting things up and tearing them down. Logistically, India would be a cost-exorbitant nightmare for location principal cinematography. The bureaucracy of India—by generating a morass of red tape, requiring many changes in the script, and even proscribing the producers from using the word *maharajah* in the motion picture—simplified an economically motivated decision to look elsewhere.

In exasperation the line producer called executive producer George Lucas for permission to change the scripted locations. Lucas had always believed that fantasy films need setting authenticity to hold them on the ground (this portion of the film had an Indian context and would need credible locations). Watts suggested that India be dumped entirely and that they instead attempt to simulate Indian culture at another location. Lucas agreed, but insisted that cultural authenticity was critical. Watts then flew down to Sri Lanka, a culturally akin island nation off the southern tip of India. There he found everything needed to establish an Indian setting. The city of Kandy, capital of the ancient civilization of Sri Lanka, was filled with architectural splendors of the past, and the people closely resembled those of India. Moreover, everything needed for cinematography was within an hour's drive, with acceptable accommodations for cast and crew. The decision to use Sri Lanka instead of India thereby saved a great deal of money and expedited production. Photographs were taken at all locations in Macao and Sri Lanka and sent to director Steven Spielberg, who subsequently flew over to see the settings for himself.

Two locale decisions remained unresolved: where to shoot the Shanghai airport (now out-of-bounds in China) and where to photograph the maharajah's palace, unavailable in Sri Lanka. On the principle that when you have seen one airport you have seen them all, they decided to use Hamilton Air Force Base in California and to paint some signs on the buildings that would make it resemble the Shanghai airport. The maharajah's palace was built on the back lot of Elstree Studios in London.

Once the locations had been determined and approved by the director, the line producer returned to Hong Kong, Macao, and Sri Lanka to hire personnel and arrange for local crews to work on constructing facilities needed for the intensive weeks of principal cinematography in each area. Key supervisory personnel were left behind in each location: set designers, construction foremen, and other technicians. The art department, con-struction crew, and visual effects artists referred to the photographs taken during the tour of India for constructing the village and the palace.

Now the momentum toward production began to build. Key technicians and crews were retained in advance so that their services would be available when required. Sound stages were booked for interior scenes. The costume designer began work. Miniature and optical technicians and cinematographers coordinated their efforts to match the coming footage created by principal cinematography. And large props needed for photography were shipped out to the locations in advance.

Watts then took a second unit director to Hong Kong, Macao, and Sri Lanka and mapped out the sequence of cinematography. Storyboards were revised, or in some instances, were created for the first time; they could then be drawn to suit the location. Instead of looking for overseas locations to match the storyboards, the storyboards were now drawn to match the overseas location. (Watts makes the point that when a screenwriter is engaged to write a script, it is a shame he or she cannot be taken along with the storyboard artist to all the locations before beginning to write so that the story may be told in the desired context.)

The next responsibility of the line producer was to put together a core production crew of technicians who could do the job and work well together. Both considerations are vital because the crew must function effectively as an organic unit under a wide variety of circumstances. A cinematographer who is excellent in studio situations or in comfortable domestic environments may be a poor sport when filming in the heat and humidity of the tropics. Willingness to cooperate is high on the scale of virtues when selecting a crew to make a film. In the end, the producer is no better than the professionals with whom the producer has chosen to work.

Casting was now underway and the casting director as well as the director were interviewing potential actors. This task proved difficult because it was a small cast with widely disparate characteristics. After the principal players had been selected by the director, the casting team searched for an American boy with Asian features, an Indian actor to play the high priest of the cult, and the hundreds of local Sri Lankans to play the roles of villagers and cultists. The final decision lay with the director, but the line producer had a share of input in the cast selection.

At this point all the technical people were coming to the line producer with their problems: The sets could not be built in time; they did not have the kind of equipment they needed to do this or that in Sri Lanka, and it would take three months to ship it there by sea; the weather experts were predicting an early monsoon, and so forth. "Somehow," Watts adds wryly, "we were always ready on time but I don't quite know how."

Now the line producer's support team were earning their money. The production manager, busily ordering and shipping every last item needed abroad, was left in London in charge of three hundred people building sets at Elstree Studios. The associate producer Kathleen Kennedy was in constant touch with both Sri Lanka and Industrial Light and Magic in California to be sure there would be a match between the footage obtained from principal cinematography and the visual effects. This she did in collaboration with the co-executive producer Frank Marshall. The paperwork required for an organization that now totaled four hundred people became enormous: paychecks, time cards, petty cash, rentals, transportation, purchases, licenses, insurance—all the headaches of running a great enterprise built in months from scratch.

Scheduling the times and places of principal cinematography was the next concern. A shooting schedule is based upon several things: the locations of the dramatic actions, the availability of those locations on the given shooting dates, the availability of the actors, the time required to build sets and ship expensive props to the required places, the vagaries of the weather, and so forth. The cinematography is planned carefully to complete the filming in the minimum number of days. But flexibility is important because everything is subordinate to the director's creative will, and changes, if necessary, should be made possible by the line producer. For overseas work in particular the production unit should be so designed that it can be moved anywhere and everywhere at minimum cost and maximum effectiveness.

In the instance of *Indiana Jones*, two classic automobiles had to be flown by private air cargo service to Macao for the chase sequences because there was not sufficient time to ship them out by sea. However, there was plenty of time to ship the cars by sea to California afterward for the conclusion of the same chase sequence to be photographed at "Shanghai Airport"— Hamilton Air Force Base.

Climate and geography play a role in scheduling an entire movie. When the locations are abroad in regions of climatic extremes (such as the tropics of Sri Lanka), the time of year for production becomes important. A person cannot conduct cinematography during monsoons or periods of enervating heat. In the case of *Indiana Jones*, the producer juggled the shooting schedule to conduct principal cinematography in the interstice between the minor spring monsoon and the major summer monsoon at a time when the heat was bearable for cast and crew.

The overall schedule is crucial because the parameter of time comprising principal cinematography is the most expensive and the most exciting in the production of a film. This is the period in which costs can escalate enormously, and the schedule must be tightly organized by the line producer to accomplish as much as can be physically done within the briefest possible period of time. *Indiana Jones* was scheduled for eighteen weeks of principal cinematography.

The overall schedule of production was planned as follows: (1) a second unit, with stunt doubles for the principal cast, first flew to Macao for principal photography of all the exteriors and the chase sequence for the Shanghai segment; (2) the main unit, later joined by the second unit team, traveled to Sri Lanka where the rest of the major cinematography for exteriors was completed; (3) everyone concerned moved to London where all the interior scenes were photographed on sound stages; and (4) everyone involved returned to California to Hamilton Air Force Base to photograph the conclusion of the Shanghai sequence photographed in Macao at the beginning. The final days of principal cinematography occurred at Lucasfilm where the visual effects cinematography took place with the actors.

When principal cinematography begins, part of the decision-making process involves selecting the order in which scenes and sequences will be photographed at a given location. Watts explained that the choice can make a significant difference in costs. For example, in *Indiana Jones* an Indian village was constructed that was seen twice in the movie. In the beginning the village—which had lost its sacred stone—

was viewed as dilapidated and run-down: The land was desiccated, the trees were barren of leaves, the people looked sickly and miserable, and the village was dying. At the end of the movie the villagers had recovered their sacred stone and with it everything else: The houses were in perfect condition, the people were happy, water was flowing, flowers were blooming, and trees were heavy with foliage. Therefore, a village had to look nasty at one time and nice at another, and the choice faced was: Which to do first?

The producer and the designer decided that it was easier and less expensive to make a nice village subsequently appear dilapidated than to make a ruined village look pristine. They chose to photograph the village in its happy state first, which meant shooting it on the first day of principal photography, even though in the completed film those scenes come at the end of the story.

Shooting the last scene first engendered other problems relating to the lead players. What would the actors look like by the story's end? The answer is that they would have been through every kind of ordeal and seem a walking shambles. At the end of the story Indiana Jones was to appear dirty and disheveled with cuts and bruises on his face. He therefore was made up to look that way in order to photograph him first in a dramatic sequence that came at the very end of the film.

Once this was done, it was necessary to ruin the village for the sequence to come at the very beginning of the Indian context of the movie. To give the art department time to devastate the village, the cast and crew then photographed all of the other locations scheduled for Sri Lanka. Once the village had been properly ruined—the trees stripped of leaves, the flowers uprooted, the people's clothing dirtied and torn—cast and crew returned to photograph the Indian sequence that falls near the beginning of the film in which Indiana Jones discovers the ruined village and the loss of the sacred stone. Therefore, for purely logistical and cost-effective reasons, the last sequence to appear in the film was photographed first.

Possible injury to an actor is a major concern during production. The filming in Macao and Sri Lanka occurred without mishap on locations where one might anticipate problems. Then, while shooting in London, an actor was injured and temporarily unable to continue. Inasmuch as all location cinematography had been completed at enormous cost, replacing him was out of the question. The film could not do without him, and while he recovered, production had to continue.

The line producer sat down with the schedule to see what could be done in the interim. Watts juggled sets and options to permit continued work for another three-and-a-half weeks while the actor recovered. The plan was taken to the director, who made some changes and then agreed to the partial solution. Everything that could be photographed without the player was filmed, and the scenes inescapably requiring this actor would be photographed later and integrated in editing.

Eventually the work ran out. The doctor attending the actor said that recovery would take another three weeks. Watts had to decide whether he should incur the enormous cost of keeping the cast and crew available on a standby basis or release them and possibly lose their services to others. The decision was made to shut down all production. Some people were therefore put on token retainers, others on half salary, and yet others returned to the United States to photograph second unit scenes. "You make the best accommodation you can," Watts comments, "because you do not want to lose the services of people who are ultimately needed for completion of the film. There is insurance taken to cover such exigencies, but the producer tries to act as if uninsured to minimize such use of insurance funds."

The actor then made a complete recovery and returned to the set. The film unit was activated once more, and the rest of the interior scenes were photographed in London during the following three weeks. The improvised plans proved successful because, although the player was unavailable for seven weeks, only five extra shooting days were required to complete principal cinematography.

Watts submits that when excessive costs are going to occur, or the line producer can perceive that they will inescapably occur, it is better to prepare the people up front at the outset rather than to spring it on them later. His policy is to state the worst possible scenario in advance and not mention those possible savings in other accounts that may be used to compensate for unexpected losses. Then he tries to save in ways that will still bring the film in on budget with optimum quality.

Financial problems sometimes arise as a consequence of the director's creative input during principal cinematography. The director may have had a set constructed to accommodate one hundred extras and, after seeing the set, decide that one hundred and fifty are needed for the five days of shooting. That increase of one third means two hundred and fifty working days of added personnel costs over the original budget, and it becomes the producer's responsibility to try to save the money elsewhere. He or she must then exercise judgment with regard to saving money and ultimate production values. Although it is not good to go a half million dollars over budget, neither is it good to come in a half million dollars under budget during the pressure-packed days of principal cinematography if the savings inflict damage on the ultimate quality of the film.

The line producer knows that there are no funds for those fifty people in the extras account, and so the producer may peruse the budget and try to find some other account that may be cut back without affecting the quality of the film, thereby making up the money to bring in the production within budget. As Watts explains, "It would be imprudent of me to tell a director that the film cannot afford those fifty extras and then come out a hundred thousand under budget to the detriment of the film. The director will then turn to me and ask, 'Why didn't you let me have those extras?'"

On the other hand, in some films, the director may ask the various department heads—set designers, cinematographers, visual effects experts—to do things the line producer knows very well there is no money for. That is not the technician's fault; these creative department heads obviously have rapport with the director and they want to help make the movie, but they must also be conscious of the budgets of their departments. The creative technician who has been asked for productions beyond the department's budget should go to the line producer and explain the situation. The producer's role then becomes that of mediator; he or she must go to the director and say, "This is too expensive. Do we really need it? Can we do it another way within budget?" In rare cases, the producer may be forced to draw the line and say, "I'm sorry, but we do *not* have the money for that effect."

Moreover, the line producer must be prepared to be critical of the work in progress. If the director is experienced but lacks empathy for the content, or is unable to evoke a performance from the talent in keeping with the spirit of the content, or is using camera movements as a substitute for ideas, or is not performing the director's function of getting the story on the screen in an involving way, it is the producer's responsibility to initiate action to replace the director by calling the executive producer, or the studio, or whoever engaged the line producer to say, "This director is not on top of the material." Then those in charge would come and look at the film footage, and if they agreed, they would replace the director. Watts hastens to add, "Nothing of the kind occurred during the production of *Indiana Jones and the Temple of Doom.*"

Visual effects cinematography frequently takes place concurrently with principal cinematography, and the resulting footage is intercut to be sure that the effects photography will convincingly match conventional cinematography in every respect. Everything is monitored at every level of production. The sound personnel channel all of the original dialogue, postsynchronous dialogue, and sound effects and plan for music.

"Once principal and visual effects cinematography have been completed, and all sound tracks recorded," Watts concludes, "it becomes the producer's final tasks to collaborate with the post-production experts in editing the rough and fine cuts of the film, adding music, postdubbing, and sound mixing. And finally, to shepherd the film through the laboratory and work with the cinematographer in grading the prints to arrive at the best photographic quality in the finished film."

And then the work is done. If the line producer has brought the film in on schedule, within budget, with production values as good as possible under the circumstances, the work will have been well done.

Watts observes, "Every decade in cinema produces a technical and aesthetic breakthrough: in the Forties it was *Fantasia*; in the Fifties it was Cinerama widescreen; in the Sixties it was *2001: A Space Odyssey*; in the Seventies it was *Star Wars*; and in the Eighties it was *Who Framed Roger Rabbit*. I feel very fortunate to have worked on the last three of these classics."

Watt's role as a contributor to the realization of *Who Framed Roger Rabbit* adds a fresh dimension to the complexities of being a line producer. He was an indirect catalyst for the film, having submitted another project by animator Richard Williams, first to Lucasfilm, then to Disney, and finally to Amblin Entertainment, where it was again declined. Steven Spielberg, however, took an interest in the extraordinary animation skill of Williams, and asked him to supervise the Amblin-Disney production of *Who Framed Roger Rabbit* with Robert Watts as line producer. The challenge was too much to pass up (Figure 1.11).

Robert Watts and Frank Marshall decided to do the line production work together. The worldwide experience of Watts and Marshall would now help them to integrate within a single film the animation created by Richard Williams in London, the visual effects achieved by Ken Ralston at Lucasfilm in San Francisco, and the live-action cinematography directed by Robert Zemeckis in Los Angeles.

The film is set in Los Angeles during the 1930s. The production team decided to build a red streetcar and install it on a street in downtown Los Angeles that had not changed significantly since the Thirties and had nothing structural in its background that was problematic.

Director Zemeckis decided against combining live action with animation in the traditional way—that is, with the camera locked down and the live-action subjects flat-lighted to complement the flat painting of conventional cartoon animation. Animator Williams agreed with Zemeckis that both live-action and cartoon characters should be modeled in-the-round with chiaroscuro lighting and insisted "We will make it work."

They made it work in this way. Zemeckis directed the live-action players, with the cartoon characters missing. Robotic arms, monofilament lines, and other mechanical devices were used to manipulate real objects—such as the baby's cigars and the weasels' guns. The photographed live action scenes were combined later with animation scenes yet to be done.

Then, each frame of live-action footage was enlarged to the size of an animator's field guide and punched to fit an animator's drawing disc. By superimposing a transparent material called a *cel*, the animators were thereby able to create cartoon characters having perfect eye contact with the actors. Equally important, they were able to model the animation in-the-round with values that matched the lighting values of the live-action footage. The animators even drew moving shadows for their cartoon characters. When the cartoons were printed together with the live-action players, the verisimilitude was astonishing.

Another dimension of this film's creation involved the Lucasfilm optical house, Industrial Light and Magic, which took what was basically two movies and put them together so the seams would not show. There were many more optical effects in *Who Framed Roger Rabbit* than in any motion picture ever done before—far more than in *Star Wars*. This required close communication along three sides of a long thin triangle, with Watts commuting almost continuously between London, Los Angeles, and San Francisco to coordinate this incredibly complex pro-

**WHO FRAMED ROGER RABBIT** (U.S.A., 1988) DIRECTED BY ROBERT ZEMECKIS.

FIGURE 1.11    *Robert Zemeckis says of making* Who Framed Roger Rabbit, *"It was what I had always dreamed of finding in a project. It was to be able to crack the nut of interaction and make me believe that the audience could be made to believe that cartoon characters and humans can coexist. Animated features always seem to be about fables and fairy stories. This was unique in its combination of genres— Looney Tunes and film noir."*

*Producer Robert Watts reminisced, "There were times during the production of* Who Framed Roger Rabbit *when I would stop and ask myself, 'Would I have let myself in for all this if I had known what I was in for?' The answer was always 'yes,' because producing this film has been the greatest challenge of my professional life—up until now."*

FIGURE 1.12 *Producers' reward. On the first day of principal cinematography, before the first setup, it is traditional to pop the corks and drink a champagne toast to the birth of a new film, as shared here by Frank Marshall and Robert Watts.*

duction. Watts gives high praise to Zemeckis for his direction of the cinematic elements that made this film work.

Normally, post-production is a less intense time for filmmakers, but in *Roger Rabbit* the animation had to be matched after the live-action footage had been edited—with blank spots left where there were cuts to a cartoon character. Moreover, the animators not only had to endow the cartoons with three-dimensional lighting characteristics, but had to render their animation so it would relate to subtle camera moves. Watts emphasized that many of these moves were not easily apparent to the eye when viewed alone, but the slightest discrepancy would be obvious on a large screen if the animation did not move in exact relationship to the camera moves. The animators made a total commitment and their achievement was an extraordinary complement to the live action directed by Zemeckis. Robert Watts and Frank Marshall saw to it that this worldwide, multidimensional film was coordinated and produced in a professionally viable way.

*Who Framed Roger Rabbit* opened to acclaim throughout the world, and critics who rarely agree on anything were unanimous in their praise of the verisimilitude of the film. Everyone associated with this fantasy film classic has received a heaping share of much deserved credit (Figure 1.12).

*Norman Corwin's writing credits include seventeen published books, five produced stage plays, and numerous television and motion picture works—including the screenplay for* Lust for Life, *for which he received an Academy Award nomination (Anthony Quinn won an Oscar for his performance as Gauguin). Corwin has also written three cantatas (one of which was performed in the United Nations), and the libretto of an opera produced by the Metropolitan Opera Company. He has received twenty-two major awards in media and the humanities and has been a nine-year member of the Board of Governors of the Academy of Motion Picture Arts and Sciences, where he now serves as First Vice President.*

# Two

# THE SCREENWRITER

*with Norman Corwin*

THERE ARE AS MANY reasons for seeing a given movie as there are people who attend, and a viewer's selection of a film is affected by age, sex, education, intelligence, environmental background, interest in certain subjects, the day's travail, and even escape from a summer heat wave. Most viewers, however, share a desire to leave behind for a few hours the banality and routine of daily existence and to live another life on the screen through identification with characters in conflict. The viewer seeks emotional catharsis through filmed stories of mystery, intrigue, comedy, history, and adventure and willingly surrenders consciousness of self with the first fade-in, often to emerge after the last fade-out, refreshed.

Elemental emotions are the attraction of narrative films, emotions that lie deeper than culture and cut across all strata of society to touch the viewer's instinctive core. Love, pity, hate, tenderness, courage, and desperation are the timeless elements of drama that transcend the topical experiences of daily life to express emotional truths. Viewers recognize these emotional truths from their own experiences; through this recognition, they identify with the players on the screen. The dramatic screenplay must have interesting characters and conflicts, themes of universal appeal, compelling action that reveals character, and a story that grips the imagination.

A screenplay is a story intended to be published in the medium of motion pictures. Therefore, screenwriting is visual and auditory rather than literary. The screenwriter is not writing words to be read by the audience, but images to be seen, sounds to be heard, and dramatized situations with which the viewers can identify. A script is a story told because it has meaning to its writer; it poses emotional dilemmas to arouse interest, gives insight into relationships, and embodies a judgment of the human condition.

The script format also communicates information to everyone involved in a film production. From the script, the producer can "ballpark" a budget in a breakdown into starring roles, second major characters, speaking parts, extras, number of interior and exterior locations, and so forth. The director studies the script for scenes to be dramatized and scope to be visualized. The players learn its dialogue and the contexts of the relationships. The designers conceive their settings from its indicated milieu. The cinematographers plan a visual look and begin to select lenses and film stock. The sound designer thinks about recording voices, music, and effects and plans to synthesize them in the final mix. The editors begin to think ahead into cinematic time and distance. All of this derives from the writer's vision expressed in a screenplay.

The professional screenwriter typically goes through these major steps in creating a production script for a feature film.

He or she begins by writing a brief synopsis (of a few pages) giving a sketch of the proposed story and its characters.

Then, the writer creates a prose treatment (of about fifty pages) containing a more thorough development of story and characterization, but without dialogue.

The writer does a screenplay schematic, which breaks down the actions into major sequences—written as bare plot—with locations, characters, and

"The writer is at square one in the process of creating films; it begins with the writer, but ends far from him (or her) after it wends its way through the assembly line of production. By nature the cinema—depending as it does on technology, electronics, and the powerful medium of photography—is the most complex of the arts. And the writer is creating in words something to be realized by many different means. Photography, for example, is in a class with music in terms of flexibility, power, the capacity to be both specific and abstract, and in status as one of the great arts. Yet its rendering in cinema begins with the written word."
—*Norman Corwin*

dramatic situations, but with little texture and no dialogue.

Finally, the writer writes the screenplay itself—rendered with full descriptions, characterization, and dialogue, often containing some directing and camera hints.

Sometimes the axiom "Scripts are not written, but are rewritten," is all too true. The screenwriter's vision seldom reaches projection in its original form but is revised again and again and again. Each revised page is given a distinctive color, according to its sequence of revision, and many a script reaches the production stage without a virgin page of original white. Moreover, the work may be taken away from its originator and passed to another writer for revision, and then to another, and another, seemingly ad infinitum. These arbitrary actions occur because a screenplay does not belong to the screenwriter alone in the same sense that a novel is the proprietary work of an author. The screenplay is not the end product—the completed film is the end product. The script is only the first stage of a production process to be realized by others. In fact, the production company frequently appears in the contract as the legal writer of the screenplay. Moss Hart's famous comment about the scribbler's trade—"Writing, like begging in India, is an honorable but humbling profession"—is all too true in the motion picture industry.

## Relationships

People in the movie industry know that a film is only as good as its script. The characters of a dramatic film, the story unfolding from their passions and problems, the milieu of their struggle, and the theme ex-

pressing some perception of the human condition spring from the heart and mind of the screenwriter. Although the director is the star of the film industry, he or she is primarily an interpreter of the vision of the screenwriter. Many great films have come from a director who was also a screenwriter, a true *auteur*, or from writer-director teams with a close professional rapport.

### Writer and Director

Norman Corwin comments on the relationship between the writer and the director and producer (Figure 2.1): "Ideally, there should be understanding in collaboration. A writer can with profit listen and be guided by the director, assuming there is mutual respect. Unfortunately, there are directors for whom the making of a film is an ego trip from beginning to end, and whose authority is more important than arriving at the highest possible artistic expression of what is intended. And the screenwriter's work may also be subject to influences by—if not actual attrition by— the star (or stars), the star's agent, the director and the producer, the producer's wife, and sometimes—as once happened to me—by the producer's gardener, who was confident that he represented the point of view of the movie-going public. That is a worst scenario, of course, and it does not necessarily obtain for the writer who, fortified by successful credits and a little clout of his own, is able to neutralize the forces of interference" (Figure 2.2).

"The writer's experience," Corwin continues, "is another factor in collaborating with a director. No one expects a new screenwriter to strike off an impeccable script on his [or her] first try any more than one would expect a composer to create a masterpiece in Opus 1, or a baseball rookie to hit a home run the first time at

FIGURE 2.1  *In Norman Corwin's screenplay for the historical film* Lust for Life, *characterization and story development were based upon what Vincent van Gogh and Paul Gauguin had actually said and done. Van Gogh's* Dear Theo, *the journals of Gauguin and Emile Bernard, and other writings of the time were the true sources of the film. The film's title came from a best-selling novel, but the film itself derived from original research.*

*Philip K. Scheuer wrote in the Los Angeles Times: "This film is remarkable for its integrity, its faithfulness to the life and work of an artist; remarkable for its sustained power in the light of having jettisoned the accepted rules in dramaturgy (beginning–middle–ending, conventional conflict and audience identification); remarkable for the single-track intensity of Kirk Douglas's portrayal of Vincent van Gogh."*

**LUST FOR LIFE** (U.S.A., 1956) DIRECTED BY VINCENT MINNELLI.

91-98.  INT.    THEATER    DAY                                    91-98.

LONG SHOT - From two-thirds of the way down the orchestra, SHOOTING TOWARD THE STAGE, which is lit only by a rehearsal light. Down around row F are three men connected with the show - the director, GRUBER, the producer, MEGLIN, and somebody's cousin from Albany. They are listening to Annie perform the same song from which we have just dissolved both visually and aurally.

99.  CLOSE SHOT of Annie singing. She betrays a lack of confidence at first, but picks up power and strength as she goes along.                                    99.

100.  INT.    CHAPEL    DAY                                    100.

Juxtaposed bar-to-bar with Annie's song we now hear a HYMN sung by a choir and congregation. The voices rise as we see:

101.  LONG SHOT from the rear of the chapel, SHOOTING OVER THE HEADS OF THE CONGREGATION toward the chancel:    101.

CONGREGATION
(singing)
Come, Holy Ghost, Creator blest,
And in our souls take up Thy rest....

102.  CLOSE SHOT of Stephanie, exalted, singing with the others.                                    102.

STEPHANIE
(singing)
O Comforter, to Thee we cry,
Thou heavenly gift of God Most High....

Suddenly, over the singing, in a moment of SUPERIMPOSED SOUND, comes the VOICE OF MEGLIN, shouting "Hold it".

CUT TO:

103.  INT.    THEATER    DAY                                    103.

CLOSE SHOT of Annie, reacting with confusion as the voice of Meglin continues from the above:

MEGLIN'S VOICE
Hold it, hold it, for God's sake!

Annie stops, apprehensive.

104.  CLOSE SHOT - MEGLIN AND GRUBER

MEGLIN
Tell me, Miss Rawlins, are you in a hurry about something? This is not a contest to see how fast you can get through it. Please do me the honor to take it at a reasonable pace, which is to say, half as fast. Half as fast! Can you do that?

FIGURE 2.2  *The screenplay format is exemplified here by a page from* The Blue Veil, *written by Norman Corwin.* The Blue Veil, *starring Jane Wyman, Natalie Wood, and Charles Laughton, won Wyman a nomination for an Academy Award as Best Actress.*

The screenplay format indicates that it is a blueprint for realization in another medium, rather than an end in itself as a piece of literature. Its component elements serve these functions.

The numbers running down the sides of the pages are cumulative "shot numbers" that go from the beginning to the end of the screenplay; they serve as reference points for everyone associated with the production of the film.

Each block of descriptive passage is introduced by an indication of whether the scene is interior or exterior, day or night, and location; the passages explain the dramatic action and its interpretation as suggested by the writer. Capital letters are used for characters' names, location references, and the writer's suggestions for cinematography.

Dialogue and its modification and each character's name follow a central column down the pages, enabling the director and the players to easily find the lines of dialogue.

The foregoing format may vary according to the idiosyncrasies of the writer, the director, and the studio, but it is essentially the structure of the master scene screenplay.

bat in the majors. There is nothing shameful about apprenticeship; a new screenwriter would be foolish not to be eager for the guidance, input, and instincts of, say, a Robert Altman.

"An experienced screenwriter, on the other hand, usually prefers to develop a concept out of his [or her] own vision, and then let the director, the producer, and other collaborators respond. Once their reaction has been studied and absorbed, the experienced screenwriter may still prefer his or her own concept; but ultimately, the screenplay must meet the approval of the director, the producer, and the studio. Also, alas, sometimes the star."

## Characters

Classic stories grow primarily out of character studies. The cleverest plot will not hold the interest of the audience long unless we care about what happens to the people in the story. They must appear cinematically as flesh and blood human beings who are interesting to watch as they act and react to the turmoils of conflict in the story. Dramatic film appeals primarily to this voyeur instinct in viewers, to their fascination for seeing what people do when their social veneers are stripped by dramatic necessity, to the profound curiosity about the only inexhaustible study—humankind (Figure 2.3).

Cinematic development of characters involves concepts and techniques that may be learned by intelligent people, but can be understood and applied to film only by those with intuitive empathy about what motivates human beings. It demands the ability to view the actions of other people with suspended moral judgment in order to ask the infinitely variable question "Why did he or she do it?" and then un-

**KRAMER VS. KRAMER** (U.S.A., 1979) DIRECTED BY ROBERT BENTON.

FIGURE 2.3   Kramer vs. Kramer *is a story drawn almost entirely from character. The story involves a family breakup and the struggle between father and mother, played by Dustin Hoffman and Meryl Streep, for custody of their son, played by Justin Henry. The conflict is triggered when the mother, Joanna, abandons her husband and son to seek self-fulfillment in a career.*

*Meryl Streep says of their roles, "Dustin is not trying to be an archetype for all fathers, nor am I trying to be like all women in such a situation. You have two very specific parents and one little boy. It's not necessary that you understand her, but she must be realistic. In the book, I hated her. I didn't understand her, and she was no one I had ever known. I wanted to make it a little harder for the audience to place its allegiance."*

derstand the infinitely variable answer well enough to present it in a dramatic film. For a truly moving cinematic development of character, the screenwriter must become that person and view another's actions from within.

Characterization and plot ideally should be intimately linked, with each aspect mutually dependent upon and closely related to the other. Without a good story, there are few interesting ways to reveal the nature of a character through action. Without interesting characters, the viewer would not identify with the life on the screen, and the most ingenious story would soon begin to pall.

The creative reality of dramatic script writing is that the amorphous blob of an idea, as it coalesces in the mind of the writer, usually takes the form of a generalized dramatic situation in which characters grow out of a dramatic situation, or sometimes the situation grows out of a dramatic character, depending upon the circumstances and the orientation of the writer. No iron-clad rules exist for developing the relationship between plot and screen character; the final film is usually conceived in pain and born in agony after innumerable revisions to both. Character and plot are warp and woof of the same narrative cloth and must be considered as an interwoven unit.

Norman Corwin's approach to character development and dramatic structure depends on the degree of fiction inherent in the subject. "If the person is a known historical figure, the writer is obliged to honor the truth, to respect historical fact. But if very little is known about the figure in a personal sense, the screenwriter's guess may be as good as anybody's, and is usually better, because he [or she] has studied the area. After all," Corwin comments, "Cleopatra did not write a column called 'My Day' and there are no filmed records of Brutus and Caesar. Shakespeare is known to have taken characters that were only sketchily documented, if at all, and he did what he wanted with them. But if the writer is developing a story about a historical figure with known characteristics—Woodrow Wilson, John Kennedy, Mahatma Gandhi—the writer is restricted by the record, so that the level of invention and creative enhancement differs from what could be done with a fictional character."

*Major and Minor Characters*

Major and minor screen characters differ in the degree to which they are given three-dimensional development, with every step away from the major roles resulting in further simplification. Major characters often have essential inner qualities quite different from the personalities they reveal in the film, and in the climax their true characters stand exposed and often transformed. Minor characters, on the other hand, do not as a rule change; their personalities and characters are presented as constants throughout the story because it might dilute the viewer's interest in the major characters if the minor ones were also developed in-the-round.

The protagonist—whose passion sends the spindrift flying—and the antagonist—whose determination resists with equal dramatic force—must be fully developed. Their physical, environmental, and psychological natures should be clearly evident. Minor characters are also created with these basic traits in mind, but they are rendered in a more understated manner. The low profile of a minor character holds true even when that person triggers the conflict or functions as an agent who makes the action work and effects change in the protagonist.

A minor character need not be a shallow character, however, and if clearly

FIGURE 2.4 *Meryl Streep comments about her development of Joanna's character: "If Joanna is a villain, if there's a white hat–black hat situation, that doesn't make for an interesting courtroom scene, which I consider the climax of the film." Joanna's testimony at the* custody hearing is one of the film's most emotionally moving sequences, in large measure because Streep avoids histrionics. So thoroughly had Streep come to inhabit her character that she wrote every word of the courtroom speech herself.

37

CHARACTERS

though briefly drawn, may be shown emotionally affected by the outcome of the major conflict. The principle of subordination of minor characters is important because they exist primarily as foils to the majors and as plot and expositional devices. A story in which all the major and minor characters believably play their proportional roles in the conflict reflects a high order of dramatic ability in the screenwriter.

### Screen Personality and Character

Personality and character are two dimensions of a role in a dramatic film that are used as contradictory foils in a major character and as complementary elements in minor characters.

*Persona* is what lies on the surface, the face we prepare to meet other faces. It is the smiles or surliness, the amiability or irascibility, the grace or grouchiness born of life experiences and the need to get along with other people that adds up to the sum total called persona. A pleasant personality, cultivated or ingenuous, is a collation of agreeable traits—friendliness, courtesy, good will—that is difficult to define, but like true love, we know it when we see it. An unpleasant persona is simply the reverse: a collation of disagreeable traits such as hostility, rudeness, ill will, and so forth.

*Character* lies deeper than persona and is usually revealed only in conflict. Character refers to the inner essential qualities of the person: honesty, duplicity, courage, cowardice—things that can be known only when one is subjected to an ordeal with something vital at stake. A primary basis of dramatic appeal derives from the interest viewers have in seeing what people do when their personalities are seared away by an ordeal and their true inner selves stand exposed (Figure 2.4).

**KRAMER VS. KRAMER** DIRECTED BY ROBERT BENTON.

When developing an original idea, Corwin tends to develop personality and character by using as models the people with whom he comes into contact. "If it is a character that I have developed, the world is very instructive. One meets so many people in life that there is seldom much hesitation in fixing upon an individual one knows as a basis for developing a character. A writer is at liberty to develop that character in such a way that he or she will be, on the one hand, real, recognizable, and identifiable and will still have the potential for fictional growth or decay. The effects that this model of a character have on the story, and the effects that the circumstances of the story have on him or her, is of the greatest importance in creating drama."

### Consistency of Character

*Credible* and *necessary* are terms that refer to the consistency and believability of a screen character's responses to the crises of a story, which in turn derive from his or her personality and character. The screen character must at all times react in a manner that is credible, given a collation of personality and character traits, and necessary, given the pressures of a conflict. In real life, the average citizen is a walking bundle of internal contradictions: He or she may be kind to children and dogs, pick the wings off flies, give generously to charities, and cheat his or her colleagues without any apparent awareness of contradictory behavior. Such inconsistency of personality and character traits is often unacceptable in a screen character. The same viewer who accepts inconsistencies in people in daily life with a shrug of the shoulders insists upon consistency in screen characters and scoffs at contradictions.

In *Kramer vs. Kramer*, a story of the custody battle for a young son between husband and wife, the divorcing adversaries did everything legally possible to win their cases, including developing closer relations with the boy (Figure 2.5). Had the husband then said, "This is too much hassle—you keep the kid," and had the wife then answered, "No, you keep him. I have the mold to make more," the responses would have been out of character for both of them.

### Character Development

Realistic screen characters are usually created by selecting only those traits for revelation that somehow relate to the structure and conclusion of the cinematic tale and by deleting all others. One does not create a believable character by literally transposing every trait of a living person to the screen any more than a landscape painter would render every twig on a tree. Such an interpretation would be true in fact but false in spirit. Film aims not at the transposition of life, but at its *dramatization*. The fact that a murderer is good to his mother or that a romantic lead may leave a ring around the bathtub is dramatically irrelevant if it does not contribute to the story. Through the selection and highlighting of relevant traits, and the suppression and elimination of others, the screenwriter creates characters that seem real in the context of the story.

A cinematic character should be developed *specifically* in terms of his or her age, sex, physical characteristics, education, occupation, religion, and social-political-economic milieu. Because the viewers can see and judge every character's action based upon their own life experiences, if the character strikes a false note in any aspect it may destroy the credibility of the story. A believable screen character should be developed in three dimensions: *physical appearance*, *environment*, and *psychology*.

A person's *physical appearance* relates importantly to his or her basic attitudes,

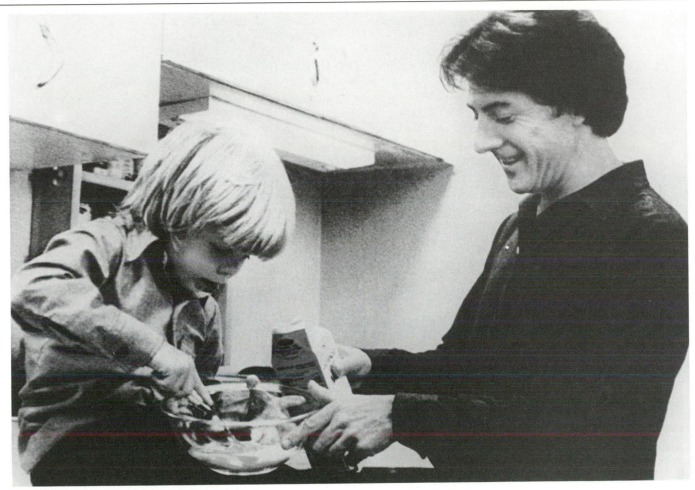

**KRAMER VS. KRAMER** DIRECTED BY ROBERT BENTON.

FIGURE 2.5    *The development of character, as conceived by the writer, may be revised considerably through the interpretations of the director and the star.*

Dustin Hoffman added his personal touch to the interpretation of the estranged father, shown here making French toast with Justin Henry in the role of the son. Producer Stan Jaffe says of the actor, "He has strong convictions to which some people have objected in the past. My advice is to listen to him. Out of our discussions . . . and even some heated arguments . . . came a better movie."

Hoffman says, "An actor is, in a sense, crippled. . . . not an innovator like a writer or composer or painter, [but] . . . treated as an interpreter . . . I ask that my ideas be considered and tried—that I get my shot."

Hoffman says of the boy, Justin Henry, "It was an emotional experience for all of us. Not only did Justin become disciplined but he was genuinely interested in helping me. When we worked together beforehand, he would pick up my rhythm and mood . . . which would carry over into the next scene. Every actor knows that that ability, to support another actor when you're not on camera, is professionalism at its highest."

aspirations, and response to any given crisis. An individual who has been attractive from infancy has probably received pampering from friends and relatives, become the teacher's favorite, been sought out by members of the opposite sex, and received preferred treatment in the world of work. Robert Frost wrote, "The beautiful shall be choosers." This unfair truism may shape the lucky individual into either a person of serene self-confidence or into a spoiled brat: one who faces life's crises with the conviction that the world and everyone in it exist to provide the anointed one with the best of everything.

At the other extreme, a person who has been unattractive from infancy may have been shaped by that experience through the indifference of playmates, relatives, teachers, members of the opposite sex, and lost opportunities in the workaday world. In the process of maturation, this unattractive individual may have acquired a full complement of inhibiting complexes, which the screenwriter may exploit, that would affect the character's response to a crisis.

In between these simplistic extremes are physical eccentricities that may engender personality quirks: A short man may develop the aggressiveness of a bantam rooster to compensate for his stature. A woman with gross ears may become so sensitive about them that she hides her ears with an unbecoming hairstyle. Moreover, people's personalities may be transformed as a consequence of physical changes: A brave man may degenerate into cowardice with age, infirmity, or crippling. A woman once serene in her beauty may become wildly neurotic with the disfigurement of a scar or the erosion of time.

Physiology is another physical factor contributing to an individual's outlook on life. A chronically sour stomach may create a chronically sour outlook. A high or low hormone level may explain why a man is dynamic or lazy, friendly or irritable, arrogant or humble, confident or diffident. Nobody escapes the burden of flesh and the ills to which it is heir; and in a dramatic film, the screenwriter may use any property of a screen character that the viewer can perceive is consonant with the role of the character in the story.

*Environment* is a second shaping influence used in the development of a screen character. A person with a given set of physical and intellectual characteristics may develop into as many different kinds of human beings as there are circumstances in which to be reared (Figure 2.6). A girl who grows up in a dirty city tene-

FIGURE 2.6 *The cruelty of an environment is a central theme of this film, and the setting is a character present in every scene.*

*Jon Voight (left) and Dustin Hoffman, playing respectively Joe Buck and Ratso, are an unlikely pair of loners who join forces to cope with a hostile world that rebuffs them at every turn. Gradually, Joe and Ratso become comrades as well as business partners. For the first time, each man begins to care about the welfare of someone else, to assume responsibility for another, to communicate. Each has found his first friend. At one point, when Joe Buck is threatening another man to get money, he snarls, "I have a family to take of." Ratso, slowly dying of pneumonia, has become his family.*

*Archer Winston wrote in the* New York Post, *"Dustin Hoffman brings to bear on his role a talent of astounding power and versatility. . . . It is a performance that, like Voight's, sticks to the mind's eye as if embossed."*

*Rex Reed wrote in* Movies, *"Jon Voight plays 'one helluva stud' from Texas . . . with such coltish naiveté that he performs the miracle of keeping the audience in his pocket during the entire film."*

**MIDNIGHT COWBOY** (U.S.A., 1969) DIRECTED BY JOHN SCHLESINGER.

ment, surrounded by crumbling walls, cockroaches, and diseased people, will react differently to a crisis than she would if reared in the charming environment of a clean suburb, surrounded by leafy trees, singing birds, and buoyant people.

The maturation of a person's character is most influenced by his or her early life at home: Were the parents living or dead, together or divorced, loving or hostile, dutiful or negligent? Did the breadwinner(s) make a good living, barely eke out a subsistence, or desert the family? Were the parents' life habits a ritual of church attendance and good works, a round of cocktail parties and bridge games, a flabby vascillation between watching television and doing nothing, or an all-out commitment to climbing the socioeconomic ladder? Although change is a rule of life and one premise of drama—and many film stories recount the breaking of family ties and matrices—the influence of family life (or the lack of it) will be felt in the individual for a lifetime. And when a character appears on the screen, his or her background should be evident unless there is to be an element of mystery.

Other environmental factors that may influence a person's reactions to a crisis include racial and ethnic heritage, religious upbringing or the lack of it, and educational background: aptitudes, good subjects and bad, and how easily he or she learned. And ultimately, we could ask other environmental questions: What became of his or her occupation? How remunerative was the job? How suitable was the person for the conditions of employment?

Unless one is dealing with a character of ambiguity, mystery, and uncertainty, all of these physical and environmental factors will usually be apparent in the person's mannerisms, speech, style of walk and gesture, and attitudes toward other people. The average adult can often assess where another individual has come from and the major influences in that person's life—a skill brought to the viewing of a film.

The *psychology* of the individual provides the real interest in drama; what draws viewers to narrative film is a fascination with how people behave under stress when they think no one is looking. By giving the viewer insight into human motivation on the screen, the screenwriter offers the viewer insight into self.

The intangible elements of personal aspiration are infinitely variable. What does the individual live for—power, money, security, prestige, God? Does the person want to contribute to country and community or be the sales representative with the highest commissions in the corporation? Is the individual an artist demanding the right to creative fulfillment or a politician expunging organized crime from the city? A person's aspirations may grow from an inner need demanding expression or it may be formulated for the person by peer groups, but it is often the strongest single element of human motivation.

Other aspects of psychology to be considered may include the individual's love life, satisfying or unsatisfying; talents and intellectual potential, developed or latent; social expertise, poised or gauche. Amusements are another index of character. During leisure hours does a person read books, play bridge, watch television, bet on horse races, go jogging, or head for the nearest bar? People reveal themselves in their pastimes, and these too may be used in the development of a screen character.

The principle of three-dimensional characters—physical, environmental, and psychological—provide the screenwriter with enormous scope for developing believable and interesting screen subjects. The manipulation of any of these elements will create a unique individual who will react in a distinctive way to a given crisis, according to what is credible and necessary in his or her nature.

### Change Within Characters

Change is the only constant we can be sure of in life. Change in a protagonist derives from Aristotle's explanation of recognition and reversal in the *Poetics*. Dramatic dialectics is a Hegelian process of effecting changes in screen characters through a resolution of their internal contradictions, as follows. The protagonist suffers the internal contradiction of wanting something he or she does not have. The protagonist strikes out to attain what is wanted in a dramatic thesis. The protagonist's desire is intolerable to the antagonist, who opposes the protagonist in antithesis. The conflict is joined and maximum effort is fought with maximum resistance. When the protagonist realizes he or she cannot have what is wanted in simple terms, the protagonist combines the original thesis with something of value learned from the adversary in a change within the self, or the protagonist dies.

The potential for change should lie within the major characters from the outset. The seeds of change are planted in their physical and emotional makeup, their temperament and backgrounds, and especially in their desires for change. The protagonist, by the nature of striking out for something not possessed, displays in action the potential for inner change. The dialectics of change often work both ways in the better thematic concepts—right versus right—as in *Kramer vs. Kramer*, with protagonist and antagonist, wife and husband, emerging fundamentally changed from their custody fight for a child.

There must also be a progressive change in the character of the protagonist as the story is told, or the final transformation may be too abrupt. In *Kramer vs. Kramer* the husband is initially crude with his young son and incompetent in domestic skills after the two have been abandoned by wife and mother. Gradually, he becomes a gentle, thoughtful father who develops the sensibilities to handle a child; he even learns how to make a decent breakfast of French toast for the two of them—a whimsical symbol of his transformation.

Change in the broadest sense should occur within the major characters as a result of the climax of the drama, when they confront the truth about themselves and are transformed or possibly die from the inability to change. The transformations of their inner natures should crystallize in the conclusion and be reflected by changes in the emotional color of the film.

> *The Informer* begins in betrayal and ends in atonement.
>
> *The Rules of the Game* begins in frivolity and ends in tragedy.
>
> *Butch Cassidy and the Sundance Kid* begins in lawlessness and ends in death because the characters cannot change.
>
> *Citizen Kane* begins in power, arrogance, and selfishness and ends in vacuity, rejection, loneliness, and death.

In each of these films the major characters experience a fundamental change in character, or death, as a result of their actions, and the emotional tenor of the films ends differently from the tone with which they began.

Self-sufficiency in a screen character makes for poor dramatic material. A person who seems genuinely able to go it alone—neither demanding nor dependent, needing nor wanting—can seldom be used as a screen character because it is unfulfilled desire and the will to act on that desire that leads to conflict.

*Motivation*

Given a conflict, the *will to win* is required in the two major adversaries for them to carry on a protracted conflict for the length of a dramatic film. In traditional American cinema no conflict means no drama. The protagonist may start weakly and gain strength with each surmounted crisis, or start strongly and weaken with each obstacle, but he or she must have the stamina to carry on the struggle to the climax. The same holds true of the opposition. Whether the antagonist starts weakly and grows in strength, or begins strongly and declines with each crisis, the pertinacity to struggle through to the end must be there. This will to win on both sides provides unity for the drama, a framework of suspense, that keeps the audience interested in the outcome of the conflict.

A weak screen character is one who cannot make up his or her mind, vascillating with each dramatic wind, never striking out, never resisting, never making a commitment despite the provocations of the story. A weak human being, however, may be considered a strong screen character if the person has the tenacity to endure in weakness no matter how abused: Stamina then becomes a form of strength. A weak screen character, however, serving a minor role as foil to the protagonist or antagonist, usually lacks the strength to be a major force in the drama.

The *issue at stake* in a serious conflict must be something of value to the viewer as well as to the protagonist and the antagonist. In *Moonstruck*, the issue is love; in *Sophie's Choice*, the anguish of a mother having to choose which of her children must die. What should be at stake is something elemental with which the viewer can

identify given the circumstances of the story. In real life, as we all know, people often fight over trivial matters. No tribe of cannibals ever pursued a vendetta more viciously than a clique of college professors or a gang of artists trying to stamp out a differing mode of artistic expression. But these same people, as film viewers, require that elemental issues be at stake in dramatic films: life, death, love, freedom.

In many stories *right versus right* in character motivation offers a more interesting form of conflict than *right versus wrong*. Viewers may become more emotionally involved in the struggle when they can understand how the protagonist and antagonist both have something right and something wrong in their points of view. In *Lonely Are the Brave*, for example, the cowboy has broken into jail to free a friend, and then broken out of jail to free himself. Most viewers respect his loyalty in wanting to help his friend and sympathize with his desire to free himself when it transpires that his friend does not want to escape but plans to serve his time.

On the other hand, the cowboy slugs one police officer, insults a second, beats a third unconscious with a rifle butt, saws through the bars of a jail, and shoots down an Air Force helicopter. Society could scarcely take this lying down. Any reasonable viewer could understand that this trail of mayhem, however nobly motivated, violates a volume of laws and has to arouse the pursuit of police officers who are also in the right. The police have the right to capture an escaped prisoner who has the right to freedom, and the audience roots for both sides.

The *time and place of dramatic attack*, as character relates to plot, should come when the protagonist is prepared to act. A person may endure the proverbial slings and arrows of outrageous fortune for many years, but until the individual is prepared to do something about it, he or she is of little dramatic interest. There are four classic points of dramatic attack having one denominator in common: the necessity of action.

*An important or traumatic event*, such as the death of someone close, a declaration of war, or a flood may release interpersonal conflicts and set events in motion. In *I Never Sang for My Father*, the conflict between father and son was joined by the death of the mother who had formerly been the arbiter of peace.

*A pending event*, such as a mission to fulfill, a river to cross, or a beachhead to assault may ignite and give direction to dramatic fires. In *The Bridge on the River Kwai* the need to construct a wooden bridge over a tropical river by a specific date draws men and nations into battle.

*A vital object of contention* means something worth fighting for: a child wanted by a divorcing husband and wife, a woman desired by two men, an important job, land for the taking, or money may arouse a conflict between those who want whatever is at stake. *The Godfather* recounts the struggle of the Corleone family to crush its enemies and become the masters of organized crime.

*A turning point in the lives of the characters*, particularly the protagonist, may have changed their lifestyles or environment so much that they could not go on living as before. In *The Grapes of Wrath* the outer forces of destitution drive Tom Joad and his family off their Oklahoma land on a trek to California. They could no longer survive on the farm they had occupied for generations.

In each of these times and places of dramatic attack, irresistible necessity compels the protagonists to act, and with that action set the story in motion.

## Orchestration of Characters

Orchestration of characters, a term originated by writer Lajos Egri, refers to the inclusion of individuals in the story who offer a spectrum of personality and character types and who have inherent conflicts of interest. If an artist, a businessperson, a scientist, a playboy, a politician, and a drug pusher were sequestered together, there would soon be friction among them because of their disparate characters and personalities. Put these mismatched human beings into circumstances of conflict—a situation in which one of them wants something the others do not wish him or her to have—and there will be a struggle. Each of the characters will react to every crisis according to what is credible and necessary in light of his or her own physical, environmental, and psychological background. Each will consider his or her own actions fully justified in terms of a personal value system. Each will relate to the protagonist or antagonist from a personal perspective. And all will provide dramatic material for the screenwriter.

## Pivotal Character

The kickoff of a story is sometimes effected by a minor character, called a pivotal character or agent. In *The Ox-Bow Incident* the organization of a posse to avenge a slain man is instigated by a close buddy of the fallen cowboy. The friend is so outraged by the killing that he swears that if there is not a vigilante group formed to exact justice, he will personally kill the three sheep men who have allegedly fired the fatal shots. His fierce determination brings about the formation of the illegal posse and begins the story that ends in the lynching of three innocent men. Those who eventually become the protagonist and the antagonist in the film are initially dragged into it by a pivotal character who ultimately is subordinated to the others in the dramatic conflict.

## Basic Story Conflicts

Screenwriters use conflict between people and events to recount stories that consist of a series of clashes between adversaries, with outcomes that are not revealed until the end. There are five basic forms, or formats, used in our cinema: *individual against self*, *individual against individual*, *individual against institutions*, *individual against the elements*, and *society against society*. The more levels of conflict the writer can utilize within his or her story, the more opportunities there are for creating the surprise and suspense of the unexpected.

### Individual Against Self

Individual against self is a theme that explores remarkable people who have unfortunate personal traits that militate against and may destroy themselves. *Patton*, for example, is a study of the American general who could not control his temper, keep his mouth shut, or show good judgment in anything except his leadership in battle. His irrational character traits culminate in the destruction of the brilliant military career that was his life.

### Individual Against Individual

Individual against individual has been until recently the most common form of conflict found in American dramatic film, perhaps because of our strong national emphasis upon competition and our fascination with who is the better man or woman in any given conflict. A classic example would be the shoot-out of the traditional American western, as seen in *The Shootist* with John Wayne or *Butch Cassidy and the Sundance Kid*.

### Individual Against Institutions

Individual against institutions presents the theme of the underdog struggling against the perversity and restraints of the society's oppressive institutions. The concept of the loner who fights against great odds to achieve a goal is immensely popular, perhaps because we identify with feelings of rebellion against the conformities imposed by society or because we share a persistent strand of individualism. In *The Graduate* Ben struggles to be himself and find love despite the pressures of materialistic parents and friends.

### Individual Against the Elements

Individual against the elements means, in the Aristotelian sense, a human being against the gods or against his or her own destiny. In American cinema the theme has most often been expressed in the story of pioneers striving to tame a wilderness in the West, as in *How the West Was Won*, with struggles against the primeval elements of earth, air, fire, and water. And, we may also see the theme in stories of the supernatural that symbolize inner conflicts.

### Society Against Society

Society against society presents a struggle greater than the individuals participating within it, with each individual resolving personal conflicts and realizing personal destiny through the victory or defeat of one side (one society) in the struggle. The format is common in many genres of film produced in the Soviet Union but exists in American cinema primarily in war films. The story is almost formulaic: First, a climactic event looms that will decide the outcome between two contenders, usually in the form of a great battle. Second, a group of people have a mission to fulfill, the outcome of which may be the key to victory, and this group is directly opposed by a comparable group on the other side. Third, personal animosities and conflicts exist among the members of each group. All three levels of conflict—society against society, group against group, individual against individual—are resolved in the final climactic battle. *Platoon* is the story of a group of American soldiers fighting in Vietnam who are deeply divided in terms of personal conflicts yet fight ferociously as a platoon against the enemy in the last battle.

## Plot

The importance of plot is directly proportional to the length of the film, the degree of character development, and the complexity of the story. A short film may present a dramatic vignette that is improvised on location, casually photographed, freely edited, and delightful to view on the screen. Its artistic and cinematic elements are easy to keep under control. A feature film, on the other hand, usually presents many characters, many conflicts, many locations—all interrelated—and requires the organization of a plot to maintain the interest of the average viewer. Once a story line has been plotted, however, the improvisation of new dramatic sequences may add the refreshing insights of the impromptu to solid dramatic structure; this offers the best of both approaches, as

Robert Altman demonstrates in *Nashville* and *McCabe and Mrs. Miller.*

Norman Corwin considers the development of the story to be more important than the concept of the screenplay. "If one were to address a convention of writers and ask each one of them to develop the same concept, one would read an entirely different story written by each writer. Let's say the concept and problem were to write a screenplay about a father, a son, and a stolen bicycle. A hundred writers would develop this a hundred ways, one of which might become the film *The Bicycle Thief.*"

However the story of a bicycle thief might be told, certain elements in every version would be used as a framework for telling the story and revealing the characters in conflict. These elements relate to *the premise or theme*; *the protagonist*; *joining the conflict*; *crisis structure*; *reversal of fortune*; *obligatory scene and climax*; and *denouement.*

### The Premise or Theme

*Premise* in drama expresses the equivalent of *purpose*. The *Oxford Universal Dictionary* defines *premise* this way: "a previous proposition from which another follows as a conclusion." As everything that lives has a purpose, so every film that is made should have a premise. The term *premise* encompasses plot, theme, goal, driving force, whatever gives the characters a reason for doing what they do and through which the screenwriter makes a statement about the human condition.

Themes or premises may derive from timeless human emotions of love, jealousy, avarice, heroism, and so forth, or they may derive from a potentially dramatic situation that needs only this core to give it meaning. The theme of *Amadeus*, a film about the genius of Mozart and the envy of a mediocre composer, is that talent will triumph despite adversity. If the writer fails to establish a theme in the screenplay, the film may drift and lack unity.

Everything presented as part of the premise must be credible. In *Lust for Life*, van Gogh's artistic genius, his rejection by the public of his time, and his mental derangement are all part of the premise that in turn evolves into personal tragedy and great art. At the other end of the spectrum, *Who Framed Roger Rabbit* supports the premise that real people and cartoon characters can interact believably in a story leading to a climax. Even that wildly improbable film has a premise that relates to the transformation of Los Angeles from a garden spot of the West into a smog trap strangled by traffic.

### The Protagonist

The protagonist is the person whose actions set all of the dramatic forces in motion and whose persistence keeps them in motion to the end of the film. The protagonist sets out to achieve his or her purposes in a way that triggers counterforces—antagonists who resist vigorously. The sustained struggle of the protagonist intensifies from the first joining of the conflict to its final resolution in the climax; he or she never gives up from beginning to end. If the protagonist were to give up anywhere along the way, there would be no story, no conflict, no drama. In *Places in the Heart*, the young widow refuses to buckle under to her tragedy or to yield to the bigots arrayed against her black friend; she becomes in the truest sense the mistress of her own destiny.

### Joining the Conflict

Joining the conflict means presenting the adversaries at the very beginning of the drama. These first five to ten minutes in American narrative films are usually packed with exposition. The point of dramatic attack contains these elements: the context of the conflict and the person who triggers the conflict; the background of the conflict so the audience will understand the forces that brought about the conflict; the event that triggers the story and joins the conflict; and typically clues to the climax that make the ending seem credible. In *Midnight Cowboy* Ratso ultimately dies of pneumonia and to make it credible he is presented in the beginning as having a cough. All of these elements of character and exposition are presented quickly—sometimes under the titles—and continue with growing intensity between protagonist and antagonist until the issue is resolved in the outcome of the story. From this point on everything is presented in terms of cause and effect. Only at the beginning is pure coincidence acceptable.

### Crisis Structure

Crises, which constitute the main body of the story in most American films, are the dramatic events that create suspense between the first joining of the conflict and their resolution in the outcome of the story. Crises are created by the protagonist's attempts to achieve his or her goals again and again, in each dramatic scene, with frustration resulting each time. This pattern continues with rising intensity until the drama reaches its peak in the climax.

Crises appear on the surface to have two dramatic forces: the drive of the protagonist to achieve a goal and the counterforce of the antagonist. However, each crisis has two or more deeper possibilities. A third force is always present, seen, or felt that gives the protagonist a dual option for action or exists as a potential threat. The third point in triangular crisis structure creates suspense by giving the protagonist two or more options in every crisis.

The crisis structure of *High Noon*, a classic western in which a retiring sheriff faces the vengeance of four gunmen, gives graphic examples of dual choices in each crisis. When the news of the killers' return interrupts his wedding, he has the choice of fleeing with his bride or staying to fight. When he chooses to stay, his former deputy offers to help in exchange for making a corrupt deal, but the sheriff refuses the offer on those terms and turns instead to the local townsmen. He has the choice of seeking help from the roughnecks most likely and able to fight or turning to the churchgoing pillars of the community. When the town toughs refuse to help, he goes to the decent men, and they give him the choice of running away or fighting alone. Finally the climax comes and he finds himself abandoned and facing the ultimate choice: flight or fight.

Triangular crisis structure may be used under as many circumstances as there are characters in conflict. The only constant in the changing triangular relationship is the point of the protagonist.

### Reversal of Fortune

Crisis structure is a means of revealing characters in conflict, their *reversals of fortune*, and their recognition of self-delusion in the Aristotelian sense. Reversals of fortune are the consequences of the crises and the climax. Each time the major character tries to achieve a goal—and seems about to attain it—something unexpected occurs to reverse his or her fortune at that point in the story. The character then has no choice but to try another alternative. This leads to fresh obstacles and new forms of opposition in each succeeding crisis until the reversal of fortune reaches finality in the climax. In *Midnight Cowboy*,

Joe Buck attempts to make money by the sleaziest means—selling himself to women as a gigolo—and each such attempt is a personal (and sometimes hilarious) disaster. After the climax (the death of his friend Ratso) he recognizes his self-delusion and throws away his cowboy outfit to look for a job. He has changed inwardly as a consequence of his struggles through the crises and the climax, and he is a different man.

### Obligatory Scene and Climax

The obligatory scene is the dramatic event the viewers are led to believe will be the climax. If viewers are not presented with an obligatory scene in addition to the climax, they may leave the film dissatisfied. These two climactic events are closely related at the conclusion of the film and usually follow one another: first the obligatory scene and then the climax. In *Lost in America*, a young advertising executive and his wife decide to drop out of the urban rat race and set out in a motor home to "find themselves" in back-country America. It is obligatory that they set out and do as he intends, but what they find is Las Vegas, and what he discovers is that his wife loses her head when gambling. Soon broke, they now set out toward the climax of *Lost in America*.

The climax of a dramatic film is that point in the story in which the protagonist gets what he or she wants or is defeated. All conflicts are resolved one way or the other. A theme is seldom realized in dialogue in traditional American cinema; instead, it is carried out by the major character in a dramatic action. In *Lost in America* the turning point comes when the young man, now reduced to being an elementary school crossing guard, sees a vision of iridescent loveliness—a Mercedes Benz—and recognizes his self-delusion about dropping out of society. He changes back to the upwardly mobile young professional he had been. He and his wife drive on to New York and he gets a job, at a 31 percent reduction in pay but with improved medical benefits. Their change goes full circle from affluence to affluence.

### Denouement

The denouement usually consists of an explanation by one of the characters, after the climax and the obligatory scene, of all the loose ends in the plot. The denouement may be printed on the screen before the end titles, as in *Serpico*, in which we learn that a police officer was fired for trying to clean up corruption on the force. Ideally, no denouement should be needed—the film should end immediately after the climax and leave the viewer with a theme expressed in action.

## Suspense

Suspense that rises unabated to the climax absorbs the interest of the viewer. As a structural plot device, suspense exists essentially at these levels: *developing complications*, *the race against time*, *the chase*, *rising intensity of crises*, and *reversal*.

### Developing Complications

Developing complications grow out of the first joining of the conflict when several threads of conflict are established in terms of character, plot exposition, theme, and settings that may weave up and down through each succeeding crisis. The choice made by a character may create outer conflict as an expression of inner turmoil. Complications may be caused by the protagonist having inadvertently made a

friend or enemy of another character, major or minor, and that character may credibly reappear later in the story, motivated to assist or frustrate the protagonist. Or, the protagonist's actions may offend customs, public opinion, or law and order, thereby provoking a reaction by the societal forces that are credible complications. At another level, events may occur at the same time as the main story—wars, famines, earthquakes—that are plausibly drawn upon to create a crisis and develop story complications.

### The Race Against Time

The race against time is a common plot device for creating suspense; it dramatizes an inevitable terminating event that will forcibly change the lives of the main characters by its outcome. In *High Noon*, the story revolves around the drama of a sheriff trying to enlist the armed support of his community before the arrival of an outlaw on the noon train. The clock is seen, felt, and heard throughout the film, even to the extent of editing the scenes to the beat of a metronome to underscore the race against time.

### The Chase

The chase is a suspense device that is a cinematic structure not found in other media. A chase is inherently exciting, perhaps because it appeals to an atavistic hunting instinct, perhaps because viewers have been conditioned to expect that the outcome of certain stories will be realized in some form of the hunter-hunted pursuit. Action-adventure films often use the chase conclusion.

### Rising Intensity of Crises

Suspense is also created through increasing the intensity of the crises. Each obstacle is made more difficult than the last, forcing the protagonist to try ever more strenuously to surmount it. With each crisis of progressively increasing intensity, the viewer's suspense correspondingly increases until the story reaches its climax. The screenwriter's job is to gradually raise the height of the flaming hoops through which the protagonist must leap in order to build an unabating sense of suspense in the viewer.

### Reversal

Unexpected deception is an important key to suspense, and it lies within the triangular structure of the crisis. Whatever the protagonist tries to do in a given situation, the audience must identify with the protagonist and believe he or she will do it; then the audience will be just as surprised as the protagonist if the results are unexpected. The audience's expectation should always be cheated from crisis to crisis if the intent is to create suspense. And if the unexpected is provided in ways that are expected, it satisfies even more the appetite for suspense.

Dramatic structure has been dissected and presented here as something rigid rather than organic for the purpose of making its elements clear. In practice, however, dramatic structure—a story told through the actions of characters—is as infinitely variable in its forms and applications as the viewers who sit absorbed in the life on the screen. The story is the servant of the content, and as long as certain elements are present, may be treated in any way the screenwriter finds exciting.

## Dramatic Elements in a Classic Film

Having defined the basic elements of character development and dramatic structure, we can illuminate their organic relationships within the classic film *On The Waterfront*, written by Budd Schulberg.

### Background and the Protagonist

*On the Waterfront* is the grim story of Terry Malloy, an ex-prizefighter, and the struggle of longshoremen to win back their union from the criminals who have usurped control. Johnny Friendly, a criminal leader who functions within a larger syndicate, has turned the harbor into his personal fiefdom with the longshoremen working as his serfs. Friendly enforces subservience by giving work only to those who are obedient and servile, by docking the pay of the recalcitrant, by lending money on loan-shark terms, and by extorting money from ship owners with cargos of perishable fruit. He boasts that he has the "fattest piers in the fattest harbor in the world." Surrounded by thugs to their trade born, he is brutal enough to send them out to slay anyone who dares to "sing" to the state Crime Commission charged with investigating racketeering on the waterfront.

Within this context is young Terry Malloy, his boxing career behind him and now part-longshoreman and part-errand boy for Johnny Friendly. Terry is kept around almost as a mascot because his brother Charlie serves as legal counsel to the boss. Terry is a willing, contented, and not-too-bright tool of the union. His lack of intelligence is dramatized by his inability to count the money the boss has handed him and by jokes about his being punchy from his brief career as a prizefighter. His brother Charlie is Terry's only living relative, the taverns and pool halls of the longshoremen are his only home, and fighting in the streets and the arena are his only education.

Location cinematography on Hoboken's sleazy wharfs, streets, and tenements renders the visual background to the conflict. The characters and setting follow Norman Corwin's admonitions with regard to this kind of a film. "When developing an idea based upon news events or social conditions, the writer has constraints similar to those in writing about a historical character. Here one must use representative types as characters, and representative locations, in order to express the themes that may have provided the original impetus for the film."

### Context and Triggering Event

Terry allows himself to be used as a decoy to lure Joey Doyle, the man about to testify to the state Crime Commission, from his tenement flat. The pretext is Terry's return of a missing pigeon owned by Joey. When Joey goes up to his rooftop coop to receive the squab, waiting goons sent by Johnny Friendly throw him off the top of the building to his death. Down below a shocked Terry protests, "I didn't know they was gonna knock him off!" When a thug jokes, "He sings like a canary, but he don't fly like one," Terry does not laugh— but prepares to change.

Joey's death is the triggering event that draws together all the main characters and begins the story. It introduces Edie, sister of Joey, who looks up from the body of her brother and cries out, "I want to know who killed my brother!" It introduces the now-troubled Terry to Edie and begins the love relationship that is instrumental in his change of attitude. It brings in a priest who, outraged by the crime and the pervasive corruption, organizes a rump organization of opposition among the longshoremen and becomes the voice of conscience to Terry, articulating themes of right and wrong.

And the killing brings forth the representatives of strength and weakness among the longshoremen: Joey's own father, an advocate of being "D and D," deaf and dumb, as a means of survival; and K. O. Doogan, who is prepared to join the priest in leading the fight against the criminals who have seized control of the longshoreman's union. Within ten minutes of the first fade-in, the triggering events have introduced the protagonists and antagonists, the main supporting characters, the settings of tenements, slums, church, and waterfront, and the joining of all conflicts in *On the Waterfront*.

### Joining of Conflicts

The joining of conflicts must reveal the nature of those conflicts. The opening sequences of *On the Waterfront* reveal four levels of conflict, with Terry as the protagonist: individual against individual, with Terry against his boss and former friend Johnny Friendly; individual against self, with Terry against himself in a change of allegiance from complacent tool to fighting reformer; individual against society, with Terry at first against the forces of law and then against his former friends and fellow longshoremen after he "hollers cop" to the state Crime Commission; and, society against society, with the state Crime Commission against the criminal syndicate in a struggle over commercial control on the waterfront. The catalyst for the change in Terry is his love for Edie, the moral urgings of the priest, and the killing of his brother Charlie.

### Crises and the Protagonist

Terry's change of character is credible and necessary because of what happens to him within each major crisis of the story. His change of character and recognition of self-delusion are revealed progressively as follows:

Servile tool of Friendly to shock at his role in the death of Joey (Figure 2.7).

FIGURE 2.7 *The protagonist young Terry Malloy (Marlon Brando—center), is revealed as less than brilliant through his inability to count the money handed to him by the mob boss (Lee J. Cobb—left) as Terry's brother (Rod Steiger—right) watches, a characteristic dramatized by action as well as dialogue.*

*Russ Burton wrote, "Brando is called upon to delineate the psychological and emotional growth of a painfully self-conscious failure who owes society nothing to an individual who accepts responsibility even though it means turning against the codes that had once been his standard. His portrayal is incisive and complete, and they can put his name on the Oscar now and save the etcher time." (Daily News, Los Angeles, October 7, 1954.)*

**ON THE WATERFRONT** (U.S.A., 1954) DIRECTED BY ELIA KAZAN. WITH MARLON BRANDO, KARL MALDEN, LEE J. COBB, AND EVA MARIE SAINT.

Shock to guilt feelings through his attraction to Edie, Joey's sister.

Guilt to awakening of conscience through the moral urgings of the priest.

Conscience deepening through his growing love for Edie.

Love to shame at being accused by Edie of being "owned by Johnny Friendly."

Shame to outrage at the murder of Doogan while unloading cargo in a ship's hold.

Outrage to confession, to the priest and to Edie, at being an accomplice to the killing of Joey.

Confession to possible willingness to testify before the Crime Commission in Joey's place.

Willingness to change to passive courage in the face of bribes and threats.

Passive courage to active courage after the murder of his brother Charlie.

Active courage to a decision to testify at the urging of the priest before the Crime Commission.

Testimony to a personal challenge to Johnny Friendly to fight it out, a fight Terry loses through the intervention of goons, but in losing courageously wins the respect of the longshoremen.

Complete transformation of Terry from servile tool of corruption to an honest and brave union leader (Figure 2.8).

The foregoing progression reveals that Terry's change is not sudden but is a dialectical process with each succeeding crisis joining the conflict until the final denouement.

## Obligatory Scene, Climax, and Denouement

The *obligatory scene* is something the audience expects to happen as a consequence of the way the story begins and as a consequence of what the protagonist is drawn into doing. It is Terry who has inadvertently prevented Joey from testifying before the Crime Commission, and it is dramatically obligatory that he take Joey's place as a witness. The story begins with the servility of Terry to Johnny Friendly, and it is dramatically obligatory that the criminal boss be brought to justice by the testimony of his former underling. This occurs in the courtroom scene when Terry not only reveals the corruption of the unions but brings about Friendly's downfall within the syndicate: A cutaway to a mysterious figure watching the proceedings on television includes the line of dialogue, "If Mr. Friendly calls me on the telephone at any time tell him I am unavailable."

The seeds of credibility and necessity for Terry's change of attitude, and his willingness to fight back when aroused, are planted near the beginning of the film. Terry protests when he discovers he has been duped into decoying Joey to his death, which suggests he would not have been a party to the killing had he known the reason for the trap. And it is revealed that he had actually been a winning boxer—a contender—until his venal brother coerced him into throwing an important fight so that Friendly could win some bets, a "fix" that finished Terry's ring career.

Terry is basically a good person and a brave man, albeit not too bright, and he is vulnerable to the blandishments of his only family, his brother Charlie. The mur-

FIGURE 2.8   *The end comes when Johnny Friendly rages and curses impotently as Terry Malloy leads the longshoremen to work, the power of the mob now broken on the waterfront. Also featured in this classic were Karl Malden and Eva Marie Saint, who received an Academy Award for best supporting actress.*

**ON THE WATERFRONT** DIRECTED BY ELIA KAZAN.

der of Charlie in an attempt to intimidate him propels Terry into a retaliatory attack that the priest then guides into obligatory testimony before the Crime Commission.

The climax occurs after Terry's (obligatory) testimony in the courtroom. Friendly is facing indictment, but he still has control of his hoodlums and, through them, power over the longshoremen. So great is his rage at Terry's testimony, however, that Friendly tells his thugs that when the time comes he will personally get even with Terry: "He's *mine!*"

The climax comes when Terry is first rejected for work on a ship and then shunned by his fellow longshoremen, who are afraid to be seen associating with "a cheese eater." Terry strides over to Friendly's office on a barge-houseboat and confronts the criminal leader before the assembled longshoremen and thugs. Terry accuses Friendly of being a coward and hiding behind a gang while robbing decent men. He taunts, "Without your pistols, you're nothin'!" Stung and at bay, the boss comes out to fight Terry in a one-on-one battle witnessed by both sides.

But Terry fights like a winning prizefighter and soon Friendly is yelping for help from his goons. Their help turns the tide in two directions: Terry loses the battle but wins the war. The longshoremen, thrilled by Terry's courage and the proof of his challenge, refuse the order of the badly battered Friendly to go back to work. They agree to work only if personally led by their new leader, Terry Malloy. In the climax the criminal power is broken where it counts, among the longshoremen on the waterfront. And the theme is realized in action: "If you stand up and fight the criminals, you can break them."

The denouement comes with the symbolic aftermath of Terry's courage in testifying before the Crime Commission and in battling Friendly before everyone.

Joey's father, the most groveling exponent of "D and D" and "Don't fight back," gives Johnny Friendly a shove that sends him tumbling into the water of the harbor to the hoots and jeers of the longshoremen. The most craven among them has humiliated the criminal leader. The thugs are now themselves intimidated and do nothing. And Terry, exhorted by Edie and the priest, rises above the injuries he has received to lead his men back to work and victory *On the Waterfront*.

## The Character Study

In most American films dramatic structure is a means of telling a story logically that reveals insight into characters and reveals a theme in action. From Europe has come a form of cinematic structure in which characters in conflict are interpreted differently—the character study.

This conceptual approach presents a series of scenes that symbolically reveal theme, character, or circumstance—without that sequence necessarily being a crisis created by a protagonist attempting to achieve a goal. In the character study events may just happen by fortuitous circumstance, as they do in real life; and they may bear little logical relationship to what has gone before or what comes after except in a symbolic sense. The story presents a cinematic equivalent of life itself. Each scene is staged and photographed as a dramatic vignette, as the director thinks of them, and they are strung end to end until the conclusion. Outstanding examples of the character study approach in American cinema include such beauties as *Places in the Heart* and *Terms of Endearment*.

The well-directed character study often has moments of exquisite insight with forms characterized by experimentation and frequently a high order of originality. Federico Fellini, a poet in cinema, creates characters dominated by their dreams who are carried away for better or worse by their sojourns of the mind. In his classic film *8½*, he recounts the story of a film director who is drained of fresh ideas but everyone expects him to create yet again. The substance of the film consists of scenes portraying his ennui, frustrations, and fantasies. And yet, many of them could have been omitted without affecting in the slightest the logic and continuity of the film. If a sequence were omitted from most American films, written as they are to reveal cause-and-effect relationships, the effect would be devastating.

European films provide many such examples of character studies and ensemble writing in which scenes are included for their symbolic values—political, social, and economic—that could be left out without affecting the continuity of the film. In an art-for-art's-sake approach, internal structures of dreams, thoughts, fantasies, and hallucinations replace traditional narrative structures by finding their formative equivalent in the potential and plasticity of film itself. For all its freshness, the improvised approach is sometimes vulnerable to illogical continuity in the story, flaccid character development, and a conclusion that is not a climax—it just happens. The richness of the European approach, however, has firmly established the character study in American cinema and added depth to what is otherwise a story-oriented national form.

"The screenwriter," continues Norman Corwin, "is in a position somewhat analogous to that of a man or woman entering upon a marriage, except that in the case of the writer it is a polygamous or polyandrous marriage. He or she is married to more than one groom or bride, and, just as in what we call life—'real life'—he or she is subject to vagaries of fortune. If the writer is unlucky he [or she] will, like some species of insect or animal, be devoured by his mate or mates. Or, he may deliver his brainchild to a host of mates or pushy members of the wedding who will decide—almost always in his absence— what is 'best' for what he has written. In this case, send regrets, send flowers.

"Fortunately," Corwin concludes, "there can be and have been reasonably frequent cases where the relationship of writer, director, editor, and cast is smooth. This happens when all are committed to seeking truths in the creation of their film. Then they all live happily ever after, or at least until the post-production phase."

Craig Noel, actor and director with experience in film and theater, has worked as a dialogue director for feature films at 20th Century Fox; directed the Ernie Pyle Theatre, Tokyo; directed more than 200 plays of all styles and produced an additional 270 plays directed by others. His vision for the Old Globe Theatre of San Diego resulted in the establishment of the Shakespeare Festival in the late '40s, expansion to two theaters in the '50s, Globe Educational Tours in the '70s and Teatro Meta (Latino outreach) and Master of Fine Arts training program in the '80s. Among his many awards are a tribute from the Public Arts Advisory Council and the mayor's Living Treasure Award. He now serves as Executive Producer with the Old Globe Theatre in San Diego.

# Three

# ADAPTATION
## *with Craig Noel*

A SURPRISINGLY HIGH PROPORTION of feature films come from sources other than original screenplays. At various times the proportion of motion pictures adapted from other media has been as high as 85 percent of the total number of films released within a given year. The reasons for the adaptive urge are understandable: Successful novels and stage plays often have vividly drawn characters, exciting themes and stories, and above all, publicity that attracts many people who have enjoyed the book or the play to see the filmed adaptation. What happens then is another kind of experience.

## Stage Play into Cinema

Stage plays are frequently thought to lend themselves to film adaptations more readily than novels because the two forms share conceptual and physical properties. Both have similar dramatic structures. Both utilize actors carrying forth dramatic actions. Both use spoken dialogue.

But adaptations of superb and popular stage plays to film have sometimes been great disappointments because perceptual differences exist between the two forms. The flow of drama across the boards that seemed so sweeping when the lights were dimmed looks closed in and cramped on film. The gestures of players that seemed so dynamic from the balcony appear overblown on the screen. The dialogue that was so rich and fraught with meaning when it came trippingly from the tongues of fine actors has become so much numbing chatter from people who, it seems, will never stop talking so we can relax and watch the movie.

The resemblance between theater and cinema is superficial and deceptive; and the nature of the resemblance is such as to make the adaptation of a stage play into film far more difficult, in many ways, than the adaptation of a novel. The difficulty lies in the irreconcilable natures of the concepts and physical properties that inform each and that at first glance make them appear alike.

## Performance Differences

The screenwriter is in large measure responsible for adapting stage plays and novels to cinema. Before treating those elements needing adaptation, however, it may be illuminating to discuss why they *need* adaptation; at the heart of the media differences is performance (Figure 3.1).

Craig Noel says, "The distance of the actor or actress from the audience affects how much the performer may physically project ideas and emotions and, indeed, affects the very form of its expression. In a theater, the public may be a distance of anywhere from ten feet in the first row to fifty yards in the second balcony. At such distances the player must communicate by projecting through louder voice volumes, bigger physical actions, stronger energy levels. Subtleties of performance will be lost to those sitting beyond the first few rows.

"In the case of film," Noel continues, "there should be little or no projection because the camera takes the viewer up to the player to perceive every nuance of meaning in the facial expressions of the actor or actress. Distance as a factor is almost nil and every subtlety is magnified.

"The performer acting for film has in common with theater and with television the creation of a character in a dramatic situation with whom the viewer can identify and live another life. The performer must recreate within himself or herself the infinite variety of complex human emotions and render them outwardly through talent and craft, so the viewer will experience oneness with the life and story being told on the screen. The differences between the two media are quite profound, however, and relate to how the story is written and the conditions of performance."
—*Craig Noel*

FIGURE 3.1   *The filmed version of the stage play stars Sidney Poitier with Ruby Dee in a rich portrayal of the pride and anguish of a black family that suddenly comes into insurance money upon the death of the father. The change of medium was effective, however, and did not affect the universality of the theme.*

*John Cutts wrote, "No matter that the Younger family are negroes—their situation, their frustrations, are universal ones. The Youngers are the stuff of life itself, and one feels their pain and discomfort, their alternating shifts of sorrow and happiness."* Films and Filming, *July 1961.*

**A RAISIN IN THE SUN** (U.S.A., 1961) DIRECTED BY DANIEL PETRIE.

Truth must be in the eyes of the player because the lens will perceive every shade of deceit. Acting for the cinema must be the very essence of directness, simplicity, and honesty, with a general axiom that less is more.

"A good example of acting for cinema was Gary Cooper. If Mr. Cooper said, 'I see the cat, the cat is black,' he sounded as if he were reading the words off a blackboard. There was little or no inflection in his voice. But if you looked into his eyes, his eyes said eloquently that he saw the cat and the cat is black. His eyes expressed his thoughts and emotions with absolute honesty. What the eyes say is of utmost importance in motion pictures and is at the core of the differences between stage and screen: the hopes, the dreams, the love, the rejection, whatever the emotion. If the eyes tell the viewer the truth, there is no need to worry about what the sound track, the dialogue, is telling you. Gary Cooper knew this and he was absolutely honest, absolutely real, without pretense or affectation. He did everything in the easiest most expeditious way because he understood that economy is of the utmost importance in motion pictures.

"But," Noel indicates, "economy is not of the most importance in stage acting. Whether under the proscenium arch or in a small experimental theater, the player must be thinking about projecting to the audience in every move, every turn, with every word. Most importantly, he [or she] must be thinking about speaking dialogue because dialogue carries so much of the characterization and exposition on the stage. In film the player is thinking primarily, in the matter of technique, about relating to the camera."

Noel concludes by submitting "There is no reason why a good stage performer who understands the differences in media cannot become a good motion picture ac-tor, but it does not necessarily work the other way around. Laurence Olivier is a case in point. He understands how to project on stage and how to pull back for films. Gary Cooper, on the other hand, was very wise in never attempting to go into the theater because he could not have done it. Mr. Cooper was one of the many excellent film actors, superb craftsmen of the art of acting for the screen, who could not have transferred their aura and magnetism to the theater because they lacked the craft to project their emotions to the balcony. Performance differences determine so much of what is required in adapting stage plays into film."

## Stage Plays into Cinema

Any successful adaptation of a stage play to a motion picture requires that the screenwriter understand what common elements of these two deceptively similar art forms lend themselves to a change of medium, what elements require a change in the mode of expression, and what needs to be eliminated. The elements the film adaptor must be concerned with are *dramatic structure*, *characterizations*, *physical media differences*, *real time and cinematic time*, *dialogue exposition*, and *the spirit of the original play*.

### Dramatic Structure

Dramatic structure is the first common denominator. Both forms join a conflict immediately, presenting the origins and circumstances of the conflict—the time, the place, and the setting—with clues to the climax and the obligatory scenes. Both present their points of dramatic attack as deriving from a traumatic event, a pending event, an object of contention, the duress of a change in lifestyle. Both tend to employ a protagonist who wants something and strikes out for it and an antagonist in some form who sets forces in opposition, forces that are either changed by the protagonist or cause the protagonist's death. And both ascend through a series of crises to an obligatory scene, a climax, and a denouement.

The internal crisis structure of the stage play and the screenplay are different, however, because of the differences between stage continuity and screen continuity. The modern stage play has been cast into the stylistic structure of the one-act, two-act, and three-act play, with a curtain fall between the acts of the longer forms. This segmentation of the dramatic action exists for practical reasons: to permit a change of sets and costumes, to allow a passage of dramatic time, and to give a respite to actors and audience alike. Although the stage concept of the *act* is an artistic convention sanctified by centuries of use, the segmentation disrupts the flow of the story—the antithesis of the continuum of cinema.

Cinematic continuity is best served by an uninterrupted flow of story and action from the first fade-in to the last fade-out without any respites along the way (except in the case of those very long films, such as *Gone with the Wind*, in which viewer discomfort may be a factor). In adaptation, the act format of the stage play should be expunged and the dramatic structure revised to provide an unbroken flow of cinematic continuity. This often requires reducing the emphasis in the high-crisis structure near the end of an act to one of progressive build. Failure to so modify the crisis structure tends to segment the film; although the story may continue without a break in physical continuity, the viewer may sense the lumbering down of the unseen curtain.

### Characterizations

Characterization is the second common denominator. In both the stage play and the dramatic film the major characters are rendered in-the-round, presenting such fully considered traits as their physical and physiological characteristics, their environmental factors of upbringing, education, occupation, and lifestyle, and their psychological factors of intelligence, attitudes, quirks, and personal premises. Both art forms present minor characters in perspective to the major—using them as foils and expositional devices—and both orchestrate their characters to enhance the dramatic conflict. The realism of character portrayal on stage and screen are different, however, because of the differing media in which they are rendered.

The stage character is a *universal type*, containing in one individual most of the elements found in a class of human beings. Because of the distance from which a stage character is viewed, the audience is never permitted to look closely into his or her eyes during moments of triumph and tragedy. The viewer seldom feels the personal emotion of an individual but sees on the broad canvas of stage characterization the common exaltation and anguish of humanity. Because of this universality of characteristics and the slightly detached quality of stage projection, the stage character tends to appear larger than life.

The screen character, on the other hand, is an *individual* because of the intimacy with which he or she may be viewed in close-up. The character's problems in the story may be those conflicts common to the rest of us in human bondage, but the outcome of the story concerns *this* individual's solution to the problem. The stage play *I Never Sang for My Father* presented a universal story of the inability of father and son to communicate in any meaningful way. But when it was adapted to film, the story became that of individuals who had to solve their problems in a unique way, a solution not necessarily having universal implications. This change was not so much a consequence of adaptation but of the differing media techniques used to present the characters.

## Physical Media Differences

The physical differences of the media are a major stumbling block in adapting the stage play to film. The play is usually presented within the confines of a single proscenium stage with only a few changes of background. Although the technique of limbo-lighting (actors spotlighted on a darkened stage) two or three settings within a given background has provided it some of the flexibility of film, the dramatic action occurs within a narrow physical scope. Within the world of the theater, with its warm, breathing humanity and player-to-audience rapport, this narrow physical scope seems more than adequate.

But when a play is photographed within a setting as strictured as the original stage, the resulting film takes on a cramped, closed-in quality. The viewer suddenly feels confined when watching a small action spread out on a large screen and deprived of mobility. The film viewer expects to see a mobile medium that moves with alacrity from person to person and setting to setting. A photographed stage play merely provides the narrowness of action of the live theater without its life—the worst of two worlds. If the film adaptor is so in awe of the original stage play that he or she is afraid to cut it with the knife of cinematic need, the adaptor will be recording only the facts thereby violating the spirit that has made the play significant. The first film version of *Death of a Salesman* (1951) was thus flawed.

Another fundamental difference is the relative control over the playgoer's gaze versus the moviegoer's gaze. A playgoer is free to look where he or she wishes. If an ensemble scene is presented on the stage, a person sitting in the audience has the options of looking at the actor who is speaking, watching the actress who is listening, or admiring the decorations on the proscenium arch. To some degree the stage director may control the playgoer's focus of interest by lighting the action as it is blocked, but the playgoer's gaze is essentially free to wander where it will.

In a motion picture the converse is true: The film determines what the viewer will see at any point in time by presenting the viewer with only one image to look at. The filmmaker decides whether the viewer's attention should be drawn to an action, a reaction, or an objective detail. The gaze of the moviegoer is subject to the centers of interest, movement, and visual control of the filmmaker.

Opening up the closed-in stage play is important in any adaptation to film. One ploy is to place the opening sequences out of doors, before the drama actually begins indoors, leaving the audience with a residual impression of openness to the extent that much interior action may subsequently occur before the spectators become aware of the cloistered context. In the Franco Zeffirelli version of *Romeo and Juliet*, for example, the opening scenes under the titles reveal the outer world of that time—bustling marketplaces and massive castles; men on horseback dressed in dashing costumes clattering through swirling crowds—to compensate in part for the fact that most of the succeeding drama takes place in small interior sets. Eventually the closed-in quality of the drama becomes obvious, but the nature of the story is such that the transition progressively enhances the rising tension of the conflict;

the story presents a dramatic flow that starts with the broad establishing scenes out of doors and ends with a tight little conflict indoors.

Exposition should be combed to find legitimate reasons inherent in the story for providing cinematic excitement in the adaptation to film. This exposition is usually embedded in the dialogue of one character to excuse the absence of another. If the original stage play contains dialogue indicating that another character has gone to the airport to pick up a third character, that exposition may become an excuse to take the camera outside and relieve the cramped quality of the original setting by showing sweeping crowds and the ruthless alacrity of conveyor belts banging up expensive luggage.

A ride in the park is another common subterfuge for getting outside. If two characters are engaged in a conversation or a quarrel in which one location is as good as any other, the two may talk in an automobile as well as in a living room, thereby adding movement as the world goes whizzing by outside. The walk in the garden is another technique for adding blue sky as relief from unrelieved walls. In *I Never Sang for My Father*, the son's confrontations with his father are interspersed with automobile drives to visit his father, talks in the garden with his sister, and arrivals at airports and railroad stations: cinematic perforations that provide exterior relief for an interior story.

The mobile camera, however, is the most common solution for leavening a cramped set, a technique used with conspicuous success in Milos Forman's film adaptation of *Amadeus*. Crane-mounted cameras prowled through the sets and among the characters during establishing scenes, transitional shots, and times of confrontation; the lenses glided smoothly after those characters moving from one part of the room to the other or one room to the next, providing variety in camera angles for editing.

Other camera techniques are used to telescope the set, such as dramatic compositions that exaggerate the depth from object to subject or subject to subject. Another is the slip-focus (or rack-focus) shot, which shifts the viewer's attention from foreground to background or background to foreground, providing movement depth when the characters are static. Movements by the subject directly toward and directly away from the camera also create the illusion that there is more room for activity than actually exists on the set. And, of course, subjective views can be used, as the character turns to look out a window at a sweeping panorama of landscape or watch the approach of another character.

Lighting techniques can also be used to contribute depth. Splashes of light may be thrown on a set wall so that they diminish in illumination level as the splashes recede in the distance. Radical changes in the lighting levels and the mood from one dramatic sequence to the next offer visual variety. Distance may be further implied by letting a character emerge from the shadows or recede through darkened doorways and by staging one scene in halftone and the next in a full flood of light.

The editing techniques used in film adaptations of stage plays differ from those used in stories having naturally cinematic material. Scenes that would be edited rather simply in more cinematic stories are often cut rapidly in adaptations in the hope that frequent changes of camera angle and scene within a brief period of time will compensate for the lack of change in the setting. An accelerated editing tempo at every crisis and opportunity is typical of the filmed adaptation.

## Real Time and Cinematic Time

Real time and cinematic time are two fundamental differences between the stage play and the film. Real time requires that living people walk across a solid stage in whatever time it takes to physically transport themselves from one place to the other. The time portrayed in the play usually corresponds to the length of the play itself, with a long passage of time (frequently) implied by a curtain fall and a note in the program to the effect that the next act takes place "two weeks later." During the course of the dramatic action, the actors are as timebound and earthbound as the playgoers watching them. Real time as a stage concept is reinforced by the dialogue that carries the bulk of the exposition and character development. There is no way to expedite dialogue—the time needed to speak the words—except to eliminate it.

Cinematic time is created by the elimination of all superfluous and intervening actions; a three-minute climb up a staircase might be reduced to seconds in a film. The motion picture is free of the bondage of the real time needed to execute a physical act and can imply transitions of time and location without being forced to reveal them. Any adaptation from stage play to film, then, would require the deletion of many of the real time dramatic actions of the play.

## Dialogue Exposition

Dialogue exposition is possibly the biggest obstacle in the transmutation of a stage play to film. Drama on the boards is essentially spoken drama in which plot, character development, crises, and off-screen actions are rendered in dialogue. The exposition is embedded primarily in *words* (not images as in cinema) and secondarily in gestures. Although some motion picture techniques have been adapted to the stage (such as limbo-lighting of separate contemporaneous actions), the substantive exposition of a stage play continues to be locked into words.

Images convey the exposition in film. Cinema requires that the story and character development be revealed primarily through cinematography and editing, rather than dialogue. Exposition is photographed, not described. The most earthbound, least cinematic moments in most films occur when the characters talk to each other and the story is locked into real time. If a stage play is inseparable from words and cinematic exposition is intrinsically visual, how then do we proceed to make the adaptation: by ruthlessly cutting out those splendid glowing descriptive passages from the dialogue and rendering them photographically, cries of outrage from the playwright notwithstanding. The verbal description of something being presented visually cannot be retained because it will create a labeling effect, a patronizing impression that is at best annoying, at worst laughable.

Shakespearean plays and other classics present the film adaptor with a real dilemma because their greatness to a large extent lies in their literary qualities. If the play is being filmed with the original dialogue, the screenwriter should select only those lines that work cinematically, should render exposition visually, and should be prepared to take the critical consequences. The adaptor cannot take liberties with the classics without infuriating the purists, yet it sometimes must be done in order to make an adaptation that is true to cinema.

The adaptor must in particular watch out for stage dialogue written to compensate for the audience's inability to see a player's face in close-up, lines such as "Mary, you are looking at me with distrust and disdain in your eyes!" In cinema, of course, viewers can see a close-up to judge the expression in Mary's eyes, and if the speaker then makes that kind of remark, the audience will be rolling in the aisles (or walking up them).

### The Spirit of the Original Play

The spirit of the original play includes the rapport between the actors and the audience (Figure 3.2). This intangible and sometimes magical atmosphere varies from performance to performance depending upon the quality and disposition of the cast, the characters and attitudes of the audience, and the traffic the latter has had to contend with to attend the performance. The excitement of an evening at the theater—the festive air—affects the performance and pacing of the actors; the interplay between the playgoers and the performers makes the play a living thing. Those who have first seen the play and then watched the screen adaptation often complain that this human presence and rapport is missing in the film. The critics may not clearly understand the essentially different natures of the two art forms. When they object to the difference in dramatic impact, they are insisting that an apple should taste like a pear because both are fruits grown in trees.

A completed motion picture and a viewer simply do not have any interaction. A finished film presentation remains the same whether it plays to a full house or an empty one, and the reaction of the viewers and the critics, one way or the other, will not modify the presentation. The spirit of the living play is one fundamental characteristic that cannot be adapted to the screen.

The best that may be hoped for in an adaptation from stage to screen is to re-create in cinematic form the playwright's premise, joining of the conflict, major crises, obligatory scene and climax, and the essential development of the major characters involved in the story. All uniquely theatrical techniques should be scrapped in favor of cinematic techniques that can express the same ideas. Stage dialogue exposition should be discarded and, whenever possible, plot, exposition, and characterization should be transmuted into motion pictures. The dialogue itself should not carry the solidity of the stage but the weightlessness of the cinema and should be used primarily when the ideas cannot be given visual expression.

The screenwriter who intends to make a motion picture true to the spirit, story, and characteristics of the original play must, paradoxically, be prepared to ruthlessly cut apart its stage qualities and reassemble its fundamental elements into true cinematic form. The adaptor must be prepared to resist the rage of the playwright, ignore the howls of the star and the supporting actors, and burn the reviews of the critics.

## Novels into Cinema

The premiere of a film adaptation of a novel is often followed by a chorus of complaints from the author, the critics, and the readers-viewers alike that the film version has butchered the novel. Sometimes this is true. More often, however, the complaints are based on the assumption that the characters, events, and spirit of the novel are freely interchangeable with the characters, events, and spirit of the dramatic film, a premise that in turn implies that the novel provides the standard from which the film adaptation deviates at its

**FIGURE 3.2** *The spirit of a film exists independently of the viewers, whereas the spirit of a
play is an interactive process between players
and audience. In this scene from the film* On
Golden Pond, *(left to right: Jane Fonda,
Katharine Hepburn, Henry Fonda, and
Doug McKeon), we, as outside viewers,
are peeking in on a happy birthday party.
If we were part of the audience at the stage
play, we would become participants in the
event.*

*Director Rydell comments, "When Jane
Fonda first read* On Golden Pond, *she not only
appreciated its humor and perception, but also
recognized a signal opportunity to present her
father in a bravura screen role playing a highly
complex character in what became his last and
Oscar-winning performance."*

67

NOVELS INTO CINEMA

**ON GOLDEN POND** (U.S.A., 1981) DIRECTED BY MARK RYDELL.

peril (Figure 3.3). This assumption fails to recognize that the novel and the motion picture represent different artistic genera, as different from each other as music and sculpture. Those who object strenuously that their film-viewing experience was different from their novel-reading experience may be unaware that fundamental elements of an intrinsic nature preclude the direct transfer of a novel's conceptual form into a dramatic film.

Differences inherent in the novel and the film determine many of the changes required in any adaptation from one medium to another, but the pattern of changes tends to be consistent, although subject to variations in the story content of the novels themselves. When transmuting novel into cinema, the adaptor is concerned with such elements as *media differences, suitability of the novel for adaptation, condensation of the novel, continuity revisions, viewpoint relationships, equivalence, leading characters, action sequences, settings, dialogue, love, sex,* and *violence, matters of taste,* and *universal issues.*

## Media Differences

Differences in the media require changing the means and modes of expressing ideas. The most fundamental of these changes is the transmutation of *verbal content* into *visual content.*

The novel is deaf and blind. The sounds of voice and music, the rustle of leaves, the din of battle, the whimper of a child, and the whispers of love are all heard through symbols that echo in the sound chamber of the mind's ear. The sight of leaves turning crimson after a frost, the first snow in a pine forest, the swath of death cut by a cannonball, the sudden blush of a lovely woman can be seen by the reader only through the stimuli of words that project their images on the screen of the mind's eye. Because readers vary in their literacy levels, they each ascribe their own interpretations to the words, creating their own sights and sounds.

The motion picture, to the contrary, is a perceptual art form that presents all viewers with identical sights and sounds. All viewers see the same images of Dr. Zhivago riding across the snow-covered taiga to a rendezvous with Lara, the Scots cavalry hurling themselves in waves against the cannons of Napoleon at Waterloo, and the supple bodies of a man and a woman making love. All hear the same sounds of hoofbeats on packed snow, the cries of the wounded and dying men as they fall, and the whispers of love. Even though each viewer tends to look for those things that are familiar and significant to him or her, the motion picture nevertheless offers a common experience far less vulnerable to variations in interpretation than does the arbitrary word.

The novel, moreover, makes use of such literary devices as tropes, which have no counterpart in film. Expressions such as "the slings and arrows of outrageous fortune" *(Hamlet)* and "she flung the javelin of her will" (John Steinbeck's *Winter of Our Discontent*) cannot, for obvious reasons, be transmuted to motion pictures. Similes and metaphors may enrich the pages of the novel, to the great pleasure of the reader, and be a salient characteristic of the author's style, yet they cannot be rendered on film without becoming laughable. The broad spectrum of colors and flavors unique to the printed word cannot be transmuted to the motion picture.

The cinema, on the other hand, has its unique modes of expression. The close-up and extreme close-up yield an emotional impact different in kind and quality from a written expression or an exclamation point, and these cinematic techniques may

FIGURE 3.3 *Whoopi Goldberg plays the role of Celie, who waits and yearns for her sister during the years she was abused by Mister. Goldberg says, "After I read* The Color Purple, *I wrote Alice Walker and told her if they ever made a film of the book, I'd like to play anything in it. . . . a piece of dust on the floor, a screen door, anything."*

*Author Alice Walker wrote of the film adaptation of her book* The Color Purple, *"My hopes for the movie are that people will celebrate the spirit of Celie and Shug and the other characters, celebrate being alive, struggling together and maintaining our connections with each other even though it can be hard to do that. . . . When I first saw her (Whoopi Goldberg), I knew she was my ideal Celie . . . incredibly smart, with a pointed sense of humor."*

**THE COLOR PURPLE** DIRECTED BY STEVEN SPIELBERG.

FIGURE 3.4   *The novel that lends itself most readily to filmed adaptation is the one that tells the story in objective actions rather than in subjective thoughts and the novel with chronological events that take place within a relatively brief span of time. Ernest Hemingway's short novel was itself almost a screenplay in its brevity and objectivity. Spencer Tracy stars movingly in the filmed adaptation as the old man, with Felipe Pazos as the boy.*

**THE OLD MAN AND THE SEA** (U.S.A., 1958) DIRECTED BY JOHN STURGES.

FIGURE 3.5 *The film portrayals of Tom Joad and his family, as well as the other major characters, are close physical, psychological, and environmental equivalents of those found in John Steinbeck's novel* The Grapes of Wrath. *Henry Fonda (left) stars as Tom Joad; John Carradine (center) portrays the preacher, and John Qualen plays Muley.*

be used in ways having no counterpart in the novel. Furthermore, seeing a subject tells more about him or her in an instant, more explicitly, than pages of exposition. The motion picture not only expresses similar concepts by means fundamentally different from those of the novel, but it may express ideas and emotions that are outside the ken of the printed word.

**THE GRAPES OF WRATH** (U.S.A., 1940) DIRECTED BY JOHN FORD.

### Suitability for Adaptation

The suitability of a novel for adaptation depends upon whether the author's style is introspective or descriptive (Figure 3.4).

The introspective novel tends to probe the psyches of its characters to reveal their thoughts, their feelings, their fears, fantasies, and phobias—sometimes with little overt action on the part of the characters. This kind of novel is difficult to adapt to cinematic form because its elements do not have the objective forms in real life needed for cinematography. A life lived inside the skull of a character cannot be transmuted to the screen without contriving some forms of cinematic action that did not exist in the novel, changes that may substantively alter the original concept of the novel. The film adapted from the introspective novel, however successful and popular the movie may be, almost invariably disappoints those readers-viewers who have looked forward to enjoying a cine-

matic portrayal of their reading pleasure.

The descriptive novel tends to tell the story in overt dramatic action, physical action, with the development of characters revealed in outward movements and dialogue (Figure 3.5). The descriptive novel lends itself best to adaptation because it resembles the classic form of the screenplay, with introductory exposition to establish the setting followed by straight dialogue and dramatic actions. Because these novels avoid getting into the minds of the characters, they lend themselves to film versions with the least amount of mutilation to the original concepts.

FIGURE 3.6 *The trek of the Joad family to California in their canvassed jalopy provides many of the action equivalents of the novel, which parodied the pioneers' bitter migration to the West. Because John Steinbeck's novel contained more events and characters than could be viably transmuted to film, condensation was vital.*

**THE GRAPES OF WRATH** DIRECTED BY JOHN FORD.

## Condensation

Condensation is frequently necessary because the scope of a novel more often than not exceeds the potential scope of a single motion picture (Figure 3.6). A novel may encompass a time span of years, even millennia, moving easily between the past, present, and future within a paragraph and without disrupting the continuity or losing the reader. Novels cast in the epic mold of James Michener's *Hawaii* that encompass the lifetimes of generations of characters cannot be filmed with anything like the scope of the original book. The best that can be done is to take one brief segment, select a few of the many hundreds of characters, and adapt that story to the screen.

Serialized versions of novels adapted for television, such as *Roots* or *War and Remembrance*, are less demanding in this regard. The need for condensation, however, is almost universal; cinematic criteria, not literary criteria, should be used in the selection of content.

## Continuity Revisions

In order to change the narrative story line of a novel into the dramatic structure of a film it is frequently necessary to make continuity revisions. In the course of making such revisions some events and characters may be moved up to the first joining of the conflict whereas other subplots, events, and minor characters may be moved back or eliminated. Chronological sequence is more often the rule in the film than in the novel; when events are shown out of chronology in films, they are usually presented by means of cinematic transition such as flashback or flashforward.

## Viewpoint Relationships

A different viewpoint relationship exists between the characters of the descriptive novel and the reader than that between the characters of a film and the viewer. In many descriptive novels, particularly mystery novels, the characters know the answers to the story and its conflicts, and the reader must complete the novel to discover what at least one of the characters knows.

In most films, on the other hand, the characters are groping toward or against each other in the film, trying to find out what the viewer already knows. The viewer can watch the separate actions of the protagonist and his or her adversaries through parallel editing and cutaways while the screen characters struggle blindly against each other. In *Lonely Are the Brave* (adapted from Edward Abbey's *The Brave Cowboy*), for example, the viewer watches the attempts of the vagrant cowboy to escape from the law while also seeing the struggles of the sheriff, the posse, and the Air Force to run him down. When the cowboy is about to run the gauntlet of a police ambush, the viewer sees its preparation and execution from the points of view of all sides, although none of the screen adversaries know for sure what the others are doing.

A film version will most often be told from a third-person point of view, the omniscient viewpoint, regardless of the narrative voice of the novelist. Almost 90 percent of the novels adapted to film have been rendered from the omniscient viewpoint characteristic of cinema, and those film versions that tried the first-person perspective have often reverted to the third-person in order to present events that would be outside the scope of a first-person narrative.

When the film uses the first-person viewpoint, it is usually handled in two ways: through the use of the subjective camera, in which the viewer sees through the eye of the subject and thereby experiences the character's perceptions; and through the use of a voice-over narrator,

FIGURE 3.7 *Director Sydney Pollack says this about his casting of Robert Redford (shown here with Meryl Streep) as the male lead in* Out of Africa. *"I have always thought of Denys Finch-Hatton as a combination of Hubbell Gardner from* The Way We Were *and Jeremiah Johnson. He is this ultimate individualist. There is a lot of the real Redford in there."*

in which the subject speaks directly to the viewer. Both of these techniques are used in Norman Corwin's classic film *Lust for Life*. The visual viewpoint alternates between subjective camera techniques and the third-person point of view in order to reveal van Gogh's perspective on the world and the world's perspective on him. In the sound track of the same film Corwin allows the artist to speak dirctly to the viewer—over scenes of van Gogh's subjects and paintings—to express his inner feelings about art in a way that could not be revealed in dramatic action.

### Equivalence

Equivalence is an important concern in most film versions of novels, authors' complaints notwithstanding. In the majority of adaptations the film versions retain the main characters, story line, and dramatic actions of the original novels; and, within the limits of cinema, attempts are made to find film equivalents for many of the literary devices of the book. The title of the novel is almost invariably retained for its publicity value. Emotional equivalence in transmuting novel to film would be ideal.

The dramatic film's need for a broader audience carries with it, rightly or wrongly, the assumption that viewer comprehension is on the whole lower than reader comprehension, with a concomitant need for simplification of content. In the course of adaptation dialogue is shortened, modernized, given a conversational rather than a literary tone, and edited so that the average fourteen-year-old can readily understand it. Characters' names are changed when they are difficult to pronounce, when they resemble the names of other characters, or have inappropriate connotations for the contemporary viewer (as in Mark Twain's Nigger Jim in *Huckleberry* 

*Finn*). Ideas and complex forms of knowledge are simplified and, if dated, made current by relating them to topical events. The explicitness of film, which renders subtleties directly into graphic perceptual images, contributes to this simplification.

### Leading Characters

The leading characters in films adapted from novels usually follow the general characterizations of novelistic characters (Figure 3.7). Certain dramatic actions may need to be transferred or omitted because of cinematic exigencies, but for the most part the screen portrayal of major characters essentially conforms to the novelist's portrayal of characters.

Actors are usually chosen to play their roles with a serious attempt at following the novelist's interpretation of characters. But modifications of a character are sometimes prompted by the need to expand a screen character's role in order to meet the demands of a star performer; this is simply a reality of the film industry. Actions that were not in the novel may be added to exploit the actor's abilities. Actions in which the actor dominates may be retained, whereas actions dominated by others may be eliminated. Actions implemented by others in the novel may be transferred to the star performer in the film. And dramatic sequences in which the star is acting may be strategically relocated in order to emphasize the star's performance; the last scene of a dramatic film seldom fades out on a minor character.

### Action Sequences

The parts of a novel most frequently selected for adaptation to the screen are action sequences. To exploit the cinema's ability to dramatize actions and move-

**OUT OF AFRICA** (U.S.A., 1985) DIRECTED BY SYDNEY POLLACK.

FIGURE 3.8 *Equivalence of settings is some-thing sought and achieved in most films adapted from novels. This image reveals a set-ting—instantly—with a lucidity requiring long equivalent passages of prose in the novel. (From left to right: Jane Darwell, Doris Bow-den, Henry Fonda, O. Z. Whitehead, and Russell Simpson.) The cinema adaptation of* The Grapes of Wrath *was scrupulously rendered by the director to evoke the themes, substance, and spirit of the original novel. A sanitized ending was substituted in deference to the pub-lic's standards for film at that time, but the movie was true in its essence to the John Stein-beck novel.*

**THE GRAPES OF WRATH** DIRECTED BY JOHN FORD.

ments, the film adaptation tends to em-phasize plot rather than character devel-opment. Passive passages in the novel are rewritten whenever possible to be revealed in action and dialogue. Static passages—such as the author's insights, implications, and philosophical commentary—may have to be deleted unless they can be given cinematic form.

New action sequences having no coun-terpart in the book are inserted in more than half the adapted novels to flesh out the cinematic qualities of the films. These action sequences may exploit the motion picture's unique modes of expression, yet they enhance the thematic or dramatic qualities of the story. Other action se-quences are inserted to allegedly enhance audience appeal—such as scenes of sexual activity and violence—sequences that are frequently antithetical to the concept of the novel.

FIGURE 3.9 *Music is used to help convey setting in* The Color Purple. *Though it had no counterpart in the novel, giving voice to this music in the film added passion and color to the adaptation. Quincy Jones, composer of the musical score, has this to say: "The music is on a parallel path with Celie's growth. It encompasses the gambit from African music, church music, blues, and jazz. The period of Celie's* personal renaissance from 1906 to 1947 is also a renaissance of black music in America."

*Margaret Avery stars as lusty blues singer Shug Avery, a preacher's daughter who helps Celie realize her own potential. Avery says, "When I first read the book, I was immediately drawn to Shug. . . . Not just because we had the same last name, but because of Shug's love for life and free spirit."*

77

NOVELS INTO CINEMA

**THE COLOR PURPLE** DIRECTED BY STEVEN SPIELBERG.

## Settings

Settings play an important role in both the novel and the film because they provide the physical and emotional context for the story and its revelations of character. Settings that require pages of exposition in a novel may be shown in seconds on the screen (Figure 3.8). Visual rendition may easily communicate settings that the viewer grasps in an instant, without effort and without awareness of even doing so.

Because of the filmmaker's concern for transmuting as many elements of the original novel as possible, the settings of the film version are often the very essence of their description in the novel. To avoid the monotony of repetition, the screen version usually supplies a variety of settings not always found in the original book (Figure 3.9). Those settings in the novel that do not lend themselves to cinematography are usually deleted.

## Dialogue

Dialogue written for the eye is different from that written for the ear. In the novel a character may deliver a declamation that runs on for pages, that is, in fact, a speech. In the novel *Lust for Life*, for example, some sentences are half-a-page long, extensive enough to exhaust the lungs of an aspiring politician. Moreover, they are written as grammatically correct statements, complete with commas and semicolons and replete with a wide range of expressions having poetic, literary merit. Such forms of written dialogue usually pass unchallenged by the reader because they do not invite direct comparison with reality and because the reader concedes the author's literary license in expressing his or her views.

Dialogue written for the ear, however, invites comparison with the tongues of reality, the speech of daily life. Unfortunately, the average viewer does not always respond kindly to speeches loaded with poetic and literary allusions that try to pass as normal conversation. Viewers may laugh aloud at the same dialogue spoken in a dramatic film that they read without cavil in the novel.

When dialogue is adapted from a novel to dramatic film, the following changes are usually recommended.

> Only use the original dialogue that is required to develop character and give exposition in the film, regardless of its importance in the novel.

> Shorten the dialogue selected for use so it can be said in one breath, and revise it so it is easy for the actors to articulate.

> Prune literary allusions to make the lines palatable to a mass audience.

> Express the author's views in action in the climax of the film rather than in dialogue.

## Love, Sex, and Violence

Filmmakers often emphasize love, sex, and violence to lure viewers away from their television sets.

The love interest of a novel is often inflated in the film version (Figure 3.10). The exaltation of romance in the dramatic film sometimes eclipses everything else adapted from the novel, even though it may have been only a minor thread in the original story. The adaptor usually creates hero and heroine roles in which their love relationship determines the inclusion or omission of other characters, subplots, and events from the novel. One of the cherished beliefs of the American film industry is the canard that the average viewer wants most of all to see a love story. As long as this belief prevails, matters of the heart will dominate in most film adaptations, even though the novel may have emphasized other things (Figure 3.11).

Once upon a time the carnal aspects of a novel's love story were gently glossed over in the film adaptation. Today, this kind of activity is apt to be emphasized to present the adult viewer with the kind of visual experience he or she is unlikely to view on television. Brutality and violence are part of the same trend—tending to be portrayed more lavishly and graphically in the film than in the book. Violence was once treated circumspectly or eliminated; now many adaptors cull the text for violence to be vividly exploited on the screen regardless of its importance to the story and to the development of characters. Profanities and vulgarities—once omitted or played down in deference to public taste—are now frequently emphasized, flaunted, and dignified by the label "realistic adult entertainment."

Social criticism is sometimes modified or deleted when it is thought to be offensive to sizable segments of the American viewing public. Religious and political in-

FIGURE 3.10   *The theme of star-crossed love for Meryl Streep in her role as Isak Dinesen is played out to its end at a graveside. Edwin M. Yoder, Jr., wrote, "Dinesen's own particular tragedy is her romance with the hunter-adventurer Denys Finch-Hatton. It ends with a burial scene on one of those unspoiled African hilltops, with vistas stretching scores of miles. Over his open grave, Streep/Dinesen reads lines from Housman's "To An Athlete Dying Young."* The Washington Post, *January 19, 1986.*

**OUT OF AFRICA** DIRECTED BY SYDNEY POLLACK.

**THE COLOR PURPLE** DIRECTED BY STEVEN SPIELBERG.

FIGURE 3.11 *Capturing the spirit of Alice Walker's novel became a passion for everyone associated with the film. Screenwriter Menno Meyjes wrote, "In order to capture* The Color Purple's *humor, depth of character, and uplifting spirit, it was personally important to give as much of myself to the screenplay as Alice Walker gave to her book."*

*Oprah Winfrey, a superstar on television, made her film debut as the robust Sofia, the proud physical woman who marries Mister's son Harpo and whose strength is an inspiration to Celie. Winfrey says, "Sofia knows who she is. She's part of the legacy of strong black women whose courage and triumph have enabled me to be all that I am." Similarly, Willard Pugh says, "Playing Harpo made me rethink the entire sphere of loving human relationships. And, by the end of the production, Harpo and I were better men because of it."*

stitutions are seldom subject to the criticism, derision, and ridicule found in the original novel. Whenever such an attack is central to the themes of the novel, the film version tends to shift the blame to an individual who is an exception and not representative of the group, such as Johnny Friendly in *On the Waterfront*, or to eliminate the attack altogether.

The same film industry that creates feature films for theaters also produces the 80 percent of prime time television, which is produced as motion pictures. Given the vastness of this maw and its insatiable need for dramatic material, adaptations from stage plays, novels, and short stories will go on and on.

## Taste

Matters of taste, however, still tend to impose some limitations upon what may be adapted from the novel to the screen. Many serious novels conclude on a note of futility, despair, frustration, or indecision. This kind of emotional tone is often unacceptable to the average American viewer (particularly the younger audiences) but is acceptable to European and Asian audiences. The film version may therefore be made with two endings to accommodate domestic and foreign tastes. For an American audience, the films have traditionally ended on a note of hope and affirmation; for the others, on a note of futility. *The Key* concludes with a man racing down a railroad platform to catch a departing train on which the woman he loves is riding out of his life. In the American version, he catches the train and implicitly regains the woman. In the foreign version the train outraces him and he loses her forever. The recent trend has been away from the happy ending in American films and toward the ambivalence typical of foreign films.

## Universal Issues

The universal issues presented in a novel are often changed in film adaptations to offer a personal solution. Seldom does the film adaptation retain the catholic character of the original novel. Instead, the personalities are particularized to such a degree as to eliminate universal meanings. The outcome of the story is most often offered in terms of the consequences to an individual character and thus drained of broader implications.

Good and evil tend to be personified. In the novel evil exists in institutions and social forces, and the villain is generally the instrument through which evil works. The novel implies that as long as evil social forces exist, evil persons will exist to do their dirty work. This relationship is reversed in the film adaptation of the novel: All the properties of evil are invested in a specific individual whose evil apparently exists without context and whose destruc-

tion provides the solution to the conflict and an end to evil. The polarized philosophy that humanity is divided into two groups—good and bad—and that a slaying of evil will leave only good can also be found in films other than screen adaptations, but recent trends in contemporary cinema are away from such simplistic interpretations of life.

Social criticism is sometimes modified or deleted when it is thought to be offensive to sizable segments of the American viewing public. Religious and political institutions are seldom subject to the criticism, derision, and ridicule found in the original novel. Whenever such an attack is central to the themes of the novel, the film version tends to shift the blame to an individual who is an exception and not representative of the group, such as Johnny Friendly in *On the Waterfront*, or to eliminate the attack altogether.

The same film industry that creates feature films for theaters also produces the 80 percent of prime time television, which is produced as motion pictures. Given the vastness of this maw and its insatiable need for dramatic material, adaptations from stage plays, novels, and short stories will go on and on.

*Dean Tavoularis (left), shown with Francis Ford Coppola, is a production designer of feature films who adds the knowledge born of experience to this chapter. His many credits include* Bonnie and Clyde, Little Big Man, The Conversation, *and* One from the Heart. *Tavoularis has received Academy Award nominations for art direction of* Apocalypse Now, Tucker, *and* The Brinks Job *and was honored with an Oscar for art direction of* The Godfather, Part II.

# Four

# PRODUCTION DESIGN

*with Dean Tavoularis*

WHEN MOVIES FIRST BEGAN, the job of the artist was to paint roll-drop settings behind the dramatic action. With time the artist evolved into the art director who showed his or her sketches to the director and, when approval was obtained, made scale drawings, supervised set construction, and then dressed those sets with furniture and bric-a-brac. From set to set the stylistic consistency of the film was a matter of the art director's good sense, carried in his or her head, and there was seldom an attempt to influence the director's vision of the film. An exchange of nods over drawings was probably enough.

The art director became the production designer when David O. Selznick commissioned one man to do a scene-by-scene visual conception for the epic film *Gone with the Wind* and insisted on posting this credit: "This film was designed by William Cameron Menzies." Although that production had three successive directors and swirled in controversy, the motion picture was artistically and commercially successful because Selznick insisted that each director in turn be true to the production designer's vision of *Gone with the Wind*. In this instance, the production designer was the director of the visual interpretation of the script. Thereafter, it became standard practice in most studios to have a feature film visualized by an artist in advance of production. With time the responsibilities of the designer expanded to impinge upon every aspect of production through the stage of principal cinematography.

Dean Tavoularis, a distinguished production designer working in the United States and Europe, describes how the designer has become a crucial link between the words of the screenplay and its visual expression on the screen; he discusses his own methods for creating environments for motion pictures. Tavoularis believes that the designer should assume responsibility for the credibility of every setting that appears on the screen.

## Relationships

The terms *production designer* and *art director* have sometimes been used interchangeably, which is a consequence of changes in terminology in relation to function. Formerly, each film had an art director and an assistant art director. The term *production designer* gradually superceded the term *art director* because of the vastly expanded role of the designer to include all visual aspects of the film. The functions are the same, but the names are changed. The production designer is responsible for the look of the film, and the art director is the designer's assistant.

Dean Tavoularis stresses, "At least 90 percent of being a production designer is organizing and creating your art department and your crew, the machinery that makes one's ideas take form in reality. The creative part is about 10 percent of the total effort. Many artists and art directors want to become production designers because they have felt exploited—perhaps some resentment that a designer has gone to the director with a sketch and seemingly taken credit for it. When given a chance to become a production designer, however, they falter. They can produce the creative part that is the 10 percent of production design and cannot produce the other 90 percent that involves the construction of a credible environment for a film. This role requires the ability

"The production designer is responsible for the credibility and emotional ambience of every visual aspect of the settings in which the drama occurs. It must look right and feel right in order to express the intent of the writer and the vision of the director."
—*Dean Tavoularis*

to work with people, to organize materials and schedules, and to assemble talent that can collaborate as a team to create a convincing environment for principal cinematography."

The production designer's team consists of these professionals:

The *art director* assists the designer in making drawings, measuring locations, and doing whatever else is reasonably required.

The *set designer*, a draftsperson, is responsible for creating blueprints that will be followed by the construction crew in making sets.

The *set decorator* obtains the furniture and related items and places them appropriately on the sets.

The *costume designer* prepares the clothing for the players.

The *prop man* or *prop woman* obtains whatever else is needed.

If the storyboards that visualize the script are not done by either the production designer or the art director, then an illustrator, a *storyboard artist*, is retained to work under supervision.

In addition, the production designer's professional relationships involve the producer and line producer, the writer (through the script), the director, the director of photography, the sound designer, the visual effects expert, and the assistant director.

To the producer the production designer is responsible for drawings and atmospheric renderings that are used first to obtain funding for the film and used later in the realization of the film. Therefore, the designer is directly accountable to the line producer for a budget for his or her bailiwick and is responsible for maintaining cost control in set construction and decoration. The issue of budgets looms large in this relationship. Tavoularis says, "The producer always wants a detailed budget at the outset before the set designs have been sufficiently developed so that I can really assess the true costs; and so I never make a budget until they scream for it. The more I can delay, within reason, the more accurate I can be in submitting the budget. The set designs must be finished before I can make an intelligent estimate of the costs of settings for a given film."

The director's relationship with the designer is the most important because the director has the final word on all aspects of the realization of a motion picture. The production designer works with the director from script breakdown, to color keying the film, to making storyboards, to making set designs, to selecting locations, to blocking action with the actors. The two consult frequently through all the phases of development up to principal cinematography.

"All of a designer's professional relationships are important, and none should be neglected, but if I had to name one that was first among equals it would be that with the director." Tavoularis explains, "The director is the one individual with whom there must be the most complete rapport, the highest level of communication. If there can be said to be two camps in the making of a film—the director's side and the producer's side—the production designer definitely belongs in the director's camp, although taking care not to go over budget."

The writer is sometimes consulted, with the concurrence of the director, when the designer thinks of a way to create a background or an effect other than that indicated in the script. Occasionally a problem arises when the writer attempts to direct his or her screenplay by detailed descriptions of settings, cinematography angles, and dramatic actions, which is fine if the director agrees that it is. Otherwise, these will be developed as the director wishes them to be realized, as expressed in the approved drawings submitted by the production designer."

Tavoularis comments, "The writer cannot say, 'This is my script and that's the way it will be shot.' It would be professional suicide to insist it has to be done one way and only one way. Realistically, everything is evaluated for its potential in creating better scenes. If a script description indicates the character exits from the side door, and if we then find a trapdoor to the roof that will make the story unfold in a more exciting way, the director will make that departure from the script. . . . Nor do we build everything in the film as indicated by the script. The screenplay is always being adapted to the locations available for cinematography, and indeed locations will often dictate changes in the screenplay regardless of the feelings of the writer."

The director of photography is important because sets must be designed to accommodate cameras, cranes, and frequently dolly tracks. The production designer goes to the cinematographer to determine what lenses are to be used (this affects the scope of the sets), the color values, the position of lights, mood, and finally the blocking of actors' movements in relation to set furniture and decoration.

Tavoularis stresses the cooperative nature of the director-cinematographer-production designer relationship. "We will spend a week discussing the look of the film. Francis [Ford Coppola] thinks visually and is sensitive to using color and lighting evocative of the story and themes. Is it a drab look? Is it a white look? Is it dark and brooding? Color, value, and lighting are always at the heart of a production designer's understandings with the cinematographer."

The sound designer needs to be consulted eventually with regard to sets. A roof or a wall at the wrong place may force the sound technicians to use a sound boom in a way that interferes with the lighting of a scene. If there is a conflict between lighting a scene and recording the sound, the nod usually goes to the visuals and the sound designer has to make the best of it.

"Sound people take a lot of kicking around," Tavoularis smiles. "The cinematographers are always complaining that their microphones are dipping down into the image area. Sound is not really a major problem for the production designer. I have had to build splayed walls and make structural changes to accommodate the sound people, but not often. There is hard sound with hard walls and lost sound when there are high ceilings, as when shooting in a location warehouse. Hard sound can be helped with fabrics, but with high ceilings they just have to make do. They complain a lot, but the sound is usually fine."

The visual effects experts must be involved with the creative design of a set when a mechanical effect is planned to occur within a set, such as a sofa making a jet-assisted takeoff through an open window. Then the production designer must become directly involved with creating a set that will meet the needs of mechanical devices. Every aspect of the set then becomes subordinate to the effects expert. Tavoularis says quietly, "I tend to avoid films that require me to be a service station for gadgets."

The assistant director is the traffic control implement for the director and is responsible for coordinating with the line producer the matters of when and how the film is to be made. The designer works with both the director and the assistant director to assure completion of all sets in time for principal cinematography.

Others who collaborate with the production designer are the construction coordinator, who works from blueprints to supervise the actual construction of sets; set painters, who render and texture sets for illusionary realism; modelers and sculptors, who create details; property clerks, who find what needs to be found; and a small army of technicians, including carpenters, plasterers, electricians, gaffers, riggers, stagehands, floor managers, and various "go-fors."

## The Designer's Role

The production designer's work extends over these purviews: *script*; *storyboards and atmospheric drawings*; *budgets*; *research for settings*; *set designs, set construction*; *decor and set decoration*; *models*; and *principal cinematography*.

### Script

"The work usually begins when the producer makes a call," says Dean Tavoularis." Then there is a series of informal meetings: First to give me a script or story outline; then, to probe more deeply into story, characters, and milieu." Careful readings of the screenplay give the designer a sense of the story, the characters, cues to the physical properties, and a feeling for its emotional characteristics. *Emotional* is the operant word here because the production designer must create settings with overtones more felt than seen.

The director is always consulted with regard to the descriptions of settings as indicated in the screenplay. The director may sometimes have plans to interpret the story in ways that are quite different from that intended by the writer, and the director has the final word. A given scene may be staged in a local bar instead of by the soft glow of a dying fire.

These early stages of a film production are sometimes very fluid. "In *Godfather II*," Tavoularis says, "Francis [Ford Coppola] was to be the writer and we actually started work without the script. As we worked on the design of the film, it influenced the writing, and in fact the script was completed after the designs for the film were done. Francis and I had a close working relationship and we often did research together for the writing and designs dealing with different periods of time. We would find these photographs of New York in 1912 and say, 'Look here, we could build a scene around the construction of the subways.' Or, 'Look at these photographs of the soldiers marching off to World War I—that would make a great scene.' Most of this came from the writer, who was Francis. It sometimes happens in conversation, however, that an idea for a scene will come up from the production designer and the script is changed or is accommodated to accept it."

When asked about the use of early sketches to sell the film to backers, Tavoularis comments, "Well, once in a while. Usually the film is financed when work begins. One of the arguments for developing the drawings so early is that they could be used to find investors for the film. Later, when a script is presented to the backers, it is always impressive for them to see something visual. Afterwards, the drawings may be used to develop the film itself."

When the production designer has a sense of the story and the director's viewpoint, the script is broken down and the scenes are collated *according to the locations* at which the dramatic events will occur. The designer studies carefully what dramatic actions will occur at each location (Plates 1 and 2 and Figures 4.1, 4.2).

*Storyboards and Atmospheric Drawings*

Tavoularis reminisces, "When I worked at Disney Studios, my film school, Walt wanted every script storyboarded on a scene-by-scene basis so he could control what was developed in live-action filming, just as he did in animation. It was Disney who carried this animation technique into general use for live-action work, primarily to put his stamp of approval on it. Storyboards were quite useful in developing the sets because we would photograph them on slides and then project the storyboards up to make the larger plans."

Storyboards and atmospheric sketches tend to emerge from the welter of discussions (Plates 3 and 5). The production designer then makes rough sketches for settings, depicting mood and composition with an indication of dramatic actions, and presents them to the director. These rough drawings suggest composition, color, lighting, and decor—with a figure included to give scale to the set. The drawings may be revised again and again until they conform to the vision of the director. Sometimes, however, it is the production designer who creates the look of the film for the director, particularly for those directors with a theater rather than a cinema background.

"It is worth noting," Tavoularis says, "that the conceptual parts come at the beginning in the script, storyboard, and atmospheric drawings. When location selections are finalized, however, all three are likely to be changed to accommodate the realities of cinematography on location. Locations may dictate the design of the

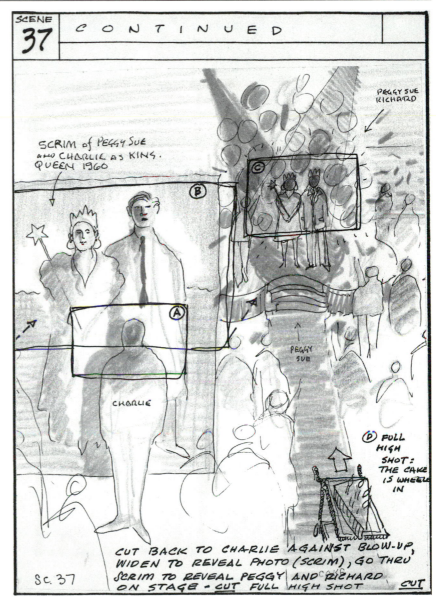

COURTESY ZOETROPE STUDIOS

FIGURE 4.1 *A storyboard panel may take proportions unrelated to actual screen dimensions but always for a functional reason. In this panel from* Peggy Sue Got Married, *the panel encompasses a crowd scene with indications of three separate shots within its borders.*

FIGURE 4.2  *This storyboard panel for a wide-screen format reveals another aspect of this useful tool. In this jungle scene from* Apocalypse Now, *the arrow and the angle indicate a low camera move up a jungle path over the face of a fallen soldier.*

CAM·LO – MOVES UP PATH.

COURTESY ZOETROPE STUDIOS

film in the sense of offering problems needing solutions before production can proceed. Many of the production designs come as a reaction to the solution of problems posed by the locations selected for shooting. Generally there are not twenty possible design solutions. Generally there is only one logical solution and we must make the best of it, changing the story and the storyboards to accommodate the demands of reality."

Storyboard drawings are a critical phase in conceptualizing a motion picture. These consist of a series of realistic drawings, 2″ × 3″ for standard screen and 2″ × 4½″ for wide screen, which depict every dramatic action in every shot from the beginning to the end of the film. Tavoularis prefers color storyboards as part of conceptualizing the movie, but they are often rendered in black and white to facilitate photocopying the sets of storyboards for every person associated with production. The storyboard drawings are begun as a script-in-hand collaboration between the director and the illustrator; the director explains what he or she wants with

arrows and swish lines to show in graphic shorthand what the dramatic actions are intended to be.

Then the storyboard illustrator makes realistic panel-by-panel illustrations that synthesize the actions indicated by the director with the settings created by the production designer (in the atmospheric drawings) to render what is to become the basic visual form of the film. The drawings are not set in cement. Those involved with production may make suggestions for changes, and during the exigencies of principal cinematography, the director may elect to depart from the actions indicated in the storyboads.

For the most part, however, the storyboards state the basic form of the film and become the reference point for everyone involved in production. The cinematographer can see what the dramatic action will be, make a selection of cameras and lenses, and decide when to plan for tripod, crane, and dolly shots. The visual effects experts start to perceive what the images are supposed to look like and begin to do what is required for impact and verisimilitude.

The set designers, the costume designers, and the set decorators can all begin to work after seeing the storyboards. When approved, the storyboards are photocopied and reduced in size so that they can be inserted into the script. A copy of the storyboards will go to every location involved in principal cinematography.

Dean Tavoularis recounts how important the storyboard was in one film by Francis Ford Coppola. "Francis decided to carry the concept of the storyboard as far as possible in the production of the film *Hammett*, using slides. First, he had actors and actresses read the script, recording the dialogue on audiotape for the length of the proposed film. Then we photographed a series of slides of the players in close-ups, medium shots, and so forth. We thereupon photographed the locations in which the players were to appear. We combined the actors with their locations by projecting them in unison on the animation stand and photographing them together with a video camera. We finally had a videotape that became our storyboard—a sketch of the entire movie—which, when combined with the audiotape, gave us a sense of timing and tempo for the entire film. The videotape could be shown to others, tested on an audience, whatever."

## Budgets

Although Tavoularis prefers to make a budget after blueprints are drawn for the construction of sets, budgets are frequently required after the storyboards and finished sketches are approved.

Budgets are computed in terms of labor and materials, generally at a ratio of about three to one, though the materials costs vary widely for each film. The cost of labor is usually computed at union scale for carpenters, painters, scenic designers, modelers, casters, and other technicians.

Construction costs are affected by the expense of raw materials, rental of properties, purchase of properties, cost of set dressing items, rental or purchase of livestock, and such ancillary costs as putting up scaffolds and creating effects like rain, wind, and snow. As the film production evolves and construction of sets proceeds, the production designer has the responsibility of keeping costs within budget. If unexpected major changes in set design and construction arise, for whatever reason, the production designer should have made provision for contingency costs for overtime and night work.

Tavoularis concedes that the shadow of the budget always looms over the production designer. "Budgets are always an influencing factor, but the designer should not be crippled by thinking first about the cost. We look for solutions to dramatic problems, then weigh the costs. Obviously, the designer cannot solve set problems with a blank check, but if one is subconsciously aware of realities there will be found a solution that meets the needs of the film and fits within the limitations of the budget.

"The production designer may need to defend himself or herself and the work from the expedient. If others argue for a solution that is stupid, or merely convenient for somebody else, he or she may need to counter that this solution is a more beautiful or evocative setting for the drama. If the cost is slightly higher and the scene is important enough to justify the extra expense, so be it. When weighing the cost considerations of a set, there is always a factor of judgment of whether this is a major scene or merely a transitional scene."

Tavoularis continues, "Budget considerations also affect the selection of locations. In *Godfather II*, I thought Ellis Island was probably a location that could

COURTESY ZOETROPE STUDIOS

FIGURE 4.3 *This research photograph of Little Italy in New York about 1912 was used by Dean Tavoularis in creating an environment for the settings of* The Godfather, Part II.

Tavoularis says, "Research is the sparking point that gets you going, particularly when dealing with a period film. The moment I have read the script and talked to the director, I begin to do research because ideas come from what I discover at an exponential rate, with ideas sparking more ideas. I pore over old photographs from archives, look at paintings in museums, and read literature about the period in which the story occurs. Films whose settings are found in the past— movies like *Little Big Man, Bonnie and Clyde, The Godfather*, and *Godfather II*— all lead one into another America. Old photographs of Indian villages with tepees that glowed like lanterns from the hearth fires within, paintings by Remington and Russell, museum artifacts of clubs and clothing, give one insights into a vanished world. Pictures of the immigrants at Ellis Island in New York in 1912, old photographs of Little Italy evoke powerful emotions. The images are very real, very poignant, and the production designer wants to capture that ambience for the film. Seeing the pictures and reading about the immigrants is a very emotional thing (Figures 4.3 and 4.4).

"Everything in the beginning is very interesting because the story begins to unfold. First there is location scouting. You make broad selections at first, then hone it down finer and begin to make tentative decisions about what will work dramatically. Then the director is brought around to look at the selected locations or photographs of the locations. We always prefer to adapt some existing location for major settings rather than to build it from

be restored to make it possible to shoot the immigrant scenes. I said to Francis [Ford Coppola], 'It's a mess there, but it could probably be used if we took a high-powered fire hose to knock off the peeling paint and clean out the worst of the dirt.' I thought we could fix up the lower part and install period furniture. Francis pointed out, however, that we would need to ferry over thousands of extras (playing immigrants) every day from Manhattan for shooting. There would be the cost of feeding them, probable delays due to bad weather for boats, and so forth. Francis made the decision to shoot those scenes at some location in Europe because of the probably excessive costs of shooting on the original site at Ellis Island."

### Research

Research begins in earnest when the designer develops scenes and settings. As

FIGURE 4.4 *This basic research photograph found in archives showed newly arriving immigrants lining up to have their papers examined. Tavoularis reminisces, "When I went alone to Ellis Island, now abandoned, to scout it as a location for* Godfather II, *I began to sense what it was like then, coming alone to a* new land, with a different language and strange customs, most often with nobody there to meet you. America got the best people because it got the most courageous, most energetic, most imaginative people. My sense of what it was like then and what they were like gave me a feeling of how the settings should look."*

91

THE DESIGNER'S ROLE

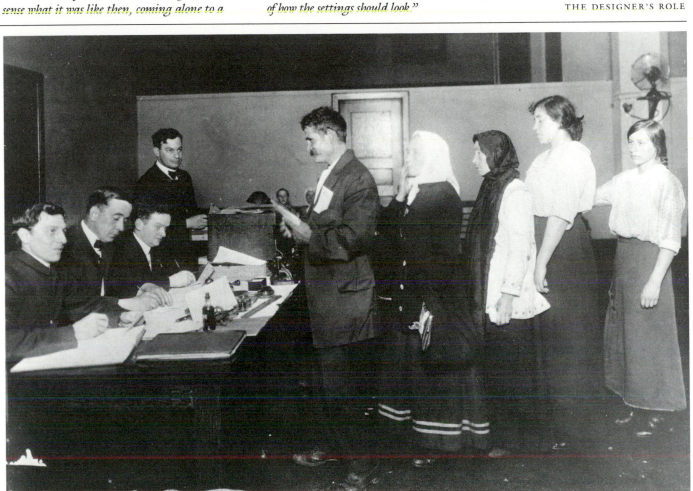

scratch, at least when period films are involved. An important consideration in location selection is whether other scenes can be photographed there. One needs to pick the main day's shooting in the same part of town where there are other shots to be picked up, out of context. At every location we discuss how every aspect of it may be utilized to shoot as many scenes as possible in as brief a period of time as possible, commensurate with quality. And, at every location, I take photographs and measurements that would enable me to make drawings that could become blueprints for set construction. Getting into the locations of a story really means getting into the life of the film itself, getting those feelings about ambience that should be given visual forms.

"*Bonnie and Clyde* was the first film in which I served as production designer, and location scouting for that took me to another part of the country. We shot that film on locations all around Texas, at Ponder and Waxahatchee, in small towns that were a mother lode of Americana from the

FIGURE 4.5 *This scene was shot at a "found location" in which the dramatic action was choreographed around the availability of the setting. Dean Tavoularis says, "We shot* Bonnie and Clyde *in Ponder and Waxahatchee and other beautiful little Texas towns frozen in time. Exquisite places with quaint stores lining* the street. I loved the old stone bank that was there, the one into which I installed an old post office structure I had found in a junkyard. Those little towns were nostalgic memories of America past, parts of us now being knocked down to make way for shopping malls."

**BONNIE AND CLYDE** (U.S.A., 1967) DIRECTED BY ARTHUR PENN.

1930s. The streets were lined with old banks and old buildings and other beautiful things (Figure 4.5). The interior scenes, such as the bank robberies, sometimes required that we rebuild the interiors to suit our purposes. I found an old English post office in an antique shop and put it into one of the banks as an interior. We photographed the motel bedroom scenes on a small stage in Dallas with beds and other set pieces we had scrounged in old furniture stores. I spent a lot of time in junkyards and antique shops as we had a budget of only fifty-five thousand dollars for the whole film."

Tavoularis pauses and says, "I worked hard to get the mood of the Depression in that film, to get at the truth of the situation. At Disney Studios when poverty was portrayed, it was always charming and picturesque and not how people really lived when poor. It was artfully poor and full of character, the sentimental kind of thing. In *Bonnie and Clyde* I wanted to convey

FIGURE 4.6 *This elevation drawing was used as a blueprint to construct a set for the film* One from the Heart; *it indicates the usefulness of architectural training for the production designer.*

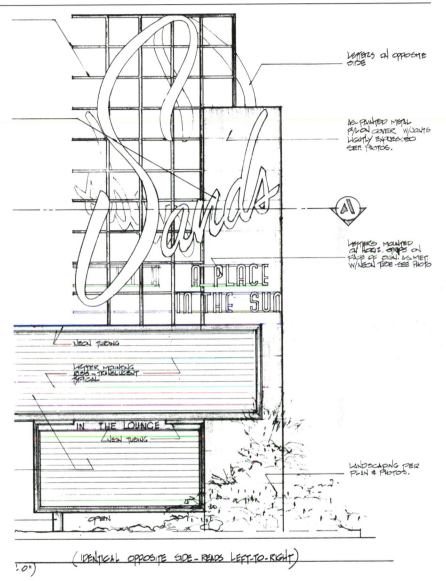

COURTESY ZOETROPE STUDIOS

the sense of what it meant to be dirt poor and absolutely desperate. The setting had to say it as eloquently as the story and the characters.

"Whenever I go to a location," he continues, "I look for specifics. I look at interiors and ask myself whether it would be as effective and less expensive to build the sets. The smaller the setting, the more likely it should be built on a stage. A lot depends in making this decision on the dramatic importance of the setting. If a scene set in a bar takes up twenty pages of manuscript, we will certainly build it because it will shorten production time to have control of all the visual elements. On the other hand, if the drama fills twenty pages of manuscript in a railroad station, the cost of building that station might be so exorbitant that going on location—and making adaptations to a real station—might be the prudent choice. The production designer must always want to spend his [or her] budget funds intelligently, and well. The bottom line is not cost, however, but the quality of the film."

### Set Designs

The lead time required to actually design and construct the sets for a film varies with the budget and the complexity of the film (Figures 4.6, 4.7, 4.8 and Plate 4). Tavoularis indicates that lead time usually ranges from eight weeks to three months, with a few big budget films requiring as much as six-months' preparation in advance of principal cinematography. On average,

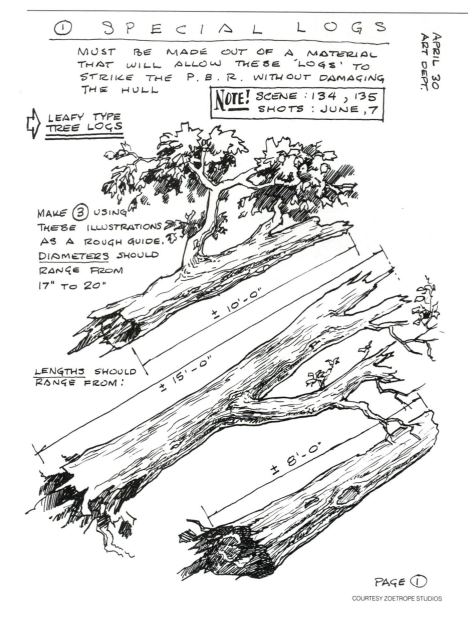

① SPECIAL LOGS

MUST BE MADE OUT OF A MATERIAL THAT WILL ALLOW THESE 'LOGS' TO STRIKE THE P.B.R. WITHOUT DAMAGING THE HULL

APRIL 30
ART DEPT.

NOTE! SCENE : 134 , 135
SHOTS : JUNE , 7

LEAFY TYPE TREE LOGS

MAKE ③ USING THESE ILLUSTRATIONS AS A ROUGH GUIDE. DIAMETERS SHOULD RANGE FROM 17" TO 20"

± 10'-0"

LENGTHS SHOULD RANGE FROM :

± 15'-0"

± 8'-0"

PAGE ①

COURTESY ZOETROPE STUDIOS

FIGURE 4.7 *The set designer makes detailed drawings for everything that needs to be constructed for the film. Here is a drawing delineating logs to be made of a material that may be struck by riverine patrol boats without damage to the hull in* Apocalypse Now.

about thirty sets are required for a film, with perhaps two or three major sets, six to eight medium-size sets, and eighteen to twenty small sets. Despite the huge size of studio stages, constructing more than one set within a stage is impractical because the slightest sound on one set will be picked up on another. Generally, large sets are built on large stages, and other sets are built on smaller stages with many of the smaller sets consisting of modification of structures found on location. When more than one set is intended to be used within a large studio, each is first set up and then struck after principal cinematography; the next is then set up. Portability has a high priority in production design.

"Set design and construction cannot be considered something that applies only to interior settings to be photographed on a studio sound stage, as if they were different in kind from location cinematography. Locations put their stamp on a film in ways that should be echoed in the interior sets. In practice, much of production design work consists of adapting existing structures on location with partial sets. In *Godfather II*, Francis [Ford Coppola] asked for a residential compound like the one we had in *The Godfather* but changed in the sense that the family had moved to California, so we started work first at Lake Tahoe. Before the script was finished we knew we needed certain locations because of where the story moved, back and forth

FIGURE 4.8 *This setting was realized from the elevation drawings for a major assault scene in* Apocalypse Now.

**95**

THE DESIGNER'S ROLE

**APOCALYPSE NOW** (U.S.A., 1979) DIRECTED BY FRANCIS FORD COPPOLA.

FIGURE 4.9 *For several months, painstaking construction in New York transformed an entire city block into a three-dimensional replica of Little Italy in 1918. Production designer Dean Tavoularis selected East 6th Street between Avenues A and B for its basic architecture. Buildings were aged, store fronts taken over, and Little Italy of 1918 arose: Italian groceries, cheese, sausage, and poultry stores; tailoring and barber shops; fruit, vegetable, and fish markets; dry goods, tobacco, and carriage shops; an immigrant employment center and an Italian social club. The street was filled with colorful sights and pungent smells.*

**THE GODFATHER, PART II** (U.S.A., 1974) DIRECTED BY FRANCIS FORD COPPOLA.

in time (Figure 4.9). We needed that street in New York where Bobby DeNiro first worked in a grocery store (Figure 4.10). He had asserted himself, in the story, by killing this local thug, and we needed a place that looked like Little Italy. We found it near Sixth Avenue and made our sets to match the character of that location (Figure 4.11). There was a cross street that had natural perspective for five miles, though all we needed to adapt was the first block—and then we had to black bag the traffic lights in the distance. The character of all the sets was determined by 'found' places."

When all the sketches for sets have been made and the dimensions indicated, they are given to a set designer to be rendered into blueprints. The drawings for set constructions are usually made at a scale of ¼ inch or ¾ inch to the foot, depending upon the size of the constructions.

Scale drawings have their planning based on stage size, the standard theater

FIGURE 4.10    *The grocery store in which the godfather worked when he first immigrated to the United States is shown here, accurate to the last vegetable crate and authentic in ambience. To play his Academy Award-winning role as the godfather, Robert DeNiro, pictured here, acquired proficiency in the Italian language and spoke with inflections unique to the Sicilian dialect.*

**THE GODFATHER, PART II** DIRECTED BY FRANCIS FORD COPPOLA.

FIGURE 4.11 *This exterior facade was created to represent the Genco Olive Oil Company, a front business for the mob in* The Godfather, Part II. *A restored automobile of that period is parked before the set as a prop.*

title, production number, and set number. The better craftspeople are artists at heart, and they may take a great interest in the set if the design and a model are displayed and discussed openly. Enthusiasm gives everything a little extra zing.

### Set Construction

There are three basic commandments in building and decorating sets: Build so the players can move easily through the actions blocked by the director, with more than one option for choreography; build so the camera may follow the characters and the recorder pick up the dialogue; build so there is visual continuity from scene to scene, and the sets make sense in construction and color in transitions from one set to the next.

Sets are built to accommodate the main dramatic actions of the players. The director may decide that a character should leap out of bed at the sound of an accident in the street, trip over a chair running to look out a window, then turn and slam open a door to go racing down a corridor. This dramatic action means that the set should represent a bedroom with a chair, a window, a door, and an exterior corridor that may be seen from inside the bedroom. If the director wants the camera to follow after the actor as he races down the corridor, the door must be large enough to accommodate the following camera crew, possibly riding a dolly cart mounted on tracks.

Should the director decide to have the

flat, camera angles, acoustics, and projection back for forced perspectives. These elevation drawings feature front, top, and side views defined in terms of their physical sizes and construction specifications and are intended for use by carpenters and others who actually build the sets. Each set may require four to five elevations, with ten to fifteen detail drawings for construction. Diagrams reveal doors and windows; they are used to plot furniture arrangements that give the director more than one option for the movements of players and are also used to plot camera movements and lighting plans. Each studio floor plan is identified by a production

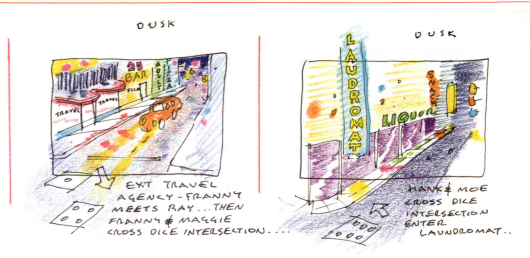

PLATE 1 (above)  A storyboard most commonly takes the form of a series of 2" by 3" drawings (approximately the proportions of the standard film screen) that visualize the story as a common reference for everyone associated with the production of a motion picture. This storyboard, used in *One from the Heart,* sketchily indicates color, ambiance, and dramatic action—essences without details for this kind of film. Storyboards for other kinds of films may include dialogue, music, and special effects described beneath the pictures. If any special effects are to be stated, they would be drawn and described in realistic detail.

PLATE 2 (right)  The storyboard is a variable tool, the format of which may be adapted to whatever visual ideas are being expressed. In this vertical storyboard (from *Apocalypse Now*), scanning from bottom to top reveals the movements of a camera; arrows indicate the direction of (first) a pan to the left and then (second) a tilt upward with the camera until it establishes the cabin cruiser.

COURTESY ZOETROPE STUDIOS

HAU FAI Staging Area.
• MATTE Shot • 25'H Cam • 35mmLens •

PLATE 3 (left) This atmospheric sketch is intended to visualize the setting for a military staging area in *Apocalypse Now*, with the stipulation that the camera (with a 25-mm lens) be mounted 25 feet above the ground. The term *matte shot* refers to a visual effect in which a subject and a background—photographed at different locations—are subsequently printed together.

PLATE 4 (right) This elevation drawing shows the layout of the Viet Cong village to be attacked during the "Ride of the Valkyrie" assault by helicopter gunships in *Apocalypse Now*. The arrow indicates the route of the helicopters and guides those involved with the production of this scene.

PLATE 5 (below) This atmospheric drawing for a temple ruins scene in *Apocalypse Now* indicates that it will be photographed with a 25-mm lens with the camera set up in a static long shot. The lens viewing angle indicated on the drawing by the production designer shows the set designer how wide the set will need to be to fit within the parameters of the shot.

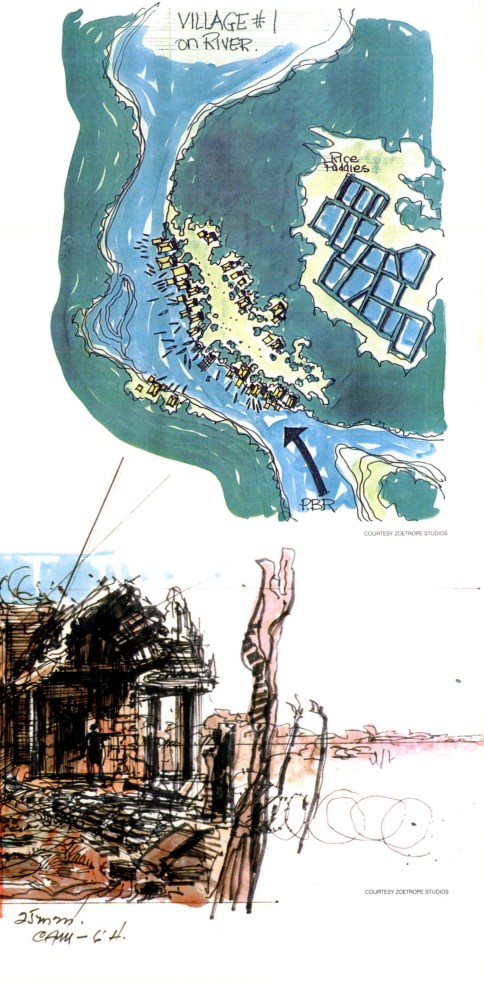

COURTESY ZOETROPE STUDIOS

COURTESY ZOETROPE STUDIOS

PLATE 6  "This scene (from *One from the Heart*) was shot on a very small stage," Tavoularis says, "and we used forced perspective to make the actual distance seem apparently like a much longer distance. The set painting begins just beyond this freeway that had cars passing by. The stage was so small that we had to have 'tormenters' on the sides to black off the edges of the set and a 'teaser' hung over the top like a proscenium arch to mask the top of the set and painted to match the color of the sky."

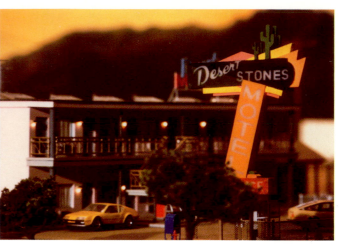

PLATE 7  Models were used to create the neon look of the Las Vegas Strip in *One from the Heart*. A 50-foot miniature replica of the Strip was photographed by a camera moving quickly enough to prevent the viewer from detecting that the buildings, garages, gas stations, vehicles, and distant mountains were in fact only models.

PLATE 8  Films that are conceived as all-interior productions frequently have a highly stylized, otherworldly quality that borders on the surrealistic. Richard Corliss wrote of *One from the Heart,* "On the Zoetrope sound stages, Production Designer Dean Tavoularis has created a show-stopping amalgam of razzle on dazzle, sending skyrockets speckling over what looks like a mile-long Strip of surreal glitter." *Time,* January 25, 1982.

PLATE 9  This model of the Stardust Hotel in Las Vegas (in *One from the Heart*) is such an accurate replica that, when seen out the window of a passing automobile, the verisimilitude is extraordinary.

PLATE 10  The real "star" of *Tucker* is this automobile, shown in the drawing and restored vehicle parked before a billboard created as a location set. The designs for the story of a man who tried to create a new automobile company were so richly evocative of the late '40s that they brought Dean Tavoularis Academy nominations for art direction in both Britain and the United States.

character run outside to see what has happened in the accident, then an exterior complex may need to be built to show a street, houses with entrances and windows, and vehicles. If the character then walks with the police officer on duty at the scene to discuss what happened, the production designer will need to measure the actual distance of that stroll and ensure that the proper extent of background be built to accommodate it during cinematography.

Main dramatic actions are usually built around a specific set item: desk, fireplace, window, kitchen sink, television set, water cooler, whatever might be a normal point of contact between the characters. In *Bonnie and Clyde*, for example, the brass bedframes found in the motels the pair frequented were almost as much in evidence as the omnipresent guns.

Lighting and lens selection are the next considerations. The set must be designed to permit room illumination so that the camera crew can move continuously through the set without throwing perceptible shadows; the set must also be wide enough so that cinematographers can pass through the door. And the set must be broad enough so that a short focal length lens will not expose the edges of the set and beyond.

Sound recording and acoustics are next in importance. If the character cries out, "Omigod! What's that?" as he leaps out of bed, a sound boom and microphone will be suspended overhead to record the story. This probably means that there will be no ceiling to the sets for this dramatic action. A related consideration is acoustics: Parallel walls without covering fabrics tend to echo slightly and modify the timbre of voices; the walls may need to be splayed slightly to preclude this effect.

Perspective modification may be needed. If the walls are splayed instead of parallel, the illusion of being square may need to be designed into the set through the addition of alcoves and windows constructed to seem in correct perspective, or through illusionary painting and textures. Forced perspective is sometimes used to enhance a sense of depth, with the front and the rear made to a different scale so the room (or exterior) will seem to diminish rapidly within a short distance. A ceiling may be added to emphasize scale and perspective and to enhance the sense of grandeur.

Set construction requires close interaction among the production designer, the storyboard artist, the set designer, the set dresser, and the construction coordinator. The designer chooses the materials and discusses structure and detailing while trying to involve the others as much as possible.

Dean Tavoularis emphasizes, "The construction coordinator is an important person. Most of them are well-educated individuals who take a keen and close interest in developing the film. In most instances they will be looking over the shoulders of the set designers to study the blueprints and anticipate what their problems will be. The new generation of craftspeople have graduated from film school in many cases and have the kind of understanding in depth that many of the older generation did not have. They are usually intelligent people who understand a complex concept and can then carry it through."

The production designer does not, however, hand over the blueprints to the construction coordinator and crew and walk away, oblivious to what happens next. The prudent production designer owns a viewing lens and appears early in the construction process to walk about the sets and be sure photography will fall within their parameters. The director of photography will have apprised the art director what lens he or she intends to use. Within an interior setting it is likely to be a 1-inch lens (25 mm) for static long shots, a 2-inch lens (50 mm) for medium shots, and a 3-inch lens (75 mm) for close-ups.

Tavoularis states, "I go down there and walk around while the walls are going up to get a feel of the space, to sense whether it is right for the dramatic action about to be photographed. I may say, 'Move that wall out a little, it feels too close to accommodate the players.' Or, 'Let's move that wall in a bit to eliminate waste space.' It's advisable to warn set construction people in advance that a wall or two may need to be moved so they can mount it only temporarily, with vice grips, to be nudged in or out later."

Good supervision is required to keep the artisans working in relays without spoiling the work of others as they rotate on the job, as in this hypothetical sequence of action:

Carpenters erect the walls of the set.

Painters then paint or paper them.

Carpenters return to install moulding.

Painters return to paint the moulding.

Carpenters return to hang the doors and install the windows.

And so forth.

The construction coordinator sets the schedules for the craftspeople and sees to it that they neither waste time nor overlap each other; and the coordinator attempts to reduce that strange animosity that sometimes arises among members of different crafts who are required to work as a team to produce a motion picture.

Tavoularis makes an important point about building sets for period films. "When making *Bonnie and Clyde* we spent a lot of time looking for doors that had the right character for the film. It is expensive to build a door and mount the hardware and so forth. It is easier to find doors, stoves, cabinets, water heaters, and so forth and then build a set to accommodate them than it would be to do it the other way around."

He continues, "It is vitally important that the production designer visit the sets under construction almost continuously to be sure that they relate to the drama taking place. In *Bonnie and Clyde* I built the sets to accommodate the camera, but I deliberately built the motel interiors small. One day I received a message from Burney Guffey, the cinematographer. . . . He poured up a couple of drinks and said, 'You've built all the sets and they're very small and tight—why?' I offered this explanation: 'Bonnie and Clyde are on the run. They're staying in little motels, crummy dives; they're gradually being trapped. They're depressed with each other in a depressing environment. Everything should feel progressively more claustrophobic.' Burney listened to me go on about the philosophical architectural concerns of designing the environment to infuse it with a visual equivalent of the theme and the story. Then he poured up a couple more drinks, smiled, and said no more about it. He understood that I had a reason for what I was doing—creating an environment that expressed the mood of the story. If I had not had a reason for making everything small but had done it out of ignorance, Burney would probably have had everything ripped out and done over. He was very cooperative from that point on."

Tavoularis says emphatically, "An important part of the job of production designer is to argue for quality in set construction. In the current film I am working on, the drama takes place for the most part on a large yacht. I want to use real teak and real mahogany for our set and not cheap pine that has been textured to resemble teak and mahogany, and there are good reasons for this. Most of the story is told in the small environment of the ship, and the viewers will have a long and close look at the setting and will eventually detect what has been faked—to the detriment of the credibility of the film. Teak, for example, turns from chalky white when dry to dark red when wet, and that will not happen with pine. This is a film about the sea, with storms that soak the ship, and the wood must respond authentically when drenched.

"As I said, an important part of this job is to argue and win those disputes about production quality when dealing with those who would do things with only cost in mind. This issue is usually faced when dealing with the production department, an arm of the producer. If need be, I will tell the producer 'It's not your job to tell me to use pine instead of mahogany. It's your job to see to it that I don't go over budget.' As a last resort, when there is an issue of quality I turn to the director, but I do so only as a last resort."

Painting and texturing the sets also come within the purview of the production designer. When the sets are constructed to the right proportions and have met with the approval of the director, the designer will present color swatches to the construction master to indicate what colors he or she wants and where. Color consistency is important from set to set and scene to scene to give the film an overall harmony. Earth colors and pastel colors tend to predominate, with black and white (not complementary colors) used to darken and lighten them.

"Painting and texturing are important in presenting form and color to the camera," Tavoularis says, "but sometimes things are exaggerated to a false effect. At Disney Studios, for example, they used to make mouldings bigger and deeper than they should be 'for the camera,' and tex-

tures were rendered grossly 'for the camera.' Then, when we went out on location for principal cinematography where mouldings and textures were of normal size and configuration, they would differ so much in character from the interior sets as to be glaring. This always bothered me. Inasmuch as there are always lighting problems on location, why not, in a sense, light the interiors a bit 'incorrectly' so they will match the exteriors when the footage is edited?

"At location interiors, in which an enormous amount of illumination is needed, shadows tend to be wiped out by the multiplicity of lights. On those occasions," Tavoularis observes, "we may actually paint the shadows in order to give proper form to interior structures. In *Rumble Fish*, for example, the shadows were painted on the sides of the pillars to enhance the contrast between the light and the dark areas when there was a great deal of light. Heavy texturing may similarly serve the function of darkening a shadow area. Incidentally, we often become obsessive about having only one shadow thrown by a subject when, in real life, multiple shadows from multiple light sources are the norm for interiors."

To emphasize shadows or to create illusionary perspectives and apparent right angles, a darker value of the same color is usually applied with a spray gun. Because of the play of light and dark on surfaces, variations of texture sometimes photograph more convincingly than different shades of colors. Texturing to enhance shadows is usually done on plaster surfaces.

An important consideration in texturing and coloring surfaces is the presence of lighting as it will occur during principal cinematography. The electricians are often asked to turn on the lights so the production designer and the cinematographer can see their effects on the rendered

FIGURE 4.12 *This composite photograph of a fish market in Trieste reveals the site found by the production designer to serve as the location for the Ellis Island immigration scenes in* The Godfather, Part II. *Portable sets, constructed in Rome, were moved to Trieste and erected in the fish market when a combined holiday-weekend offered the best opportunity to set up for principal cinematography.*

textures. When a film demands something extra in subtlety of performance from the actors, the production designer has the responsibility of creating an environment in which the players feel they are living their parts.

Consultation with the cinematographer, as well as the director, becomes increasingly important as the days of principal cinematography approach. Discussions with cinematographers are initially unstructured—discussing color and mood and so forth—then become concrete in terms of individual scenes. The cameraperson may ask, "If you could put a lamp post outside the window so I can motivate the lighting, it would help." Motivational lighting (providing the scene with apparent sources of light) by means of windows and lamps is a frequent request. This sometimes becomes a problem when shooting on location. (Cinematographers tend to like restaurants because they have table lamps and many places to set up lights.)

"Aging a set" is something of a creative

process. It is better to construct the building and then inflict creative dilapidation on it than it is to build a ruin, which somehow always seems to look contrived and picturesque. Results are more convincing if a set is built up and then knocked about the edges.

The effect of aging rooms and walls may be achieved by sponging moist-seeming patches on surfaces to connote dampness and decay, flaking paint off woodwork, putting cobwebs into corners, dabbing rust color on metal drums and ironwork, chalking graffiti on the inner walls of abandoned buildings, and generally fouling things up. A door that falls off the hinges at the entrance of the character says "dilapidated" with a bang.

Sets are made to be taken down or *struck*, as well as to be photographed.

However solid and formidable a castle's medieval stone wall may seem when photographed, the surface illusion has usually been created by paint on wood—canvas-and-plaster-coated flats that are secured by vice grips, with bracing every 5 to 10 feet that prevents the stone wall from shaking when the drawbridge goes up or down. Sets are not usually struck until the rushes are in to ensure that they are available in the event of retakes. If a temporary strike is mandated to make way for another set, the first set is photographed before striking to be sure that when re-established, it will convey exactly the same configuration to the camera for the retake.

Sometimes sets are specifically made to be portable because they are to be used on locations with very limited access for principal cinematography (Figure 4.12). Dean

**LITTLE BIG MAN** (U.S.A., 1970) DIRECTED BY ARTHUR PENN.

FIGURE 4.13 *Dean Tavoularis recalls, "We made all fifteen tepees as the Indians did and stained the designs with authentic colors. Research opened up all sorts of possibilities. We made their shields, their arrows, their utensils the Indian way, and they were as finely made as the Indians did them. Dorothy Jenkins, our wardrobe mistress, made jewelry and quill-work for the moccasins and other clothing. There is plenty of information on these things and . . . no excuse for not being authentic. When we had our screening in New York with people from the National Geographic Society in attendance, they said it was the first narrative film they had seen that showed real respect for the Indians and was genuinely authentic." Fine performances were given by Dustin Hoffman and Chief Dan George.*

ily when we had the opportunity to shoot: a platform where a doctor examined a patient, cattle guards to control the crowds of immigrants, a huge chandelier to hang from the ceiling, crosspieces for the windows to make them resemble those of Ellis Island. The fish market closed in the early afternoon, and we moved in with what we could leave standing and hanging. Then, when we had a weekend and a holiday back-to-back, we moved in quickly to set up for principal cinematography."

Tavoularis recalls, "When we gave up on the idea of using Ellis Island for *Godfather II*, we decided to look around Europe to find a place that might be used to replicate Ellis Island. We looked at two or three places, but found them unusable. Then we heard of a place in Trieste that was similar enough to Ellis Island but found it was a commercial fish market for the port, available only on weekends and holidays. We decided to build portable fixtures and settings that could be moved in and out read-

### Decor and Set Decoration

Decor is a vital consideration in the verisimilitude of a film. *Little Big Man* had to be historically accurate to the curve of a war club, the finest quill-work on a moccasin, the colors used to paint a tepee (Figure 4.13). *The Godfather, Part II* had to be ethnically authentic to the antimacassar on the overstuffed chair, the gilt picture frame on the wall, the flowered wallpaper (Figure 4.14). *One from the Heart* had to be credible to the last neon

FIGURE 4.14 *Props can frequently add subtle notes of irony and nuances of meaning, as does the picture of the Madonna and Child hanging next to the face of the godfather (Robert DeNiro).*

**105**
THE DESIGNER'S ROLE

**THE GODFATHER, PART II** DIRECTED BY FRANCIS FORD COPPOLA.

sign in the glitz and glitter of Las Vegas (Plate 6).

A major consideration for the production designer then is the authenticity of the backgrounds, the settings, the set decorations, and the wardrobe. The designer and the designer's associates—set designer, set decorator, and costume designer—are always browsing in libraries and bookstores looking for subjects and illustrations that will give insight into the surroundings similar to those in the story (Plate 10). Those professionals involved with settings for period films usually acquire large libraries dealing with major epochs of the past. If a valuable book on the subject of the ancient Maya appears in the bookstores and it is well illustrated, the book may be bought on the spot and shelved for the day that *Popul Vuh* is put on film.

"Set decoration is something I am involved with early on," says Tavoularis. "Initially, I go by myself to seek locations adaptable to the film's needs. Once I have found two or more locations that are suitable as is, or are readily modified, I bring in the decorator and show that person suitable atmospheric drawings to indicate what I want in furniture or other items for the setting.

"Then the decorators go off to browse through prop shops, antique shops, and junkyards, and they take Polaroid photographs of the items to show me. When I have reviewed their photographs, I take trips with them to look at the likeliest prospects. When I find individual pieces that have true authenticity and character—a table, a vase, a desk set—it gives the set decorator a sense of what I need. It enables him or her to pull together items having the same look and feel. Then we'll pick out the drapery, carpets, and upholstery and select a paint color for the room that is appropriate: forest green, teddy bear brown, or whatever.

"Props are often used as a point of dramatic focus in the film, and actors and directors love props to handle to ward off nervousness and add topical interest. In *The Godfather*, Clamensa showed Michael how to make spaghetti, instead of just sitting around, after the mob had 'gone to the mattresses.' I often put things into actors' pockets to make them seem more human and credible. Why shouldn't a screen character have loose change and keys in his [or her] pockets? Actors are so often absorbed in the craft of acting their roles that they forget the elements of reality that add to the believability of their performances. An actor will play the role of a man lugging suitcases through the door—supposedly tired after three weeks on the road—and then carry suitcases having nothing in them. The suitcases are feather-light and this diminishes the credibility of his performance. Players seldom think of things like that. They all like props, however, for 'busyness.'

"Details are very important in decoration," he continues. "When we made *The Conversation*, a film about a professional snooper and wiretapper, we subscribed to the magazine that private investigators read, bought items that they use to tap telephones, and then used the magazines and invoices sent to us for the products as props in our character's office. The items were authentic and they added authenticity to the office.

"The production designer is responsible for making the actors feel comfortable on the set. The sense of smell does not show up on the screen, certainly, and yet scent is important to playing a scene. The actor or actress should be immersed in the scenes in which the drama is supposedly taking place rather than in the smells of paint and varnish that usually surround a newly finished set. In the grocery store scene of *The Brinks Job*, we built the set and spent the whole night dressing it to look right for the camera. Then, just before principal photography began, we crushed sprigs of garlic, oregano, and paprika around the set so the context would feel right to the players in that setting. The production designer must not overlook anything in the broadest design of the set or the finest detail of decoration that may contribute to a convincing performance.

"The wardrobe of the actresses and actors is very important because it is right up front, on the backs of the players. Costume designers are all different, and the freedom the production designer gives to that person depends on how well one knows the individual. A costume designer cannot be given the option of a personal choice. There should never be a nasty surprise for the director on the first day of cinematography in terms of how the players are dressed. The costumers must be supervised at least to the extent of always knowing and approving of their selections and designs. An advantage of working in Europe is that there are all those fantastic wardrobe places where one can find all the national forms of dress, such as we used in *Godfather II*. We dressed our immigrants in ragtag portions of Turkish, Danish, Greek, Italian, and Ukrainian national costumes.

"Another advantage," he adds, "was that we had extras by the thousands with truly European faces. Europeans have an expression on their faces that is different from the expressions typically found on Americans, another plus for authenticity in this instance."

### Models

Models may be built for planning or production at either end of the production process. When used at the outset for pre-production planning, a model may enable

complete understanding among director, designer, and cinematographer as to the choreography of the scene. This may be of particular importance to the director of photography because lighting is often affected by complex moves; the cinematographer thereby becomes aware of overhangs and recesses that may affect illumination of the scene. Similarly, the need for a crane or for dolly tracks will be made apparent through scrutiny of the model before the set is actually built.

Tavoularis recounts, "Models are sometimes made for the information of the director and others who are concerned with production because some things are easier to understand when shown than when explained. Francis [Ford Coppola] had us make a model of the temples in *Apocalypse Now* that were about one-tenth scale so we could study the structures for dramatic possibilities before erecting the actual buildings (Figure 4.15). Models are also useful to the sound designer because a model enables the sound designer to plan where to put microphones in relays for those pauses in action between characters in which there is an exchange of dialogue.

"Occasionally we make models intended to be photographed and incorporated into a live-action film. In *One from the Heart*, Francis gravitated to the premise of making the film entirely in the studio (Plate 8). With that decision made, I did not want to photograph the Las Vegas Strip and cut it into what would otherwise be an interior studio production. We decided to make a model of the Strip for principal cinematography in order to give it a 'studio look' consistent with the rest of the production.

"Consistency," he says, "is the key word here. The important thing for any production designer to do is to look at the film and solve its most difficult problem first and then apply that solution to all the

FIGURE 4.15 *"Francis had us make models of these temples so they could be studied for dramatic possibilities before they were actually constructed. This model was carefully studied by everyone associated with this sequence before we moved a block of stone. Then," Tavoularis continues, "we had to construct these temples on location just the way they were made during the time of Angkor Wat. Because of the mud, we could not use our machines to build anything. We had these huge blocks that were pulled by carabao on sleds through the mud to the site. The Filipinos made this cantilevered bamboo tripod to raise the blocks with a bamboo scaffolding around the building, just as they did it a thousand years ago."*

**APOCALYPSE NOW** DIRECTED BY FRANCIS FORD COPPOLA.

other problems. One cannot solve the easy ones first and then come back to the hard problems and expect aesthetic consistency in the film.

"In *One from the Heart*, I decided to solve the hardest problem first by making a model of the Las Vegas Strip with miniature buildings and gas stations, like toys, with pink mountains in the background (Plate 7). We were trying for a state of mind, not for reality. This male character had one state of mind when he drove down the Las Vegas Strip to the airport to catch his girl, and another state of mind when he came back. When he failed to persuade his girlfriend to stay, he shuffled back to the car—having lost his girl—to find that he had left his car top down in the rain, he had been given a parking ticket, and he was totally defeated. We gave the Strip a whole different look as he drove back wet and bedraggled. The change from hope—as he drove to the airport—to despair—as he drove back—was echoed in the model (Plate 9).

*Principal Cinematography*

"The production designer's work is done only when the film is in the can," Dean Tavoularis concludes, "and principal cinematography is as tense a time for the designer as it is for anyone else. As often as not, the set decorator and I will stay up half the night—sometimes all night—to be sure that everything is as it should be when the director and the players appear on the set. Sometimes, even during principal cinematography, the director or the cinematographer will ask for modification of the set or its decorations, or ask for props for improvised dramatic actions, and I see to it that whatever is requested is done as quickly as possible. It is up to the production designer to complete the settings so they are visually authentic to the camera and professionally viable to the director and players. Only when the director calls 'cut' after the last take of the last scene is the work of the production designer concluded."

*Mark Rydell, shown here with Sissy Spacek, began his career as a director on the "Ben Casey" television series and has since directed nearly seven hundred one-hour shows. His feature film credits include* The Fox, The Rose, The Reivers, Cinderella Liberty, The Cowboys, The River, *and* On Golden Pond, *for which he received a nomination for an Academy Award.*

# Five

# THE DIRECTOR

## *with Mark Rydell*

MASTERY OF THE LANGUAGE of cinema is the hallmark of every major director—a realization that cinema does not involve a rendering of the written word but a transmutation of its ideas into images and sounds in a unique art form.

The film director is now the star of the movie industry. The director's name appearing above the film title may offer more public appeal than the names of the talent appearing in the film. The reputations of George Lucas, Steven Spielberg, Alfred Hitchcock, Mark Rydell, Francis Ford Coppola, and other luminaries have frequently created box office magic.

The director deserves this high status because the director conducts all the elements comprising the cinematic orchestra. He or she must have the artistic integrity and toughness of mind required for making the final decisions on the screenplay as an equal partner with the writer and producer; playing a decisive role in the selection of cast and staff; directing the acting, cinematography, lighting, and other aspects of production; supervising the visual effects; and exercising the right of the first cut in editing. The director must cope with unions and a staff of cinematographers, gaffers, stagehands, and electricians; set designers, scene painters, costume designers, and makeup experts; major and minor performers. The director must charismatically inspire them all to do their very best. Finally, the director must complete all this within the limitations of the budget and the uproar of an ongoing production.

This filmmaker must have a vision of the finished film before it has been photographed in order to understand how all the complex elements of this multivarious art form relate to the whole. With that concept in mind, he or she oversees the creation of each component of dramaturgy, cinematography, sound, editing, and visual effects—synthesizing them to the end effect that the public watching the film will emotionally live the life portrayed on the screen.

Each director offers unique dimensions that are expressions of his or her own personality and character—choice of subjects, themes, and filmic style. This stylistic signature embraces almost every decision made in the creation of a film. The director's personal interests manifest themselves in preferences for doing certain kinds of subject matter (as in John Ford's legendary penchant for westerns); an interest in given themes (as in Ingmar Bergman's concern for the relationship between human beings and God); a development of certain forms of conflict (as in Alfred Hitchcock's classic tales of terror and suspense); a preference for expressing serious ideas in genre form (as in Billy Wilder's comedies).

Cinematic techniques are also molded and filtered by the director's style as the film takes form. The interpretation of a script may be expressed primarily in dialogue or rendered in action; the texture of images may be softly gray or lusciously colorful; the tempo of the film may be edited with long sweeping scenes or quick staccato cuts; the sounds may represent reality or be expanded to a rich listening environment that complements the most imaginative special effects. The dimensions of *mise-en-scène* go on and on—shaping, molding, and filtering content and technique through the elements of a talent. And always it is the director's sure knowledge of how to mix the technical and artistic elements of cinema, as a

**"At the heart of every drama is an action genuinely achieved. Acting is about behavior: creating emotionally credible events under imaginary circumstances. Cinematography and editing are important interpretive tools to record the creation of an event, but I never think about them at all while creating the event with the actors. Once the actor knows what he [or she] is about, then one can bring the other craft elements to bear during rehearsal and principal photography."**
—*Mark Rydell*

111

FIGURE 5.1 *Three of the most celebrated figures in motion pictures—Jane Fonda, Henry Fonda, and Katharine Hepburn—starred together for the first time in the stage-to-film adaptation of* On Golden Pond *under the direction of Mark Rydell.*

"On Golden Pond," *says director Rydell, "is* a drama built on the abrasion of fundamental relationships—parents and children, *their children, divorce, aging, love—certain issues that are timeless conflicts that exist in all human beings. There are no exterior elements in this story; all the drama is drawn out of character."*

**ON GOLDEN POND**   DIRECTED BY MARK RYDELL.

FIGURE 5.2 *Cinderella liberty* is sailors' slang *for a pass that expires at midnight. Marsha Mason, who received an Academy Award nomination for Best Actress for her role, plays a prostitute with a heart of brass; she is shown here with her sailor-lover, played by James Caan, under the direction of Mark Rydell. Marsha Mason plays tender, tough, sexy, funny, and pitiful without missing a beat, and James Caan is a perfect complement as the gentle, kindly sailor.*

*Richard Cuskelly wrote, "There is a powerful sense of lives going on before we've arrived and after we've left the theatre. Never does Rydell let us feel performed to."* Los Angeles Examiner, *December 19, 1978*

CINDERELLA LIBERTY (U.S.A., 1973) DIRECTED BY MARK RYDELL.

painter mixes medium and colors, that transforms celluloid into art.

Four basic elements are used in the language of cinema: the actions of *players*; the vision in motion of *cinematography*; the *editing* of lengths of film to create a logical sequence of events and imply meanings; and the *sound track* presentations of narration, dialogue, music, and sound effects. Although the director need not know the technical aspects of production, he or she must understand how each mode functions to create emotional impact in order to shape picture and sound to a vision of what the film should achieve. This chapter surveys the basic concepts of cinema and their interrelationships and explores how one director uses them to create his films.

Mark Rydell is a distinguished director whose skill and sensibilities in eliciting fine performances from actors and actresses have sent many of them to the podium to receive Academy Awards (Figure 5.1). Rydell has an *auteur*'s view of filmmaking. He submits that every element that goes into the creation of a film should be an expression of the director's will and ideas. Although he insists on the aesthetic authority of the director, he freely concedes that many creative professionals contribute vitally to the success of a film. "A director would be a fool not to listen to actors, cinematographers, and editors—people trained in their art and craft—for fresh insights into the realization of the story. But the final selection of what to include in the film and what to leave out, decisions that determine the success or failure of the film, are the responsibility of the director from first to last in the creative process."

Many films are initiated by a director, and Rydell's experiences in finding ideas for films is illuminating. His first feature film, *The Fox*, was inspired by a novella written by D. H. Lawrence. *Cinderella Liberty* sprang from one chapter in a novel (Figure 5.2). *The Cowboys* was based on

FIGURE 5.3  *Director Rydell observes, "The Cowboys is a western seen through the eyes of boys, eleven through fifteen, who, by a stroke of glorious fortune, suddenly find themselves in a real cattle drive in the Old West.*

*"Casting," says Rydell, "involves finding those persons who enjoy expressing themselves physically in those kinds of behavior required to create events before the camera, as with this* group of boys engaged to ride with John Wayne in this high adventure. The director's real work is to put his [or her] cast in the frame of mind in which they are not 'acting' their roles but have achieved transfiguration into the characters they portray. Their transformation into the persona of their roles must be so complete that, in being themselves, they have become the characters."

**THE COWBOYS** (U.S.A., 1972) DIRECTED BY MARK RYDELL.

an unpublished manuscript (Figure 5.3). *The Reivers* was transmuted from a William Faulkner novel. *The Rose* evolved in part from his own past as a jazz musician. *The River* came from a clipping in a newspaper. *On Golden Pond* was adapted from a stageplay, the rights of which were bought by Jane Fonda as a present for her father Henry Fonda in his last and Academy Award-winning performance. In each instance Rydell was inspired to create a film based upon some element of theme, story, and character that touched his artistic being. Film ideas come from everywhere.

Rydell works with the screenwriter to create the story he wants for every film he directs. A screenplay is, to this director,

"an architectural form for creating believable events. The story must present a series of emotional behaviors by human beings that will be accepted by the viewer as being as real and as credible as anything experienced in daily life. Dialogue is usually subordinate to, and supportive of, actors and actresses behaving as naturally in the fictional context of the story as anyone the viewer may encounter on the street. Dialogue becomes important only when it—and the expression of ideas—are significant components of the conflicts in the story."

Once a viable screenplay has been written, most directors then assign a storyboard artist and a production designer to give the first visual forms to the story. The storyboard artist creates a series of small sketches depicting every major sequence in the film, with some written indications of dialogue. The production designer creates paintings that define the settings and costumes and color key the film. The look and feel of a motion picture should always derive from the story, theme, and setting of the film (Figure 5.4). Storyboards and production designs are mentioned here because of their role in the creative efforts of the director, but these elements have been treated at length in Chapter 4, "The Production Design," and will be discussed again in Chapter 12, "Visual Effects."

## The Players

Dramaturgy must be part of the skills and instincts of a director of cinema. He or she must be able to decide how the screen characters would react in the dramatic circumstances portrayed in the script, diagram the players' movements in relation to the camera, and rehearse and elicit perfor-

FIGURE 5.4 *This scene reveals a dusty encounter between an old-fashioned team of mules and a new-fangled motor car, a dirt farmer and an automobile full of yahoos; the scene places this rollicking adaptation of a William Faulkner story in the South at the turn of the century.*

*Andrea Maletz wrote, "The Reivers effec-* tively straddles two different kinds of films. As a piece of pure action, it has elements of suspense and adventure. As art, it's a visually pleasing and innovative work. And as a recreation of time and memory, it touches a sense of nostalgia that rarely emanates from the screen."
Films, *January 7, 1970*

**THE REIVERS** (U.S.A., 1969) DIRECTED BY MARK RYDELL.

mances from the actors that will conform to a vision of the edited film. This the director does by explaining each camera angle and scene size to give the players confidence; by relating their moves to framing, the director shows them how to work within the given scope of cinematography. He or she reveals when to use the controlled pause and when to project the emotional intensity of the player's performance. And, the director must have the delicacy of human understanding to engender a moving performance from the talent in a scene acted out of context, out on location, on an overcast Monday morning (Figure 5.5).

Directing film actors seems deceptively simple because the performers need only be believable before the camera. Directing performers for the cinema, however, may be more difficult and complex than directing for any other dramatic form because of a unique production requirement: out-of-sequence cinematography.

Dramatic actions in films are not photographed in the continuity order of the script—as are theatrical and videotape productions—but are shot out of context according to location in order to save money in production costs. If scenes 1–12, 35–70, and 105–119 occur at a given location, all will be photographed at virtually the same time even though the dramatic situations may involve such differing emotions as those of watching a baseball game, making love, and committing murder. Each performance will appear in widely separated portions of the edited film, and it is the director's responsibility to create the right mixture of art, craft, and emotion to obtain a performance for each scene that is suitable for its place in the edited film.

"Acting should not be the imitation of an event," Mark Rydell submits, "but the emotional experience of the event itself.

There can be no faking—no faltering in concentration—when playing a role before the intense scrutiny of the camera. The player must become the character in the role being portrayed in order to arouse the passions of the viewer. The director's responsibility is to help the players achieve the genuine experience of the role being lived in the circumstances of the story: loving someone, fearing someone, hating someone, truly realizing the spectrum of human emotions in the actions of the character."

Casting a role is, for Rydell, a matter of finding a player who is physically sensitive and enjoys creating behavior in the context of the story being filmed. Casting for a film such as *On Golden Pond* required finding verbally agile and sophisticated players to express the wit and subtlety of mind found in educated, retired schoolteachers. In *The Reivers* Rydell required talent who could be comically physical in the hilarious story of the South. In *The River* Rydell chose a cast who could be lyrical and sensitive yet physical in a drama rooted in the earth (Figure 5.6). And sometimes the story requires all action. When casting boys for the film *The Cowboys*, Rydell selected the sons of rodeo riders and budding young actors who had never sat on a saddle—trained the former to act and the latter to ride—then directed them to ride with John Wayne and herd horses at breakneck speed across the plains in a splendor of youthful adventure.

## Cinematography

The director works closely with the cinematographer in the selection of what is to be filmed and how it is to be visually interpreted. The director is the decisionmaker, however, because he or she must have a

**THE ROSE** (U.S.A., 1979) DIRECTED BY MARK RYDELL.

**THE RIVER** (U.S.A., 1984) DIRECTED BY MARK RYDELL.

FIGURE 5.6   The River, *expressing Mark Rydell's interest in human character and portraying his concern for the plight of farm families, centered about a young couple played convincingly by Sissy Spacek and Mel Gibson.*

*"This film is full of fundamental differences that don't need to take place on a farm," says Rydell. "There is a contest between two men for a woman's love, there's a child who has to say goodbye to a friend who leaves, there are parents passing traditions down to their children, and children listening at the bedroom door while their parents make love."*

clear vision of how the footage is to be photographed to be effectively edited. That close-up must be there when the story requires a close-up, a full shot must be available when the drama requires a full shot, and these decisions must be made at the time of principal cinematography—by the director.

An appreciation of visual interpretation is hard won by those with a background in related disciplines. Rydell recounts how, as part of his self-training, he bought a 35-mm still camera and experimented by photographing the same objects with various lenses and forms of lighting to see the differences in interpretive values. He prowled through museums studying composition in paintings by the masters, observing what created aesthetic balance, what generated tension, what achieved mood and atmosphere—thereby learning how best to tell a story through artfully designed images. "Studying the masters of art," Rydell says, "helps one to master directing."

The visual dimensions of cinema have several aspects that must be learned as constituent elements in order to understand how they function as a whole language. The director, when he or she walks about and peers through the director's eyepiece, will have the following concerns in mind.

FIGURE 5.7 *An establishing shot, sometimes called a long shot, is an introductory image used at the beginning of a film or at the start of a scene to reveal where the following action will take place and to indicate something of the mood and the character of the story. It is most often a wide-angle view that reveals a relatively large expanse of locale to the audience. The classic use of the establishing shot is found in the western, which traditionally opens on an immense spread of rugged terrain and the figure of a horseman riding into the scene, as shown here with Jimmy Stewart in* How the West Was Won.

**HOW THE WEST WAS WON** (U.S.A., 1962) DIRECTED BY JOHN FORD, HENRY HATHAWAY, AND GEORGE MARSHALL.

© 1962 METRO-GOLDWYN-MAYER, INC. AND CINERAMA, INC.

## Setting, Shot, and Scene

The settings, the shots, and the scenes are primary considerations of principal cinematography; they are reviewed carefully in terms of the dramatic focus in the story (Figure 5.7).

A *setting* is where dramatic events occur and refers not only to the location and the physical properties of the environment but to its ambience and feeling. A mediocre director may mutter the old joke, "A tree is a tree, a rock is a rock, shoot it out in Griffith Park," meaning, of course, that any setting will be acceptable that one can slide by the viewer. This may have worked in the days of the Saturday afternoon westerns, but given the sophistication of today's public, this will no longer be acceptable. Today's director will try for settings that are fully evocative of the themes, characters, and textures of the story. And each setting within the story will embody the emotional color of the dramatic event.

A *shot* is defined in cinema as that length of film footage exposed in one uninterrupted roll of the camera. Theoretically, a shot may be as brief as one frame or as long as the roll of film that may be practicably photographed. In practice, the length of the shot is usually determined by how the director plans to use the shot in editing. If the intent is to create suspense as in a mystery film, the shot may be quite long (without a cut) so that the viewers experience rising tensions as they watch. If the event is intended to be one of violence and excitement, the shots may be short with the aim of creating the excitement in editing. Alfred Hitchcock has gone to both extremes in his films: *Rope* is a feature length film consisting of footage photographed to seem like one uninterrupted shot; *Psycho* contains one event—the knifing of the woman in the shower—with more than one hundred shots. First the director thinks through how the film is to be edited, and then he or she plans the shots and scenes.

A *scene* in cinema corresponds conceptually to an act in the theater or to a chapter in a book. A scene consists of a series of shots constituting a complete dramatic event within the film—each containing a beginning, a middle, an end, and a dramatic crisis. Theoretically, a scene may have an unlimited number of shots, and a film may have an unlimited number of scenes. Pragmatically, these factors are determined by the scope of the story and the limits of viewing endurance.

### Scene Sizes

The lens is the eye of the camera. It differs from the human eye, however, in rendering everything within its scope and depth of field with equal emphasis and failing to distinguish between what is important and what is not. The director must use the lens to approximate the selectivity of the human eye—photographing only what is important at a dramatic moment.

*Dramatic focus* describes what the director will choose to emphasize on the screen at any given point in the story. The dramatic focus may be the environment in which the dramatic events are to occur, to give the flavor of the setting. The focus may be a close-up of a person's face revealing an emotional reaction to an event. It may be a detail inserted to add exposition, such as a pistol or a vial of poison. The dramatic focus may be upon movement itself to add visual excitement to the screen, as when presenting a stampeding herd of buffalo or an automobile chase. The dramatic focus must always be what is most meaningful at that point in the story. And, in every context, the director selects one primary element on which to focus the viewer's attention.

There is another dimension. With the evolution of cinema, the viewer has come to infer certain meanings from the way a subject is cropped and framed in cinematography. Moreover, there are emotional properties inherent in the camera's apparent distance from the subject, which, when synthesized with framing and cropping, imply to the viewer how to interpret the subject.

Scene sizes may range from a wide-angle shot that seems to encompass half the world to extreme close-ups that reveal only the iris of the eye. In between are a wide array of scene sizes that have acquired the following connotations:

An *establishing shot* is used at the beginning of a film—and the opening of a scene within a film—to establish a setting (Figure 5.8).

FIGURE 5.8 *The social context of* Midnight Cowboy *is expressed through this scene in which two homeless men—Joe Buck and Ratso, played respectively by Jon Voight and Dustin Hoffman—try to keep warm in winter in a* cold, unheated, abandoned tenement building. *This interior establishing shot shows the filth and peeling paint, the degrading dinginess in which these two men cling to survival.*

**MIDNIGHT COWBOY** DIRECTED BY JOHN SCHLESINGER.

FIGURE 5.9 *A full shot (below) is most frequently used to introduce a character near the beginning of a film or the beginning of a scene, as in this full shot of Cher in her brilliant portrayal of a beautiful but drug-addicted mother of a deformed child in* Mask. *Rita Kempley wrote, "Cher, after remarkable performances in* Jimmy Dean, Jimmy Dean *and* Silkwood, *offers a third superb performance here as Rocky's Mom."*

FIGURE 5.10 *The medium shot (right) is usually a waist-up image that reveals the subjects doing something with their hands, as in this mutual embrace between mother and son, played by Cher and Eric Stoltz.*

*Director Bodganovich says of his choice of Eric Stoltz as Rocky Dennis, "He's a brilliant actor. And not only is he brilliant, but he is relaxed and natural. These two things combined are dynamite."*

A *full shot* presents a full-length figure (Figure 5.9).

A *medium shot* reaches to the waist and most often reveals an actor doing something with his or her hands (Figure 5.10).

A *close-up* is the size of a human face; it shows a reaction to an event, as well as a host of functions in exposition (Figure 5.11).

An *extreme close-up* serves as the cinematic equivalent of an exclamation point or as exposition (Figure 5.12).

A *tight two-shot* presents two subjects and implies a meaningful relationship (Figure 5.13).

A *tilted camera angle* implies that something in the scene is askance (Figure 5.14).

The foregoing definitions are basic to the language of film, but like all such generalizations, are sometimes violated by a creative director to achieve a dramatic effect. Such meanings are visual in nature and can best be studied in the illustrations that accompany the text.

### Point of View and Camera Angle

The director may interpret the subject from any of three points of view, depending on how closely the viewer is intended to emotionally identify with one of the characters. These are the *objective*, *subjective*, and *performer's viewpoints*, and a selection of *camera angle*.

In the *objective viewpoint* relationship the viewer takes no part in the action but views it as a spectator from the outside, eavesdropping into the lives on the screen

**MASK** (U.S.A., 1985) DIRECTED BY PETER BOGDANOVICH.

**MASK** DIRECTED BY PETER BOGDANOVICH.

**YOU'RE NO GOOD** (CANADA, 1965) DIRECTED BY GEORGE KACZENDER.

© 1965 NATIONAL FILM BOARD OF CANADA

FIGURE 5.11  *The close-up has many uses in film, an important one being the reaction shot. In cinema, meaning is ascribed to events as much by the reactions of characters as by the events themselves. A glance at this close-up of a youthful Michael Sarrazin shows the resentment he portrays in his role as a delivery boy who has been treated like dirt by a receptionist in a poshy foyer. Close-ups also serve the functions of giving the viewer an opportunity to study something closely, of showing inserts of details, and of forming dramatic emphasis—a cut from a full shot to a close-up is a shocker.*

**THE PASSION OF ANNA** (SWEDEN, 1970) DIRECTED BY INGMAR BERGMAN.

© 1970 UNITED ARTISTS CORPORATION

FIGURE 5.12  *The extreme close-up is used at those points of greatest importance or emotional crescendo in dramatic films, as when Anna Fromm (Liv Ullmann) screams with terror when her lover Andreas Winkelman (Max von Sydow) threatens her with an ax.*

**FIGURE 5.13** *The tight two-shot primarily suggests a special relationship between two persons or a person and an object. In this tender scene between Sophie (Meryl Streep) and Nathan (Kevin Kline), the relationship is one of love and passion.*

Charles Champlin wrote of Sophie's Choice, "Meryl Streep is not Meryl Streep being Sophie, she has become Sophie, a Polish survivor with fleeting resemblance to a well-known actress. There is a crucial difference between the actor playing the character brilliantly and the actor disappearing within the character totally." *"Critic at Large,"* Los Angeles Times, *December 11, 1982*

**125**

CINEMATOGRAPHY

**SOPHIE'S CHOICE** (U.S.A., 1982) DIRECTED BY ALAN J. PAKULA.

**REBEL WITHOUT A CAUSE** (U.S.A., 1955) DIRECTED BY NICHOLAS RAY.

FIGURE 5.14 *A tilted camera angle, in which the subjects and their background are slanted on the screen, may be used to imply that something is awry, as in this shot of a youth (Sal Mineo) confronting an adversary in a gang fight. The tilted angle is most often used at times of emotional confrontation or when some individual is behaving irrationally—drunk, frightened, hysterical, on drugs—to let the viewer know that the subject, like the horizon line, is off-balance. The tilted camera angle is also applied during scenes portraying disasters of war, earthquake, riot, and shipwreck to add another dimension to the turbulence of the scene.*

(Figure 5.15). This storytelling technique gives the viewer a choice position from which to watch—through every camera angle and scene size—what is taking place within the story. The objective viewpoint is by far the most widely used in cinema because of its flexibility in presenting the best view of every dramatic event.

The *subjective viewpoint* places the viewer in the position of a screen character, seeing as the character sees, through the lens of the camera (Figure 5.16). This changes the viewer's relationship to the story from that of spectator to that of participant. The subjective camera technique is used in dramatic films at points of high emotional intensity—when the romantic lead is about to receive a kiss from a lovely woman or a fist in his face from an adversary—changing the emotional impact on the viewer from impersonal to personal.

The *performer's viewpoint* is a hybrid of the objective and the subjective viewpoints (Figure 5.17). The camera is placed to look over the shoulder of one of the performers so that the viewer sees the dramatic action very nearly from the viewpoint of a character—but not quite a

FRANCES (U.S.A., 1982) DIRECTED BY GRAEME CLIFFORD.

FIGURE 5.15  *The objective viewpoint puts the viewer in the position of being a third person peering unseen into the lives of other people, as in this courtroom scene in which Frances Farmer, played by Jessica Lange, fights her commitment to a mental institution. The objective viewpoint is the relationship that tells the story in the overwhelming majority of American films because it permits cutaways to other scenes, other persons, and other locations without the restrictions imposed by a personal viewpoint.*

*Molly Haskell wrote about Jessica Lange in* Frances: *"It would be a mistake to see* Frances *as a classic martyr, a woman-as-victim. She was a creature of uncontrollable violence, who couldn't make her way through a cocktail party without offending someone. Yet there was something emblematic about her too, and Jessica Lange, blonde, nervy, witty, with huge restless hands, captures, without self-pity, the haunting quality of the eternal misfit."* Vogue, *February 1, 1983*

FIGURE 5.16 *In the subjective viewpoint the viewer becomes a participant in the film, seeing through the lens of the camera as if the viewer were a character in the movie. In this subjective shot from High Noon, the sheriff has just en-* *tered the church to plead for help from the townsmen against the gunmen who are coming to kill him. At this moment, the viewer has become the sheriff, looked at askance by the townspeople.*

**HIGH NOON** (U.S.A., 1952) DIRECTED BY FRED ZINNEMANN.

**FIGURE 5.17** *The performer's viewpoint places the camera so close to the side of one character's head as to nearly make the angle a subjective viewpoint—but not quite. The performer's viewpoint blends the emotional qualities of objective and subjective angles to make the viewer feel almost as if Jane Fonda were making a personal greeting, playing her* Academy Award–winning role in Klute.

*When asked why she chose to portray a prostitute, Jane Fonda said, "I'm trying to show a call girl as a human being, not what one imagines a call girl to be, but a girl who could have done any number of things, a girl who is intelligent and attractive."*

**KLUTE** (U.S.A., 1971) DIRECTED BY ALAN J. PAKULA.

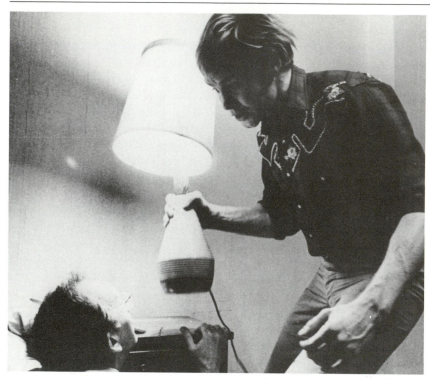

**MIDNIGHT COWBOY** DIRECTED BY JOHN SCHLESINGER.

© 1969 UNITED ARTISTS. COURTESY OF THE ACADEMY OF MOTION PICTURE ARTS AND SCIENCES.

FIGURE 5.18 *Strength, power, and violence may be implied by a camera angle that looks strongly upward at the subject. In this scene, the threatening action of Joe Buck (Jon Voight) is reinforced by the upward camera angle and the harsh contrast of the lighting.*

creasingly strong and aggressive, perhaps arrogant (Figure 5.18). Raise the height of the camera—looking downward at the subject—and the subject will appear increasingly weak and vulnerable (Figure 5.19).

*Composition and Dramatic Focus*

Although the fine points of composition and design are the prerogatives of the cinematographer and production designer, the director controls certain elements of composition to place dramatic focus within the frame. Indeed, it should be emphasized that it is the director, not the cinematographer, who has the last word on visual control of the center of interest. The primary concerns of the director in controlling visual perception in this regard relate to *space, dominance of talent, dominance of lips and eyes,* and the *composition of foreground and background activity.*

*Space* is an important compositional element for creating psychological tension. A character seen in tight close-up, or framed by bars, guns, or other characters, is psychologically confined, which in turn sets up tensions within the viewer that need release.

Increasing the amount of space around the character—allotting more visual territory—enhances the character's sense of authority and prestige and connotes more

subjective viewpoint. More intimate than the objective viewpoint, the performer's viewpoint does not offer the viewer participation of eye-to-eye contact with a character.

*Camera angles* are similarly used by the director for interpretation of the subject to give power implications to the viewer. A simple eye-level view of the subject is essentially neutral and narrative; it renders the subject in scenes that are often without heavy dramatic overtones. Lower the camera in relation to the subject—looking upward—and the subject will seem in-

FIGURE 5.19  *Weakness, passivity, and vulnerability are implied by a camera angle that looks down on the huddled figure of Celie, played by Whoopi Goldberg.*

**THE COLOR PURPLE** DIRECTED BY STEVEN SPIELBERG.

FIGURE 5.20 *Space is used here as a composi-tional element to connote authority. Henry Fonda (left), playing the role of Tom Joad in the Depression epic, is accorded the deference of leadership in a composition that places him* *in the clear whereas the followers, portrayed by Frank Darien, Russell Simpson, and Ed Waller, are huddled together awaiting his decision.*

**THE GRAPES OF WRATH** DIRECTED BY JOHN FORD.

FIGURE 5.21 *Neither the written word nor any form of measurement could define the ineffable shades of meaning found in this close-up of Hanna Schygulla. This close a close-up violates the personal space of the viewer and engenders an emotional appeal that depends on the content. The face of a lovely woman this close may seem enticing to a man; the face of a child may seem appealing to a woman; the face of a mugger may seem threatening to both, with possibly different reactions aroused in a man than a woman.*

**THE MARRIAGE OF MARIA BRAUN** (GERMANY, 1979) DIRECTED BY RAINER WERNER FASSBINDER.

© 1979 NEW YORKER FILMS. USED BY PERMISSION OF ALMI PICTURES, INC.

freedom (Figure 5.20). This may be illustrated in several ways. An authority figure among a large number of people would be accorded the deference of space whereas others may be crowded together. A prisoner attempting to escape might be rendered in a series of close-ups and medium shots to build pressure. When the escape comes, long shots and wide-angle shots could visually echo the sudden freedom.

The space allotted to characters within the picture frame may be changed constantly to reflect the shifting polarities of the drama. A character rising in power may be progressively given more space and an upward camera angle, whereas the person sinking is penned in by tighter environments and less room in which to maneuver. The design of space within the picture frame can be varied to connote freedom and power, or conversely, entrapment.

Personal space, the acceptable distance among people in our culture, relates to cinema when a subject is viewed in close-up from the subjective camera viewpoint (Figure 5.21). A lovely woman leaning nearer may seem intimate to the male viewer. A villain cursing into the lens violates the life space of the viewer and thereby becomes repulsive, frightening, or infuriating. A child seen in close personal view may arouse protective instincts that become elements of viewer identification. This invasion of personal space permits the closest perceptions of subtle expressions in moments of emotional truth: Pathos, humor, malice, and mystery are apparent with an intimate view whereas they are not perceptible from afar.

Conversely, distance tends to diminish the dramatic force of a person. Figures placed within a vast panorama seem small, however rapidly they may be moving. The

FIGURE 5.22 *Dominance in a triangular composition is often achieved by placing one person above the other two, as in this arrangement with Katharine Hepburn higher in the image area than Katharine Houghton and Sidney Poitier.*

**GUESS WHO'S COMING TO DINNER** (U.S.A., 1967) DIRECTED BY STANLEY KRAMER.

FIGURE 5.23 *Geometric shapes found on location are often useful in establishing dramatic focus. In this scene a large triangular shape formed by the beams and the horizontal sign in the background lead the eye directly to Joe Buck, played by Jon Voight. Whether he is speaking or listening, he is the dramatic focus of this shot.*

environment itself then becomes the point of dramatic focus.

The left and right areas of the image frame are frequently used as adversary positions, with the polar extremes of the screen echoing compositionally the conflict of two dramatic forces. With expansion of wide-screen techniques, the outer sides may creatively imply menace or mystery: "Someone may be out there."

The top and bottom of the image area similarly connote meanings. A figure looming near the top, whereas all others are below, becomes threatening or omnipotent. The bottom of the frame is the nadir in terms of its power implications: Weakness, helplessness, and vulnerability huddle near the base. If a lower figure is prostrate, the weakness is further emphasized even if no other character appears within the image area because we anticipate the proximity of another more dominant person.

Abstract compositional shapes may be used to comment on the dramatic action taking place. The director may use a triangular arrangement of subjects to imply a shaky relationship among two men and one woman, with the triad of compositional points shifting with the power dynamics of the relationship (Figure 5.22). Triangular compositions are useful for creating dominant and subordinate relationships in many kinds of dramatic situations (Figure 5.23). Geometric shapes of other kinds—*S* curve, circle, and cross—often underlie powerful compositions (Figure 5.24).

*Dominance of talent* means putting dramatic focus on one of the performers in a two-shot or three-shot composition (Figure 5.25). The most obvious example is an over-the-shoulder position, which makes dominant the person who is standing nearly full-face to the camera and makes subordinate the person whose face is turned away from the camera.

The principle of full-face dominance holds true even as the two-shot arrangement swings around to a profile angle on both subjects. The face turned slightly toward the camera tends to dominate

**MIDNIGHT COWBOY** DIRECTED BY JOHN SCHLESINGER.

**SLAUGHTERHOUSE** (U.S.A., 1987) DIRECTED BY RICK ROESSLER.

FIGURE 5.24 *A fence can be useful in a rural setting to bring the dramatic focus to the desired center of interest, in this instance Joe Barton enjoying civil conversation with his friends.*

over the pure profile, given equal lighting on both subjects. The more into profile a subject turns, the more it becomes subordinate.

Dominance may also be created in a two-shot by manipulating the mass, height, and lighting relationship between two subjects. Dominance may be given to one subject and subordination to the other by placing a large figure opposite a small one, a standing figure over a seated figure, and a brightly lit subject over a dimly lit one. Dominance may be shifted from one subject to the other by asking the performers to change positions in relation to the camera lens, by using a crane-set camera to swing around to a different angle, and by reversing the actors' positions within the setting. A performer may also dominate by movements, but this aspect will be treated later when we consider the concepts of movement.

The *dominance of lips or eyes* seems to derive from a voyeur instinct in the viewer. People want to know what other people are saying even if it is none of their business (Figure 5.26) The director may put a screen character in the darkest recess of the composition and fill the rest of the screen with psychedelic color, yet the viewer will strain to read the moving lips of the speaking character, ignoring the rest of the cinematic pyrotechnics. In practice, this means that only the character in dramatic focus in a given scene should, under most circumstances, be shown with moving lips. The exception occurs when everyone is talking at once—except for the central

FIGURE 5.25 *Dominance of the role played by Dustin Hoffman is achieved by having his face turned three-quarters toward the camera, whereas Meryl Streep's face is in profile, slightly away from the camera. Even though the character played by Streep may have been speaking dialogue at the time, the dramatic focus will be on Hoffman because we can see more of his face, and his reaction becomes the dramatic focus.*

**KRAMER VS. KRAMER** DIRECTED BY ROBERT BENTON.

FIGURE 5.26 *This charming film tells the story of a youthful offender being introduced to the joys of life on his way to prison. In this scene, the lips become dominant as we strain to see as well as hear what is being said. Here Jack Nicholson (center), in his role as the shore patrol officer determined to show his charge what life is all about, is introducing his prisoner, played by Randy Quaid, to a friendly madam.*

**THE LAST DETAIL** (U.S.A., 1973) DIRECTED BY HAL ASHBY.

**FRANCES** DIRECTED BY GRAEME CLIFFORD.

FIGURE 5.27 *The eyes allow us to read the thoughts and inner feelings of another person. In this scene, both characters are three-quarters faced toward the camera, but the eyes of Jessica Lange are open—drawing our attention—whereas those of Kim Stanley are downcast, placing her in a subordinate position in terms of dramatic focus.*

character—at which time the viewer will watch his or her lips and await words.

Moving eyes are second in dominance to moving lips (Figure 5.27). The eyes are called the windows of the soul because they reveal so much about the inner feelings of the person and may be used to interpret his or her spoken words. We are accustomed to reading the eyes of other people to determine whether they are saying what they mean, or just the opposite. A complete dramatic sequence, without a single spoken word, may reveal the relationships between people solely through the meanings expressed in their eyes.

Dramatic focus may be controlled through the *composition of foreground and background activity*. The viewer's gaze tends to go first to the nearest subject primarily because of its large mass area on the screen (Figure 5.28). This generalization is subject to some compositional "ifs." If the foreground subject is out of focus, the viewer may glance beyond it to a more clearly defined subject. If the nearer subject is heavily cropped, whereas the farther subject stands in the clear, the viewer's eye may drift to the farther subject because it is more easily comprehensible (Figure 5.29).

Any movement by a character will draw dramatic focus. In most scenes the subject moving the quickest in a horizontal direction across the screen will first attract the viewer's attention, and the closer to the foreground the stronger its attraction. The same holds true of a subject moving diagonally from background to foreground, thereby growing in image area on the screen. If the two movements are occuring simultaneously in two subjects, the more dynamic subject in mass and speed will tend to dominate the dramatic focus. An exception to the dominance of mass and thrust occurs when the character is static and all others are in motion, or when the subject is moving against a countervailing tide, such as a person pushing through an opposing crowd.

The director, in consultation with the cinematographer, blocks the movements for the talent. The shapes of the movements are as important in cinematic com-

FIGURE 5.28 *Foreground objects tend to draw the viewer's gaze first, as with the slain man in the foreground. Moreover, the white triangle of the coat lapel—contrasting sharply against the dark uniform—further attracts the eye of the viewer to the foreground, in this scene with Claude Rains and Humphrey Bogart.*

**CASABLANCA** (U.S.A., 1942) DIRECTED BY MICHAEL CURTIZ.

FIGURE 5.29 *The visual dominance of Humphrey Bogart in this scene with Katharine Hepburn is achieved in several ways: the shape and contrast of the dark awning draws the gaze to his face; he is standing whereas she is seated; his face may be seen in three-quarters view whereas hers is in profile; and his face is fully lighted whereas hers is modeled flatly. This image sums up, in many ways, the techniques used by the director to control the focus of attention in each shot.*

"I don't think any of us knew how much of a comedy the picture was," John Huston admitted. "I think its being funny had largely to do with the relationship between Bogart and Hepburn. They are just funny together. One called forth that quality in the other, so that the scenes invariably turned out to be uproarious where the original intention had been for adventurous drama."

**THE AFRICAN QUEEN** (U.S.A., 1951) DIRECTED BY JOHN HUSTON.

FIGURE 5.30 *Movements by the performers are, of course, the gross dimension of film and the aspect most noticed by the viewer, as in this scene with Gene Hackman. Each movement may carry shades of meaning modified by content and lens selection as well as by movements of the camera. Cinema is vision in motion through time, in which compositions are constantly being reframed, modified, and changed according to the dynamics of the subjects and the cinematographer at the will of the director.*

**BONNIE AND CLYDE** DIRECTED BY ARTHUR PENN.

position as the shapes of the subjects and their backgrounds. Throughout the path of movement at each point of pause, it is the cinematographer's responsibility to assure proper illumination and exact focus on the subject. While a performer is in motion, movement itself becomes the subject and photographic factors become less critical. When the performer stops, pauses, or turns—when the viewer has a clear view of the subject—photographic precision again becomes important.

## Movement

Movement is the essence of cinematography and takes two primary forms: *movements by the subject* before the camera and *movements by the camera or its lens over the subject*, with variations in effect implied by variations in shutter-frame rate speed. (Implied movements created by splicing scenes together will be treated later in "Editing.")

*Movements by the subject* before the cam-

FIGURE 5.31 *Movement itself has become the subject in this scene. Add the danger of men tumbling from a falling water tower to a herd of stampeding bison and the sum total of activity equals an exciting episode in which the viewer responds emotionally to movement and danger.*

**HOW THE WEST WAS WON** DIRECTED BY JOHN FORD, HENRY HATHAWAY, AND GEORGE MARSHALL.

era is the first form. So strong is the attraction of the human eye to movement within a scene that it largely nullifies the laws of artistic composition (Figure 5.30). A shot may be composed with very strong directional lines and massive shapes and forms, yet if there is one small person in the setting—moving—the viewer's gaze will dart to the subject.

*Movements by the camera or its lens* over the subject, or to follow the subject's actions, is the second form. The movements may be those of the camera itself as it follows horses, vehicles, or moving people. Or the movements may be implied by a change of focus, from one subject to another, or a change of focal length, such as a zoom-in to a close-up of a woman's eyes (Figure 5.31).

An extensive array of camera movement and lens movement concepts has evolved, each having a specific name and generally accepted usage within the language of film. The camera movement concepts are

FIGURE 5.32 *This photo demonstrates a pan after movement shot. In most scenes the subject moving the quickest in a horizontal direction across the screen will first attract the viewer's attention. Similarly, subjects moving diagonally from background to foreground will become dominant as they grow in image area on the screen, as in this scene with Jane Fonda (left), Red Buttons, Susannah York, and Michael Sarrazin.*

*Jane Fonda comments on her desire to play the role of Gloria in this film: "Actually, I turned down several other films because it was something I wanted to do. In France the original novel can be found on every bookstall of the Left Bank. Did you know that McCoy's hero influenced Camus's* The Stranger?*"*

the *pan, swish-pan, tilt, trucking shot, dolly shot, crane shot,* and *shoulder-mounted (Steadicam) shot.* Lens concepts are the *zoom* and the *rack focus.*

A *pan* is a horizontal scan of the camera from a pivotal point, usually that of a tripod (Figure 5.32). The pan is used for many dramatic purposes:

To follow the actions of a moving subject, such as a soldier racing horizontally across a field of fire to attack an enemy position.

To relate two subjects having an important content relationship, such as a woman's discovery of an intruder in her room.

To create a first-person point of view, such as that of a sheriff scanning the cliffs of a mountain wilderness for a glimpse of an escaped convict—an effect that allows the viewer to gaze out through the eyes of the sheriff.

To make a *pan discovery* shot that reveals unexpected information near the tail of the shot—information that may create suspense, provide motivation, prefigure an upcoming crisis, or be dramatic punctuation.

To add to the viewer's developing awareness, which may be controlled through movements of the camera, pausing at items that reveal exposition about an event or a person.

The *swish-pan* is a panning camera movement, but the movement is so fast as to reduce the image to flashing blurs—in effect smearing the subjects to abstraction. The swish-pan is not used to follow a subject but is used as a transitional device to imply a change of time or location or to show disorientation when used as a subjective shot.

The *tilt* is a vertical version of the pan, an up-or-down scanning movement by the camera from a pivotal point. The tilt has three main purposes:

To follow the ascending actions of a subject—such as the takeoff of an aircraft.

To relate two subjects with an important content relationship—such as a scientist watching the rise of a missile—within one shot.

To let the viewer experience the rising gaze of a screen character, as when Meryl Streep, in her role in *Out of Africa*, gazed longingly into the sky for the airplane of her lover—who would never come.

The term *trucking shot* derives from the silent film practice of mounting a camera on a truck to enable the cinematographer to keep pace with the man on the white horse at the head of the posse. The trucking shot is used to follow those fast and far-ranging horizontal actions of a subject that exceed the scope of a pan—running, riding, driving—and to obtain close-ups of the performers.

The *dolly shot* is another technique in which the camera is moved on wheels from one position to another. Its purpose is simply to move the camera closer to a subject or to follow the walk of a subject.

The *crane shot* consists of mounting a camera at the top of a highly mobile crane—with seats for director and cinematographer—and with the capability of changing heights, directions, and movements in a fluid continuous manner. In *Love Story*, the exchange of nonreligious marriage vows between the boy and girl was solemnized by a crane shot that circled about them expressing their oneness cinematically.

The *shoulder-mounted camera* (Steadicam) is an excellent means of portraying the subjectively unsteady feelings of a per-

**THEY SHOOT HORSES, DON'T THEY?** (U.S.A., 1969) DIRECTED BY SYDNEY POLLACK.

son in an emotionally distraught condition: frightened, drunk, psychotic, fleeing from an assailant, fighting in the chaos of battle. A hand-held or shoulder-mounted camera can subjectively render unstable emotions in a way that could not be equaled by any other mobile camera technique.

A *zoom-in* is the illusion of a continuous approach by the camera to the subject, with a resulting reduction of the area being photographed—an effect made possible by the variable focal length or zoom lens. The zoom-in is used primarily to draw attention to a detail having special meaning while enabling the viewer to remain aware of the detail's relationship to the whole context. The speed of a zoom-in depends upon its use: In dramatic film, in those situations where impact is more important than information, a zoom-in is usually fast for a shock effect on the viewer. On the other hand, when a growing sense of horror or realization is intended, a fairly slow zoom-in is used, alerting the viewer to look for information or exposition. Creative filmmakers find many uses for the zoom-in.

The *zoom-out*, the reverse of the zoom-in, is a progressive retreat from the subject, gradually expanding the area being photographed. Again, the speed of the move depends upon its use, slow moves for exposition or a growing sense of realization, fast moves for emotional impact. (Zoom shots and panning actions are frequently abused by novices to add specious excitement or imply meanings in a dull vacuous shot.)

Changes of dramatic focus within a scene may also be achieved by a change of lens focus, called a *rack* (or shift) *focus*. This means in practical terms focusing first on a near subject and then a far subject, or the reverse. The rack-focus technique is often used when one person

speaks and another responds. Perhaps the most common example is the situation in which a woman is seen seated before a mirror, conversing with a man who is found in the reflection of the mirror standing behind her. One may speak (in focus), and the cinematographer will then rack focus through the mirror reflection to the other person responding or reacting to what has been said.

The mobility of the camera itself—through pans, tilts, trucking, and dolly shots, hand-held and shoulder-mounted and with the zoom lens—offers the constant temptation to make gratuitous moves that say nothing in terms of content or interpretation. Mark Rydell comments in this regard, "The director must be sure that camera movements are always motivated by the dramatic actions—themes, story, and character conflicts—and not added for their own sake."

### Master Scene Technique

When a competent director blocks the actions of the performers playing a scene, it is always done in relation to a hypothetical placement of the camera (Figure 5.33). The cinematographer is usually present during rehearsals to interact, when asked, on the matter of camera placement. The director may turn to the cinematographer and ask, "Well, what about camera and lighting problems?" It then becomes a discussion in which the director may say, "I want a close-up here and a medium shot there." The cameraperson may then come up with the suggestion, "What if we start with a wide-angle shot and then move in?" The director may think about it a moment and say, "I'd rather save the long shot to use later for suspense." This discussion is essentially the approach for planning the master scene technique.

The master scene technique consists of

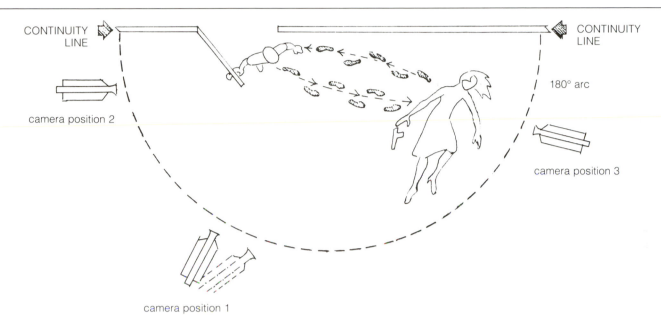

CONTINUITY LINE

camera position 2

CONTINUITY LINE

180° arc

camera position 3

camera position 1

FIGURE 5.33  *Master Scene Technique*

*1. Camera position 1 would be used to photo-*graph three scenes of the dramatic sequence: an establishing shot *of the room, complete cinema-*tography *of the whole dramatic action from be-*ginning to end, and panning *after the subject as he walks toward the body and away from the body. This provides the film editor with a cover-ing master scene to which the editor can cut if he or she has trouble editing any of the other scenes.*

*From the same camera position, the film-*maker would probably photograph a medium shot *of the man as he picked up the gun near the body and looked over his shoulder in panic.*

*Also from camera position 1, the filmmaker would photograph a* close-up *of the man's face as he paused on his way out the door to look back at the body.*

*2. Camera position 2 would be used to pho-*tograph two shots of the dramatic sequence: a subjective camera shot *through the eyes of the man as he discovers the woman, probably fol-*lowed by a zoom-in *to a full shot of the body.*

*Furthermore, from camera position 2 there would be a* full shot *of the man as he rises from the woman's body and runs toward the camera into a* medium shot *as he opens the door.*

*3. Camera position 3 would be used for four shots:* a low-angle shot *looking past the woman's body, to a full shot of the man standing at the door,* rack focus *as he walks forward and kneels beside the woman, and is reframed with her in a tight two-shot.*

*A complete dramatic sequence has been pho-*tographed from three camera positions—with camera movements, matching action, and a full spectrum of scenes to offer good potential for dynamic editing.*

photographing a dramatic action in segmented scene sizes—full shot, medium shot, close-up, and so on—so the individual shots may be edited later into a complete scene of dramatic action. The component elements of master scene technique are control of *screen directions*, *matching the action*, *matching the look*, and the *continuity line*.

Consistent shot-to-shot *screen direction*, by movements of the subject or the camera, should be maintained from one shot to another, or the changed screen direction should be explained visually. An establishing shot of a man driving his car into a parking lot, followed by a cut to a medium shot of him getting out of his car, followed by a cut to a close-up of his hand locking the door should have consistent screen direction in order to reveal the action logically. Any change in the screen direction not explained visually will confuse the viewer. The instant the viewer asks "What's happening?" the film has lost its grip.

Changes of directional continuity may be explained visually by one of three cinematic techniques. The first means is the obvious one of having the subject change direction within the shot.

The second technique is that of photographing a scene having a neutral direction—the subject moves directly toward the viewer in a head-on shot or directly away in a tailaway shot. A neutral direction permits the subject to subsequently begin anew in either screen direction when edited to another directional shot.

The third means of changing screen direction is through the use of a cutaway. A cutaway is a subject having a logical but not visual relation to the main dramatic action—for example, a person who is a spectator to the action. A cutaway is presented long enough for the viewer to forget what the screen direction was or long enough for the screen direction of the dramatic action to have plausibly changed. For example, if a fight is being photographed in which two men are struggling for possession of a gun lying on the floor, and the director has inadvertently flipped the screen direction during principal cinematography, the film editor could cover up the error by presenting a close-up of the gun long enough to make it seem plausible that the fight being heard on the sound track had changed its screen direction.

When two separate but contemporaneous actions are planned and intended to be intercut later in editing for dramatic suspense, each dramatic action should have a consistently different screen direction. An example of this would be two armies marching toward each other to battle. One army should be consistently moving from left to right, the other from right to left, so when the two parallel actions are intercut, the viewer may instantly understand, from its directional movement, which army is being watched. Another example would be the hunter and the hunted, in which both may be moving in one direction, but the hunted is always looking back at the pursuer.

*Matching the action* consists of photographing the component scenes of a dramatic action so that the resulting footage may be edited into a single smooth flow of action. For example, if a dramatic action consists of one man lunging forward to wrest a gun from the hand of another, his movements would probably be photographed in their entirety in three scene sizes: an establishing shot as one leaps forward and tears the gun from the hand of the other; a medium shot of the aggressor as he lunges forward and seizes the weapon; and a close-up of the gun as it is wrenched from the hand of the second man. Each of these shots would record the

FIGURE 5.34 *Controlling the directional gaze between two characters—photographed in separate shots—can be achieved so the two will seem to be looking at each other when the scenes are edited together. The eye-lines must match, as in this conversation between actors Laura Zimmett and David Zarella.*

CHRISSY OGDEN

same complete movements, but only short lengths of each scene would be used to edit a composite dramatic action that would appear to the viewer as a single continuous flow of action.

The dramatic action thus photographed must be repeated three times, or photographed simultaneously with several cameras, in order to have overlapping action in the three shots suitable for proper editing.

*Matching the look* refers to matching the directional gaze of two subjects—when photographing them separately, out of context—so that when the shots are edited together the subjects will appear to be looking at each other (Figures 5.34 and 5.35). During principal cinematography it is not uncommon for two subjects appearing in the same scene to be photographed at different times with their interactions being created entirely by the film editor. This practice makes it imperative that the look be matched carefully by

**FROM THE TERRACE** (U.S.A., 1960) DIRECTED BY MARK ROBSON.

FIGURE 5.35 *The false directional gaze occurs when a character in the foreground is talking to a second character standing behind with both people facing the same direction, as in this shot of Joanne Woodward and Paul Newman. She is glancing sideways with her gaze apparently directed at him even though they are facing the same direction. This placement of players permits the foreground character to display emotions different from the content of what is being spoken.*

*James Power wrote of their performances, "Paul Newman has force and considerable sympathy in the central role. Joanne Woodward achieves a catlike grace and rather sad menace as his wife."* Hollywood Reporter, *June 27, 1960*

the director during cinematography, or it may appear in editing as if the actor is looking over the actress's head while she is smiling adoringly at the third button of his shirt.

Mark Rydell is one director, however, who insists that all players appearing in a scene be present during principal cinematography. He submits that the presence of everyone elicits a more sensitive performance from each player.

The *continuity line* is an invisible stage line (a 180-degree arc) from which all the shots of a scene having a consistent screen direction should be photographed. Camera positions may be set up anywhere within this 180-degree continuity line, and the resulting film footage may be properly edited in terms of screen direction. Whether there is one subject or a hundred, whether the action is a single character walking across the room or a rampaging mob swarming through the city, whether the shots are photographed from a tripod or a mobile crane, the resulting footage can be edited with correct relationships among the subjects if the director remembers this continuity line.

Make the mistake of photographing one shot beyond that continuity line, however, and edit it into the sequence photographed within the continuity line and the viewer will be instantly confused. The orientation of the whole scene will be suddenly reversed and logical continuity will crumble.

How master scene technique is applied for interpretive values—which is the responsibility of the director—may be exemplified by two bedroom scenes photographed in Mark Rydell's film *The River*. This story about a young farm couple trying to wrest a livelihood from raising crops and livestock on the banks of a river in Tennessee portrays what happens to them and to their marriage when everything seems to go wrong.

In the first bedroom scene, the bleak melancholy of very late at night is shown with a mood of isolation between husband and wife who have had a disagreement about an offer from an agribusiness to buy their farm. Rydell felt that even a single cut in this master scene would break the mood of the sequence. He therefore blocked the action of the husband and staged the moves of the crane-mounted camera to follow after him—framing carefully at every point of dramatic pause—so that the entire scene could be rendered from several camera points of view without change by the editor. Director Rydell rode the camera as the husband read the offer under a lamp by the window, then lay it aside to join his wife in bed, turning out two other lamps, and the scene concluded with a view of their two profiles in bed in the dimness of moonlight. This long uninterrupted roll of the camera produced a full master scene that was used in the film exactly as photographed—as required by the story (Figure 5.36).

During a later bedroom scene in a hotel in Birmingham, when husband and wife are reunited after several months separation while he works in a steel mill, he finds himself so physically and emotionally battered as to be unable to respond to his wife. This bedroom sequence was directed differently by Rydell, with many camera positions and shorter scenes intended to be edited for tempo to reveal the progressive interplay between man and woman.

As the husband voices his pent-up feelings, his wife begins to gently kiss his wounds: the burns on his body from the hot coals that had spewed from the crucibles; the bruises on his face from a fight with another man at the steel mill. As husband and wife draw closer together emotionally the cinematic interpretation shifted. The initial static shots, long in time and slow in tempo with little camera movement, changed to increasing camera movements and tighter scene sizes as their emotions rise.

The two foregoing bedroom sequences were directed, lighted, photographed, and edited differently by director Rydell to correspond to the changed mood, content, and relationship between the characters: the first, with one uninterrupted roll of the camera to reflect mood; the second, with many shots to create tempo in editing. In each instance the story dictated the interpretive values.

### Multicamera Technique

The alternative to the master scene technique is the use of the multicamera camera setup in which the dramatic action occurs without interruption while being photo-graphed by two or more cameras running simultaneously. The advantage of this technique is that unrepeatable actions may be photographically captured with several scene sizes suitable for editing. The disadvantage is that the lighting of the scene may be ideal from one camera position and substandard from another.

Mark Rydell used the multicamera technique in a scene in *The River* in which a deer wanders into the furnace area of the mill and panics, running desperately back and forth in an attempt to escape. The director, in order to get matching action on moves that could not be restaged, set up cameras all over the steel mill and had the deer photographed simultaneously with different lenses from different angles to achieve the staccato editing that would be evocative of the doe's terrified scrambling to escape.

The director has certain practical, mundane considerations to keep in mind when directing principal cinematography, aspects relating more to cost than to quality but nonetheless important.

How can each sequence be photographed most effectively with a minimum number of lighting and camera setups?

Is the sequence covered to excess? This issue relates both to the importance of the sequence within the film as a whole and to a responsibility for completing principal cinematography within budget.

Is the dramatic action blocked in a way that will obtain the best performance from the actors? If the director does not evoke a performance and block the dramatic action in a way that reveals the player at his or her best, the most dramatic performances may occur off-screen.

FIGURE 5.36 *Cinematography and editing were fused within one roll of the camera in this bedroom scene from* The River. *Believing that a cut anywhere would have broken the solemn mood, director Mark Rydell had the cinematographer follow actor Mel Gibson as he read and put down the offer to buy the farm, then turned off the night lights, and retired to bed—all in one long uninterrupted scene. This technique created a palpable tension.*

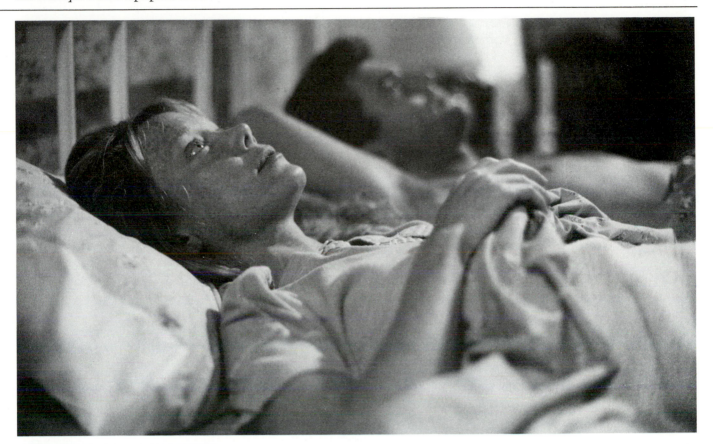

**THE RIVER** DIRECTED BY MARK RYDELL.

## Editing

Editing is what gives dramatic focus to every sequence in the film. This is the phase in which the director decides what shots will be included in the film and what will end up on the cutting-room floor. Every director is entitled to what is called *the right of the first cut*, and it means that he or she can insist on the director's interpretation of the story before anyone else intervenes to change that interpretation, perhaps at the behest of the producer or studio.

Mark Rydell comments about editing,

"Rhythm is a vital instinct for the director as well as the editor: that intuitive sense of when and where to move; when and where to hold; when and where to cut. Rhythm is at the core of every creative artist working in whatever medium. However technically competent a director may be, if he or she lacks the artistic sensibility to know what scenes should be on the screen, and for how long, and [to] know what music and sound effects are needed to complement the edited image, that person will never become a director of the first rank. Rhythms of shape, form, mass, color, and movement are near the heart of every art form, and this is particularly true in the cinema."

All the filmic elements that precede editing—writing, set design, directing, acting, lighting, cinematography, special effects, sound recording—are brought to fruition when orchestrated into a motion picture by editing.

The physical act of splicing two pieces of film together is not editing. Film editing, as art and communication, is defined by the relationships between the content of two shots, their internal movements, the screen directions of their subjects, their associated image shapes, and the lengths of each shot used to create tempo.

Each shot is selected and edited into a scene for what it says about the subject and the story at that point in the film: dramatic focus. A single dramatic scene is photographed as many bits of action in different scene sizes later to be edited into one movement. The psychological impact of the scene may be heightened in editing by eliminating the superfluous and emphasizing first one detail and then another to make the edited action more vivid than the original performance before the camera.

### The Third Meaning

The edited position of any shot, in relation to the shots that come before and after, is what gives that shot its cinematic meaning within a scene. When two related shots are edited, they take on a third meaning not inherent in either of them. This third meaning may be *narrative* (visualized on the screen) or *implicit* (created in the mind of the viewer).

*Narrative editing* simply means telling a story in a continuity order. If the film editor presents a close-up of a man looking intently at something and then splices that shot to one portraying a T-bone steak,

the narrative third meaning would be: a hungry man about to eat. The two related shots, when spliced together, acquire a third narrative meaning not inherent in either of the original shots, and each scene assumes a different connotation in the presence of the other.

*Implicit editing* means presenting two unrelated scenes together to create a symbolic meaning in the mind of the viewer that is not intrinsic to either of the scenes or to the narrative continuity. If the same close-up of the man were followed by a brief shot of lava bubbling in a volcano—when a New York setting has been established—the implicit third meaning would be that he is smoldering with inner rage, not that a natural disaster has come to Times Square. If our close-up were followed by a shot showing a hawk soaring up in the sky—in the context of a prison cell on Death Row—the implicit meaning would be a wish for freedom.

The third meanings created by implicit editing are not necessarily narrative but expressive of the inner feelings of the subject. The extent to which implicit editing may be used depends upon the film literacy of the viewer and his or her familiarity with the symbolism intended by the filmmaker.

### Transitions

The average viewer has been conditioned to understand that certain ways of changing from one shot to the next, one scene to the next—through editing—convey implied meanings connoting transitions of continuity, time, or location. These continuity and transitional concepts are the *cut*, the *fade*, the *dissolve*, the *wipe*, and the *superimposition*.

The *cut* is an instantaneous change from one shot to another—the basic technique of film editing. The cut is used to portray a continuous flow of action within an uninterrupted span of time, usually within a scene. For example, a dramatic sequence presenting two people engaged in a quarrel would be directed and edited with a series of cuts from one person shouting to the other person reacting to represent a continuing flow of action in an uninterrupted flow of time.

The *fade-in* is the gradual appearance of a scene from the black, darkened screen. The fade-in is universally used at the beginning of every motion picture to introduce the film and serves as the rising curtain of cinema. The length of the fade-in implies the emotional flavor of the film to follow: A heavy drama may be introduced by a fade-in as long as a minute to connote a foreboding quality. A comedy may fade-in with a snappy six frames, little more than a soft cut.

The *fade-out*, conversely, is the gradual disappearance of a scene to a black, darkened screen, an effect used to end a scene, a sequence, or conclude the film. As with the fade-in, the longer the fade-out the more emotionally laden the effect. Fades may be used within the body of the film to separate major scenes. In this context, their occurrence is reversed, becoming a fade-out, fade-in. In *Rear Window*, for example, Alfred Hitchcock used the fade-out, fade-in technique to denote the passage of time while Jeffries (Jimmy Stewart) sat immobile in his wheelchair. Viewers have been conditioned to accept the fade-out, fade-in as signifying a major change of time or location, from one scene to the next.

A *dissolve* combines the fade-out of an outgoing scene with the fade-in of an incoming scene—simultaneously—within the same length of film. The images of the second scene materialize and take posses-sion of the screen. Dissolves are most often used as a transitional device within the body of the film to imply either a minor change of location or a short lapse of time.

A long, long dissolve is sometimes used in dramatic films to create the effect of a slow awakening to reality. In *The Diary of Anne Frank*, the two lovers became aware only gradually of the approach of the jack-booted Gestapo, an implication made through the use of a dissolve minutes long.

The substitution of a cut for a dissolve or a fade, when making a change of time or location, is a recent trend among directors. The effect on the viewer may be an instant of confusion as he or she is thrust into a new scene without warning unless the new setting is so clearly established that immediate reorientation can occur.

A *wipe* is a transitional device in which the outgoing scene is physically displaced on the screen by the incoming scene, with both scenes sharply visible on the screen for the length of the effect. The wipe is used in a manner similar to the dissolve to suggest a minor change of time or location, but it does so with these liabilities. First, the wipe is a kind of split-screen effect, with two centers of attention, forcing the viewer to move his or her eyes back and forth to keep track of them both for the length of the effect. Second, because the wipe effect is contrived, it tends to draw attention to itself as an effect, distracting the viewer's attention from the content of the film.

*Superimposition* is the simultaneous printing of two or more scenes in the same length of film to connote usually a stream of consciousness. Most often, the effect presents a close-up of a person with the superimposure of another scene revealing what that person is thinking.

## Sound Track

The sound track, consisting of synthesized *voice*, *sound effects*, and *music*, is the fourth major dimension of the role of the film director. The evolution of the sound track has reached new levels of sophistication, however, which far transcend the original uses of sound for realistic effects. More than a hundred sound tracks may be recorded and mixed to fully complement in emotional impact the effects of acting, cinematography, and editing. In this latest wave of cinema, those directors having a background in music—as does Mark Rydell—have an advantage in supervising the final creative phase of filmmaking—sound mixing—than do those directors without such experience.

### Voice

Voice on film takes the two forms of *dialogue* and *narration*, with these differences between them. *Dialogue* is lip-synchronous; the viewer sees the player speak the lines and simultaneously hears the words in the closest approximation to earthly realism in the picture-sound relationship. Dialogue is used in dramatic films because it adds credibility to see the characters speak. Dialogue in drama is not truly realistic, however, but is used functionally to develop character, to offer plot information, or to get a laugh when these things cannot be done visually.

*Narration* refers to the voice of an unseen speaker who comments upon the visual events being shown on the screen. In *The Reivers*, the film begins with the voice-over (V.O.) narration of an older man introducing the film as a story of his own boyhood. V.O. is often used in dramatic films for remembrance.

### Sound Effects

Sound effects are most often used as realistic elements of the sounds we normally associate with whatever is being portrayed on the screen: The image of a police car racing down the street is usually accompanied by the sounds of an automobile motor, a screaming siren, and squealing tires. At a more sophisticated level, sound effects may be used to imply a nonexistent location. A soldier wading through a shallow pond in a city park may be implicitly placed in a tropical jungle by including the sounds of monkeys and exotic birds. The use of effects for realism has given way to the concept of *total sound*, in which all of the elements of sound are synchronized to complement the impact of the visuals.

### Music

Music, on the other hand, is used more for emotional reinforcement than for exposition—an element to be felt rather than heard in dramatic films other than musicals. Music is commonly used at moments of crisis or suspense, as a transitional device when slipping from one scene to another, and as thematic emphasis intended to be identified with a character or location in the mind of the viewer. In *Dr. Zhivago*, whenever Dr. Zhivago thought about Lara, the screen revealed a close-up of him while the sound track carried the music of "Lara's Theme."

A film is more than the sum of its concepts. Cinema is about people and their passions. The language of film is a means to elicit kindred passions and identification in the viewer. The skillful film director makes conscious use of the elements discussed in this chapter to express thoughts and evoke emotions as naturally as the rest of us speak and write our native language.

The master of the cinema would no more mutilate that language by ignorant usage than an educated person would use bad grammar in his or her professional life.

However much the director must be concerned with acting, cinematography, editing, and sound, these are only a means of plumbing the well of emotions. Mark Rydell understands the distinction between means and ends when he says, "An important thing to remember about the film industry is this: the paraphernalia of recording picture and sound—the camera, microphone booms, lights, all the equipment, the trucks, the crane, the dolly—are all what amounts to a highly sophisticated recording device that is there to document and interpret a dramatic event, a moment of behavior created by an actor. Too often, there is excessive attention given to the recording device and not enough to the event. And what is achieved, in that instance, is a very sophisticated recording in image and sound of a mediocre performance. That makes for bad films. Good films require a fine performance by talented actors and actresses whose gifts are nurtured by the director, and then recorded in image and sound. . . . Having said that, however, let me conclude by adding that the director had better know what he [or she] is about when [working] with his images and sounds."

*Paul Newman has received Academy Award nominations for his roles in* The Hustler, Cat on a Hot Tin Roof, Hud, Cool Hand Luke, Absence of Malice, *and* The Verdict, *and has directed such notable films as* Rachel, Rachel *and* The Effects of Gamma Rays on Man-in-the-Moon Marigolds. *He has received Academy Awards for Lifetime Achievement and for Best Actor for his role in* The Color of Money.

# Six

# THE PLAYERS

## *with Paul Newman*

KONSTANTIN STANISLAVSKI, WHOSE BOOK *The Actor Prepares* so influences contemporary acting, submitted a dramatic methodology for performing artists to create their magic. He suggested that the player draw an imaginary circle of concentration around himself or herself and another imaginary circle around the other performer, and then achieve truth in art by playing the scene as genuinely and forthrightly, as convincingly and humanly as possible.

A fine theory, that, and one that undoubtedly works effectively when continuous performances are possible, such as in the theater or on videotape made for television. To be able to draw that mental circle, however, when the scene lasts only seconds, when the other character is not within the other circle but is away playing golf, when the actor is being viewed within inches by a lens, when the actor scarcely dares to move for fear of affecting the composition within the picture frame, or when that circle has scarcely been circumscribed before the director yells "Cut!" Under such conditions, acting for film requires talent, skill in the art and craft of acting, and a general understanding of the concepts and technology of making movies.

For the reader interested in cinema, it is worthwhile to learn something about what goes into that great performance on the screen that so moves an audience to tears and laughter.

## Relationships

Acting evolved from the theater into cinema and along the way changed in its elements and its emphases for the players. Some actors and actresses are effective in one and not the other, a few are competent in both media (Figure 6.1).

### Screen and Stage

"The difference between acting for film and acting for the stage," Paul Newman says, "is primarily a matter of scope. The impulse that is generated for one is the same as the impulse generated for the other. It is a matter of scale. When acting for film, the camera will record the most intimate performance; when acting for the stage, the same performance must be projected to the second balcony. The physical projection of the character is a consequence of where the talent is playing the role. Acting for the theater emphasizes the matter of technique.

"There's a difference, too, in gratification for the performer. In a theater the reward is immediate in terms of feedback from the audience. The actor and the audience are emotionally part of each other, and if the actor performs well, the appreciation is intense and immediate. In acting for the screen, on the other hand, the emotional reward for the performer is much delayed. During principal cinematography, for example, there are only thirty or forty people out there, professionals doing their jobs, people too busy to be an audience for an actor. In critical reviews as well, the success or failure of a stage performance is known immediately, . . . [whereas] the critiques of a film will come often after the film has been edited and released, sometimes a year or longer after the performance. That's a long time to wait for audience feedback."

"The important thing to remember is that the first relationship is between the player and the character, not between the actor and the director. This first relationship is developed in the privacy of wherever the actor or actress studies the script and does research to get inside the character. That homework is done long before the talent has contact with the director, and sometimes even before a director has been picked for the film. . . . If George Roy Hill had directed *The Verdict* instead of Sidney Lumet, my performance would have been pretty much the same. There might have been a whole different texture in the way the film looked; how it was photographed; how it was edited; how the music and effects were used to complement the visuals. But my portrayal of that lawyer would have been the same performance, based upon my own interpretation of that character."
—*Paul Newman*

157

CAT ON A HOT TIN ROOF (U.S.A., 1958) DIRECTED BY RICHARD BROOKS.

FIGURE 6.1 *Paul Newman plays Elizabeth Taylor's romantic opponent in this film; he is a rugged individualist who puzzles, "I had to ask myself—do I want my wife?" Newman's performance as Brick brought him his first nomination for an Academy Award, although the film as a whole did not equal his acting. This adaptation of Tennessee Williams's play deleted the key to understanding the character of Brick, compromised the playwright's language, and tended to transform a drama drawn out of character into a melodrama.*

## Actor and Director

Much has been said about film being a director's medium; Newman's perception of the actor-director relationship provides insight into this topic. "The actor creates the character, not the director. Where a good director is really useful is when the actor is in trouble and cannot see what he or she is doing wrong for the character at that point in the film. And he [or she] can elicit shades of meaning in the performance with the cinematography and editing of that performance clearly in mind.

"A bad director is essentially a traffic cop. Most of them have the sense not to destroy the actor's interpretation and will permit [the actor] to render . . . [the] performance without interference.

"The director is particularly important in defining the performer's relationship to the camera. A good director will tell the actor how he is being framed by the camera and how he is being lighted. . . . [The director] can define and refine the player's limits of movement within the frame. He can say, for example, 'Don't lean back in the chair or you will be out of the frame. Pause at the mark as if you are thinking about something before you move on,' and so forth.

"The differences . . . [among] directors are more important to the texture of the film, as a whole, than to the performances of the actors or actresses. The differences . . . [among] directors lie in creating a milieu, in their visual conceptions, in the way the film is edited—the orchestration of picture and sound. These differences in feeling and detail may vary widely from one director to the next and be crucially important to the success of the film, but will not seriously affect the player's performance. The competent player essentially creates the character independent of the director."

### Method and Technical Acting

Acting for cinema is based upon two classic approaches used by most of the great screen performers according to their talents and training.

*Method acting* is a term used by Lee Strasberg to define a conceptual approach to acting based upon the work of Stanislavski in *The Actor Prepares.* The method involves drawing upon emotional recall in playing a role. For example, most players have never killed anyone, yet in playing a murderer, an actor would have to recreate the state of mind and emotions of someone at the threshold of murder. The player must ask the question, What is it within one human being that evokes the desire to murder another human being? The actor must delve into memory to find those moments of passion or anger or jealousy and recall its essence in order to make the emotion useful when playing a part. Every good performer is a method actor in attempting to find, within memory, emotions he or she has personally felt, but it does not mean that all players use the same method for finding these emotions. The *method* of method acting is whatever the individual performer needs to do to get inside the part emotionally and become

the living character. When Meryl Streep's eyes welled with tears as the lead character in *Sophie's Choice*—remembering her decision of which of her children was to die in the gas chamber—the emotion created by the actress was probably drawn from the well of her own experience under some other circumstance but applied to this role.

Paul Newman distinguishes between technical acting and method acting in practice. "A technical actor is basically cerebral, a method actor is basically visceral. A technical actor thinks through the effect of every move, every gesture, and concerns himself [or herself] with the image he [or she] will project. In dramas that were written with consciousness of acting style—and here we go back to Molière, the dramas of Shakespeare, and other classical plays—one's acting techniques would supercede one's visceral feelings in giving a performance. Acting styles of that period were essentially stylized, even mannered, and the techniques for expressing certain emotions were defined. It was considered less important to 'feel the part' than to project a performance considered good in the style of that period in time, and this was a function of conscious technique.

"In the modern dramas," Newman continues, "such as the plays of Tennessee Williams, Arthur Miller, Eugene O'Neill—the actor is better off if the viscera occupies the better part of his [or her] persona. The performances come not out of style and tchnique, as such, but out of feeling and emotionally becoming the character living the role at that point in the story. Once into the role, the visceral method actor then allows [the mind] to control and give finish to what might otherwise be an uncontrolled performance.

"At a certain point in a performance they can either fuse or cross over, with a cerebral actor allowing his viscera to occupy his persona, with a visceral actor becoming cerebral as he articulates and projects his role. I consider myself a cerebral actor who, by consciously thinking through a role, usually finds my emotions then filling the persona of that role."

## Elements of Acting

Given the intimacy of cinema, with its revelation of the finest shades of meaning in a close-up, the player must lose the identity of self and become another human being on the screen. The potential for portraying another person on the screen lies in the commonality of emotions, instincts, and insights one shares with all human beings, however differently they may have been shaped by the forces of culture. By unlocking within his or her own soul those emotions that are shared with the screen character, the player is able to portray the life of another before the camera. The conceptual elements from which the player draws in creating a role for the screen are essentially these: *awareness, sense memory and emotional recall, motivation, selectivity, change in the character, rhythm,* and *dialogue.*

### Awareness

Awareness is perhaps the most important of traits, next to talent, for the screen performer because intimacy of rendering is one of the salient features of film. The perceptive actor learns to create a convincing role by constantly observing the specific mannerisms of people of every age and walk of life. When waiting for the bus, for example, the player should study others waiting for transportation: How is the fifty-year-old woman behaving as

compared to the eighty-year-old woman? What is the young executive doing as compared to the aging factotum? How do they move in relation to their physical characteristics? Why do they sit in a certain way as an expression of mood? How much support do they need from arms and elbows to push themselves up to a standing position, or do they pop right up to their feet? This kind of study pays off ultimately in the player being able to portray people from many walks of life with a sense of reality.

Newman comments on the validity of constant observation as preparation for a young player. "I gave a great deal of conscious thought, then, to the authenticity of a role. I studied people of every age in bus stops, airports, parties, wherever I happened to be. Now, after twenty years of experience, I give less intellectual thought to structuring the performance and more or less step into the role after once having studied the character in the script."

When asked whether he still studies people in airports, Newman replies, tongue-in-cheek, "That's hard to do when *they* are studying *me.* I no longer have the blessings of anonymity."

### Sense Memory and Emotional Recall

Acting means responding to dramatic circumstances and conflicts in ways appropriate to the character in a given situation. It means responding to imaginary circumstances without emotional handicaps, such as being judgmental about the character or the theme. To achieve this mastery, the screen actor uses (method) exercises in emotional memory, sense memory, concentration, and imagination.

The performer then does not respond parrotlike to cues spoken by other players or mimic mannerisms intended to represent certain emotions, but plays the role from within, using those personal experiences that are emotionally appropriate. A player who performs from within seldom worries about remembering lines because he or she will become the character and speak the lines as they should be spoken under the given dramatic circumstances of the story.

Newman confirms the importance of this aspect of screen characterization. "Sense memory and emotional recall were important in creating believable roles when I was starting out and learning the craft of acting. Then I gave meticulous thought to every aspect of characterization and to the expression of a given emotion. To portray fear, for example, I would pretend that I was unable to breathe, and what would come across on film was a character who was afraid. Similarly, there were other kinds of emotions that I could imagine or draw from experience to give the impression of other kinds of emotions in the characters."

## Motivation

*Motivation* is a vital word in the player's development of a character because it determines every thought, every move, every cinematic interpretation. Motives may take the major forms of love, hatred, vengefulness, fear, or jealousy, or the minor ones of pique, contrition, or one-upmanship, but everything is done for credible reasons given what is probable and necessary in the role.

A screen player must understand what the character's motives are at all times because one cannot really fake a performance in a close-up. The viewer is usually perceptive about the slightest falsity or misinterpretation of emotion in a screen character. If the motives are unclear in the screenplay, then the director should discuss them with the player until the interpretation is clear. It may transpire that the director knows what he or she wants the dramatic focus to be in the edited film, prefers to create that performance through editing, and could not care less whether a player understands why a specific move is made as long as what is done conforms to the director's vision. A player should always, however, have a profound understanding of the role from within the psyche of the character in relation to other characters and in relation to every sequence in the film.

The axiom "Screen actors don't act, they react" illustrates the truism that every facial expression and body movement before the camera must be motivated. The reaction to a crisis must be plausible as a condition of credibility.

The basic motivation of a screen character is usually cast in terms of two questions: What does he or she want? What is he or she afraid of? When asked about the extent to which this axiom affects his motivational techniques in acting, Newman cites his portrayal of the attorney in *The Verdict*. "I thought only in terms of what he wanted, because, in that particular character, fear would have been a passive emotion. I confronted every scene in *The Verdict* in terms of what the character wanted from the situation because the film was an examination of someone who had two basic emotions: He either felt good about himself or bad about himself. He was an unsuccessful lawyer, and, as a human being, had little sense of personal worth. Through the conflicts of the story he rose to feel a sense of his own reserve, a sense of his own resolve and his own resources.

"To play that part," Newman continues, "I had to assume his persona and feel either good about myself or bad about myself, depending upon the given point in the story. I would 'think myself' into feeling good or bad whenever I was ready to go before the camera. This attorney wanted to give meaning to his life by winning this case, and every scene was emotionally directed toward that goal. It is too simplistic to cast each role in terms of either desire or fear because people are not that simple. In some characters the driving impulse may be more than one desire, in another, more than one fear, or some composite of other emotions."

### Selectivity

*Selectivity* means deciding what traits of a given character would reflect the intent of the screenwriter and director. The player, like the writer, would no more attempt to render every detail of a character than a landscape artist would attempt to paint every leaf on every tree in a painting. There must be a selection of only those character traits that relate to the story and the theme, with a pruning of everything irrelevant. An interesting screen role is created a brick at a time through a collation of selected, revealing actions.

The sense memory of an emotion may be used by an actor to generate a similar emotion in reaction to a crisis in the story called for by the role. But the expression of that emotion must be selected in the form of the *character's reaction*, not the player's own personal response to the given situation. The emotion generated from within by the player will be his or her own, but the forms of performance giving expression to that emotion should be as written in the role.

### Change in the Character

Change is at least as certain in life as death and taxes. People change as a consequence of what happens to them in their struggles through life, and a believable protagonist must similarly have some potential for change as a consequence of what occurs in the drama. Changes of some kind must occur to the protagonist within each sequence and over the length of the story.

Although it is conflict that creates drama, it is change that implements the conflict and makes it believable. And the inner transformations should be apparent in the player's outer physical actions, in the player's changes of makeup, and in the way the player thinks while playing the role. The player must evolve with the character through the story. Each crisis should end with the protagonist slightly changed by some reversal, and the climax should find the person profoundly changed (in typical American cinema). The matter of progressive change, and the degrees of change, derive from the script.

### Rhythm

The rhythm of behavior varies with every individual. Some are quick in mind and body; some are quick in mind, slow in body; others are every permutation of extremes and in-betweens. Rhythm affects pacing, and both are important to character development. Players should take their time about responding to cues. A player should respond to another's lines in a film as a person in real life would respond to a similar remark: hearing the words and how they are said, absorbing the meaning, reacting emotionally to the meaning, and then responding naturally—with or without words.

*Dialogue*

Dialogue is an important tool in cinema; players must be acutely aware that words are not always meanings in cinema, and may, indeed, mean the opposite of what is intended. Great dialogue is crucial for the theater, where exposition and characterization are often embedded in words, but in film it is the image that gives words much of their true meaning. To the film player it is the emotion behind the dialogue that is the primary concern.

Consider how inflections may change the meaning of the ubiquitous statement, "I love you."

*I* love you (even if nobody else does).

I *love* you (honest I do).

I love *you* (not somebody else).

I love you? (that's news to me).

I *love* you? (I *like* you, but *love*—come on).

I love *you*? (anybody but you).

The same three-word statement has ranged the gamut of meanings from tenderness to insult solely through emphasis and inflection. Each of these variations would in turn be changed or modified according to the object of love: a spouse, a lover, a parent, a child, a dog. With each change of object there are changes of meanings and nuances almost without end. Moreover, a gesture of the head, the hand, the body will in turn add or subtract dimensions of meaning. The dictum that great dialogue makes great actors is less true in cinema, where a player may say very little, yet say everything.

Related to variations of interpretation of dialogue is the concept of acting *against* the spoken words. If the lines are strong and meanings clear, the player may decide to introduce other elements to give the role deeper dimensions. Again with the ever-popular phrase "I love you," the line may be said through a yawn, while crunching on granola, above the roar of a washing machine, while squeezing someone in an interesting place, as well as over candlelight and dinner, giving it shades of meaning not inherent in the words.

## Getting into a Part

Donning the persona of another person in a film means ascertaining the intent of the screenwriter. Paul Newman's approach is to first peruse the script carefully to acquire a sense of the character and the story. Then, he submits, the actor must figure out which precedes what in emphasis. The player makes an intellectual judgment about what the intent of each scene is, absorbs that, and then finds some way to give physical form to that emotion. With his approach, the technical-intellectual aspects precede the emotional-visceral response to the situation. He describes to himself, in actor's terms, what the character's emotions are, and then knows precisely how to give it expression.

"The amount of work required to develop a character," says Newman, "depends upon how close the role is to the player's own personality, character, and experience. This is what determines how much work must be done because he has to climb out of his own skin and into that of another human being. This is the phase in which the performer draws on emotional recall, sense memory, and other actor's methods. If the character is very different from the player, to the point where they have little in common, the actor or actress will need to resort to other

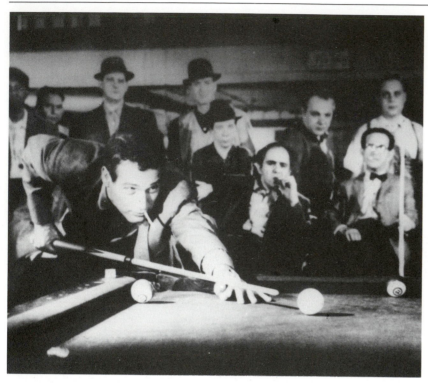

FIGURE 6.2 *"For the lead role in* The Hustler, *I lived in pool halls for about two weeks. I am not sure that I learned a lot about the character, but I learned a lot about hustling and how the pool sharks do it. The feel of the environment soaked into me and maybe I absorbed some of the mannerisms of the pool hall crowd. . . . I wish I could do that part over again in the light of twenty years' experience in acting."*

The role of Fast Eddie Felson gave Newman a part requiring depth, subtlety, and intelligent shades of mood and emphasis. Although he grumbles about being able to do better now after years of acting experience, his performance transcended his charm in this near-great film about an artist with a pool cue obsessed with being best, and beating the best: Minnesota Fats (played by Jackie Gleason). The Hustler *is an allegory of what it means to be an artist: purity and integrity of purpose, the meaning of success and failure, and the vulnerability of those with great talents.*

**THE HUSTLER** (U.S.A., 1961) DIRECTED BY ROBERT ROSSEN.

devices. This could mean research, this could mean travel to the milieu in which the drama occurs. The player must do whatever is necessary to feel and live the role" (Figures 6.2 and 6.3).

When studying a script and creating a role, Newman scribbles small notes to himself in the margin as interpretive thoughts occur. He calls them "notes of intent" and uses them to indicate shades of feeling and meaning in the character's performance. Some, he says, "are physicalization notes," indicating to himself possibilities for giving form to the performance. These reminders, written in the serenity of his study, are useful aids when playing the scenes out of context, out on

location, during the frenetic weeks of principal cinematography.

When asked whether he thought through the role in the script stage to the extent of planning such details as the gesture of a hand, the cadence of a walk, the inflection of a voice, Newman answers, "I have seldom played a character in which I thought through carefully how he walked, how he moved, as an expression of what he felt. If I have assumed the persona of that character with a clear understanding of the writer's intent, the details of those moves will come spontaneously as an expression of his emotion.

"The only exception to that generalization occurred when I went to a reservation

FIGURE 6.3 *"To do research on milieu and mannerisms in Cool Hand Luke,"* Newman says, *"I went down and lived with a tomato farmer in Appalachia for a couple of weeks to get a feel of the atmosphere and the people. I looked around and searched for ways, within myself, to relate to those people."*

In Cool Hand Luke Newman (center), with Morgan Woodward (left) and Arthur Kennedy, plays the title role of a felon who lives and dies without a friend, an absolute loner whose cool defiance creates his name. Luke's repeated attempts to escape, stoicism under beatings—and superhuman achievement in eating fifty hard-boiled eggs at one sitting—make him a legendary figure with the other inmates. And yet Newman's portrayal was never lugubrious, but always infused with self-mockery and amused courage. This was a story of how mythical figures are created.

**165**

GETTING INTO A PART

**COOL HAND LUKE** (U.S.A., 1967) DIRECTED BY STUART ROSENBERG.

in preparation for the lead role in *Hombre*, in which I was to portray an Indian (Figure 6.4). I discovered that the reservation people moved with a marvelous economy of motion, seldom making a nonfunctional move. This trait imparted dignity and a deep sense of reserve to their presence. That economy of movement was at the core of the role I played in *Hombre*."

## Casting a Role

The first meeting between the director and those auditioning for lead parts may contain discussions about the story, the characters, and the relationships between them. The director usually explains how he or she sees those relationships and how he or she intends to interpret them. This is the time—before production is under way—to iron out conceptual differences.

The relationship among actors and directors is complex, with factors of personality, skill, character, and stature entering the working dynamic. Theoretically, the director has the authority and the vision to cast a part and to determine how a character is to be portrayed in order to realize the entire film as a work of art or entertainment. In reality, a distinguished actor is usually given considerable latitude to interpret the role. A director of sensitivity may spend days with the lead actor discussing the character and ideas of the film and welcoming creative interaction with talented performers.

In the case of a well-known star with specific performance characteristics, whose stardom is the result of an acting style, the player will probably interpret every role in that proven style. The star may resist attempts by the director to encourage adaptation to the peculiarities of a role. Indeed, the star may have been picked for the part because of a dramaturgical style. If the film was financed on the condition that a bankable name be cast in the role, the director may be forced to limit his or her directorial talents primarily to cinematic interpretation.

Casting players for their roles brings other considerations into play besides talent. The physical characteristics of the actor must obviously be compatible with the role and the timbre of the voice appropriate to the character. More latitude is usually given in the selection of lead players because these roles will be developed dramatically in terms of personality, character, environmental background, and so forth. In the casting of supporting characters, however, the less central the character, the more he or she is likely to be stereotyped.

Playing a part in which a character is intended to age greatly during the story, or a role in which the player differs by decades from the age of the character, requires talent and skill. A gifted actor, such as Orson Welles in *Citizen Kane* or Cicely Tyson in *The Autobiography of Miss Jane Pittman*, can portray the decline of vitality and elan that comes with the passing years and be wholly credible, but that requires a truly accomplished artist.

An impromptu reading of a script is often required of a performer when he or she is being considered for a part in a forthcoming film. If the actor is well known to the director, the cold reading is often to refresh the latter's memory about the talent's acting style and to see how the person being considered has survived the attrition of time. Such a performer is seldom judged for competence but reads to reassure the director that his or her preference is still vital.

An unknown actor or actress, however, will need to deliver a reasonably convincing performance after a brief perusal of

**HOMBRE** (U.S.A., 1967) DIRECTED BY MARTIN RITT.

the script. In that time the player must comprehend what the scene and the characters are all about and give a portrayal that reveals the essence of the role. A competent performer can create a generalized character that may not be quite the same interpretation as he or she would give after a full grasp of the screenplay, but will still give an indication of the performer's potential after thought and preparation. An experienced performer makes a point of reading the script quite slowly in order to give himself or herself time to think about interpretation of the dialogue.

### Screen Test

A screen test is a three- to ten-minute filmed sequence in which actors being considered for parts are tested for their potential ability to perform the roles and to see how they look on the screen. The set for the test is often improvised, just an approximation of what it will ultimately become, but those players being considered for the roles usually do everything possible to look their parts.

The performer should approach the screen test with a complete understanding of the character in all ramifications in every sequence that will precede and follow the scenes for which the player is being photographed. The player must perform as if already cast in the role and as if this were a sequence like any other to be performed, no matter how much pressure there is to make this appearance something special. If the player's interpretation conforms to the director's vision and that person looks right on the screen, the role may be won.

Why not perform on a stage before the dirctor instead of having it photographed and projected? The answer is in part technical: Film does not always perceive as the human eye sees, and it is the interpretation of camera, lens, and emulsion that counts. A screen test also allows the director to see how an actor appears with makeup, in costume, and under a variety of lighting conditions and filters.

### Typecasting

Typecasting simplifies interpretation for the actor as well as for the viewer. If the screenwriter develops a character to achieve certain effects, such as a tycoon who is arrogant and bullying, and the writer stipulates that the character be 6 feet 3 inches tall and weigh 230 pounds, it is preferable that the character be cast by those physical terms because the effects intended by the screenwriter are easier to achieve by the typecast actor. An actor who is 5 feet 8 inches and weighs 145 pounds would have to be a different kind of bully from that intended by the writer. A large man imposes his presence in different ways from a smaller man and would be a hulking bully instead of a bantam rooster bully. A player who looks the part described by the screenwriter will tend to play the role as written more comfortably and easily because he *is* the same physical type.

Typecasting, however, relieves certain personality actors of having to observe how other physical types behave because they never portray any persona but themselves. John Wayne was always John Wayne, Clark Gable was always Clark Gable, Gary Cooper was always Gary Cooper—in virtually every film they ever played. If John Wayne had been thrown a script in which he was to play a coward during the Civil War who fled when the first shot was fired, he would have tossed it back and said, in effect, "That's not my image, and you will have to change the script or I won't play the part. My public would not accept my image on those

FIGURE 6.5 *"I seem to like to glamorize the wrong kind of people,"* Newman says, speaking of his roles in Hud, Cool Hand Luke, *and* Sometimes a Great Notion. *The cumulative effect of these and other roles has been to give him a unique persona, however, conveying attractive emotional qualities to the public. The composite aura of Paul Newman is that of the Great Individualist. Be the role that of outcast, iconoclast, martyr, or alienated modern hero, the nature of his stardom is that of a personable but strong man going his own way and doing his own thing regardless of the price of loneliness.*

terms." This is one of the major differences between the personality star and the star actor who can play a broad spectrum of roles based upon talent and observations of human behavior.

This is not to belittle the personality actor. One is born with an innate potential of talent and there should be no denigration ascribed to limitations unless they are transcended by pretensions. Indeed, it is a mark of astuteness when a player perceives where strengths and weaknesses lie and the player builds up strengths, however circumscribed.

### Star and Superstar

The terms *star* and *superstar* have one central connotation: a person liked so much for his or her known qualities that the audience will be cheering for any character portrayed by that person (Figure 6.5). Paul Newman is that kind of actor: Any role he plays, any film he appears in, has a head start toward success by virtue of his appearance in that film. Part of his success is due to talent, part is due to his singular good looks, part is due to his meticulous care in creating a role, and part is due to

HUD (U.S.A., 1963) DIRECTED BY MARTIN RITT.

FIGURE 6.6 *Newman playing Hud snarls, "I always say the law was meant to be interpreted in a lenient manner, and that's what I try to do. Sometimes I lean to one side of it, sometimes I lean to the other. . . . This is our land and I don't want any government man on it anytime, anyplace, anywhere."*

*Hud is a film rich in thematic values with Paul Newman in the title role uttering the philosophy of the unvarnished cynic: "This world's so full of crap that a man's going to get into it sooner or later whether he's careful or not." Set against him is his father, the role of Homer played by Melvyn Douglas, who retorts, "You don't care about people, Hud. . . . You just live for yourself and that makes you not fit to live with." Hud's crude selfishness costs him love and friendship, and the last view we have of him is a man swilling liquor behind a screen door— shut in by willfulness and shut out of life— through a fade-out into loneliness.*

the wise selection of scripts suited to his gifts and image.

Paul Newman has acquitted himself well in a wide spectrum of roles. In *Hud*, he played the part of a rat on the cattle range (Figure 6.6); in *Hombre*, an individual of incorruptible integrity; in *Harper*, a detective with a sharp comedic instinct; in *The Hustler*, an arrogant punk with the pool-table perceptions of an artist; in *Sometimes a Great Notion* (which he also directed), a rugged individualist (Figure 6.7); in *Cat on a Hot Tin Roof*, a brooding neurotic with baffling indifference to the charms of Elizabeth Taylor; in *Butch Cassidy and the Sundance Kid*, the most likable outlaw ever to rob a train and kick an adversary in the groin (Figure 6.8); in *The Verdict*, a failure struggling to redeem the value of his life. As protean and demand-ing as these roles have been, none involved playing a person of unmitigated evil— such as a child molester, a Cuban drug smuggler who butchers people with a chain saw, or someone of similar ilk. This does not detract one whit from the skillful preparatory work of an actor who spares no pains to fully realize his roles. Those roles, however, are not antithetical to the image of a man of charm, vulnerability, and deep human decency, which is the reality of Paul Newman (Figure 6.9).

*Acting Styles*

Ideally, style in acting is the player's realization of the writer's themes, characters, and stories. One need only to view films made a few decades ago—movies that were then enormously popular or critically

FIGURE 6.7  *Paul Newman says of the hero of this film, "Hank Stamper is a dinosaur. He should be extinct, but he refuses to lie down and die. Hank is a victim of circumstances and shows worthy independence, but he's unwilling to make any sacrifice for his community — he thinks he's still living in the nineteenth century."*

*Sometimes an actor becomes a director when a film is foundering, as Paul Newman did during principal photography of* Sometimes a Great Notion. *This is an unusual story about a family of lumberjacks, people of unyielding pride whose personal morality sets them at odds with the rest of the foresting community. The film's thematic statement — sometimes criticized for its political content as being anti-union — was actually pro-integrity in its essential message. The film was directed by Newman with fine visual flair.*

**SOMETIMES A GREAT NOTION** (U.S.A., 1971) DIRECTED BY PAUL NEWMAN.

**BUTCH CASSIDY AND THE SUNDANCE KID** (U.S.A., 1969) DIRECTED BY GEORGE ROY HILL.

FIGURE 6.8    *The public and some critics differed over the artistic merits of this enormously popular film about two middle-aged robbers who have outlived their time with the passing of the Old West. The reality that they no longer have the right to exist does not make them less lovable as the graying galoots they are. An important part of their characterization lies in their immaturity, shown in childish horseplay, as in this scene in which Newman, as Butch, is pursued by a bull as he tries to ride a bicycle. Those critics who can surmount their prejudice against westerns might have to admit that this film is a classic.*

*Richard Schickel wrote about ". . . lively performances in the title roles by Paul Newman and Robert Redford. The former imparts to Butch the easy good-nature of the most popular guy in the fraternity house; the latter gives Sundance the cool competence, the canny reserve of a star athlete. Both are more interesting than your standard good-bad guys and there is between them something quite rare in our films, a real masculine relationship, the depth of which is greater than they know." "Movie Review," Life, October 24, 1969*

FIGURE 6.9 *Paul Newman read the script for* The Sting *and told George Roy Hill, "Maybe I'm not old enough and I don't want to ruin your movie, but I'd play the part in a minute." Like every memorable character in Newman's gallery of screen portraits, Henry Gondorff the con artist is unique to his period, to his peers, and to himself. Newman considers Gondorff a complete original.*

*Casting against the type has its limitations. There is no way this actor could be cast as the wielder of chain saws in* Scarface *or* The Texas Chainsaw Massacre. *This ingratiating con man might fleece another crook of a significant bundle of cash, but he is thereby serving a humanitarian function in keeping with his real-life character.*

**THE STING** (U.S.A., 1970) DIRECTED BY GEORGE ROY HILL.

acclaimed—to realize that time does not always deal kindly with mannerisms in performance. What may be seen in its own time, values, and culture as real, may be regarded later as unique to the perceptions of a moribund era, hopelessly mannered if not actually laughable. Acting in America has, over the years, gravitated away from stylized performance and toward the closest approximation of realism except for those films having distinctive genre characteristics.

Acting styles develop for specific reasons. The art of silent film acting evolved its style to compensate for the absence of sound, as in D. W. Griffith's *Intolerance*. Foreign films, such as Japanese or Italian movies, have characteristics born of their traditional theaters or national temperament, as in Akira Kurosawa's *The Seven Samurai* or Lina Wertmuller's *Swept Away*. Political or cultural reasons may be behind stylized acting, such as the tendency for the Russians and Chinese to use characters to represent political or social ideas, as in the protagonist of *Slave to General* from the People's Republic of China. Performing style may be imposed by the traditional forms of a genre, such as a musical, a western, or a gangster film, which tend to require that the players execute the roles in stylized ways. Or, acting may take expressionistic forms under the demands of a director who has something to say that requires a stylized form of acting, such as Ingmar Bergman's *Fanny and Alexander* or Werner Herzog's *Aguirre: The Wrath of God*.

Improvised acting before the camera enjoyed a worldwide flash of popularity during the 1960s under the influence of the New Wave filmmakers of France because it supposedly enhanced the sense of realism. This approach fell into disuse because it proved difficult to relate the performance of a given scene to the vision of the film as a whole; moreover, to edit the film footage of such a performance into an exciting tempo was troublesome because of the frequent lack of matching action.

The style of acting that dominates in American dramatic films is essentially that of method acting, conceived by Stanislavski, promulgated by Strasberg, and discussed earlier in this chapter by Newman.

## Planning for Cinematography

Once the parts in the film have been cast, a shooting script goes through a breakdown procedure, with each scene and sequence listed on a production board according to the location at which it will be photographed. This source cites a day or night location, the cast needed for those scenes, a description of the dramatic action, a listing of equipment and livestock needed, and the number of script pages comprising the scene to be photographed.

The determination of whether to photograph interior or exterior scenes in a given film may depend upon weather. Standard practice is to photograph exteriors first if the weather is right with the rationalization that interior scenes may be done whenever the weather is inclement.

Scripts are marked "interior" or "exterior" to indicate whether they will be played on a sound stage or on location. Interiors offer the most controlled environments for creating pictures and sounds.

Scenes for the majority of films made today are played out and photographed on interior stages. These sets may include complete apartments, hotel foyers and restaurants, offices, factories, subways, airplanes, and life rafts floating on a tank of stormy water. The actor may need to eat, fight, make love, tumble down a flight of stairs, chase a dog, or make a desperate climb up an icy cliff in an interior sound stage. An "exterior-interior" may be the back lots where vintage towns and cities have been built, the facades of which have provided the settings for countless adventures from the shoot-out at sundown of a western to swordplay in the glory that was Rome.

Acting for exterior locations requires excellent physical condition and coordination. The performer may be asked to ride horses, run over rock-strewn meadows, leap streams, fight adversaries in the mountains, forest, or desert. Or the exterior location may be a real street in New York City, blocked off by the police for a motion picture production through a permit arrangement. Here, the performer may be required to race through a crowd, scramble up a staircase, leap from rooftop to rooftop, or drive a car wildly through city traffic in a chase sequence. And all of these actions must be carried out while giving the performance of a credible character, with the finesse to permit quality images and sounds to be recorded by camera and microphone.

Paul Newman indicates that he does not modify his performance according to whether a sequence is being photographed in an exterior or an interior setting. He affirms that he gives essentially the same performance in both contexts and lets the cinematographer and sound recordist worry about capturing picture and sound. Newman feels strongly that the actor should be concerned solely with giving a convincing performance on the player's own terms and should let the technicians do their jobs of recording the performance.

### Rehearsal

Newman says firmly, "I will not be caught off-balance in developing an interpretation of the character for the screen. There must be time for me to study the script and get into the part prior to working with the director. Only when I am thoroughly into the character will I work with the director, and then I have always demanded two weeks of rehearsal prior to principal cinematography."

Rehearsing for film is a different art from that of theater rehearsal because the goal is not a perfect rehearsal but a perfect take. At this point, command of dialogue, understanding of the character, and knowledge of the actions are assumed. The actor should not overrehearse because it may stale the freshness and spontaneity of the performance on film. Some actors may, in fact, give their best play the first time through and from then on decline in sparkle. Others, disciplined in their craft, improve the interpretation of the character and add nuances after each consultation with the director. A general rule is to have two full rehearsals before a take.

The director will, of course, check out the player's performance through the camera viewfinder to ascertain whether the rendition is what is desired.

The actor-director relationship becomes critical during rehearsals and cinematography because, like the take, performances are done out of continuity and without the feedback of any audience but the production crew. Some players tend to overproject, to perform at a higher emotional level than is required, and the performer should be responsive to the will of the director in order to have a scene that works in the edited version of the film.

A tactful director who is not getting what he or she had in mind and wishes to avoid embarrassment to the actor will resort to harmless subterfuges such as reminding the performer of something said or done correctly during earlier rehearsals. This is a game that both understand and play to permit honorable changes and save

face. Criticism is best made when there is also something good to say. Negative comments ought to be made as privately as possible.

A performer who is going through rehearsals and cinematography has reason to expect this information from the director:

> *Framing*: the scene size and camera angle that is being photographed, and why.
>
> *Lighting*: how the lighting will interpret the face.
>
> *Action*: what moves are to be made within the image area and what are the outer parameters of the action.
>
> *Interpretation*: the emotional shading and pacing of the acting performance at each point in the story.

### Blocking Action

Blocking action—as described in Chapter 5—means planning the moves of the players before the camera. In a feature film two groups of performers called the *first team* and the *second team* plan out the moves. The first team comprises the principal and support players who will appear on film. The second team is those people who are engaged to stand-in for each member of the first team while the details of lighting and camera action are being worked out by the director of photography and the gaffers.

Paul Newman indicates that the input of the player into such matters as blocking action for master scene technique varies tremendously with the nature of the show and with the director. In his experience, the actor is allowed first to play the role as he or she feels it, giving spontaneous form to the moves and gestures appropriate to the character at that point in the story. If the director accepts the player's interpretation and the player's moves, the director will then work with the performer and cinematographer to refine the relationship for the camera. In the interest of good framing, the player may be asked to modify some of his or her movements. But the moves usually take the forms preferred by the actor unless, for some reason, the performance lacks something desired by the director.

Matching the action for differing scene sizes of the same dramatic action is important for the editing of the film. Newman comments, "For the director to have the freedom to edit the film in the best way, the actor or actress must give perfect matching action in tighter shots. An actor can actually manipulate how a sequence is edited by not giving matching action on scenes he [or she] does not agree with. But that's dumb! The director may wish, in editing, to come in on a close-up of the actor or actress, and cannot do so unless the talent has provided the director with matching film footage. If the close-up will not work because the move is wrong, the director and the editor may need to settle for a long shot in editing when the intimacy of a close-up is needed, to the detriment of that actor's performance. The director may need to get the camera off the player at a certain point in the story—perhaps a cut to a reaction shot—and cannot do it because of a lack of matching action, and the dramatic sense of the scene will be damaged.

"It is the responsibility of the actor or actress," Newman continues, "to find some nonrestrictive way to express the meaning of the scene so it can be properly edited. If the master scene is very long, with many gestures, pauses, and turns, the actor should work with the director in simplifying them so they can be matched in tighter shots. It is to the player's own best interest to give the director the best possible matching action so that the director can edit the best possible interpretation of the actor's performance."

The more complex the dramatic action, the more carefully the performer's movements must be blocked in relation to the camera and locked into memory. If the actor becomes so emotionally involved with playing his or her role in the master scene that he or she cannot remember how to duplicate actions in the tighter shots, the sequence is in trouble. Having a videocamera record the action helps, but principal cinematography should not have to stop for repeated playbacks. Script supervisors are also present to keep notes on what happens, and that too helps. If movements are simplified and rehearsed until set in the memories of performer and director, recorded by the videocamera, and noted by the script supervisor, the blocked action should result in film footage with good coverage for the film editor: establishing shot, full shots, medium shots, close-ups. Only when the director decides that a given master scene is not to be used is the player free to change his or her movements and ignore the requirements of matching action.

When more than one person may play the same role in the same dramatic scene, such as a character and a stunt double, both must memorize the actions blocked for master scene cinematography. Some stunts required for a sequence are too dangerous to risk the performer, or require specialized skills, or indeed are so mundane as to be a waste of expensive talent's time. For these assignments, there is usually an extra who functions as a physical or lookalike double. A stunt double is used in such dangerous actions as hand-to-hand fighting, falling off a horse, leaping from rooftop to rooftop, and so forth. Interaction between player and double is important. The player studies the double's action in the stunt and the double watches the mannerisms of the actor, so that each can emulate the other sufficiently in movements to pass for the same person when

FIGURE 6.10 *The charm of Robert Redford (right) and Paul Newman were joined again in the comedy-spoof* The Sting, *a cinematic piece of cake they did as much for fun as for money. As Johnny Hooker, Redford becomes a protégé to Henry Gondorff and makes his graduate step to the big con. Playing the "steerer" to Gondorff's "inside man," Hooker learns that landing a mark involves a highly complicated interplay of personalities. All concerned, including director George Roy Hill, were surprised by the magnitude of the box office earnings generated by this filmic lark.*

**THE STING** DIRECTED BY GEORGE ROY HILL.

the stunt footage is edited into the master scene footage.

Sometimes the director may be dissatisfied with how the actor is moving in relation to the camera. The player may then be asked to take the camera position in order to better understand the dramatic action from the lens's point of view. This may mean looking through the viewfinder, standing in the director's place, or simply standing next to the camera. On occasion the director will demonstrate what he or she wants by actually going through the moves as the player watches from the camera position.

When actions have been blocked in, the key positions for standing or moving are marked on the location or the set floor of the cinematography area. Outdoors, the mark may be an anonymous rock or twig that indicates the key spots for the actors to relate to the camera yet blends into the background. Or the reference point may be a fencepost, automobile, or house corner that the player can use without an obvious glance. Indoors, the sound stage may be marked with tape, chalk, or props such as furniture to position the actors. The player cannot, however, glance down at a mark or look at a prop in order to find the correct position. A professional actor

develops a sense of peripheral vision and instinct that enable him or her to find the correct position without any outward manifestation of searching for it (Figure 6.10).

### Terminology on the Set

Certain aspects of acting for film can be described by the terms used on the set during the shooting of a scene.

The terms *upstage* and *downstage* have

roughly the same definition as when applied to the theater. *Downstage* means nearer to the camera; *upstage* means farther from the camera. If an actor is directed to move upstage, she will move toward the rear of the set; if directed downstage, she will move closer into the foreground.

A *clean entrance* is a player's movement in which there is no evidence of his presence before his appearance in the scene. A clean entrance means no sound, no shadows, no hint of existence before entering the frame to be seen.

Making a *clean move* means completing action without dialogue. Because it is often too difficult to speak lucid dialogue while engaging in movements or exertions of any kind, it is standard practice to speak dialogue before, between, or after dramatic actions. When a comment was made to Newman that he seemed to speak his dialogue before or after moves, Newman exclaimed, "God—I hope you're wrong!"

*Clean speech* refers to understandable delivery of dialogue. In most American films the directors do not want one performer's lines to overlap the delivery of another's because it limits what can be done with the sound track in editing. If the director wants overlapped dialogue, he or she can do so during the sound mix where pitch and placement may be controlled for dramatic effect.

*Close-ups* offer the player the greatest opportunity for a fine cinematic performance. A basic principle all players should insist upon—and professional directors and camerapeople will know—is that the camera should photograph them in close-up at their own eye level unless there are narrative reasons for looking up or down, such as peering up at an airplane or down from horseback at someone on foot. A close-up in which the eye-line is up or down will seem patently false when inter-

cut with another scene in which the object of the player's gaze is at eye level.

*Loosen the frame* means that the director believes the players are framed too tightly for the desired visual interpretation—there is too much emotional tension. This request asks that they move in depth away from the camera, which in effect provides more space around the subject and thereby lowers the emotional temperature of the shot.

Conversely, the director may say *tighten the frame*, which means moving closer to the lens and thereby filling in the frame and dramatically heightening the tensions. In a progressive dramatic action in which two players move upstage to downstage—without a cut—the two quarreling characters will move closer and closer to the lens; the emotional and visual temperature of the scene rises with their anger as they move from a long shot into a tight two-shot. In both loosening and tightening the frame, the depth of the movement is affected by the focal length of the lens.

Paul Newman indicates that he does not vary his dramatic performances to suit the characteristics of the lens focused on him, in part because there would be perceptible differences in movement when the shots are edited into scenes. This harkens back to matching action for editing. He emphasizes that the intimacy of the lens requires intimacy of performance, and it is the job of the cinematographer to capture the essence of the player's subtlest performance; the actor has no responsibility to project a performance to the camera beyond being cooperative in the matter of compositional framing.

Newman gives one exception to this rule. "If I am on a mountain five miles away and am being photographed with 50-mm lens, I might wave my arm to let the . . . [cinematographer] know where I am."

*Blending in* is a term of movement in which a second performer is required to move with a first performer and keep herself or himself within view of the camera but subordinate to the lead. This may require fancy footwork and skillful performance to make the scene play naturally.

*Drifting* refers to an unobtrusive move by a player from one part of a scene to another, into or out of a set, without drawing attention from the viewer. A performer may be asked to drift to another position in order to be removed from the camera's field of view, to be subordinated as another actor becomes the center of attention, or simply to be repositioned for a later reaction shot.

*Beat* refers to reaction time. In comedies such as *Some Like It Hot*, a player may take a long pause in response to something that has happened in order to give time for a funny line to sink in. Or, a beat may be taken in a serious film to give the viewer time to grasp a new dramatic focus.

*Business* is a term to describe performance activities that supplement the main drama, such as lighting a cigarette, pouring a drink, glancing slyly to one side for a beat. The business of using hands and eyes may provide richness to a performance: A long poignant pause before giving a response or the visual drama of a thoughtful glance down at the hands can enrich a scene.

Moves about the set are another dimension of business: The camera follows with a loose full shot, next a two-shot, then moving in concert with the dolly, settling into an over-the-shoulder shot, next twirling to provide a reverse angle. This choreography of movement for the camera lens allows the performer to give his or her role a cinematic dimension not possible by acting alone. Ideally, the viewer is never aware of the movements of either camera or player.

## Acting for the Camera

When the time comes for an actor to be in a scene, the professional will approach the mark already settling into the emotion required for the role in that scene. Seldom does an experienced performer march up with an off-stage attitude to plunk down cold where the scene is to begin. Instead, the player mentally and physically eases into the character as he or she approaches the proper place before the camera.

Every actor is aware of the angle from which he or she is being photographed. Many stars are quick to protest when being photographed from a bad angle for their features or one that does not show them at their best. The director determines the camera angle, but this has not prevented clever performers from playing to the camera during moves and falling into positions photographically favorable to themselves.

The actor should place himself or herself unobtrusively but clearly in the scene, unobscured by props or foreground actors, yet fully integrated with the overall group as seen through the viewfinder. Some directors use the technique of placing the main character in a crowd and letting the actor draw attention through distinctive gestures. The player may, at the will of the director, perform to make himself or herself prominent. Otherwise, it is important that the actor confine all gestures to ensure that he or she in no way distracts from the emotional orchestration of the scene but is purely supportive at the level indicated by the director.

Controlling the directional look of the actor in relation to the camera is an important consideration because, after the scenes are photographed out of context, the visual relationships in the edited film have to make sense. On occasion a player will be directed to confront the camera as if it were another person speaking in subjective viewpoint. The director may ask him or her to look at *camera left* or *camera right*. This refers to the cinematographer's left and right, as the cameraperson views the player and the scene through the camera viewfinder.

A moving actor must often relate to a moving camera during the course of filming a scene. The actions of the two should be carefully coordinated so that the subject will remain in focus as both subject and camera move from position to position for cinematography. The camera—mounted on a crane or a dolly—would move toward or away from the subject, or parallel to the subject on tracks, always at the exact pace of the performer. The player has the professional responsibility of pacing movements to conform to the limited mobility of the camera, and the cinematographer has the responsibility of making it appear that the camera is in fact leading the actor.

## The Take

The important moment for the film player arrives when a scene has been rehearsed to everyone's satisfaction and the relationship to the camera is clearly understood. The first assistant director momentarily takes command on the set calling out "Quiet on the set!" and asking for the sound stage to be put *on the bell*.

The sound recordist presses a button to emit one long ring both inside and outside the sound stage to signal that a take is about to begin. The ring of the bell also activates blinking red lights over exterior entrances—which continue to flash warnings to forestall interruptions—until the scene is concluded by the sound recordist with two long rings of the bell.

After the call for quiet, the first assistant director calls out "Roll 'em!" The

sound recordist electrically starts both camera and sound recording units; when both are running synchronously at sound speed, which is 90 feet per minute, the sound recordist calls out "Speed!"

A slate board is then held up before the lens—citing the film title, scene number, take number, and the names of the director and cinematographer—to be photographed by the camera. A wooden clap hinged on top of the slate is banged down to provide an audiovisual synchronous mark to be used later by the film editor. Picture and sound are also electronically tail-synchronized at the end of the shot.

While the crew and their units are gearing up, the performer will be emotionally entering the persona of the character so as to be mentally and physically prepared to act for film when the director calls "Action!"

"Cut!" is the command given by a director to conclude a scene, an order that ends the player's performance and results in the shutoff of cameras and recording systems. To cut a scene is not the option of the actor. Even if the scene is going badly and the performer really is clinging to a cliff by the fingernails, the actor must hang in there until saved by the director's cry of "Cut!"

Another dimension of this command is "cut and hold," which does not conclude the scene but requires that players stop and remain fixed in their positions. This order is most frequently given to permit the director to check the scene through the viewfinder, make some minor changes in action, and continue the take from that point without having to rephotograph the scene.

If the scene does not work to the director's satisfaction, the player may be asked to "take it from the top," a request to perform the scene from the start through to a given point. If the scene is successful except for one small line or gesture, the performer may be directed to perform only

FIGURE 6.11 *The Color of Money dominated the fall theater schedules in 1986 with Paul Newman's second stellar performance as Fast Eddie Felson and fine acting by Tom Cruise and Mary Elizabeth Mastrantonio.*

*The story is not, however, about money. "The Color of Money is about what makes you happy," says Newman. "Felson has been compromising all his life and has become the very* thing *he hated. In the final analysis, compromise is what he liberates himself from." In the last line of dialogue in the film, Felson racks up the balls and says, "I'm back." He has remade himself into the top professional he had been as a youth. This sequel to the memorable film in 1961,* The Hustler, *is one of the few to surpass the original in every respect.*

**181**

THE RUSHES

the erroneous part in a pickup shot.

Sometimes—through nervousness, inadequacy of preparation or rehearsal, inability to empathize with the role, or lack of talent—the player gives a performance unsatisfactory to the director. When the director says, "Get inside the part," he or she is evoking Stanislavski in asking the player to become the role the player is portraying: Absorb that person's traits, realize the persona, adopt the motivations and forms of expression from the inside out as the character being portrayed. Innumerable slang terms are used to urge better performances: *color it more*, *juice it up*, *give me 20 percent more*, and so forth. Whatever forms of jargon are used, the director will make it clear when the player is falling short of a satisfactory performance, and the performer must learn to give the necessary sparkle and brilliance in order to remain in the role.

Once into an emotion, the best way for a screen actor to portray it is not to act at all, but to just let it happen with simplicity and honesty. If the player is feeling an emotion, trust the camera to perceive its natural expression in face and body. Any attempt at conscious physical projection in the theater sense will seem grotesque and melodramatic on the screen. When the player feels the part, the player should be permitted to continue through every shot required in the master scene, with the thoughtful support of everyone present.

## The Rushes

Viewing the rushes in a projection room means judging the unedited footage. Many players wish to be present at this time to view their raw performances, and many directors refuse if principal cinematography is still in progress.

Performers naturally want the opportunity to view the film to see how well they

**THE COLOR OF MONEY** (U.S.A., 1986) DIRECTED BY MARTIN SCORSESE.

have interpreted the role. If the talent has some objectivity, lessons may be learned from mistakes and improvements may be made in the portrayal of the role—from the actor's point of view. The director, on the other hand, often regards the filmed performance as only a means to the end of footage edited to a vision. Therefore, what the actor may regard as a flawed performance may be perfect for the director's concept of what that role in the film should be and the director does *not* want the player to change. Performers are sometimes locked out of the rushes while cinematography continues.

In conclusion, Paul Newman was asked if he had any good advice to give young thespians aspiring to the screen. "Only the obvious things: Learn your craft, study people, and act whenever possible for the experience" (Figure 6.11).

Jack Lemmon—*actor or director in more than forty-five films, nominated for an Academy Award six times, winner of the Academy Award for* Days of Wine and Roses *and* Save the Tiger—*adds his expertise to this chapter.*

*Billy Wilder, director of Jack Lemmon in* The Apartment, *said,* "The Apartment *was written for the light* farceur *talents of Jack Lemmon, who can bring off a crazy comic-tragic role better than any other film actor today."*

# Seven

# COMEDY AND HUMOR

*with Jack Lemmon*

THE CLUMSY TUMBLE OF A caveman was probably the first knee-slapper; laughter at the humiliation of others has continued ever since to leaven the tedium of good times and bad. Literature is filled with puns, jokes, parodies, tall yarns, and humorous essays. Comedy has grinned and chuckled its way through the rise and fall of Rome, the Renaissance, the Restoration—in every kind of performance through contemporary films and television programs. And in every epoch, the comedy has dealt with life not as humanity would like it to be but with life as it is.

Laughter, prized by people everywhere, has been used for diversion, subversion, joy, and hostility, as well as the subject of study in theses and dissertations. Scholars have been probing into the nature of laughter since the inquiries of Plato, Aristotle, and Aristophanes, with generally dismal results. E. B. White commented, "Humor can be dissected as a frog can, but the thing dies in the process and the innards are discouraging to any but the pure scientific mind." A sense of humor is not born of study, knowledge, or understanding, but of perception. It is a way of looking at things. Perhaps it will do no harm to look at what has proved to be funny on film.

Film comedy began with a sneeze. *The Sneeze*, produced in 1894, showed a man sneezing. The film was no longer than it took to sneeze and revealed how hilarious it is for someone else to have a cold. Two years later, in 1896, the Lumière brothers demonstrated the delights of giving someone else a cold: A gardener was sprinkling the yard with a hose. A child stepped on the hose, stopping the flow of water. When the gardener, puzzled, stared into the nozzle, the child stepped off the hose.

Film comedy was then expanded into a genre primarily by one man, Mack Sennett. In 1911 he wandered onto a film set where D. W. Griffith, creator of the language of cinema, was shooting a film. He returned to watch every day thereafter and applied what he learned to film comedy. Sennett created a zany world in which nothing was sacred and corruption abounded: Lawyers were crooks, policemen were stupid, churchgoers were hypocrites, honest men were fools, the villain got the girl, and all social problems could be solved with a good kick in the rump. Sennett's stable of comedians included Charlie Chaplin, W. C. Fields, Harold Lloyd—a veritable who's who in the creation of film comedy. Mack Sennett's world was a caricature of life in which events that would ordinarily be tragically disastrous had no more effect than a custard pie flung in the face, and they were so wildly improbable that even the police laughed at the Keystone Kops. Sennett's sight gags and satires were so delightful that he never received a single complaint from any special interest group.

The advent of sound was the first blow to the great era of the pantomime slapstick comedian. The second blow was dealt by Mickey Mouse and Donald Duck, whose animated pratfalls were wilder and more extreme than anything mortal flesh could endure. The first to fall from the dual blows were the innocent comedians who could not tell a joke, or whose style of humor was blunted by words—deadpan comics like Ben Turpin and Buster Keaton. Laurel and Hardy, however, succeeded in making the transition to sound, as did W. C. Fields and the Marx Brothers. The style in film comedy evolved into a team of one comic and one straight man,

"I like best to do those movies that are a blend of comedy and drama, films of ideas like *The Apartment*. To this day I would not know how to classify that film. I would not consider it a comedy, although the studio did. I would call it a comedy-drama, or a drama with comedy, or a comedy with drama. It was the kind of film Billy Wilder did so brilliantly, a wonderful blend of laughter and tragedy. . . . I search for roles like that."
—*Jack Lemmon*

**183**

one to tell the jokes and the other to take the pratfalls—a tradition that came straight from vaudeville and still persists on television. Laurel and Hardy were followed by Abbott and Costello, who were followed by Dean Martin and Jerry Lewis, who were succeeded by Desi Arnaz and Lucille Ball, and so forth.

## Relationships

Jack Lemmon comments that the production of a successful film comedy is an absolute miracle—"analogous to creating a baby"—requiring the meshing of many diverse talents, all of whom have one thing in common: the comic instinct. Most important among them are the player, the writer, the director, and the editor.

"Comedians are born and not made," says Lemmon. "The player is either born with an intuitive sense of what is funny, with an instinct for comic timing, or he is not. There are many wonderful dramatic actors—gifted performers—who are not that proficient at all when it comes to comedy. . . . [Although] it is also true that there are actors and actresses who can do comedy well who cannot play drama well, it is far more often the case that someone proficient in comedy is also proficient in drama. There are special demands in comedy—the sense of timing, the instinct for when to exaggerate slightly—that add a special dimension to any other kind of performance. The comic instinct is like being born with red hair—you either have it or you don't."

Good writing is crucial to good comedy. Lemmon mentions that Billy Wilder considered writing so important that he felt that 90 percent of his work was done in the final draft of the screenplay. The rest was the drudgery of putting it on film. "The difference between mediocre writing and fine writing," Lemmon observes, "is the difference between a stage flat and a brick house. Flats have the semblance of reality, but the other one is really there. Any time you see a terrific performance, remember that it was the writer who created the characters and scenes that made the great performance possible. If a script is epidermal, there are only one or two ways to play the part and make it funny. If the characters are richly drawn, in interesting situations, there will be twenty ways to play the part and eighteen of them will be legitimate. The actor can then play the role in a way that will be most moving to the audience, and it should be, always, to express the intent of the writer."

The director must have the gift for comedy: inventiveness, timing, and most importantly, overview. A film comedy should progressively build layers of laughter to higher and higher crescendos; this requires that the director have a gift for directing comedies. Lemmon says, "To make a great comedy in film requires a great director. We have all seen films that did not quite make it, yet when analyzed scene by scene, each one was an absolute pearl. The difference came when the scenes were all strung together and the beautiful pearls were somehow *not* a beautiful necklace. For some reason the pearls now seem lumpy, varied in size, and don't match to make a beautiful whole. The difference between a comedy that makes it as a whole film and one that doesn't is the difference between a good director and a great director. Billy Wilder had a genius for directing comedies, in his prime, that showed up in classics such as *The Apartment, Some Like It Hot*, and many others."

The film editor is important in a comedy because comic effects are so often a matter of timing. The player may take the right beat and time his or her lines and moves to perfection, but if the editor lacks the sensibility to perceive the humor in the pacing, and interprets a pause as a blank spot—cutting it out—the laughs may end up on the cutting-room floor. As Lemmon comments, "I know I must have a beat before this line or the line is only going to be half as funny. I must have that beat, and I pray to God that some idiot doesn't cut it out when he [or she] is editing the film. Remember, the actor is long gone when the editor has his [or her] hands on what is supposed to be funny."

Comedy films should not be edited to death. Lemmon recounts, "Every time I have done a comedy, and we have had a preview and the laughs are all there, I go through the tortures of the damned when someone says, 'Now all we have to do is fine tune it.' I have seen comedies hurt or even ruined by fine tuning in editing. I have seen successful films that I did not play in—where I am really being objective—in which comedies that were damned good in preview were distributed in final form having a lot fewer laughs than they had in the first cut. They had cut the wrong things, the wrong way. Having the right editor is vital in film comedy."

## Comedy and Humor: Defined

*Comedy* and *humor* are often used interchangeably, but each has a unique meaning and application.

*Comedy* is based essentially on human foibles, self-delusions, and weaknesses. Comedy pokes fun at duplicity, hypocrisy, and vanity; it parodies people pretending to be more than they really are. It is the tale of a confident approach to a situation, an unexpected fall, a realization of what has happened, and a sense of humiliation. Comedy is essentially timeless; the silent film pratfalls are often as funny today as they were a half-century ago.

*Humor* is based upon content and is

therefore topical and transient. The humorist gleefully hurls satirical barbs at politics, politicians, and issue crusaders, pricking the balloon of difference between form and substance. Humor, like comedy, derives from unexpected weakness and has as its goal the humiliation of the subject. In topical humor the audience must be fully aware of all the ramifications of a situation for a joke to be funny. Otherwise, the light steps bounding to a leap of laughter may be mired in the tar pits of explanation and never get off the ground. Humor changes quickly with the times and soon becomes dated. *Alice in Wonderland*, a masterpiece of satirical humor, has survived because of its literary qualities, but much of its humor has become meaningless with the passage of time and the burial of its original targets. The Disney animated film *Alice in Wonderland* is a virtuoso cinematic abstraction whose meaning is virtually lost on the modern audience.

### The Comic Spirit

What's funny? The question is difficult to answer because laughter lies in the viewer rather than in the event, and one man's buffo is another man's boredom. Almost everyone prides themself on having a sense of humor; only slightly less insulting than a slur on the beauty of a man's wife is the implication that he lacks a sense of humor. And laughter there is for almost everyone according to his or her likes and tastes—a ladder of laughter that begins with the crudest jokes about genitalia and excrement and ascends to the subtlest visual-verbal satire in the world of ideas. Not all things are funny, laughter is unique to a given event and its perception by the viewer.

Tradition holds that the world is a comedy for those who think and a tragedy

FIGURE 7.1 *Jack Lemmon comments on the ludicrousness of this scene. "One of the things that made Charlie Chaplin so great, and so popular, was the fact that he never lost his dignity. The Tramp never had a nickel, he had to fight for everything, but he never felt sorry for himself no matter what the circumstances. When he was starving to death he didn't show*

for those who feel. Actually, laughter is evoked by situations having elements of both comedy and tragedy, and as often as not the world is a comedy for those who feel and a tragedy for those who think. This paradox was exemplified in the films of Charlie Chaplin. The essence of his cinematic comedy lay in the pathos that tripped into absurdity, the laughter that died into tragedy, the recognition that comic elements are present in life's most profound moments.

Jack Lemmon distinguishes between a sense of humor and an appreciation of humor in this way. "A sense of humor is creative." A sense of humor is the ability to know that certain lines, which are perfectly straight, may become terribly funny gag lines when used by certain characters in given situations. Neil Simon's screenplay *The Out of Towners* gave a superb example. Sandy Dennis played my wife in that film, and every time some horrendous thing would happen to us, all she would say was, 'Oh, my God.' Now, nobody can tell me that 'Oh, my God' is a funny line. And yet Neil Simon knew it would be funny as hell coming from her in situations that were progressively more outrageous. Today I cannot walk down the street in a major city without someone spotting me, laughing, and saying, 'Oh, my God.' It is this ability to know in advance what will be funny in a certain situation that is truly what I consider a sense of humor.

"An appreciation of humor is something else," Lemmon continues. "Let's say that you tell a joke and tell it pretty well, and the man just looks at you after the punch line because he doesn't get it. We say, 'He has no sense of humor.' To me, what he lacks is an appreciation of humor because he cannot perceive that the joke is funny. Again, a true sense of humor is one that can creatively combine characters and context in ways that will be funny, as Neil Simon did in *The Out of Towners*."

Attempts to explain what is funny tend to fail if the explainer takes himself or herself and laughter, seriously, in relating fun to serious life. Being funny means playing around, abandoning the sober dictum that life is grim, life is earnest. At the heart of evoking laughter is the importance of not being earnest. Even animals sense the mood of play and will romp through mock battles that are understood not to be taken seriously. A playful dog may be flung this way and that, and will react with loud snarls, barks, and mock ferocity, but the wagging tail will be laughing out loud.

### The Comic Elements

What's funny about a given comic figure or a situation? Three elements tend to make people laugh: the *ludicrous*, the *incongruous*, and the *unexpected*.

Anything *ludicrous* is out of proportion; it is exaggerated (Figure 7.1). A ludicrous trait in a comedian means that something is the matter, something is out of normal proportions. It may be a physical exaggeration: A comic figure may be too fat, too thin, drunk, dumb, big-nosed, big-eared, big-mouthed, big-footed, or speak with a funny accent. Or, it may be a personality or character trait that is disproportionate. He or she may have prejudices that are commonly known but never discussed and exaggerated to the point of being ludicrous.

A ludicrous situation is one that has elements of normality, or begins normally, but has been exaggerated out of proportion. When Stan Laurel, of Laurel and Hardy, attended a formal dinner, he found himself unable to scoop up a maraschino cherry that had fallen off the top of his dessert—a relatively minor mishap. But when Laurel pursued the cherry in dead earnest around the rim of his dish about ten times, the situation became amusing. When the cherry fell off his plate and he hunger pangs or sit around with a woebegone expression; he looked around for a shoe to eat. . . . That's class."

Charlie Chaplin had the most extraordinary appeal of any comedian in film history. The Little Tramp was kicked from pillar to post but put up a fight every step of the way in a battle for his dignity. His appeal was universal: To children he was the eternally mischievous boy. To adults he was a champion who could outwit his oppressors, shrug off defeats, and optimistically seek new adventures. To social critics he was a living protest against the crushing of the little guy by impersonal social forces. To idealists he was a dreamer searching for beauty and gentleness. To everyone he was funny.

**THE GOLD RUSH** (U.S.A., 1925) DIRECTED BY CHARLIE CHAPLIN.

FIGURE 7.2 *The incongruity of two male stars in drag—with musical instruments perforated by machine-gun bullets—compels laughter in this scene with Jack Lemmon and Tony Curtis (left). Lemmon comments, "Everyone in the industry thought that Billy Wilder had gone crazy because he was taking a five-minute burlesque sketch—two male musicians disguising themselves as women and joining an all-girl orchestra—and stretching it into a two-hour farce. Within a week, two weeks, I knew we were in something special, but I felt great trepidation. Would we be laughable, or would the audience laugh because we were good?"*

pursued it in front of the gentleman seated beside him, the situation became absurd. And when he spooned his way furiously around the edge of the formal dinner table, climbing over the laps and working around the heads of dowagers and tycoons—to get a maraschino cherry—it became utterly ludicrous. And funny.

Lemmon comments, "Exaggeration in almost all of comedy at times is what makes it laughable. The important thing for the actor *not* to do, however, is to play the exaggeration. The humor lies in the character's belief that the situation is important, when it is not. The loss of a thumbtack can seem as important as the H bomb about to go off, the fall of Rome, the end of the world. It becomes funny because the character honestly gives exaggerated importance to something as trivial and dumb as a lost thumbtack."

A sense of proportion is an indispensable element in keeping a comic action plausibly ludicrous. W. C. Fields played a sequence on the golf course in which he spent eighteen minutes preparing to hit the ball and then retired without ever swinging the club. Had Fields dragged out his eighteen-minute warmup to twenty minutes, the comic effect might have mired down into ennui and died with a yawn. There are no guiding principles in having a sense of comic proportion; the individual either has or has not the instinctive knack for the ludicrous.

Mel Brooks's approach is to play off the truth and exaggerate only slightly, as in his interview with a two thousand-year-old man. Brooks achieves hilarious comedy with such trifling chips off the truth.

The *incongruous* in comedy and humor means discovering mismatched characters in a normal setting, or normal characters in a mismatched setting (Figure 7.2). The relationship must be visually or verbally a square peg in a round hole. Laurel and

Hardy were funny on sight because they were physically incongruous together: Laurel was small and skinny, Hardy big and fat. In *The Odd Couple*, one character is prissy and fastidious, the other a booze-swilling, cigar-chomping slob; any context in which the two appear together is humorous.

The relationship of a character to his or her situation can be equally incongruous: W. C. Fields was filmed in a scene in which he accidentally falls out of an airplane to what is apparently his death. On his way down he decides to enjoy one last cigarette but can not decide whether to smoke a regular or a king-size cigarette before ending in a puff. His entire descent is given over to a sober, rational discussion of the relative merits of regular and king-size cigarettes—an incongruous and funny situation.

Neil Simon says that one of his secrets for comedy is to place naturally incongruent forces of people, desires, personalities, or characters into an intolerable situation and let the sparks fly. The sparks so generated by Simon have yielded some of the funniest plays and screenplays ever written and a record of being perhaps the most successful comic playwright of the twentieth century.

Incongruity refers to the discovery of a weakness, foible, or inconsistency in a character who, on the surface, appears to be other than he or she really is. If a heavyweight boxing champion were shown rubbing a tattered remnant of his baby blanket between rounds of a title fight, it would be funny because of the incongruity of a professional fighter needing this kind of reassurance.

The *unexpected* is the third dimension of laughter, and it may take two forms: The unexpected may be something unforeseen that the viewer does not anticipate but the comedian does, as is true of

**SOME LIKE IT HOT** (U.S.A., 1959) DIRECTED BY BILLY WILDER.

FIGURE 7.3   *Reversal of characters is at the heart of* The Odd Couple —*placing two mismatched characters in an intolerable situation to hilariously funny effect.*

*Jack Lemmon's rollicking role of Felix Unger may well have been the funniest and most touching one in a brilliant career that has included some of the most popular and highly ac-*

verbal gags; or it may be something the viewer expects but the proxy victim does not, as is often true of sight gags.

In *M\*A\*S\*H* the discovery that the beautiful nurse has a lover stimulates a spirited discussion over the weighty issue of whether she is a natural blond or a bleached blond. Bets are taken among the civilian doctors, and a project is implemented to ascertain whether Hotlips, as she is now called, is blond all over. The only way to find out for sure is to catch her in the altogether, and the only reasonable place to do this is the women's shower. The doctors rig the shower's outer curtain to an overhead pulley, weight the other end of the pulley rope, and then line up on chairs to await the viewing of Hotlips. She arrives in due course and enters the shower, disrobes, and begins to bathe. A signal sends the shower curtain soaring up and reveals Hotlips as she really is. Before she can double up and hide, all lean forward to confirm that Hotlips is indeed an honest blond. This scene has all of the classic comic elements: It is ludicrous, incongruous, and unexpected to the humiliated but unbleached lady.

*Reversal* is a comic synthesis of the incongruous and the unexpected in which the elements considered normal are exactly reversed. The technique may be used in dramatic situations, characterization, and plot.

Reversal in a dramatic situation is exemplified by two men who live together, separated from their wives, in Neil Simon's *The Odd Couple* (Figure 7.3). One man is a slob who drinks too much, eats too much, smokes smelly cheroots, leaves clothing flung about the apartment, arrives tardy for dinner, stays out late and returns with slamming doors. The second man is prissy in his lifestyle, eats moderately, never smokes or drinks, is fastidious in his clothing, keeps appointments precisely, and goes into a huff when the slob shows up late for dinner and spoils his meat loaf. Their mutual hostilities are those of the traditional husband and wife, and the reversal—and humor of the situation—lies in the fact that the excesses of each of them are what have estranged them from their wives.

Reversal in characterization is a major premise in Billy Wilder's *Some Like It Hot*. Two musicians, fleeing from the guns of gangsters, are forced to dress and act like stereotypic women. They parlay their masquerade into jobs with an all-girl orchestra; much of the comedy derives from their parody of the alleged mannerisms of women.

Reversal as a plot device is found in *Splash*, a contemporary film fantasy of Hans Christian Andersen's *The Little Mermaid* (Figure 7.4). A mermaid from Cape Cod sprouts legs (when she is dry) to follow a young man whose life she has saved and come to love. A scientist who has seen her while scuba diving is determined to make his reputation by proving that mermaids really exist.

The reversals of plot occur to the scientist who follows her about Manhattan, determined to prove she is a mermaid by splashing water on her legs, which would make them revert to fins. The first bucket of water he heaves at the wrong woman, and her escort punches out several teeth. The second time he hoses down a well-dressed couple in an elevator, and the gentleman breaks the scientist's arm. The third liquid assault occurs at a dinner being given in honor of the President of the United States. Secret Service agents grab him by the arms and drag him into the street while he screams, "There's a mermaid in there! There's a mermaid in there!"

Each of these plot reversals results in progressively higher levels of laughter, claimed performances in screen annals.

Walter Matthau, who repeats his stage role in The Odd Couple, is equally at home in comedy or tragedy. He belongs to the school that says that an actor can play any part.

The casting of characters is critical in comedy because having people who "click" together is like having a third star on the screen. This film is a successful comedy in part because the talents of Lemmon and Matthau work well together. As Lemmon comments, "Walter and I know without saying a word what the other is doing, or about to do, and can act intuitively for funny effects."

**THE ODD COUPLE** (U.S.A., 1968) DIRECTED BY GENE SAKS.

FIGURE 7.4 *Reversal as a plot device occurs in this comedy in the form of repeated attempts by an obsessed scientist to douse mermaid Daryl Hannah with water and thereby transform her comely legs and feet into tail and fins. By drenching other people by mistake, and acquiring new victim-inflicted injuries on himself with each attempt, the scientist creates ascending levels of belly-shaking laughter from audiences who are delighted by his humiliation.*

**SPLASH** (U.S.A., 1984) DIRECTED BY RON HOWARD.

with the mounting exasperation and humiliation of the scientist. Ultimately, of course, he does succeed in dousing her legs and sprouting her fins—proving that (at least in the film) he is not crazy. The anticipation created by each of these reversals triggers the expectation of further humiliation to come, and the audience is prepared to laugh hilariously at each succeeding surprise and debacle.

### Targets of Comedy and Humor

Every social code and authority figure is a legitimate target of laughter; those most easily ridiculed are the ones trying to preserve society's order: doctors, lawyers, professors, judges, politicians, government officials—all solid citizens to the core. Add to these big government, the Pentagon, the CIA, the FBI, social welfare programs, the local police, and the Parent-Teacher Association. If fathers are honored, then Dad is an incompetent boob. If mothers are sacred, then Mom is an interfering pest. If thrift and diligence are exalted, then spendthrifts and lazy oafs are enormously successful, setting a terrible example for the young and impressionable. Comedy celebrates every form of sincerity and the decline and fall of every form of pretentious authority. Somerset

FIGURE 7.5 *Harpo (left), Groucho (center), and Chico Marx combine all three comic heroes into one madhouse team. Harpo is the Fool who wrecks almost everything he touches, misunderstands every situation, chases women with embarrassing lewdness, yet plays the harp with the sublime sensibilities of an artist. Groucho is the Scroundrel—a cigar-chomping cynic who is the ultimate con man and bottom-pincher, full of treachery and self-serving sophistries, stooping to almost any deceit for personal advantage. Chico is the Innocent, an immigrant who can barely speak or understand the language or cope with the customs of his new homeland. The unleashing of all three at once means the humiliation of all that is dignified, a triumph of the anarchic spirit of comedy.*

**193**

COMEDY AND
HUMOR: DEFINED

Maugham wrote that judges should preside over the court with a roll of tissue paper on their benches to remind themselves that they are only human. This tongue-in-cheek jibe is the essence of the debunking comic spirit. It has been comedy, not tragedy, that has brought down the wrath of church and state on the fools of truth who undermine the stability of the powers that be.

Some revered figures are unsuitable targets for ridicule, however, because their images correspond to their reality. A comedian who parodies Abraham Lincoln delivering the Gettysburg Address may be damned with a cold silence from the audience; it would not be funny because Lincoln embodies greatness with humility, not pretentious humbug.

### The Comic Hero

The traditional comic hero takes three conceptual forms: the Innocent, the Fool, and the Scoundrel, all of whom may be traced from the earliest dramas to the latest films (Figure 7.5).

Charlie Chaplin is the classic Innocent. Naive, decent, sentimental, with an inner spirit untainted by corruption, he spunkily confronts a nasty world in a fight for dignity and self-respect. Chaplin is the lit-

**ANNIE HALL** (U.S.A., 1977) DIRECTED BY WOODY ALLEN.

FIGURE 7.6 *Woody Allen, shown here with Diane Keaton, is a latter-day version of the Innocent. His neuroses, bungling inadequacies, gleeful ironies, and the battering he receives by modern urban existence has been synthesized into a character almost as universal as Charlie Chaplin's Little Tramp. So strongly has Woody Allen evoked contemporary identification with bruised innocence that the words of film critic Richard Schickel spoke for us all: "Woody, c'est moi."*

tle guy who could somehow outfox Mr. Big: He is the eternally mischievous boy who would defiantly kick the bully in the slats and then run like blazes; and he gives the viewers hope in their own lives by outfoxing his corrupt superiors on the screen, shrugging off defeats, and walking away alone but undaunted to optimistically seek new adventures. The Tramp made the best of every situation and faced life with picaresque optimism. The Innocent as a lover and cultural hero is a persistent strand in American comedy (Figure 7.6).

The Fool is the second persona of the comic hero and not far removed from the Innocent in certain respects (Figure 7.7). The Fool is one who has slid from the childlike wisdom of Charlie Chaplin to the mindlessness over matter of Jerry Lewis or Mel Brooks. The Fool is a simpleminded survivor who thinks from the neck down, dashing from mayhem to carnage in a rampage of destruction that leaves nothing intact but the Fool. The Fool's success is the success of dumb luck and circumstance. Where the Innocent often asserts profound insights and values, the Fool offers chaos as a way of life in a zaniness that appeals to the very young— and to the French—but less so to the sober public because the Fool does not really know what he or she is doing, which is disturbing. The Fool tends to be like a speeding car without a driver unless controlled by someone else as part of a comic team, as was true when Jerry Lewis was teamed with Dean Martin or Stan Laurel with Oliver Hardy. The Fool alone is unnerving as power run amuck without a guiding brain.

The Scoundrel is the third major persona of the comic hero and is embodied in the old con artist of *The Flim-Flam Man*

FIGURE 7.7 *Jerry Lewis has been a classic Fool in the movies: as a nutty professor who concocts a brew that transforms him into the campus heartthrob; as a bookkeeper-fisherman who reels in a frogman with knowledge about diamond* *smugglers, followed in turn by not one but two gangster mobs; as an unemployed bumbler who stumbles through occupations at which nobody could possibly fail, but who bungles them all with hilarious results.*

**195**
COMEDY AND
HUMOR: DEFINED

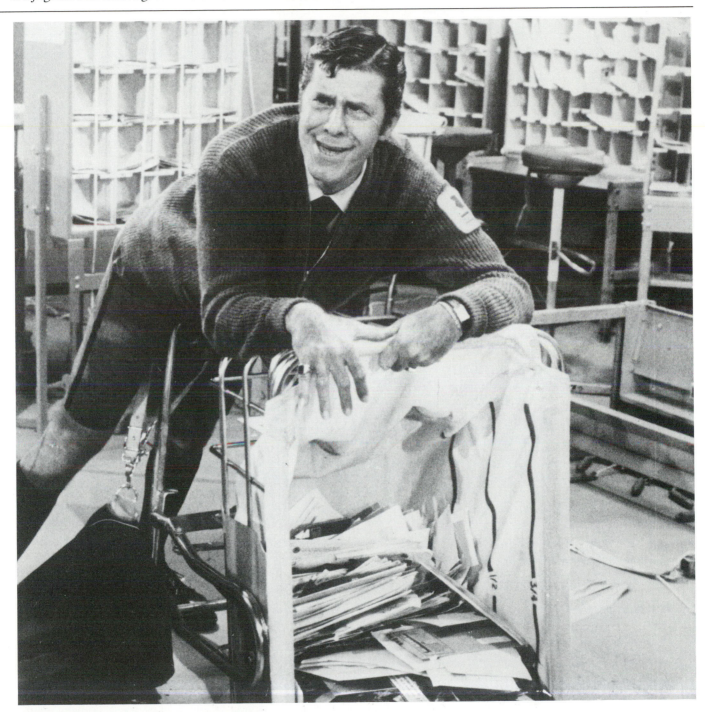

**HARDLY WORKING** (U.S.A., 1981) DIRECTED BY JERRY LEWIS.

FIGURE 7.8 *"Greed's my line," crows the Flim-Flam Man, with George C. Scott as the Scoundrel who gleefully fleeces the self-righteous and hypocritically respectable. He is teamed with Michael Sarrazin, playing the Innocent, as they infuriate the forces of propriety and righteousness.*

*Charles Champlin wrote, "George C. Scott is the con man of legend, on permanent exile from polite society, a missionary bent on depriving suckers of an even break, a master of the vanishing Queen, the predetermined dice, the found-wallet ploy, the salted gold mine, and anything else that will engender a dishonest sawbuck." Los Angeles Times, October 23, 1967*

**THE FLIM-FLAM MAN** (U.S.A., 1967) DIRECTED BY IRVIN KERSHNER.

(Figure 7.8). He tricks and fleeces the public for fun and profit, considering himself an educator to the corrupt and gullible elements of conventional society. His machinations confound the other characters, complicate the plot, and unite the young lovers, and he escapes the outraged forces of truth, justice, and right amid gales of audience laughter.

The Scoundrel is often linked in partnership with a Fool or an Innocent. Laurel and Hardy yoked the Fool with the sly schemer, as did Bud Abbott and Lou Costello. The Scoundrel is always pretending to be what he or she is not, is usually on the make for a shady deal, and generally has an eye cocked for a comely young woman. The con man or woman of the team is usually full of sly innuendos and corrupt wisdom, sending the Fool out to

FIGURE 7.9  *A sight gag is the only phrase to describe a scene in which the character strains spaghetti through a tennis racket and then eats it, one loopy strand at a time, as in this picture of Jack Lemmon wolfing down pasta the hard way.*

implement risky adventures while basking in the relative shade of safety. Scoundrels are often rendered in films in the form of rogue lovers—such as Clark Gable and Burt Reynolds—or cheeky women—such as Jane Fonda.

### Sight Gags and Verbal Gags

What is the comic element? Aristotle defined it as something ugly or distorted, but not painful. Immanuel Kant defined it as an expectation that suddenly comes to nothing. Within these two definitions lie the skeletons of the sight gag and the verbal gag. Sight gags and verbal gags are the two major kinds of film and television jokes, with variations in the way they are handled in counterpoint dependent upon whether they are intended for theatrical or televised release.

A *sight gag* is a visual joke, an extension of the unexpected slapstick pratfall in which the payoff makes the subject look ludicrous (Figure 7.9). The heyday of the sight gag was the era of the silent film, when a joke had to be visual or it was no joke at all. Pantomime, not wisecracks, is the basis of the sight gag, with all the surprises the comedian can incorporate and all the situations the comedian can concoct. When Jack Lemmon strains his spaghetti through a tennis racket in *The Apartment*, the sight gag sends waves of laughter rippling through the audience. The ultimate form of the sight gag may be found in the animated cartoon because

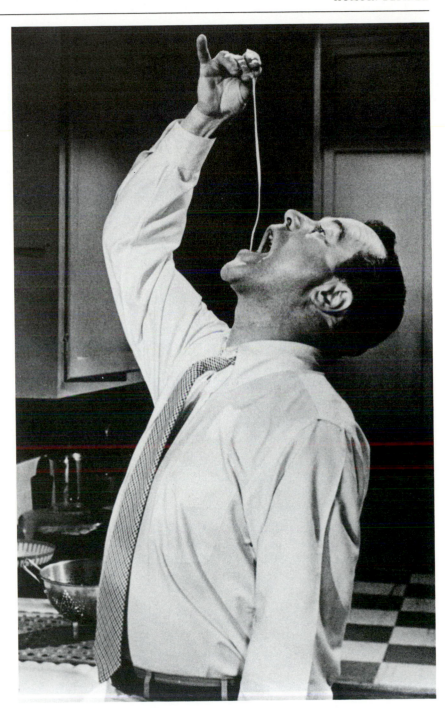

**THE APARTMENT** (U.S.A., 1960) DIRECTED BY BILLY WILDER.

FIGURE 7.10 *This sight gag of Tony Curtis (left) and Jack Lemmon impersonating women for their roles in Billy Wilder's classic comedy is the basis for the movie and the source of its fun. Commenting on his need to wear dresses in Some Like It Hot, "They didn't teach me this in drama school," Lemmon says, and he adds, "this is no burlesque. We have to be believable or the whole farce falls apart. . . . In Some Like It Hot, the audience is in on the gag and therefore must make allowances for credibility if they're really going to enjoy the fun."*

**SOME LIKE IT HOT** DIRECTED BY BILLY WILDER.

FIGURE 7.11 *Having Sugar Kane (Marilyn Monroe, center) confide to Jerry (Tony Curtis in drag) that she wants to marry that millionaire who owns "the company with the Shell sign" (also Tony Curtis, straight) provides the sight gag with the verbal wit to make the situation hilarious.*

**SOME LIKE IT HOT** DIRECTED BY BILLY WILDER.

there are no limits to the pratfalls to which the characters can be subjected: Characters ricochet off walls and each other, are dismembered and reassembled, metamorphose with the explosion of each stick of dynamite, and generally indulge in acrobatics that defy the laws of man and nature.

*Verbal gags* are practical jokes on the mind. They lead the listener down a logical corridor of expectation toward an unexpected banana peel waiting in the dark, and then drop him flat. For example:

"Daddy, can I go out and play?"

"Shut up and deal."

This gag is purely verbal and is contingent upon the absence of vision for its unexpected twist. Purely verbal jokes are usable in film and television primarily by the stand-up comedian telling an anecdote. But our concern is with humor and comedy that relate to and support the living image: the sight gag that requires verbal wit to make its point, the verbal joke that is meaningless without its visual point (Figure 7.10).

A delightful example of a sight gag linked to verbal wit is found in *Some Like It Hot* (Figure 7.11). Jack Lemmon plays the part of a seedy musician from Chicago who has to impersonate a female and flee to Florida to escape from being the machine-gun victim of a gangster. In Florida the quasi-female catches the lascivious eye of a dirty old millionaire, who pursues him-her with less than honorable intentions, a ludicrous and incongruous relationship. The absurdity of this courtship grows in hilarity as the millionaire becomes more and more persuasive, to the point where the quasi-female forgets he is not a female and begins to listen seriously to the millionaire's propositions and proposals. When the millionaire offers to marry him and make her an honest woman, she forgets himself and consents.

The millionaire and his confused bride-to-be depart on a motorboat to begin a honeymoon on his yacht. On the way, the female impersonator remembers he is not a female and exclaims, "Hey—I'm not a woman!" And the millionaire answers, "Nobody's perfect." The visual absurdity of their relationship and the impossibility of their marriage—a sight gag—is capped by delicious verbal wit, each of which is laughable only in context with the other.

### The Viewer's Motivation

What is it in a comic situation that releases inner tension in the viewer and dispels it into laughter? Malice. Relief. Feelings of superiority. It is that sudden tremendous sense of satisfaction and glee that comes with the realization that humiliation has come to a proxy victim and not to the viewer. A dirty word blurted in a polite social setting, a pratfall leading to a loss of dignity, a faux pas in a tense social situation, a prank at someone else's expense—these are the crimes without punishment, except for the humiliation of being laughed at, that delight the average viewer. The viewer sees a hapless character in a situation with which he or she can identify, doing something he or she has done or might have done, and when that person is humiliated the viewer laughs.

In *M*A*S*H*, a film comedy about the doctors and nurses serving in the Korean War, the beautiful blond nurse serves as a proxy victim. She is superficially prudish, correct, and very Regular Army, and her arrogance rubs all the civilian doctors the wrong way. Also in the medical unit is a Regular Army doctor, who agrees with this nurse that the slovenly civilian surgeons are a disgrace to the service, and he too antagonizes the civilian doctors with his superior attitude.

One night in her tent, the two are talking in a way that is clearly leading toward intimacy, when they are overheard by a civilian doctor passing by outside. The civilian obtains a microphone, slips it under the edge of their tent near the bed, and connects the plug to the camp's public address system. Immediately their passionate words and kisses, grunts and groans, squeaks and squeals are broadcast to the thousands of personnel in the camp. When the two lovers begin to hear the vibrating echoes of their own words, they search for and are horrified to find the hidden microphone. The audience laughs uproariously at their humiliation.

Laughter's friend is cruelty and its enemy is compassion. Jesus, Moses, and Muhammad are never known to have joked; they took serious pity on people in distress and were therefore humorless. Their compassion was as boundless as their souls. A person must have a slight streak of sadism to take pleasure in the sights and sounds of anguish in others. There are a few aristocrats who can genuinely laugh at a humiliating joke on themselves, but not many. There is no shortage of those who take delight in the other person's humiliation.

Malevolence underlies most forms of comedy and humor, with one qualification: We laugh only when the malevolent situation is not really true. A slapstick comedy in which the comedian is knocked cross-eyed when hit in the head by a thrown brick may evoke a gust of laughter—the viewer knows it is only playacting. A documentary film showing a man knocked senseless by a maliciously thrown brick will arouse indignation in the average viewer—the injury is real, and it is not funny. This distinction is important; laughter may have a sadistic substratum, but real physical injuries to people and animals are not funny to the normal viewer.

Public acceptability is an important factor in comedy and humor. Laughter derived from ridicule of the alleged foibles of race, creed, sex, or physical deformity are no longer acceptable to civilized people. Racist stereotypes—such as Stepin Fetchit roles, which are cruel and stupid—are banished forever, we hope, from American comedy.

## Acting for Comedy

"The best definition of acting I have heard," Jack Lemmon asserts, "came from George Burns. We were attending a banquet and the air was full of the noise and hubbub that attends such affairs. Unaccountably, as sometimes happens, everyone fell silent and you could hear a pin drop. Into that silence came George's voice saying, 'The secret of acting is honesty. If you can fake that, you've got it made.'

"The basic difference between acting for comedy and acting for drama," Lemmon continues, "is essentially no difference at all. The thing I learned by the time I played in my first film, a comedy with Judy Holliday entitled *It Should Happen to You*, was that an actor—if he knew what he was doing—would not approach a comedy role any differently than he would approach a heavy dramatic part. For all the jokes we make about faking honesty—'Reality! What a concept!'—the nub of what acting is all about is the creation of some form of truth, of seeming truth and reality to an audience. The audience must believe that the funny situation is *real* in order to get those laughs."

Having the talent to act to comic effect is innate and not acquired. Lemmon states, "Those who have comic talent can sharpen the tools they have by working with good actors, good writers, and good directors in comedy, and by gaining experience before an audience. They can sharpen the attributes they have, but they cannot go to drama school and learn how to be a comedic actor if they do not have a natural talent for it.

"Consciously or unconsciously," Lemmon cautions, "an actor may unfortunately be all too aware that what he is doing is funny. He struts about implying 'Here comes the funny stuff.' And the moment that the viewer becomes aware that the actor thinks that what [is being done] is funny, . . . [it] isn't. It's gone. The performance is illegitimate. The audience may not be able to put their finger on the difference, but they don't like it, and if there is laughter it will be much diminished. The broader the comedy the more seriously it must be played. It is the essence of farce to be *real*, and the characters must be serious about it."

Three of the most important elements of acting for comedy involve taking a beat, timing the laugh, and performing comic business. Lemmon says, "The comic player must instinctively know, innately and through . . . experience, that if he [or she] takes a beat before . . . [saying] a certain line, the line will be funny. . . . [Without] the beat, it will not be funny. If he [or she] reads the dialogue a certain way, it will be funny. . . . [Without reading] the line a certain way, it will not be funny. One cannot verbalize it at all. It just has to be done."

Timing a laugh means knowing how

long to wait between the first gag line and the second, and these are quite different in the media of theater and cinema. As Lemmon says, "In the theater the actor uses the audience to time the laugh. The joy of doing comedy on the stage is that the actor can wait for the laughter to roll and, just as the laugh is beginning to die off—whack!—come in with the next line. The proficient actor knows how to time that next laugh by the feedback he [or she] gets from the audience."

When the laughter from a first funny line overlaps a second funny line, and the audience misses it, that's part of the problem of timing laughs for cinema. "That is the disease," says Lemmon, "you hope to suffer from. And it is not necessarily bad. A large percentage of the box office attendance in *Some Like It Hot* came from those paying to see it a second time because they had missed many of the funny lines the first time through." Lemmon tells the story of a youthful Billy Wilder who was sitting in an audience to watch the premiere of his first film comedy. The man sitting before him persisted in laughing through the second funny lines until an irate Wilder pounded on him yelling, "Shut up! You are laughing on my lines!"

"Audience attendance at a film comedy, believe it or not, affects the timing of a laugh," says Lemmon. If there is a fully packed theater at, say, the 7:30 or 8:00 showing, you will get belly laughs and the house will be roaring. Now the same movie in the same theater goes on for the midnight showing, and even if the film is a smash hit, the laughs will be half as long and loud. There seems to be an embarrassment in people that comes out when there are empty seats around them—when they're not jammed together—that inhibits laughter even if they are enjoying it just as much. Suddenly the scene that was filled with roars of laughter in the earlier show-

ing is beginning to lay there in the later show. In theater, we would pick up the pace, speed up the timing, but in film the timing is set in celluloid.

"Timing a laugh in film production is nearly impossible. The only audience is the crew and they are busy doing their jobs. Each scene is shot in bits and pieces instead of in a continuous flow. And a lot depends on how a scene is cut. If the editor does not perceive the beat and sense the timing for a laugh, it's out. You've lost a terrific laugh."

The closest Lemmon has come to timing laughs for cinema was in a film he directed entitled *Kotch*, starring Walter Matthau. Lemmon recounts, "It was a sweet gentle story about an old man that did have some comedy in it. I would actually ask the crew to watch certain scenes because I wanted to find out whether it would get any chuckles. If it got a laugh from twenty people—a big one, a mild one, whatever—it was at least an indication. But the director should never be thrown off by a reaction from the film crew because the bottom line is that you can never really time a laugh on film."

Sometimes a scene requires reaction time for one character to understand what another character has said or done. This pause may slide perilously close to a chuckle-smothering silence unless it is filled by performing comic business. "The actor must never fall into the trap of waiting and allowing the scene to congeal," says Lemmon. "Unless he can fill the pause with comic business, he will sit there with egg on his face. . . . [The actor] must fill the moment with legitimate activity so that if no laugh ever comes the scene won't die. And here I have a wonderful example from *Some Like It Hot*.

"In the bedroom scene where I talk things over with Tony Curtis, after just having returned from dancing with Joe E.

Brown, and Tony has been with Marilyn [Monroe], he asks, 'How was your evening?' I answer, 'I'm engaged.' The line in that situation was absolute dynamite, and it takes Tony a few moments to realize that I, as the character, had forgotten that I was a man and could not get engaged to another man. To fill the time it takes for this realization to sink into Tony's head, Billy Wilder handed me a set of maracas and said, 'Jack, take these damn things and twirl them around between every line. Whenever you say something, twirl afterwards until Tony answers.'

"As a result," Lemmon concludes, "I could go fifteen seconds, twenty seconds—a long time between lines—and meanwhile Tony could wait and think. I was able to fill the pause legitimately and humorously, and the audience waited in anticipation to laugh at the next line. Tony Curtis played the straight man brilliantly: He never waited too long and he always waited long enough. Without the brainstorm of using the maracas, which was not in the script and was conceived by Billy on the set, the reaction time might have murdered the laughs. That bit of business was, in its simplicity, a kind of directing genius—the greatest example I can remember in the forty-five or so films I have done."

*Levels of Laughter*

Comedy and humor play to every level of intelligence and every class in society. There are jokes related to age, sex, level of education, political, social, and economic milieus. There are jokes understood and appreciated only in hippie communes, faculty meetings, student unions, and doctors' conventions, jokes that are lost on those who are not members of the select group. More often than not, the jokes are at the expense of others to whom that group is somehow related. The liberated throw barbs at the straights, professors joke about students (and the reverse), and obstetricians have their parturition puns. The joke is on the outsider, but listeners must be on the inside to appreciate the humor.

Certain patterns of visual and verbal humor have proven to be consistently funny to great numbers of people watching film and television programs. They share the elements of the ludicrous, incongruous, and unexpected discussed earlier, aimed for the most part at the humiliation of a proxy victim. The patterns ascend in degrees from the visual to the verbal, the physical to the abstract, the denotative to the connotative. This ladder of laughter includes *anatomical jokes*, *physical mishaps*, *plot devices*, *verbal wit*, *high comedy*, *satire*, and *deus ex machina*. Each step up the ladder may include elements from the rungs below—they are cumulative.

*Anatomical jokes* between mother and child may be the first exchange of amusement in the human experience, and they relate to the omnipresent potty. Euphemisms about weewee and doodoo are innocently funny jokes based upon anatomy that are reborn with each new generation. Vulgar humor continued more or less respectably in the media when Archie Bunker flushed a toilet in the television series "All in the Family" and Mel Brooks's cowboys released the exhaust from eating beans in *Blazing Saddles*.

Obscenity in film humor, however, features sexual comedy of every conceivable kind—heterosexual, homosexual, and bestial. Obscenity is a crude form of comedy based upon genitalia and sexual activity that, even in these tolerant times, walks a fine line in public acceptability. Although we are not concerned here with the legal ramifications of obscenity in film, this type of humor occupies the lowest rung in the ladder of laughter.

*Physical mishaps* is the next level of comedy (Figure 7.12). In the silent film days comedians were expected to be half-stunt man, half-imbecile as they floundered through pratfalls, drove off cliffs, sat on detonated bombs, and fell down elevator shafts. Comedians were clobbered by custard pies, knocked into wet cement, brained by rocks and swinging beams, chased by hornets, dogs, husbands, and policemen, and blasted into low orbit by the ubiquitous banana peel.

Another form of the physical mishap is the slow-building sight gag that progressively becomes more insane. Each event is plausible in terms of what preceded it, and logical in terms of what follows, but the climax is so wildly improbable as to be hilarious. The story usually takes the form of an average person innocently getting involved in some situation with slightly embarrassing overtones, and in his or her efforts to extricate himself or herself the situations become wilder and wilder.

The *plot device* is a third level of humor common to all film comedies. It consists of planting visual or verbal clues that seem to have no point until they culminate near the end with a humiliating sight gag. The dramatic value of the plot device is that it progressively builds a tense social situation that prepares the viewer to laugh at the ultimate humiliation.

In a film comedy called *A Shot in the Dark*, Inspector Clouseau (Peter Sellers) is shown from the beginning to be developing his judo skills and reflexes in order to be able to fight off surprise attacks. In obedience to Clouseau's orders, his assistant Kato pounces on him at unexpected times and unusual places and launches savage judo attacks that Clouseau tries to fight off, invariably without success. Later in the film Clouseau finds himself the lucky subject of a beautiful woman's romantic interest. She draws him close with the tenderest of words and gentlest of embraces. As Clouseau kneels amorously over her, feeling himself to be the luckiest man in the world, his assistant strikes with a wild judo attack and drags him off the woman—a humiliating sight gag that paid off the earlier visual clues.

*Verbal wit*, puns, and plays on words are the next rung up, and they, too, emphasize the ludicrous, incongruous, and unexpected. In Steven Spielberg's comedy *Back to the Future*, a teenaged youth (Michael J. Fox) finds himself projected back in time through a time warp device into the high school environment of his parents; he becomes an object of interest to his future mother. When informed of this, the youth gasps, "You mean, my mother's got the hots for me?"

*High comedy*, fifth rung in the ladder of laughter, is based upon human foibles in culturally stressful situations recognizable to a given national or ethnic audience (Figure 7.13). The television situation comedy has become the essence of this form; it is a cultural comedy that pokes fun at problems familiar to a broadly based segment of the public and gives people a chance to laugh at themselves through identifiable proxy victims placed in ludicrous and incongruous situations.

Identification is important in cultural comedies; the audience must see itself in the themes. Therefore, each new television season brings forth a fresh crop of time-tested situations. Daily life is the stuff of situation comedy—life as it really is rather than as one might wish it to be—and offers the most mundane dimensions of existence for a chuckle: the relationships of husband, wife, and children; divorced parents and children; dating and mating games; good jobs and bad cooking; clothing and crockery; minutia and trivia in

FIGURE 7.12 *The pratfall did not die with silent film comedy, but slogs on in this sticky scene in which river gumbo has replaced the custard pie. Steve McQueen (right) laughs uproariously at the gooey humiliation of himself and Rupert Crosse, and we laugh together at the messy downfall of two charming scoundrels who have it coming.*

**THE REIVERS** DIRECTED BY MARK RYDELL.

**MOONSTRUCK** (U.S.A., 1987) DIRECTED BY NORMAN JEWISON.

FIGURE 7.13 *Moonstruck is an Italian-American story set in New York, featuring a near-spinster (Cher) and her wild-eyed, one-handed lover (Nicolas Cage).*

*Cher says about acting for* Moonstruck, *"Comedy is a lot harder than drama. It's not easy for me to be funny at the drop of a hat; the dynamics are very different from drama, which is what I've done on the screen before. As a result, I was very dependent on Norman [Jewison] and quickly learned to trust him completely."*

variants of *Harold and Maude, Four Seasons,* and *I Love My Wife.*

A high comedy film may be universally popular in its originating nation, yet die in another country. A Japanese film shown in the United States (*A Cat, Shozo, and Two Women*) recounts the story of a man so henpecked by his wife, mother, and mistress that he seeks true friendship and understanding in the companionship of a cat. The Japanese viewers laughed until tears streamed down their cheeks. The American viewers, reading the subtitles as they watched, sat stony-faced at the lines that drew the greatest laughter from the Japanese. The comedy was so bound to cultural factors recognizable only to the Japanese that it was entirely lost on the Americans.

*Satire* is a world of ideas—a humorous lampoon flung at the pretensions of society, puncturing the cushion between what pretends to be and what really is. Satire must be audacious to be funny. The court jester was the only one who could launch barbs at the king with impunity, so long as the jester speared only his vanity and not his vital organs. This is the basis of delight in satire directed at important people; their pretensions are deflated and they seem cut down to size. Yet the barbs are funny only when they do *not* cut to the marrow. Satire must be aimed at the differences between the target as he or she is and as he or she pretends to be. Taste is involved in the selection of a subject fit for satire. A satire on law enforcement may be in order, but a satire on the murder of a police officer killed in the line of duty is unacceptable.

*The Apartment* hurls a barrage of barbs at the Great American Dream of hard work, individual initiative, free enterprise, and personal integrity as the means of achieving success in a modern corporation. This saga recounts the rise of an insurance clerk to a high post in his firm by turning his only capital, an apartment, into profit by exploiting the interest of his superiors in having a discreet rendezvous place for their paramours. The clerk lends the key to his apartment to his bosses, who, in turn, write glowing reports about his work; promotion follows promotion as he leaves his integrity in a file drawer with his night school diploma and rises to the top through the reversal of every Horatio Alger virtue. And what is his reward in the room at the top? The keys to the executive toilet.

*The Apartment* does more than tell a comic story about a pandering relationship; it knifes our urban way of life without mercy until the American Dream lies bleeding from laughter—but always with the light touch of revealing the incongruity between facade and reality. When the young man on the make asks the fair young maiden how many men have loved her, she answers, "Three," but unwittingly raises four fingers.

Satire must not be too bitter or it becomes hot and heavy scorn. Once the light thrust of the rapier is exchanged for the heavy chop of the saber, the playfulness that makes satire funny disappears into sober contemplation of the facts. The rapier of satire punctures the skin of pretension, the saber of drama slashes through to the bone and muscle of reality. The saber may be justified under some dramatic circumstances, but it cuts at the price of laughter. The satirist is most effective if he or she clearly remembers the phrase "make fun of." Charlie Chaplin made a cinematic spoof of Adolph Hitler's personal quirks and foibles that was hilarious in many sequences of *The Great Dictator.* As long as the film dealt lightly with the pretensions of those carrying the banner of the double cross, the lampoon was funny to most viewers. When the film changed character, however, and got to the flesh and bones of the true meaning of the Nazi and Fascist movements, it became self-consciously melodramatic, embarrassing to watch, and undid much that had been said effectively in moments of levity.

Reformers have often tried to use laughter as a means of attack against corrupt institutions and officials. For the most part, however, such attempts have only made their audiences uncomfortable. Reformers tend to be in dead earnest, and humor is incompatible with a crusading attitude. Satire works best against petty sinners—the petty sins of the great or the pretensions of the highly placed. Satire seldom pierces the substance of corruption, only its camouflage. The reforming satirist can achieve some goals by flaying the victim of all the features that might inspire sympathy in the viewer (petting a puppy, being kind to old ladies) and by avoiding emotional involvement—but not by being in earnest.

The concept of *deus ex machina* originally referred to the intervention of a deity in the lives of young lovers and other foolish mortals. It has been used in melodramas in which the heroine is saved from eviction by the appearance of a lost will, or when the unexpected patronage of a wealthy industrialist rewards the patient merit of a young impoverished Horatio Alger with a new life of prosperous industry. The *deus ex machina* is universally condemned as a plot device in tragedies as evidence of weak writing. Yet its very irrationality may sometimes fit in hilariously in comedy, as occurs in the Buster Keaton classic *The General*, when the *deus ex machina* of a train moving out of control and a cannon taking aim of its own volition on the hero create situations that still evoke belly-shaking laughter from audiences.

Two more contexts for comedy are important: *comic relief* and *comedy in tragedy*.

### Comic Relief

Comic relief is important in serious feature length dramas, especially in psychodramas. If the tension created by heavy dramatic actions is not relieved from time to time with a touch of humor, the viewer may burst into laughter during a love scene, a murder, or just as the pathological vampire sinks his teeth into the succulent throat of the lovely young heroine. Comic relief may appear at interludes between major crises and may be no more than an unexpected kitten chasing a fallen ball of yarn or the reappearance of the same panhandler whining the same appeal to the same character, as occurs in *The Treasure of the Sierra Madre*.

Jack Lemmon recounts the importance of comic relief in one of his own dramas. "Serious drama needs comedy at various points to provide relief from the heavier stuff, to round it off in the human sense. In *Days of Wine and Roses*, a film about the unfunny subject of alcoholism, Blake Edwards [the director] and I dreamed up all kinds of things to weave in as comic relief that were legitimate to the story. The lead character would get drunk and walk into a plate-glass window, or try to pay the cab driver through the wrong car window—dumb things that would be funny but true to the situation. Once he had a fight with his wife and went out to get drunk. He returned with flowers for his wife, only to have the blossoms cut off by the closing elevator door, and he was unaware of what had happened. When he presented them to his wife, he realized that all he had in his hands were stems. It was kind of pitiful, but it got a small laugh in the middle of a downward spiral for these two. It gave the audience a breather from the heavy stuff with comic relief."

## Comedy in Tragedy

"Comedy is part of real life and is therefore part of serious drama," Lemmon says. "Injecting it into tragedy legitimately and making it work so it doesn't seem imposed or tasteless is extremely difficult. Wilder did a courageous thing in one scene of *The Apartment* and achieved comedy in tragedy. He had me get drunk in a bar, pick up this lady barfly, and bring her back to my apartment. In the meanwhile, the character played by Shirley MacLaine had taken an overdose of drugs, trying to kill herself, and was near death in my bedroom. Wilder had me running back and forth between the bedroom and the living room, trying to help a near-suicide on the one hand and trading gag lines with this dizzy tart on the other. I ran back and forth, back and forth, with no break in continuity. Billy not only got away with this outrageous mixture, he had the audience soaked in tears and laughter at the same time.

"Sometimes the most serious dramas will get the biggest laughs. I saw *A Streetcar Named Desire* when it first appeared on Broadway, and there was not a comedy in New York that got as many laughs as Marlon Brando did when he played that wonderful character. And yet, strangely enough, when that play was adapted to film, only the tragedy came through. There were very few laughs in the audience.

"There is a reality about film, a lack of theatricality that can change the level of comedy. There are no sets, as such. And everything becomes so real when that camera comes in close and looks into the actor's eyes. In *The Prisoner of Second Avenue*, we had the story of a middle-aged man out of work, unable to get another job, and having a nervous breakdown. Peter Falk gave a fine performance in the theater and got laughs in his broad stage presentation. But when it was adapted to film (and I played the lead part), the reality of the situation on film hit the audience very hard. Although the elements of comedy were there, the circumstances were so pitiful that the audience was not sure it was supposed to laugh."

Comedy is part of living, and people will always want to laugh. Little distinguished comedy and humor have come from totalitarian states, which suggests that the people living there may lack the perspective that comes with a healthy dose of ridicule. Wherever people can enjoy a good laugh at their own foibles and pretensions, as Americans do, there is a bright prospect that things may be seen as they are, with hope of betterment in the future. In laughter there is truth.

VILMOS ZSIGMOND

*Vilmos Zsigmond, distinguished director of photography, adds his expertise to this chapter. Zsigmond's many credits include* Deliverance, McCabe and Mrs. Miller, *and* The Witches of Eastwick. *He has been nominated for an Acad-* emy *Award for Cinematography for his work on the* The Deer Hunter *and* The River *and was awarded an Oscar for his filming of* Close Encounters of the Third Kind.

# Eight

# THE CINEMATOGRAPHER

*with Vilmos Zsigmond*

CINEMATOGRAPHY—LIKE EDITING—HAS emancipated the audience from the bondage of a single location or point of view. Every scene on the screen presents the viewer with a new position or angle from which to see through the roving eye of the camera. Fundamental to understanding the nature of film is the realization that *the mobile camera keeps the viewer always in motion*. Although the viewer may be comfortably seated on a fixed chair, he or she can nevertheless fly from an aerial view of a battlefield, to a close-up of an actor's face, to an object at which the actor is peering, to a parallel race with a vehicle in which the spectator shares the emotions and experiences of its riders. The viewer is carried along to see the action instantly from the best points of view, whether it is a creeping microbe, the kiss of a woman, the gallop of a horseman, or the silent trajectory of a spaceship hurtling through intergalactic time (Figure 8.1).

The cinematographer must draw the viewer's attention to what the director has indicated is the dramatic focus of the story at any given moment—this is the essence of cinematography. The subject most important in a scene, at any given point in time and space, may be a performer, an object, a setting, a landscape, or even a mood—whatever the director has decided in advance he or she wants the dramatic point to be—but the cinematographer must understand the intent before setting up the camera.

The primary functions of the cinematographer (formally called the director of photography) are the lighting of scenes and the setup of camera positions within the scene in relation to the talent. The cinematographer lights the scenes based on his or her own experience, with reference to the work of the production designer; the setup of the camera positions is done in collaboration with the director. From the outset the cinematographer is involved with the selection of locations, budget problems (Is the dramatic action worth the cost of an expensive setup?), making lighting charts, blocking camera movements, selecting lenses and filters, and exchanging information with the director. The cinematographer is more than the photographic hand of the director while shooting is in progress. The director of photography typically knows the script as well as the talent in order to think through the best cinematic interpretation and to anticipate moves by the player to be properly followed on film—one reason why so many former cinematographers have successfully made the move into directing films.

Artistic style is an expression of personality, and many cinematographers have a mien that pervades their work. Some camerapeople take a realistic approach to their films, a documentary style in which the viewer can almost taste the dirt and feel the grime (Figure 8.2). For films about mean streets and debunking westerns, this grainy interpretation is an enhancement of the content. Other cinematographers prefer rich colors, voluptuous textures, rippling glitter, and a sense of classical relationships, exquisitely composed and lighted, with the character moving into and out of "just so" compositions. This approach would be fine for musicals and historical films. Still others render life in stark and expressionistic terms—with Gothic shapes and sterile landscapes as an expression of a bleak view

"The director and the cinematographer are partners. It is these two . . . who are responsible for making the movies. The fight for the look of the film is usually with the studio. They often don't understand what the director and the cinematographer are attempting to do. The studios eventually understand what we are doing when the Academy Awards are given out and there are box office profits in the millions and millions of dollars."

—*Vilmos Zsigmond*

211

FIGURE 8.1 *Vilmos Zsigmond emphatically states, "I consider lighting not as turning on lights, but rather as taking it away from the object that you're shooting. I light with shadows. . . . Silhouettes, shadows, and light are more important than color. Color is like visual sound effects."*

**CLOSE ENCOUNTERS OF THE THIRD KIND** (U.S.A., 1977) DIRECTED BY STEVEN SPIELBERG.

FIGURE 8.2   *"The Deer Hunter is probably one of my most realistic pictures,"* says Zsigmond. *"I wanted everything to look very real. When you think of a steel mill town, it's smoky, hazy, with bluish tones outside. Inside the mill, you have the warm tones of the furnaces and the lighting in contrast to the outside. The Vietnam footage was very sharp and had a newsreel quality to it. Up in the mountains, I wanted to create the feeling of freedom and freshness. There was no flashing or diffusion there."*

**213**
RELATIONSHIPS

of life—a style suitable for psychodramas.

The techniques of cinematography are also expressions of artistic temperament. Some individuals make use of the mobile camera. Some prefer static shots to facilitate dynamic editing. Some prefer the zoom lens and others an array of prime lenses. Some like to use many filtered effects, and others leave effects for the film laboratory to create. The professional cinematographer can, of course, adapt concepts and techniques according to the themes and textures of the film and the will of the director, as a skilled artist may work in many styles. Most of them, however, become noted for doing a certain kind of film extremely well with a visual consistency that becomes a professional signature.

## Relationships

Cinematography for feature films is an art form on a par with painting and sculpture. The best camerapeople are artists who are sought out by directors with scripts containing content that is suitable for the style of a given cinematographer. Sometimes great directors become partners in association with great cinematographers in the production of classic films so intimate was the understanding between them. One recalls D. W. Griffith with cameraman Billy Bitzer, Sergei Eisenstein with Edouard Tissé, William Wyler with Gregg Toland, Woody Allen with Gordon Willis, Alfred Hitchcock with Robert Burke. Each enriched the other's work, the two achieving more in creative synthesis than either might have done without the other.

### Cinematographer and Director

The interaction between director and cinematographer is often critical to the suc-

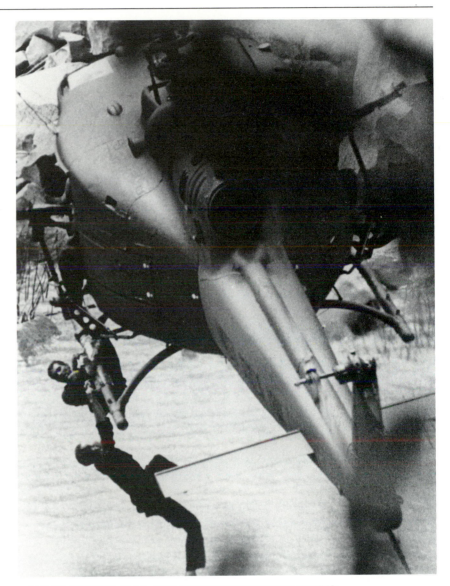

**THE DEER HUNTER** (U.S.A., 1978) DIRECTED BY MICHAEL CIMINO.

**MCCABE AND MRS. MILLER** (U.S.A., 1971) DIRECTED BY ROBERT ALTMAN.

FIGURE 8.3  McCabe and Mrs. Miller *is an unflinching look at the Old West in which corporations hire killers to destroy those who stand in their way, widows are forced into prostitution, and drug addiction rivals drunkenness as an escape from misery. Warren Beatty gives a brilliant performance as the erratic poker player who loses at cards and life, whereas Julie Christie is the convincing embodiment of the madam who does what she has to do in running a brothel, then retreats to the solace of opium dreams.*

*Flashing the film was first used in color film in American cinema by Vilmos Zsigmond in* McCabe and Mrs. Miller. *Flashing means giving the film a slight exposure to reduce the contrast and bring up the shadow areas of a film. Director Robert Altman told Zsigmond to begin photography early in the morning, so early that there was no reading on the light meter. The director said, "Shoot it anyway." The forced processing required to get an image on the exposed footage also meant Zsigmond had to underexpose shots rendered under full illumination in order to preserve a grain consistent with those photographed under low light. This yielded a slight coarseness of image texture that enhanced the gritty themes of* McCabe and Mrs. Miller.

cess of the film. "Much depends," according to Vilmos Zsigmond, "upon the temperament and the experience of the director. The cinematographer must never push his [or her] perception of how the film should be photographed, or assume the functions and prerogatives of the director—or even make suggestions—until it is apparent that such is willingly accepted by the person designated as the director. This is a matter of professional judgment, and the cinematographer should help only as much as the director is willing to let him [or her] help. Some directors, such as Stanley Kubrick, insist upon controlling every aspect of cinematography from the beginning to the end of the film, essentially without input from the director of photography. Other directors, such as Robert Altman are flexible and improvisational. He begins with a script but creates freely while on location and accepts ideas from others that may greatly enrich the film. In situations of the latter kind, the . . . [cinematographer] may offer welcome suggestions that add unexpected dimensions to the motion picture" (Figure 8.3).

Zsigmond continues, "Some directors are newcomers from other disciplines—

FIGURE 8.4 *The cast of* The River *went to Tennessee a month before production. Director Rydell asked Mel Gibson to learn to drive a tractor, and Sissy Spacek literally moved into the main farmhouse where she baked breads and pies and served them to the crew. Rydell said he chose Mel Gibson for his "exciting, rough but vulnerable qualities."*

*In* The River, *Zsigmond had a director who shared his convictions about the importance of poetry and realism in lighting. Rydell, in fact, uses the term* poetic realism *to describe his overall directorial approach to this film.*

theater, writing, editing—and need guidance to be sure that the footage being photographed may be suitably edited later. In the latter instance the cinematographer may actually be teaching a fledgling director how to photograph in master scene technique until that phase of competence is reached where the new commander-in-chief turns and says, 'I'm the director and we'll shoot it this way.' Then the cinematographer should withdraw and let the director handle it alone.

"The novice director sometimes forgets to look through the lens to see what the camera sees," Zsigmond explains. "This is not true of the experienced directors, who set up every camera position and are aware at all times of the camera. Some of the less experienced ones, however, have their hands full dealing with the performance of the talent and leave much discretionary judgment to the . . . [cinematographer]. The cinematographer often knows a great deal about editing and can see the movie being cut as it is being photographed. He [or she] can often perceive that a certain scene will be edited too slowly if played in full and knows that the editor will need to cut to something else at a given dramatic point. Moreover, the inexperienced director may think that a close medium shot is a close-up when it is a medium shot, and

**THE RIVER** DIRECTED BY MARK RYDELL.

so forth. The cinematographer may need to suggest that while we are getting this excellent performance, can we also come in a little tighter for a close-up? This is necessary only until the new director quickly grasps what is required and assumes command of the situation. Most are receptive to suggestions that will help them make the transition to full directorial control" (Figure 8.4).

### Cinematographer and Others

Vilmos Zsigmond makes it clear that any attempt by a cinematographer to influence a dramatic performance for the sake of visual effect would result in eviction from the set. "Usually, there are excellent relations between talent and cinematographer. The players are keenly aware that how they are photographed may affect how they are perceived by the viewers, which in turn may affect their entire careers. A temperamental performer may fight with the director, but not with the . . . [cameraperson]. The cinematographer in turn tries for a good relationship with the talent, to make the actor or actress feel that the lighting and the camera angle will show them at their best. In the case of veteran performers—sensitive about the encroachments of age as revealed in a close-up—the kindly cinematographer will use a diffusion filter without being asked. The relationship between director, player, and cinematographer may become quite close during rehearsals and principal cinematography."

The production designer works closely with the cinematographer in creating sets and providing motivation for interior lighting. "Without a good production designer for interiors," says Zsigmond, "a cinematographer is in trouble." The production designer is the person who creates the mood and ambience of the film, and it is often the responsibility of the director of photography to recreate the *mise-en-scène* of a design on film.

The production designer is extremely important to the work of the cinematographer. This art director creates the milieu of the film and provides most of the opportunities for plausible lighting for the director of photography on those scenes involving interior settings. The illustrations that accompany this portion of the text reveal a setting in three stages of completion and show how carefully the execution may follow the original painting.

These illustrations display the original conception of the throne room for *Camelot*, conceived by art director Ed. Carrere (Figure 8.5), construction of the sets (Figure 8.6), through final use as an interior set for principal cinematography (Figure 8.7). The execution of the final form is changed only in the respect that the suspended crown of the drawing has been changed to five windows that suggest the crown without stating it. Note how the diffused lighting at the midpoint of the completed set has greatly enhanced the sense of depth and majesty.

Sometimes the production designer may influence a story while filming is in progress. Vilmos Zsigmond recounts how, during the location shooting of *McCabe and Mrs. Miller*, the production designer Leon Erickson suggested that the brothel sequences of the film would not be authentic unless they included a functioning bath house. Director Robert Altman thought it over, appreciated the advice of an expert, and requested construction of a usable bath house. Some of the most charming sequences of the film depicted harlots and customers running in and out of clouds of steam. Moreover, cast and crew enjoyed having a hot bath themselves every night after a day of hard work on location. The work of the production designer frequently goes beyond drawing a conception of the sets to actually supervising their construction to assure authenticity, as Erickson did in the making of *McCabe and Mrs. Miller*.

The cinematographer works with two other persons: the storyboard artist, whose drawings are the basis of master scene cinematography; and the assistant director, who handles the traffic.

"The director is in charge of the talent," avers Zsigmond, "and the cinematographer is in charge of the set."

FIGURE 8.5 *This is the original design for the Great Hall and Throne Room of Camelot, created by art director Ed. Carrere.*

**217**
RELATIONSHIPS

**CAMELOT** (U.S.A., 1967) DIRECTED BY JOSHUA LOGAN.

FIGURE 8.6 *The Great Hall and Throne Room, shown here under construction, arches over an area of twenty thousand feet, giving a cathedrallike aura of splendor.*

**CAMELOT** DIRECTED BY JOSHUA LOGAN.

FIGURE 8.7  *Crowds now throng the completed Great Hall and Throne Room of Camelot with principal cinematography underway.*

**219**
RELATIONSHIPS

**CAMELOT** DIRECTED BY JOSHUA LOGAN.

## Rehearsals and Blocking Action

During rehearsals the director-player-cinematographer relationship comes together (Figure 8.8). The director will block the action and rehearse the talent in relation to the hypothetical placement of a camera under the watchful eyes of the cinematographer. The latter can see where the talent will move and stand, how the lights should be placed and directed, what lenses will be required, and how to plan for the laying of dolly tracks if necessary. The dramatic sequence is then broken down into master scenes and camera positions in a dialogue between director and cinematographer, with a determination made of the chronological order in which the shots will be photographed: now a master scene, now a panning shot, now a two-shot, now a close-up reaction, and so forth. The cinematographer must be present during rehearsals to smooth out lighting and photography problems so that when principal cinematography begins everyone may concentrate on the players' performance.

## The Screen

The screen is the canvas of the cinematographer. Ideally the framed proportions of a scene should be modified as a painting is to suit the proportions of a subject; the screen proportions of a redwood tree would be tall, a river would be wide, and so forth. A verity of the medium, however, is the fixed proportions of the aspect ratio of a given film, regardless of its changing proportions of content—a parameter within which the filmmaker must work. The standard aspect ratio of films used to be 3 to 4, but most theatrical aspect ratios today range between 1 to 1.65 and 1 to 1.85, with Cinemascope at 1 to 2.33. The format chosen depends upon the nature of the subject and the financial factors but once chosen all the content within the image must relate to that aspect ratio.

The advent of wide-screen cinema generated immediate concern for the desecration of artistic elements hitherto developed, as had the innovation of other new technical developments. The broad horizontal spread would, it was feared, lead to cluttered compositions at opposite extremes. It would fill the screen with more details and centers of interest than the viewer could absorb, destroying the sense of intimacy in close-ups. And above all, it would diminish the dynamism of editing.

The initial impact of the wide screen justified these concerns. With time however, filmmakers made the width work for them; they designed the extremes of the screen to enhance the center of interest and not distract or create multiple centers of interest; they created a greater sense of realism for the viewer; they filled the viewer's peripheral vision; and they exploited the expressiveness of the human face in even tighter close-ups. Editing did suffer, however, in the sense that real time and distance returned, and dynamic montage was displaced in emphasis by exquisite cinematography. Epic productions, in particular, are suitable for the use of wide-screen techniques because the wider format fills the peripheral vision and enhances the viewer's feeling of being there.

## Film and Filters

Film stock adds a significant dimension of aesthetic and psychological connotation to an image through the perceptibility of the grain. The coarser the grain (within reason) the greater the sense that life is grim,

FIGURE 8.8 *The cinematographer strives for a good relationship with the actors, such as John Cryer, because they will perform better if they feel comfortable and that they are among friends. Zsigmond says, "They should feel every minute that you are trying to light them nicely, take care of them visually so they will look their* best. *The ideal situation is when the cinematographer gives them no instruction at all at the time of cinematography so they can concentrate on their roles, their lines, their characterization. If I were to tell an actress to move over so I could see her better, the director would throw me off the set."*

**221**

FILM AND FILTERS

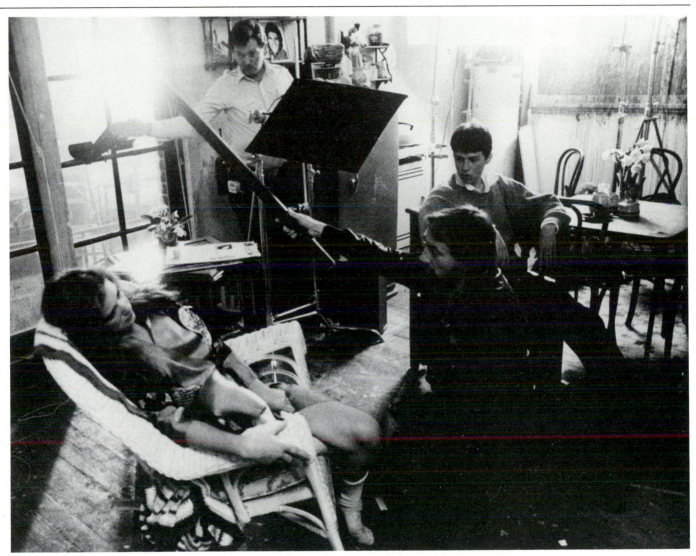

life is earnest. War films, such as *The Killing Fields*, are typically made with an essentially coarse film grain to enhance the documentary sense of reality. Fine-grain film stocks are used whenever the subject calls for a polished interpretation. A film with music, *Amadeus* was exquisitely fine-grained to capture the richness of court life in the days of Mozart with all its pomp and glitter. In both instances the texture

of the theme and story dictated the texture of the film grain.

Similarly, the exposure and processing of the film stock will modify its color and grain. If a film is slightly underexposed at the time of cinematography, it will maximize the color potential of the film stock and render it with voluptuous richness. *Yentl*, a film with music, was slightly underexposed throughout to enhance the color chroma. Films may be slightly over-exposed to connote a sense of sterility and flatness in the lives of the subjects, as in *The Last Detail*. Vilmos Zsigmond comments, "The remarkable image quality of *Butch Cassidy and the Sundance Kid*—a sense of the glaring light of the open West—was achieved by overexposing the film and underprocessing it to bring up the details in shadow areas."

*Flashing the film* means giving the film stock a slight exposure at the laboratory before using it during principal photography in order to reduce the contrast and bring up the shadowed areas of the film. Preflashing film stock ensures consistency of tone throughout the film. According to Zsigmond, "Postflashing, after the film is exposed but before it is processed, achieves the same effect but with better control. . . . All of these subtle manipulations of grain, color, and tone add sophisticated nuances of meaning to interpretations of the story."

Filters may be used to induce a wide variety of effects. If the clouds in the sky are too wispy during location cinematography, and the director wishes to emphasize their presence for dramatic effect, the cinematographer may insert a polarized filter to enhance the clouds' contrast against the blue sky. If the director wishes to connote the warmth of a love scene, he or she may call for the director of photography to add a warm-colored filter to the lens or warm-colored gels before the lamps illuminating the scene.

The latter approach was taken a step further by Vilmos Zsigmond during principal cinematography of *Cinderella Liberty*, a rather seamy story about a prostitute with a heart of brass and a sailor with a heart of gold (Figure 8.9). He says, "The interior scenes were grubby to capture the texture of the theme and the story, yet the subjects seemed more vital and alive than their environment. This effect was achieved by means of putting a warm gel over the main light and a blue gel over the fill (shadow) light, heightening the color of the subjects within the somberness of a slum environment." The uses of filters and their interpretive values are extensive, exceeding the parameters of this book: diffusion filters to soften age lines, day-for-night filters to shoot a night scene in broad daylight, and so on.

## Milieu

Locations and settings are important in creating the proper environment for a character; every aspect of the scene should say something visually about the story and the theme. A mediocre director or cinematographer will settle for the expedient (a tree is a tree, a rock is a rock, and so forth) and photograph in settings that are convenient rather than convincing for the texture of the film. The artist will seek out locations or create settings that are the very essence of the mood and theme at a given point in the story. In the conclusion of *Citizen Kane*, for example, the tycoon's home at Xanadu is an enormous high-ceiling castle with polished floors and ornate fireplaces, cluttered with statuary and a beautiful wife who is also a prop. The house is not a home but an ostentatious facade, connoting success without savor.

The meanings of context may be extended into symbolic clothing or even personal grooming to reveal states of mind. A woman may appear at the beginning of a film to be beautifully coiffured and personally composed. But, as her self-assurance disintegrates under the stress of successive crises, she becomes unravelled visually in loosening strands of hair, indif-

FIGURE 8.9 *Regarding James Caan, director Mark Rydell says, "He has enormous gifts and is terribly true as an actor. I felt that he could give the character of the sailor something very male, very strong—silent strong—and solid."*

*In this film Zsigmond created an interesting separation of his characters from their settings through lighting. The two lead characters were lighted with warm and cool gels, to enhance their sense of vitality, whereas the dinginess of the backgrounds were lighted normally or with available light. Charles Champlin wrote, "The acting and the top-rate moody-cinematography by Vilmos Zsigmond are everything in* Cinderella Liberty." *Los Angeles Times, December 9, 1973*

**CINDERELLA LIBERTY** DIRECTED BY MARK RYDELL.

ference to makeup, and mismatched clothing carelessly worn. The crumbling of her poise may be visually echoed in the settings of her life in which a well-kept home or place of occupation grinds down from order into slovenly disarray.

Zsigmond observes, "Viewer expectations of how polished the characters and settings should be have changed since the glory days of studio production when everything was rendered to perfection in every detail. Heroines would climb out of vats of boiling oil with their makeup perfect and every hair in place, dressed for breakfast at Tiffany's. Thanks to decades of news magazines, documentary films, war movies, the filmed civil rights disorders of the Sixties and Seventies, and, importantly, the many feature films made with documentary film techniques the public has come to accept and expect films to be closer approximations of reality. Location cinematography is now the rule rather than the exception, and filmmakers do not hesitate to scout the entire world to find just the right settings to express the milieu and atmospherics for their story."

In addition to settings and clothing there are props that may acquire special significance. Glass, for example, is a popular device in German cinema for use as a Brechtian distancing device between people who can see each other and talk to each other but are separated spiritually. In *Paris, Texas*, a film written by Sam Shepard but directed by German Wim Wenders, the divorced man and woman converse with each other (in a brothel) through glass—sitting three feet apart. *Paris, Texas* is really a German film and gives the typical European intellectual's perception of American life as rootless and ruthless. Scene after scene presented prop after prop symbolizing despair and sterility, including a painting of the Statue of Liberty on an alley wall facing the back entrance to a brothel. A little of this goes a long way. Symbolic props may add richness, however, if done tastefully.

## Lighting

Lighting serves two equally important functions: to illuminate the subject for cinematography; and to interpret the director's themes, characterizations, and story at a given point in time. Artificial lighting is sometimes as important for exteriors as it is for interiors.

Zsigmond says, "The cinematographer is responsible for lighting the set, with the assistance of a gaffer, an electrician, and, like an artist, he [or she] 'paints' with illumination to create mood. The most astonishing range of interpretations is possible through the manipulation of light intensities, colors, angles, textures, and patterns of light and dark. One actor or actress, posing without expression, may be given a dozen identities, a hundred personalities, a thousand shades of emotional meaning through evocative plays of light and shadow. One cannot exaggerate the importance of lighting in creating emotional qualities in cinema."

### Basic Lighting Concepts

Certain principles of illumination must be understood in order to appreciate lighting for cinema and to perceive what is intended by various kinds of lighting.

The *key-to-fill lighting ratio*—the proportionate amount of light falling on the subject from the primary source as compared to the amount coming from the secondary source—affects the mood of the scene and the interpretation of the subject.

FIGURE 8.10  *In this scene with Meryl Streep and Malick Bowens, the two figures are lighted from below eye level in part to indicate the horror of having been mauled by a lion. Ordinary lighting—with the key light above—would have changed the extraordinary event to something ordinary. The performances by Streep and Bowens were very moving.*

*Richard Schickel wrote of Streep's performance, "Always at her best when challenged to leave her own time and place for regions more passionate and generous, Streep embodies an aristocrat's arrogance toward the unknown and an artist's vulnerability to it." "Cinema,"* Time, *December 16, 1985*

**OUT OF AFRICA** DIRECTED BY SYDNEY POLLACK.

The more harshly lighted a face is, in its key-to-fill proportions, the more turgid its expression seems (Figure 8.10). Faces contorted with fear or anger in a quarrel are often harshly lighted to reflect the emotions of the confrontation. If a person's face is illuminated with little plastic modeling, the lighting creates an impression of candor, good will, gaiety. Move the direction of the key light around toward the rear of the subject, throwing the person's face into shadow, and the subject acquires an aura of mystery or menace.

The height of the key light also affects the viewer's interpretation of the subject. The normal direction of illumination is by overhead lighting from the sun. Any lowering of this height to eye level or below begins to give the person an unnatural appearance. In psychodramas in which surface normality is underlain with mental aberrations or evil abnormality, the subject is frequently key-lighted at shoulder level—in a setting otherwise lighted from a normal direction—to make the viewer feel uneasy about that particular person.

The more the event taking place suggests horror—for whatever reason—the more appropriate it is to illuminate the scene with the key light below eye level.

### Tonality

Tonality, the overall proportion of light to dark in a scene, is important in creating mood and atmosphere and interpreting the subject to the viewer. Emotional connotations are created according to whether the scene is illuminated in *low-key, high-key,* or *narrative tonality.*

*Low-key tonality* means that more than half the image area is devoted to darks and

**SOPHIE'S CHOICE** DIRECTED BY ALAN J. PAKULA.

FIGURE 8.11 *The deep brooding melancholy of Sophie, played by Meryl Streep, is echoed in the low-key tonality of the lighting, with most of the image area in darkness. Here the lighting complements the tragedy of Sophie's memory of having to choose which of her children would die in a Nazi gas chamber.*

*Charles Scott wrote, "Make no mistake about Meryl Streep. She is one of the most genuinely great actresses of our time. Her talent is far more than the total of the accents she has mastered, and her expertise with accents is merely prologue to the depth of characterizations. She is resourceful, inventive, many-sided and immensely gifted." Parade Magazine, January 22, 1989.*

halftone values (Figure 8.11). Low-key tonality creates an aura of ominous foreboding, of implied menace, of imagined fears of the night. Or, given a man and a woman as camera subjects, it may offer the suffused mystery of romance.

*High-key tonality* means that more than half the image area is committed to light, bright values (Figure 8.12). High-key tonality most often implies cheerfulness and gaiety, the tonality that characterizes most comedies and musicals. When carried to extremes, however, high-key tonality may be used to create a sense of barrenness and sterility, as in a desert scene or a science fiction film about the antiseptic world of a technological tomorrow.

With both low-key and high-key lighting, the illumination of the subject remains at the same level of intensity except in a night scene. The illusions of low-key and high-key tonality are created by changing the proportions of the image area given over to darks, halftones, and light areas, not by changing the intensity of illumination on the subject. Reducing the light level on a subject in a low-key scene would make it appear underexposed; increasing the light level in a high-key scene would make it appear overexposed.

*Narrative tonality* falls between the other two extremes in its allocation of light and dark tonalities (Figure 8.13). As the term implies, narrative tonalities are used in straightforward action devoid of extreme emotional overtones in which the subjects are illuminated simply so that the viewer can easily follow the action.

FIGURE 8.12  *The high-key tonality of the set-* *ting echoes the comic overtones of this scene in* *which a young man (David Villalpando, left)* *discusses his plans to find work in the United* *States with his older friend and mentor* *(Rudolfo Alejandre). The earnest young* *Guatemalan learns that in order to pass for* *being Mexican he must leaven every sentence* *with profanities and obscenities.*

**EL NORTE** (U.S.A., 1983) DIRECTED BY GREGORY NAVA.

FIGURE 8.13  *The narrative tonality of this scene contains balanced values from light to dark. A young woman (Zaide Silvia Gutierrez) relaxes alongside a Guatemalan moun-* *tain lake while washing clothing for her family, before she undertakes the trek to the United States to seek work with her brother.*

**EL NORTE** DIRECTED BY GREGORY NAVA.

*Motivation*

Lighting should be as motivated as the subject's performance and not exist merely so that the viewer can see what has been photographed. Illumination should imply something about the story, theme, and characterization at each point in time. Lighting should arouse interest, build emotion, create mood and atmosphere, and direct the viewer's gaze to whatever is in dramatic focus. As a rule, the filmmaker uses these working principles:

Dark against light for simple narrative statements (Figure 8.14).

Light against dark for mood and atmosphere (Figure 8.15).

Splashes of light or dark for depth and mood.

Abstract patterns of shadow to connote disturbed emotions (Figure 8.16).

Within this formula characters may, according to the emotional content, be photographed as follows:

FIGURE 8.14 *The value contrast of a darker head against the lighter lampshade helps to bring the dramatic focus to the candidate, Robert Redford, seen here with Karen Carlson. Redford says about the film, "This one . . . will be entertaining and authentic to the last detail [in its treatment of] the underlying charade of 'real' political campaigning."*

**THE CANDIDATE** (U.S.A., 1972) DIRECTED BY MICHAEL RITCHIE.

FIGURE 8.15 *Spencer Tracy is the dramatic focus on the screen in large measure because his white shirt is the lightest spot on the screen. In a scene having a broad spectrum of values from light to dark, the lightest area will draw the gaze of the viewer.*

**GUESS WHO'S COMING TO DINNER** DIRECTED BY STANLEY KRAMER.

**THE BALLAD OF GREGORIO CORTEZ** (U.S.A., 1982) DIRECTED BY ROBERT M. YOUNG.

FIGURE 8.16  *A converging pattern of iron bars and shadowed bars gives expressionistic form to the terror of a boy being clapped into a jail cell in this shot of Mico Olmos as the son of Gregorio Cortez, played by Edward James Olmos.*

*This film is based on a popular* corrido *(ballad) that is sung along the Mexican border where the events of 1901 actually took place. Cortez, a cowhand, kills a sheriff in self-defense, triggering a manhunt led by the Texas Rangers and six hundred pursuers who are unable to capture him. Only when his family is thrown into prison does he surrender to authorities.*

If two persons are facing each other in a conversation or a love scene, the lighting may be motivated from a single direction—the lens softened by a filter—to imply that this relationship is innocuous if not loving.

If the same two persons are confronting each other in a quarrel, they may each be lighted from opposite directions—harshly—with a dummy light bulb hung between them to motivate the lighting. As one character gains dominance over the other, the change in relative strength may be implied by lighting a performer's movements and subordinating the loser's features into shadow.

Lighting techniques are used to control the viewer's gaze through the use of light and shadow patterns such as these:

Blocks of light may lead to a subject's head, shadows may be used to frame it, with the shapes of each directing the viewer's gaze (Figure 8.17).

Wall shadows may substitute for a poor filmmaker's set—shadows from a venetian blind creating an office, shad-

FIGURE 8.17 *The powerful shadow slashing across the picture leads the viewer's gaze directly to the center of attention, the face of Isabelle Adjani. This strong abstract shape is representative of the ways a cinematographer may use design to control dramatic focus in a scene that is otherwise cluttered, in this instance with rats.*

*Lucy Harker wrote, "Intense, brooding, and willful are the adjectives most commonly applied to Isabelle Adjani, the star of* Nosferatu the Vampyre. *Her beauty and immense talent are of course also mentioned, but they have been rather taken for granted—by the French—since her teenage years at the Comedie Française. This independence of spirit has characterized her every move since that time."* Pressbook, 1979, 20th Century-Fox.

**NOSFERATU THE VAMPIRE** (GERMANY, 1979) DIRECTED BY WERNER HERZOG.

**GONE WITH THE WIND** (U.S.A., 1939) DIRECTED BY VICTOR FLEMING.

FIGURE 8.18 *Broken light patterns on the wall connote the disturbed, uncertain situation as Vivien Leigh, in her role as Scarlett O'Hara, confronts a Yankee deserter bent on looting her home in this epic film about the Civil War.*

ows from a tree branch transforming the corner of a parking lot into a park.

Splashes of light down a darkened corridor wall may imply depth and enhance perspective.

Light or shadow patterns irregularly splashed on a wall in low-key lighting may engender a mood of confusion and uncertainty (Figure 8.18).

The curse of multiple shadows, when the performer opens a door to pass from one room to the next, may be ameliorated by illuminating the next room decisively lighter or darker than the exit room.

Even crowd control is possible through lighting techniques. A *scrim* (piece of gauze mounted before a lamp) may be cut to illuminate the subject more sharply than the same light falling on the rest of the crowd and thereby draw the viewer's gaze by a subtle difference in the texture of illumination.

*Recognition Factors*

Lighting a subject for cinematography is governed by four factors of viewer recognition: *line* (Figure 8.19), *mass and value*, *texture*, and *color*.

*Lines* and outlines tell the viewer the most about the subject. The configuration of a woman with a given hairstyle and clothing style may enable a friend to recognize her a long distance away simply

FIGURE 8.19 *Linear lighting may be used to create a delicate, almost lacy mood, as in this romantic scene with Jarl Kulle and Bibi Andersson. Linear lighting often comes from behind the subject and enables the cinematographer to suggest more than he or she illuminates by the simple expedient of breaking up space areas with splashes of light. Here a splash of light on the flowers and the lattice-work of light on the windows and walls psychologically fill the spaces.*

**THE DEVIL'S EYE** (SWEDEN, 1960) DIRECTED BY INGMAR BERGMAN.

COURTESY OF JANUS FILMS

FIGURE 8.20 *Mass, modeling, and values may be used to create a sense of depth even though the dramatic focus is confined to an area no larger than one corner of a restaurant table. The glasses and shakers on the tablecloth create a distinct foreground: the subject Wallace Shawn—leaning on his arm and fully modeled—creates a middle ground; the reflection of Andre in the mirror adds the background, for an effect of depth. The dramatic focus on the subject is further enhanced by the linear thrust of the mirror frame and the diagonal thrust of the arm and hand. This seemingly casual scene was in reality composed with care.*

**MY DINNER WITH ANDRE** (FRANCE, 1981) DIRECTED BY LOUIS MALLE.

FIGURE 8.21 *Textures add what might be called the culinary dimension in the lighting of a scene. We can sense the dark-brown taste of poverty in the jumbled mess and junk, the grubbiness and squalor—picked out by the light—in this scene with Sophia Loren.*

**TWO WOMEN** (ITALY, 1960) DIRECTED BY VITTORIO DE SICA.

through the familiarity of her outline. Let that woman adopt a radical change of hairstyle or differing mode of dress and the friend may fail to recognize her until she is close enough to see her face. Lighting a subject for quick recognition means lighting for linear configuration.

*Mass and value*, next in importance, are related factors that involve lighting the subject with chiaroscuro modeling and a range of values from light to dark that emphasize the three-dimensional form of the subject (Figure 8.20). The illusion of depth in a scene may be enhanced by progressively reducing the fullness of the lighting of each subject as it recedes in the distance, lighting foreground subjects with a strong sense of mass, middle-ground subjects with a flatter rendition, and background subjects with nearly a one-dimensional silhouette.

*Texture* is important as a recognition factor because of what may be termed the culinary appeal of realism (Figure 8.21). Emphasis on the textures of a subject can make it seem so real the viewer can almost touch it, feel it, taste it. The more intimate the dramatic mood, the closer the scene size, the more important becomes the factor of textures. A scene may be enhanced in appeal by visual textures that range from silk on a woman's skin to mud caked on a soldier's boots.

*Color* is an eye-catching element that contributes greatly to a film's enrichment and the public's enjoyment. Some narrative films—such as musicals, historical films, and others requiring pageantry—receive an emotional shot in the arm by color. And yet, color must be kept under control by the proper use of gray-scale contrast relationships—lines, masses, and values—to be sure the image is easy to understand and the chroma (intensity) of the colors does not detract from the center of attention in a scene.

Vilmos Zsigmond insists, however, "I am not one of those who yearn for black and white cinema, and mourn for an art form lost. Any emotional effect a director might want in monochrome, I can achieve in a color film. I can make it feel like black and white by controlling the colors in the settings through the use of gels on the lamps and filters on the lenses and by the way it is processed and printed in the laboratory. *Deliverance*, *Cinderella Liberty*, and *McCabe and Mrs. Miller* were given a black and white look by these means but rendered on color film stock. I would almost go so far as to say that there is little or no place for monochromatic film in contemporary filmmaking."

## Lighting Environments

Illumination of a setting presents different kinds of problems depending upon whether the cinematography is exterior or interior and whether the story's dramatic action occurs during the day or night.

### Exteriors

Superficially we might assume that cinematography outside would offer fewer problems because the great Fresnel in the sky provides the key light. The sun, however, presents as many problems as solutions (Figure 8.22). In early morning and late evening the rays of the sun are filtered by the atmosphere so that more red comes through in the spectrum of light than is true during the middle of the day. Moreover, the sun ducks behind clouds, hides behind overcast, changes patterns of light and dark in the landscape as it arcs across the sky, and acts capriciously, preventing the filmmakers from photographing individual scenes over a period of days and weeks that are supposed to represent a brief continuum of time when edited together. And, the sun may depart in a squall and leave a dampened cast and crew staring forlornly at a week of steady rain.

Moreover, altitude, latitude, and time of day may be a problem in location shooting. Cinematography in the high mountains produces footage with color heavily skewed toward blue because of the thinner atmosphere. When filming in the far North in the winter, the sun may not rise until nine or ten o'clock in the morning, and color temperature problems may be subordinate to getting an exposure.

Lighting continuity and consistency in daylight exterior shooting separates the fine cinematographer from the mediocre cinematographer. Whether the scenes were photographed in early morning, high noon, or sinking twilight, if the footage is intended to be edited as a short continuum of time it must be photographed to appear on the screen as if the cinematography were completed in five minutes.

With new film stocks that have more sensitive film emulsions, colored gels on exterior lamps to modify color temperatures, and increased sophistication of film laboratories in making color corrections the skilled cinematographer can compensate during exterior cinematography to ensure consistent lighting throughout the footage.

Night exterior cinematography on lo-

**DELIVERANCE** (U.S.A., 1972) DIRECTED BY JOHN BOORMAN.

FIGURE 8.22    *Exterior shooting in a shadowed environment, such as the forests that were the setting for* Deliverance, *involved problems of consistency at different times of day. To resolve the problems, Zsigmond picked the time of day he wished to be the defining atmosphere of the film. The sun during the noon hours gave the forest an interesting dappled pattern of light and shadow that was to become the lighting style. The morning and late afternoon light in a forest is, however, diffused light because it is deflected and absorbed by the foliage.*

*Cinematography could not, for obvious reasons, be restricted to the noon hour, and it was decided to bring in high-intensity lights and a power generator in order to direct lights down through the trees and onto the stream to create the same dappled effects of foliage from early morning to late afternoon. This enabled principal cinematography to proceed from morning until dusk every day in the forest without regard to the de facto position of the sun.*

*Jon Voight, shown here, says, "I lost some fifteen pounds paddling that canoe. I spent so much time underwater I thought we were doing a Jacques Cousteau documentary."*

cation is analogous to interior cinematography in the sense that everything must be illuminated by artificial light in a way that is convincing (Figure 8.23). Obviously, a cinematographer cannot hope to illuminate the sky at night; on the other hand, the cinematographer cannot leave vast black holes in the image area. To create a sense of realism, the areas of dramatic action are fully illuminated and those areas that are inherently dark are broken with light flecks that seem plausible. Large dark areas in city and country can be broken by pinpoints of unexplained lights that imply that something is out there. Moonlight may be simulated during daylight photography by using filters and then printing with a deep-blue gel in the film laboratory.

Vilmos Zsigmond had lighting problems of epic proportions when illuminating the night scene landing of a huge spaceship amid hundreds of people in *Close Encounters of the Third Kind*. Director Steven Spielberg had discarded the option of using special effects to combine the images of people with that of a small model, photographed separately and printed together, because he did not want the degraded image quality that comes from a second generation negative. Therefore, it was decided to do everything lifesize and illuminate the entire landing as a single scene. A set about three hundred feet in length was produced along with the bottom half of a spaceship about two hundred feet wide. Cables lowered the spaceship to the thronging crowd and artificial lights illuminated the entire set (Figure 8.1).

*Brute lights*, the most powerful illumination lamps available, were arrayed in banks a hundred feet above the ground, and mirrors and reflectors enhanced the effect so that the spaceship seemed to come down in a blaze of lights and power.

Cinematographer Zsigmond comments, "I had to turn on three brutes before there was the slightest discernible difference on the ground. We used all the electricity that Alabama could give us and it still was not enough." But it was enough. Spielberg's confidence in his director of photography was vindicated by an Academy Award for cinematography and profits of over a hundred million dollars in the studio's coffers after the release of *Close Encounters of the Third Kind*.

Vilmos Zsigmond concludes, "Location cinematography is not the financial bargain one might think, depending on where the location is and how much of it is to be rendered with dialogue. Ambient noise on location often requires that dialogue be rerecorded in the studio after production. Moreover, the cost of transporting and supporting cast and crew in the field are high, and location cinematography may end up costing more than building a set in a studio."

*Interiors*

Most professional cinematographers prefer to work on a set than to work on location because they have better control over the conditions of lighting and cinematography. An interior set is constructed to be disassembled to permit lighting and cinematography from any angle. This breakdown capability speeds up production and, in the end, lowers production costs. On location the cinematographer may be required to improvise with inadequate or poorly controlled light. Or, the cinematographer may be backed up against an immovable wall and forced to use a wideangle lens that induces distortions in the image. In feature films other than those needing a gritty documentary look, the trend is toward producing films in the tra-

FIGURE 8.23 *"People were brainwashed in the big studio days,"* Zsigmond says, *"to believe that everything would be glass-smooth in all aspects of cinematography. All that changed, however, when people got used to seeing images that were imperfect through publications like* Life *magazine and by watching documentary films shown over television. Over the past twenty years small imperfections have come to be tolerated, expected, and indeed exploited to* enhance the sense of realism."

This night scene was illuminated almost entirely with exterior studio lamps erected at the direction of Vilmos Zsigmond; the "rain" was provided by overhead sprinklers.

Zsigmond adds, *"I like to use kickers or backlight, and I like to separate people from the background, but if I cannot justify the lighting, I will not do it. For me the reality is more important."*

VILMOS ZSIGMOND

ditional studio setting so that all elements may be controlled (Figure 8.24).

Zsigmond says, "The first consideration in lighting a set is the nature of the story and the mood of the scene. The same room would be lighted quite differently for a tragedy, a comedy, or an action film. The mood of the scene within the story is equally important: love scenes, murders, and slapstick pratfalls require, under most circumstances, different kinds of illumination for the same interiors. Those who are particularly interested in lighting for mood would be well-advised to study the paintings of Rembrandt, Vermeer, Ter Borch, and other Dutch masters; they thought in terms of painting with light for dramatic effects.

"The light that establishes the mood of the set," Zsigmond continues, "is the first lamp I turn on, and all other illumination is subordinated to that. It may be the key light coming through a window, a fill light coming from another room, a background light throwing the subject into silhouette, a bounce light to create the diffused ambience of daylight. But I do that first and work from there."

That first light on the set is like the first sketch of an artist. If visual justification for the mood light is not there, the production designer may be called upon to provide such motivation so the cinematographer can create the proper mood. Most production designers are tuned in to such things, but if not, the director of photography may ask him or her to provide the necessary windows, room lamps, or skylights to motivate the desired effects.

Creating the illusion of depth within an interior—foreground, middle ground, background—is done by stratified values in lighting. For example, the foreground may be shadowed dark, the middle ground may be light, the background may

be halftone. Clear separations in depth will then be apparent. Whenever dealing with crowd scenes, such as the wedding sequence of *The Deer Hunter*, Zsigmond uses stratified lighting to achieve visual order in what might otherwise seem a chaotic scene. "It is important to think in terms of black and white value contrasts when lighting for color. When a film finds its way to television, or for some reason has to be viewed in black and white, the images should be as clearly perceived as when originally projected on the screen in full color."

Many directors of photography prefer to experiment for effects—to improvise Rand move lights about the set—rather than to follow a strict formula of key, fill, and background lights. Others like to plan their lighting positions in advance, note them on paper, and give them to the gaffer as instructions to follow—after which the cinematographer makes adjustments while working with a light meter.

Experiments sometimes take place on the set against the wishes of the cinematographer. In one film, director Warren Beatty walked about the set turning off lights to achieve unusual mood effects, much to the consternation of the director of photography. Every time a light was turned off, the cinematographer wrote on the slate, "Filmed under protest." The motion picture he filmed under duress eventually brought him an Academy Award for cinematography, which he did not protest.

"The litmus test for good lighting is," Zsigmond says, "how the players look in the scene as they appear on the set for rehearsals and principal cinematography. Levels of light are adjusted and moved, if need be, to be supportive of the talent and to play its role in the final composition of the scene before cinematography."

VILMOS ZSIGMOND

FIGURE 8.24    *This picture gives some grip-level insights into the techniques used by Vilmos Zsigmond in illuminating a set with lamps, gobos, and reflectors to create the illusion of natural lighting from a window. The first lamp he sets up is the one that creates a proper mood for the scene according to the ambience demanded by the dramatic situation. His selection may range from a key light on the subject for exposition to bouncing light off the ceiling for low-key background mood illumination.*

*"Painting is a great influence on my lighting of interiors. Whenever I can I go to mu-seums and look at the classics, the Dutch masters. What they did with light are the basics for . . . [cinematographers]. We can learn from them."*

*When questioned about the absence of sound equipment in this scene, he says, "Of course sound is very important. But I would definitely develop the visuals more and the sound would be like music or effects. Take* Gandhi *or* Amadeus *and you will see the visuals so well done that you are overwhelmed by them. That's the kind of film I would like to direct."*

## Composition

The performers are intended to be the dramatic focus in most of a film's shots. If the scenes are badly composed, however, the viewer's gaze may wander all over a wide screen in an establishing shot before it finds the director's intent. Making the talent the *artistic* center of attention in a composition—so the viewer's gaze goes instantly to the intended dramatic focus, even a person in a crowd scene—requires that the cinematographer use elements of design similar to those used by a painter. Among these are *dominance of the lightest area, sharply focused over softly defined subjects, composition in depth, larger subjects over smaller,* and *brighter colors over duller.*

### Dominance of the Lightest Area

The dominance of the lightest area on the screen is reflected in the hoary Saturday afternoon serial-western practice of putting the cowboy-hero under a white hat or over a white horse (Figure 8.25). No matter how large the posse or how much dust it raised, the audience full of yelling boys was transfixed by that white spot thundering across the screen.

The same principal of light dominance holds true at more sophisticated levels. Given a scene with a normal range of values from light to dark, the viewer's gaze will go quickly to the lightest point. And the darker the tonality of the scene, the more quickly the viewer will see the lightest value. The exception occurs when the story takes place in an environment with light or white values, such as a snowy winter scene, in which a dark subject will attract the eye. The danger here is that any secondary dark subject may distract the viewer's attention. The spectator may look first at the background forest, second at a stone outcropping, and third at the subject of the scene. Light environments with a dark subject are more vulnerable to distraction than are dark or halftone settings with a light subject.

### Sharply Defined over Softly Defined Subjects

Sharply defined subjects tend to dominate over softly defined subjects, primarily because they are easier to see and understand (Figure 8.26). Trying to perceive a fuzzy subject is hard work, and if there is another subject on the screen that is easier to understand, the audience will probably look at that.

Controlling the viewer's gaze by sharpness of focus is accomplished in two ways.

The cinematographer may use a lens with shallow visual properties (a long focal length lens) so that the subject will be in focus, but everything before and behind the subject will be out of focus.

The shift-focus (or rack-focus) technique may be used to focus first on one subject, as he speaks, and then shift to a second subject, as she responds, with each subject taking a turn at being in and out of focus according to his or her dramatic dominance.

### Composition in Depth

The arrangement of shapes on film is an attempt to create the illusion of three dimensions on a two-dimensional surface. Design in cinema has certain elements in common with painting: the arrangement of lines, forms, values, textures, and colors

FIGURE 8.25 *The white square towel fram-ing the head of Akousa Busia draws the view-er's gaze to her first. It is the lightest area in a normal narrative scene and therefore the first seen. Here we see Danny Glover as Mister peer-ing over the clothesline at the girl given to him for his wife (Whoopi Goldberg), and her sister. Busia says, "Celie's sister Nettie is Celie's touch-stone. There is a deep love, the kind few people ever know. Nettie is a character I feel very blessed to have played."*

**THE COLOR PURPLE** DIRECTED BY STEVEN SPIELBERG.

FIGURE 8.26 *The dramatic focus goes instantly to the dark figure in pursuit, rather than to the intended victim, because (in part) it is in sharp focus whereas the distant figure is in soft focus.*

FIGURE 8.27 *Geometric shapes (right) are powerful forces in controlling the center of attention. Here the ellipse of the hat brim and the rectangle of the podium bring the viewer's gaze inexorably to the compositional confluence of the scene:* Citizen Kane *(Orson Welles). The genius of Orson Welles made* Citizen Kane *one of the great seminal films in the evolution of modern cinema.*

**THE HOUSE OF WAX** (U.S.A., 1953) DIRECTED BY ANDRÉ DE TOTH.

for aesthetically pleasing effect. Movement is an element found in cinema that is not found in painting; all of the following concepts may be modified by any movement on the screen.

Geometric shapes are the common denominators of compositional structure underlying all of the visual arts (Figure 8.27). Any perceptive viewer who studies great art will perceive compositional skeletons in the forms of triangles, squares, *S* curves, circles, and *x* directional lines as a means of controlling the viewer's gaze and unifying a composition.

The thrust of a major shape or line brings the audience's attention to the subject in dramatic focus.

Perspective lines and composition of subjects in depth send the gaze of the

**CITIZEN KANE** (U.S.A., 1941) DIRECTED BY ORSON WELLES.

FIGURE 8.28   *Perspective lines, architectural lines, and a low camera angle combine here to make Orson Welles seem joined to his wife played by Ruth Warrick only in ostentation in their loveless marriage. Here the setting is the* dramatic focus, and it has more to say about the relationship between husband and wife than anything said or done by the two characters at this point in the story.

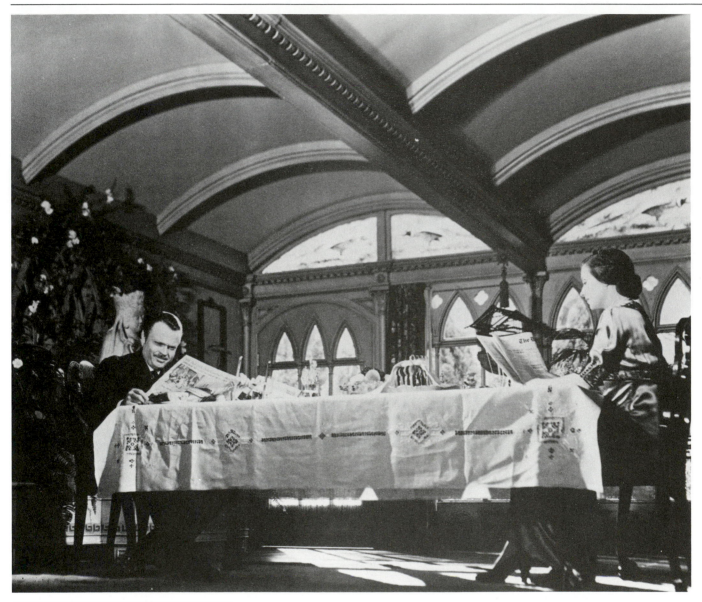

**CITIZEN KANE** DIRECTED BY ORSON WELLES.

FIGURE 8.29 *Depth may be added by photographing one person over the shoulder of the second, rather than merely presenting a close-up of the person speaking, as in this view of Lupe Ontiveros, as Nacha. This technique is so strongly identified with films made in the United States that it is known in Europe as the "American shot."*

**EL NORTE** DIRECTED BY GREGORY NAVA.

© 1983 CINECOM INTERNATIONAL FILMS. USED BY PERMISSION.

spectator to the subject in dramatic focus (Figure 8.28).

Creating the illusion of depth on film is an art within an art, with five major principles:

Place subjects in a foreground-middle-ground-background depth relationship, using their diminution of size to create the cinematic illusion of three dimensions on a two-dimensional screen.

Select camera angles that emphasize natural perspective lines, such as those of buildings, streets, and landscapes. A three-quarters view of a subject or even a slight angle presents the strong modeling and perspective lines that enhance three dimensionality.

Require people or other mobile subjects to move from background to foreground, or foreground to background, thereby expanding or reducing their mass area on the screen and effecting an apparent change of distance.

Photograph over-the-shoulder shots of objects as well as people to emphasize depth (Figure 8.29).

Select lenses with optical properties to expand or contract the illusion of depth in photographing the scene.

The viewer's perceptions of the life on the screen may also be implicitly extended beyond the limits of the image area. For example, by having the hand of a performer—standing outside the scope of the lens—thrust into the image area, an impression is created that an entire figure, an entire world, exists just beyond the limits of the screen. With the enhancement of off-screen voices, music, and sound effects, the viewer may be made to feel that the framed area of the screen is no boundary to the screen world.

Location cinematography tends to be approached differently from studio work in the matter of compositions. The arrangement of shapes on location is more often a matter of discovering natural elements to be exploited than it is forms to be created. Location settings are open arrangements of landscape in which the filmmaker finds a point of view that best

**INTOLERANCE** (U.S.A., 1916) DIRECTED BY D. W. GRIFFITH.

FIGURE 8.30 *When principal photography is to be shot on location, it becomes important to find natural compositions in the landscape. In this scene the director and cinematographer are exploiting the long diagonal tree shadow to create—with the two columns of horsemen—a compositional shape in the form of a giant Z to unite excitingly what would otherwise be a scattered and undramatic composition.*

reveals the dramatic action and achieves required atmospheric characteristics. Location cinematography is usually worked out in discussions between the director and the cinematographer, and there is seldom a serious attempt to make formal arrangements for aesthetic effect (Figure 8.30). The result is spontaneous rather than artfully controlled and as such offers a segment of reality that implicitly extends beyond the frame. People and objects are freely cropped in segments and sections, compositional effects that most viewers accept as part of the world out there. Location cinematography seems to invite camera movement, as if trying to embrace life.

Studio scenes, on the other hand, tend to be conceived and controlled in every shape, line, form, value, and color, with exquisite lighting that creates a feeling of a world complete in itself (Figure 8.31). People and objects are carefully arranged, aesthetic concepts artfully balanced. Such scenes are usually creative, formal, contrived, and to some degree expressionistic. The viewer has the feeling that any action occurring elsewhere will also take place on a designed set that has also been composed in an attractive arrangement of shapes. In some of the higher expressions of the studio approach, such as the interior scenes in *Blue Velvet* and *The Godfather, Part II*, the viewer seems to be watching a fine painting in motion. The studio approach tends to lend itself to dramas that are expressions of ideas and themes because every aspect of the image may be subtly controlled to enhance nuances of meaning.

### Background Shapes

The design of background shapes can keep the attention of the viewer on the subject, but the degree to which the shape controls the viewer's eye depends upon the

FIGURE 8.31   *No one can out-Hollywood Hollywood when it comes to the studio lushness of interior settings. This scene was richly evocative of the themes, characters, and story of a moribund class of American society—the decline of a great family—in its elegance of decor and perfection of design and composition. This is so artfully done that the viewer is tempted to have it enlarged to the size of a painting, frame it, and hang it on a wall for contemplation. Settings like this are intentionally stylized to communicate intellectual as well as emotional ideas.*

**THE MAGNIFICENT AMBERSONS** (U.S.A., 1942) DIRECTED BY ORSON WELLES.

scene size (Figure 8.32). A close-up reveals little context, in most cases, and the background is relatively unimportant. As the scene size increases in scope, however, design of the background shapes becomes increasingly important.

Wide establishing scenes involving vast landscapes or swarming city streets are backgrounds in which the subject may be difficult to see unless the lines of the mountains or the buildings lead to or near the subject. In settings with strong perspective lines, the compositional thrust may carry the viewer's gaze irresistably toward the horizon. In all such cases the subject should be placed so that the compositional thrust is toward or near the player, not away in another direction. Crowd scenes in particular require that the people be arranged so that the abstract shape of each group provides graphic directional lines leading directly to the subject or the player in dramatic focus may be hard to distinguish from the others.

### Larger Subjects over Smaller Subjects

Larger subjects tend to dominate smaller subjects because of their intrinsically greater mass on the screen. This generalization may be modified compositionally as follows: If the larger subject is cropped, whereas the smaller subject stands in the clear, the viewer's gaze will go to the smaller subject. If the smaller subject is in motion, whereas the larger subject is static, the viewer's attention will go to the smaller subject. If both large and small may be clearly seen, however, the larger subject of the two will tend to dominate the scene.

### Brighter Color over Duller Color

Brighter color is dominant over duller color in most circumstances. The specta-tor's gaze will gravitate toward whatever is the lightest and brightest area on the screen. The linking of *lightest* with *brightest* is intentional and important because color has intrinsic values of light to dark, in addition to its intensity of chroma. A person wearing a bright red shirt that has the same value as the background will be more difficult to perceive than if the shirt and the background differ widely in light values.

## Cinematography

Everything discussed to this point leads up to the moment when the director calls out "Action!" and the cinematographer begins to record the behavioral event called acting on film. It all comes together with lens and camera.

There are essentially two ways to photograph a subject at a given scene size. The first is to set up the camera at a suitable distance from the subject to crop the subject—full shot, medium shot, close-up, and so on—to the desired proportions with that particular lens. The second way is to change lenses on the camera, selecting a focal length lens that will have optical characteristics that create the desired image size of the subject on film without changing the camera-to-subject distance. The second alternative is obviously the easier means, but most lenses optically distort the reality that the normal eye perceives.

The camera lens differs from the human eye in that it is undiscriminating: It cannot see true depth, it distorts perspective, it gives false emphasis, and it has only a fraction of a normal person's scope of vision. The human eye, on the other hand, tends to perceive only what the person is interested in—a subjective

**JULIUS CAESAR** (U.S.A., 1953) DIRECTED BY JOSEPH L. MANKIEWICZ.

judgment—not noticing anything considered unimportant.

The cinematographer must therefore use the lenses of the camera, within the limitations of each lens, to approximate the selectivity of the human eye, making the value judgment of what is important to see in a given scene. Then, movements by the subject, the camera, and the lens are fused to approximate human selective perception—and feel *psychologically true*. The filmmaker's need to approximate normal human vision and use optical distortions for emotional effects has led to the development of a wide array of lenses, each having unique properties and uses.

## The Lens

Lenses are generally grouped into four categories according to their *focal length*, a term relating to a lens's magnification power, depth of field (focus), and scope of vision. The four categories in 35-mm are: the wide-angle lens (under 25 mm), the normal lens (25 mm to 65 mm), the long focal length lens (65 mm to 180 mm), and the telephoto lens (180 to 200 mm and longer). Each of these fixed focal lengths has a unique set of optical distortions that may be used to simultaneously photograph and interpret the subject to the viewer. Fixed focal length lenses such as these, also known as *prime lenses* and *hard lenses*, are preferred by many traditional cinematographers for their sharpness of resolution.

Other cinematographers, relatively new to the scene, are selecting the zoom lens for reasons to be discussed later.

### The Wide-Angle Lens

The wide-angle lens has the widest scope of vision, the greatest depth of field (focus), and the strongest proclivity to bend the lines and distort the proportions of the subject (Figure 8.33). At its shortest focal length extreme, the 5-mm fisheye lens presents a wildly distorted view of the world, with all lines bowed and all subjects grotesquely warped in their relative proportions, perspectives, and relationships. The fisheye lens is used when distortion is psychologically desirable, as when presenting the point of view of a person who is drunk, drugged, or mentally disturbed. At the other extreme of the wide-angle length, 25 mm, the optical distortions are reduced nearly to the point of normality but still warp the images enough to hint that something is awry.

The excellent focusing depth of the wide-angle lens makes it useful whenever two subjects at different distances are to be kept in focus simultaneously. Another use relates to its tendency to exaggerate the feeling of distance. A small room may appear much deeper on film when photographed with a wide-angle lens, and any movements by a subject from foreground to background will tend to be exaggerated.

### The Normal Lens

The normal lens is so called because it most nearly approximates the perceptions of a normal human eye as it sees the relative proportions of people and objects in perspective (Figure 8.34). Its depth of field and ability to resolve content before and behind the subject roughly approximate human vision.

When changing from a wide-angle to a normal lens, the effect is that of moving closer to the subject, narrowing the scope of vision. It also reveals the subject in greater detail and softens the focus on the foreground and the background. Linear distortion does enter in, subtly, at both ends of the normal spectrum. At the short focal length end there is a slight tendency to warp and distort all subjects in the image area; at the long focal length end there is a slight tendency to flatten perspective, localize the subject, and reduce apparent movements in depth. For most narrative filming intended primarily to tell a story or reveal a process without strong emotional implication, the 40-mm lens—right in the middle—is possibly the most commonly used lens; it is the workhorse of lenses.

### The Long Focal Length Lens

A long focal length lens begins to distort many visual elements from the way they are perceived by the normal human eye (Figure 8.35). When changing from a normal to a long focal length lens, the effect is that of moving even closer to the subject, narrowing the scope of vision, revealing more minute details, and further reducing the depth of field.

One effect of the long focal length lens is to make those subjects in focus appear crowded together as perspective becomes apparently shallower. A second effect is to diffuse those visual elements that lie before and beyond the subject's depth, tending to lift the subject out of context; this effect is used in dramatic films to make young lovers appear in focus only to each other, oblivious to a busy but diffused world. A third effect is to flatten out apparent movements in depth, making them appear slower than they are, an illusion familiar to anyone who has watched a newsreel of racehorses rounding the far turn with their hooves pounding the turf without perceptible progress.

### The Telephoto Lens

A telephoto lens is at the far extreme in focal length from the wide-angle lens and offers, of all the focal lengths, the narrowest scope of vision, the shallowest depth of field, the strongest crowding of visual elements, and the sharpest reduction of apparent movement in depth (Figure 8.36).

The telephoto lens seems to bring the viewer so close to the subject that he or she can see fine details that are barely perceptible to the unaided eye. Those visual elements surrounding the subject in the immediate foreground and background seem to be so densely packed that it often appears as a two-dimensional picture to the viewer. Foreground and background are diffused to abstraction. Movements in depth are flattened to the apparent degree that a character may appear to be running toward the camera for a long time without making perceptible progress. Foreshortening is visually reduced to one-half or two-thirds of its real distance.

In *The Graduate*, the young man Benjamin is running to the church to prevent the marriage of his sweetheart to another man. To reveal Ben's inner feeling of running his heart out but getting nowhere, the director used an extremely long telephoto lens to photograph his desperate race against time. Ben's arms and legs churned furiously, but he was apparently suspended in time and space.

### The Zoom Lens

Vilmos Zsigmond prefers to work with a zoom lens for these reasons: "Because I work in the kinds of movies that use actors and actresses, there is often an element of vanity present in the talent when shooting a close-up: The players want to look as good as possible, and, with a prime lens, a diffusion filter is required. With a zoom lens a slight softness is built into the image quality and less induced diffusion is required. Whenever I find it necessary to mix prime and zoom lenses in a film, I use a diffusion filter with all my prime lens cinematography in order to create a match

FIGURE 8.33    *The four photographs of actress Laura Zimmett (Figures 8.33, 8.34, 8.35, 8.36) were taken at the same camera distance from the subject and illustrate the progressive approach to a subject the cinematographer may take by simply changing lenses.*

*Figure 8.33 was taken with a 25-mm lens; Figure 8.34 was taken with a 50-mm lens;*

*Figure 8.35 was rendered with a 75-mm lens; and Figure 8.36 was photographed with a 100-mm lens.*

*The first photograph (8.33), taken with a short focal length lens, reveals a great deal of the setting and much detail in foreground and background, with Zimmett seeming relatively small in the setting. With each change of lens*

FIGURE 8.33

CHRISSY OGDEN

FIGURE 8.34

CHRISSY OGDEN

to a longer focal length, there is a progressive increase in the apparent size of the subject and a diminution in the importance of the setting, both in relative size and sharpness of focus.

The dramatic focus of a scene is often controlled by the properties of a lens. Short focal length lenses are used when the environment is important. Long focal length lenses are used when the subject is to be separated from his or her background. When photographing interiors, cinematographers must take care to use consistent focal lengths or the backgrounds will pop in and out of focus, changing the dramatic focus.

FIGURE 8.35

CHRISSY OGDEN

FIGURE 8.36

CHRISSY OGDEN

FIGURE 8.37 *Location photography of some-one running or riding sometimes requires that tracks be laid on which to mount a dolly to carry the camera. Many of the trucking shots are not photographed from trucks, but from* *a dolly mounted on tracks. The decision of whether a scene is worth the expense of laying tracks often comes after a huddle between the director and the cinematographer on the ways and means of achieving an effect.*

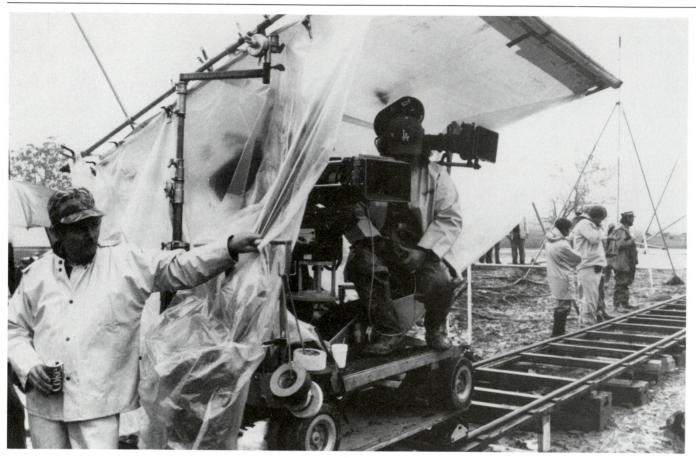

VILMOS ZSIGMOND

of resolution with the zoom lens shots.

"Moreover," Zsigmond says, "I prefer the zoom lens because I can work more quickly in setting up shots and photographing them. A dolly shot, for example, must be set up far more carefully with a prime lens than with a zoom lens because the former does not have the adaptive capability for minor changes (Figure 8.37). If the dolly tracks are not exactly right, or there is a slight difference between what is seen through the viewfinder and what is actually photographed, the dolly tracks must be rebuilt and the scene rephotographed. If a scene requires a 21-mm lens instead of a 20-mm lens in order to be

framed just right, a slight adaptation with the zoom lens will line it up to perfection. There is, moreover, greater adaptability with a zoom lens in dealing with actors. While following two actors in a parallel move, the cinematographer can if desired zoom in a little bit or pull back in order to maintain proper framing. A prime lens, on the other hand, requires that the players and dolly move carefully to prevent the actors from moving into a bad-framing relationship.

"A zoom lens of 20 mm to 100 or 120 mm is most versatile. Given today's high cost of production in which time is money, the zoom lens offers the opportunity for

FIGURE 8.38 *Vilmos Zsigmond comments in passing on the union regulations that stipulate that director of photography and camera operator are two different functions. "There are times in difficult or special circumstances when it is necessary for me to operate the camera myself in order to lead the subject in a certain way,* invest a move with a certain timing, frame up the subject at the beginning or end of a move, and give the shot an aesthetic feeling that can only come with personal operation of the camera." Usually, the photography is done by a camera operator under the supervision of the director of photography.*

257
CHOICES

excellent and efficient cinematography with image quality approximating the selective perception of the human eye."

## Choices

Prime lenses are preferred under certain circumstances. Whenever light levels are extremely low the prime lens should be used because it better transmits available illumination than does a zoom lens. And, whenever there is a wide-angle scene that presents a great deal of detailed information—such as an aerial view looking down at New York City—the prime lens is better able to resolve the small details. Whenever a film is photographed that requires the use of both prime and zoom lenses, it is prudent to use a diffusion filter on the prime lens to ensure matching footage. Otherwise, some perceptive viewers may detect a difference in image resolution.

The decision of when to use a lens in a straightforward narrative fashion and when to use distortion for its interpretive value and emotional impact on the viewer is a matter of artistic and technical judgment by the cinematographer. The optical distortions created by lenses of different focal lengths—linear distortion of perspective, definition control of foreground and background visual elements, and manipulation of apparent movements in depth—are important cinematic considerations discussed in depth with the director. So important is the interpretive value of a lens, however, that a professional cinematographer may select the lens first, and then compose and light the scene.

A second camera with a different lens may be set up beside the first in order to get perfect matching action in two scene sizes with two different lenses used concurrently (Figure 8.38). In a prize-fighting sequence, such as the smashing climax

VILMOS ZSIGMOND

**THE WITCHES OF EASTWICK** (U.S.A., 1987) DIRECTED BY GEORGE MILLER.

FIGURE 8.39 *Vilmos Zsigmond says of his filming of* The Witches of Eastwick: *"Altering reality is where my strength lies as a cameraman. Sure, I can go out and shoot just what is there, but I prefer to create things, to dream things. It is the poetic reality, rather than the natural, that I capture on film." And he adds, "I like using the anamorphic (wide-screen) pro-cess, which I experimented with in Eastwick."*

*Famous for his leading ladies and boudoir mien, Jack Nicholson stars as Daryl Van Horn, the wealthy, eccentric, and charismatic stranger, who takes up residence in one of East-wick's historic mansions and confronts three stunning women upon whom he casts his insidious spell.*

**259**

CHOICES

of *Rocky*, when the situation makes matching action difficult, the use of a second camera is an efficient solution. Zsigmond notes, "A second camera must be used with discretion because of possible lighting problems. What is optimum lighting from one position may be less than optimum from the second camera position, and may result in mismatches of lighting when editing one shot to another. The usual pattern is to have one camera shooting the large master scene and the other the close-up, with the in-betweens photographed in various camera positions."

One more important consideration is deep focus photography, in which the foreground, middle ground, and background are all in sharp focus. This effect is created by using a small f-stop (a small aperture hole) and is used when the environment is thematically important. The interior settings of Xanadu in *Citizen Kane* made a visual statement of the hollow glory and surface success of Kane through deep focus photography of the settings. Careful design of sets and lighting become critically important in deep focus photography. And consistent f-stops must be used in every shot within a scene in order to preclude constant changes of focus in the foreground and background.

Although this information is somewhat technical, we cannot really understand the medium of motion pictures without understanding the rationales and means for creating effects. Why an effect is used and how it is created are part of understanding cinema as art.

Vilmos Zsigmond says in conclusion, "We live in a world of *feelings*. And it is the responsibility of the cinematographer to give visual forms to the feelings that express the director's intent. You know, we . . . [cinematographers] are like painters, but we paint with light and mix with lenses to render our images on film" (Figure 8.39).

*Peter Zinner has a luminous record of achievements in editing for cinema and television: an Academy Award, the British Oscar and the American Cinema Editor's Award for* The Deer Hunter; *an Academy nomination and the American Cinema Editor's Award for* The Godfather, Part II *and* The Professionals; *an Academy nomination for* An Officer and a Gentleman *and* The Godfather, *with an A.C.E. nomination for the latter; and many other feature film credits, which include* A Star Is Born, Lord Jim, Running Brave, *and* In Cold Blood. *His television credits include the miniseries* War and Remembrance *and* The Winds of War, *for which he was nominated for an Emmy.*

CHRISTA ZINNER

*Nine*

# THE EDITOR
## *with Peter Zinner*

THE PIONEERING GIANTS OF CINEMA—D. W. Griffith, Sergei Eisenstein, V. I. Pudovkin—were as much editors as directors. While directing the actors for cinematography, they sought to achieve the effects they would create in editing. All the phases of the production process were kept in mind by these filmmakers. Cinema was not then compartmentalized into highly technical purviews of almost autonomous specialization, as is true today. When Eisenstein directed two shots that were apparently unrelated, he knew the meanings that he would create when they were spliced together into a sequence.

The autonomy of the editor has changed since the days when director and editor were one filmmaker. The advent of sound narrowed the control of editors over the creative elements of cinema by expanding the number of people involved in an increasingly collaborative industry. Where the director-editor was once responsible primarily to the producer and to his or her own creative instincts, the strong administrative control required for creation and distribution of a multifaceted feature film has now placed the editor in a position of being only a part, albeit a vital part, of the film production team.

Today the editor usually has little to do with directing or cinematography, and sometimes does not play a role in productions until the footage is delivered and screened for his or her perusal. To use the metaphor of the hourglass, the editor's role is presently at the narrowest point in production. Above and before the editing phase are the elements of script, acting, directing, lighting, cinematography, and sound recording. The editor then pulls it all together, selecting and eliminating, and gives it the desired form and content as a narrative film. Below and after the midpoint of the hourglass are the postediting additions of music, sound effects, and mixing as indicated by the editor in collaboration with the director. If the director has provided ample coverage, the editor may realize the film in any of a dozen ways.

Nevertheless, it is the editor who "makes the film." Only when the film editor sits down to the Moviola with the photographed scenes and begins to create a continuity order—with actions and reactions and a tempo to which the viewer responds at an almost subliminal level—does the film begin to come alive as cinema. The best-directed, best-photographed film footage may be intrinsically beautiful, but it is seldom a cohesive motion picture that will hold the viewer's interest for long unless it has been creatively and dynamically edited. Conversely, footage mundanely directed may sometimes be transformed into an excellent film by a fine film editor. Editing is near the heart of cinema art, and more than one fiasco has been elevated to the Academy Award level through the imagination and artistry of its editor.

The editor, because he or she understands the elements required to make a viable film, often goes on to become a director of feature films. From the ranks of film editors have come such distinguished directors as Robert Wise, Hal Ashby, Dorothy Arzner, David Lean, John Sturges, and Carol Reed. In the tradition of the total filmmaker, they direct scenes understanding clearly what shots are required to edit a dynamic motion picture.

> "Editing is essentially an art. When to cut, where to cut, and how to cut may be learned in the forms of studied techniques, but the ultimate decision comes from within the artistic sensibilities of the editor. In the end fine editing, as in every art form, is an expression of skill and cultivated talent. The best film editors create what 'feels right' from the fiber of their aesthetic instincts."
> —*Peter Zinner*

## Relationships

The film editor theoretically begins work after the end of principal cinematography, but in reality he or she often works with the writer, director, and producer throughout the realization of the motion picture (Figure 9.1).

### Editor and Director

Because most creative directors conceive their principal cinematography with editing constantly in mind, they may have a clear vision of how they want the film edited so they ask the editor to wait until principal cinematography is completed in order to be present for editing. The director has, under guild regulations, the right to dictate the first edited version. If director and editor have worked together before and both are on the same conceptual wavelength, the director will concede more latitude to the editor.

When a fledgling director is shooting his or her first film, the cinematographer will often assist the novice in shooting footage that can be properly edited. If the film is complex or a high-cost production, the studio may retain the editor to go out on location during principal cinematography to help the new director with setting up some of the scenes and camera angles, and with the preparation of shot lists. A relatively recent trend is to send the editor on location, even with experienced directors, so that plans for editing may be underway while the footage is being photographed, thus enhancing the fluidity of the creative process from beginning to end.

### Editor and Others

Although writer and editor do their creative functions at opposite ends of the production process, a creative relationship exists between them. This may involve dialogue revisions, character changes, post-recording and line dubbing to create voice-over sound for reaction shots and story line.

Peter Zinner comments, "Dramatic emphasis and characterization sometimes change during production and post-production, and the writer may be needed to intensify another story point. Rarely does one find a finished screenplay that has been photographed and edited to end the way it was written. Most scripts will be changed significantly during production and post-production. The final cut of the film is, in reality, the final draft of the screenplay."

Sometimes an editor may be caught in the middle between stubbornly conflicting perceptions of how a film should be edited. There may be conflicts between the director and the producer, the producer and the studio, the studio and the director, or some other permutation. For example, it is axiomatic among major studios that feature films should not exceed two-and-a-half hours in length, and the director may insist on a length of three hours. This sometimes means that the editor stands between impossible demands for loyalty to the director and responsibility to the studio.

When these differences of opinion occur between the powers that be, the editor may act as mediator. A resolution may depend upon how much status the editor has, how convincing he or she can be, and how diplomatic the editor is. Tact ranks high among the required virtues of a film editor.

## Cinematic Editing

The first dramatic films were photographed stage plays in which each player's movements were filmed in their entirety.

FIGURE 9.1 *"A fundamental principle of editing,"* Peter Zinner stresses, *"is that one should form a clear vision of who is carrying the dramatic life of the sequence and edit every scene toward the dramatization of that character."* He admits that cutting toward that end is mostly an intuitive process in which changes are made until it plays right in dramatic form and emotional impact.

*Robert DeNiro made intensive preparations to develop his portrayal of Michael in* The Deer Hunter. *He spent six weeks tramping throughout the Ohio River Valley steel-producing region, talking with mill hands and recording their speech patterns, drinking with them in local bars, and having dinner with them in their homes.*

**THE DEER HUNTER** DIRECTED BY MICHAEL CIMINO.

FIGURE 9.2 *Running Brave is the story of American Sioux Indian Billy Mills, played by Robby Benson, who overcomes the stigma of race and drunken parents to win the ten-thousand meter race at the 1964 Tokyo Olympics. The film was funded by the Ermineskin Indians and photographed at their insistence in Alberta, Canada.*

Presenting dramatic actions in real time and real distance, however, was soon found to be the dullest of film forms. Only when the dramatic actions were broken up into small scenes and edited together to create a sequence more exciting than reality was cinema born as art.

American films are perhaps the leanest films in the world. Every scene and sequence in a film is there for a functional reason: to tell the story, to contribute to the development of a character, to give exposition, to provide humor, to develop mood and atmosphere. Any scene not serving some contributory function to the film story is usually discarded, no matter how succulent the cinematography, for any scene that does not add to the substance of the film detracts from it. The fundamental concerns of cinematic editing relate to *continuity, cinematic time and distance, tempo and suspense, flashback and flashforward, montage,* and *visual simile and metaphor.*

### Continuity

Logical flow or continuity is the essential framework for narrative editing in most dramatic films because the viewer must be oriented at all times to follow the story and be absorbed into the life on the screen. Breaks in continuity often mean breaks in credibility. For simple storytelling the traditional editing approach is long shot, medium shot, close-up, long shot. The long shot establishes the player and his or her setting. The medium shot introduces the player and presents the player doing something typical to reveal his or her character and personality. A close-up gives the viewer an intimate look at the player's face. And then, once more, a full shot to reveal a new character or begin a new dramatic action.

Motivation is an equally important basis for a change of scene. If a woman turns her head to look at something, the next shot should reveal what she is looking at. If what she sees is frightening, it should be followed by a reaction shot revealing her emotions. If her emotion is that of panic, her reaction may be that of flight, and this should be shown in action. In each instance a cut to another scene is motivated by what has preceded it—motivated visually, logically, and emotionally—unless the intent is to create the shock of the totally unexpected.

### Cinematic Time and Distance

Real time and cinematic time are often two different concepts. Real time in film or videotape form presents a full-length visual record of an event that requires as long a time for the viewer to watch as the event took to occur. When real time is used, it yields a film presentation only as exciting as the event staged before the cameras and little more. Real time is used primarily in dialogue scenes with actors who have such a moving presence that their own tempo is the best tempo. But real time, from a cinematic viewpoint, makes pedestrian use of the medium compared to the stimulating quality of edited cinematic time.

Cinematic time consists of holding a shot on the screen only long enough to reveal character, develop plot, make a dramatic point, and then move on to the next shot before the viewer loses interest. The real time of the events being dramatized is almost irrelevant. What counts is that the viewers be shown the significant and dramatic aspects of an event only long enough for them to understand the scene and remain interested. The next shot is then held on the screen for only as long as it takes to

*The first cut of the film, however, was described as "really a mess" by producer Ira Englander. "It was more of a jock film about running than a film dealing with the sensitivity of Billy Mills as a human being."*

*The footage was sent to Peter Zinner for re-editing. He inserted and subtracted shots, revised the tempo and the dramatic focus,* inserted narrative sound bridges with actor Benson reading actual Billy Mills letters to his sister about being an Indian in a white man's world, and so forth. Indians and whites alike applauded at the preview of the Zinner version of Running Brave.

make its dramatic point, and so on, to the end of the film. In this way, events that take days, weeks, months, or years to occur in real time may be compressed into hours or even minutes in cinematic time.

Emotional time is an expression of cinematic time, and as such may be longer or shorter than the real time of the event. For example, the headlong dash of a soldier charging a machine-gun nest lying across fifty feet of open meadow, a matter of seconds in real time, may be lengthened to minutes in cinematic time to express the emotional eternity it seems to the soldier having to make the charge. And the instant of death, in which the hopes, dreams, and aspirations of a person become nothing, may be edited as an event of majesty or as a snuffing out of no consequence by its extension or compression in emotional cinematic time.

Apparent distance is also subject to change through editing. In real distance, for example, a filmed sequence of a businessman leaving his office for the day would depict him clearing his desk, donning his coat, giving last-minute instructions to his secretary, joking with his associates, riding down the elevator to the ground floor, walking across the foyer and through the revolving door to the street—recorded every step of the way by a camera.

In cinematic distance, however, only those events needed to tell the viewer that the businessman was leaving his office would be rendered. There would probably be a scene of him rising from his desk, followed by his arrival home, with the intervening distance eliminated and the transition implied by a dissolve.

Apparent speed may also be modified by editing techniques of cinematic time and distance. A running man in an uncut full shot would seem to be running at no

**RUNNING BRAVE** (CANADA, 1988) DIRECTED BY D. S. EVERETT.

© 1988 ENGLANDER PRODUCTIONS INC. COURTESY OF THE ACADEMY OF MOTION PICTURE ARTS AND SCIENCES.

faster a pace than he is actually running. The man running in a race, as rendered in short cuts of flying feet, flaring nostrils, straining-churning arms, and flying hair will seem to be racing at incredible speed, as in the race for Olympic gold in *Running Brave* (Figure 9.2). Apparent speed may be vastly increased by glimpses of

FIGURE 9.3 *Director Michael Cimino describes his film* The Deer Hunter *in this way: "My movie is basically about friendship and courage and what happens to those qualities under stress. It deals with the extraordinary qualities that so-called ordinary people are able to bring to the face of a crisis, and of their ability to build meaningful lives out of the wreckage brought by events over which they have*

movements whose full portrayal would be slower in effect.

### Tempo and Suspense

Tempo is controlled in film editing by the length of time a shot is held on the screen. As a rule, the longer the shot, the more relaxed the tempo. The shorter the shot, the more exciting. Each extreme and those in between have their proper uses. The classic method of building suspense in dramatic films is to start with long shots and gradually shorten them in order to accelerate the tempo as the film proceeds toward the climax. A climactic finish with a great deal of action is usually cut into very short shots, almost a kaleidoscope of flashing images, in which movement itself becomes the subject.

Conversely, an extremely long shot within the context of a dramatic film is used as a suspense device because the viewer is conditioned to expect a change averaging one every ten to twenty seconds. If a shot is held on the screen for much longer, a tension begins to arise within the viewer and a visceral feeling cries out: "Cut!"

The content of a sequence most frequently determines its editing tempo (Figure 9.3). Scenes of emotional intimacy are often rendered in long moments of quietude with images lingering on the screen to be evocative of the narrative mood. Action films and action portions of any dramatic film may be cut in a snappy fashion that accelerates with the dynamics of the story.

The emotional quality of a scene within a story also determines the length of the shots used in editing it. A sequence displaying a mood of ennui, boredom, or dreariness would probably be cut with long slow-moving scenes, whereas a sequence of shrill excitement, such as the

cossacks' slaughter of the innocents in the Odessa Steps sequence of *The Battleship Potemkin,* would be rendered in short shots of frenetic action.

Suspense is created largely by the editor who, like a magician, manipulates the interests and emotions of the viewer by the way he or she presents some shots and holds back others. The film editor selects and arranges the scene sizes as much for their flavor and impact as for their narrative content.

To gradually quicken the viewer's interest in a person or a subject, the change in scene sizes is slow and progressive: full shot, medium-long shot, medium shot, medium close-up, close-up. This editing concept is useful in crowd sequences when the intent is to single out one person for the viewer's attention without the rigorous impact of a zoom or a radical change of shot size.

For suspense leading to shock, an efficient approach is this: close-up, close-up, close-up, long shot. The series of similar scene sizes lulls the viewer's visual expectations, then the long shot is shocking by its contrast. The principle of building suspense to a shock effect through the repetition of scene sizes followed by a radical change applies to almost any scene size. The progression may be long shot, long shot, long shot, close-up, to the same effect of startling the audience.

Suspense may be further enhanced by delaying the inevitable (Figure 9.4). Adding extra scenes before the dramatic high-point, or having a character make an elaborate ritual of what he or she is about to do, or staging unexpected delays—such as a ringing telephone—can arouse suspense within the audience to the degree that they are literally sitting on the edges of their seats.

Suspense may also be created by the reverse technique of fast-paced editing.

little or no control." John Savage (right), shown here with Robert DeNiro, plays the vulnerable Steven in the close friendship between these two comrades.

Zinner emphasizes the intuitive nature of editing in this example from The Deer Hunter. Two American prisoners of war listen to the Viet Cong enemy, upstairs, force other POW's to play Russian roulette with a loaded revolver. The dramatic focus in editing was an emotional buildup to the point of their decision to somehow escape. The exchange of glances between the prisoners, the fears, the apprehension, the looks of understanding grew to a crescendo. Not a word was spoken between them, but the sequence was edited to create a growing symphony of emotions fused into one meaning: escape!

**THE DEER HUNTER** DIRECTED BY MICHAEL CIMINO.

FIGURE 9.4 *In this suspense film a blind housewife (Audrey Hepburn) is trapped in a dark apartment with a psychopathic killer. Repeated close-ups revealed her frightened face as she crept around to evade him in the dark.*

*Then a wide-angle shot was cut in just as the killer leaped at her from a doorway—an editing technique that made the audience scream with shock.*

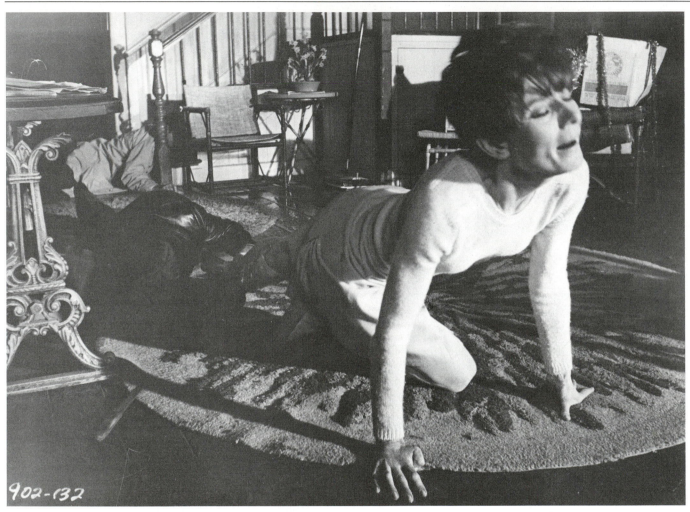

**WAIT UNTIL DARK** (U.S.A., 1967) DIRECTED BY TERENCE YOUNG.

For a chase sequence, such as the smashing conclusion of *The French Connection*, the scenes should vary radically from one to the next for a staccato effect: long shot, close-up, full shot, extreme close-up, medium shot, and so forth (Figure 9.5). Any viewer who has ever seen the portrayal of a cattle stampede, with its rapid cuts from a full shot of the entire herd to a close-up of horse's hooves, from a sea of horns to cowboys' spurs, will recognize this fast-tempo suspense editing concept.

*Flashback and Flashforward*

The flashback is an expositional device used to portray an event that occurred at an earlier time than the present dramatic action shown on the screen. Traditionally, a screen character begins to narrate what happened at that earlier time, a visual effect such as a dissolve provides a transition, and the story of the earlier event is then recounted as if occurring in the present. When the flashback incident has been

FIGURE 9.5 *A battle of wits may be echoed in editing tempo through move and countermove, cut and counterthrust, action and reaction. In this action thriller the adroitness of the Ameri-can detective Popeye Doyle (Gene Hackman) and the French drug smuggler Marcelle (Peter Nicole) were thus played out on the screen through the sharpest editing.*

**THE FRENCH CONNECTION** (U.S.A., 1971) DIRECTED BY WILLIAM FRIEDKIN.

told—in the past-present tense—another visual transition returns the viewer to the original time dimension. Then the dramatic action picks up the story where it left off when the flashback began. Sound as a transition may greatly facilitate the flashback.

The flashforward portrays an event that may occur in the future. Again, a visual transition such as the dissolve may be used to transport the viewer into tomorrowland, and he or she will then witness a sequence that may occur in the future as if it were transpiring in the present.

Peter Zinner favors the use of flashbacks and flashforwards because he considers these concepts a cinematic way of telling a story. These methods were used by him at length in *The Godfather, Part II* to recount the Sicilian childhood of the Mafia chieftain, as well as to reveal his rise to criminal power in America (Figure 9.6).

The kind of flashback Zinner is concerned with preserves the emotional reality of the present with the introduction of the past. Any flashback that dissolves to a story set in the past but that expunges the emotional reality of the present is a poor use of the concept. One frequently finds this ponderous approach in older films in which calender leaves fluttered away to start a new story of twenty years ago, retaining only a remote connection with the emotional present.

A proper use of the flashforward is seen in *The Godfather*. When Marlon Brando in his role as the Godfather is wounded by a gunshot, he can barely whisper, "Where's Michael?" Another son reassures him, "Michael's all right, he's safe." As Brando shakes his head in disbelief, there begins a long, slow dissolve to Sicily where Michael is walking with bodyguards, one of whom will try to assassinate him. The transition to Sicily fuses a flashforward to the com-

ing menace with the emotional context of the present.

### Montage

A *montage*, as defined in American film, is a series of relatively short shots, which, when viewed as a whole, convey a single unified meaning. A montage may be used to connote the passage of a long period of time or cataclysmic events when those elements need to be accounted for in the story but are not intended to be emphasized. Slavko Vorkapich shot and John Hoffman edited the earthquake sequence of *San Francisco* to create, in montage, the violence and excitement of the day-long event in minutes.

Similarly, Peter Zinner created a four-minute montage in *Mahogany* to recount the rise of a woman in the fashion design business. Shots of Diana Ross drawing clothing designs, models displaying her clothing, and Ross herself walking were superimposed over images of Rome, Paris, and New York; the images were unified and cut to the pulse of music.

The montage concept in American film is actually an extension of implicit editing. Dissolves are generally used to connect scenes to imply the passage of time or to create a stream-of-consciousness effect. Dreams and fantasies are almost invariably fused with dissolves to achieve a sense of continuum.

Russian filmmakers, on the other hand, use the montage to portray events of momentous importance rather than as fill-in for short episodes that cannot be accounted for in straight dramatic continuity. In *War and Peace* (1956), for example the climactic battle of Borodino was extremely long; a montage rendered the agonies of two armies locked in mortal combat.

The rest of Europe and many other

FIGURE 9.6 *Peter Zinner recounted the rise of the Godfather in a story that moved back and forth in time, ignoring the traditional chronological approach to storytelling. Using dissolves of varying lengths, related content, similar shapes and forms in the outgoing and incoming scenes, he created lyrical ambience in a tale that fused family loyalty with criminal brutality. Here we see Robert DeNiro as the youthful Godfather killing an adversary who had been extorting money from local merchants, thereby establishing himself as the man in charge. DeNiro received an Academy Award for his role as young Corleone.*

**THE GODFATHER, PART II** DIRECTED BY FRANCIS FORD COPPOLA.

parts of the world use the term *montage* in the same sense that Americans use the term *editing*. For the purposes of this book, however, *montage* is used in the restricted American sense, whereas *editing* is used broadly to define that phase of film production concerned with the selection, cutting, and splicing of scenes into a motion picture.

### Visual Simile and Metaphor

Visual simile and metaphor—the edited visual comment on one subject made by intercutting it with a scene of another subject—was widely used during the silent film days. During one sequence of the Russian film *October*, the strutting portrayal of Kerensky, then premier of the provisional government, was intercut with scenes of a peacock spreading its tail to reveal his allegedly preening vanity.

Visual commentary of this kind (related to implicit editing) fell into disuse in America with the coming of the sound film because the approach is cinematically slow and reflective rather than quick and narrative. Moreover, it lacks dramatic momentum and tends to seem self-consciously arty in a medium characterized, in America, by realism. Visual similes and metaphors are still used frequently by a number of European filmmakers.

## Editing Techniques

Cutting the footage begins in most feature films while principal photography is still in progress. This generally means that all the footage photographed at a given location may be delivered to the editor as raw daily rushes. Inasmuch as the footage shot at a given location comprises a complete sequence, it enables the editor to be-gin working with script and storyboard to make a rough cut of that scene. Footage not yet photographed is represented by white leader in the continuity cut until the footage of those sequences is delivered. Sometimes editing is actually necessary during principal photography in order for the second unit team, the special effects cinematographers, or even the first unit filmmakers to render additional matching cinematography.

Given the complexity of editing film footage, the editor's first job—in association with the director—is to eliminate unusable footage by culling the film rushes for bad takes, duplicated actions, poorly acted close-ups, muffed lines of dialogue, and all superfluous scenes. If several scenes are acceptable from a technical point of view, the selections are narrowed on the basis of three visual criteria:

The content should graphically reveal the script's desired action with economy of viewpoint and simplicity of expression.

The photographic quality should be excellent in terms of composition, exposure, focus, and smoothness of camera and lens movements.

The continuity relationship of a scene should work editorially in relation to those that precede and follow in terms of screen direction and matching action.

When the film editor is concerned with lip-synchronous sound and has narrowed his or her selection of scenes according to the above visual criteria, the editor makes the final selection according to the following considerations: the best sound in terms of clarity, rate of delivery, and naturalness of expression.

Sometimes a scene that is good visually will have poor recorded sound quality. Or, a good sound recording may have a poor

FIGURE 9.7 *Peter Zinner relies on instinct to tell him how long a shot should dominate the screen when the dramatic focus is on the talent. He asks himself, always, "Is she holding the interest of the audience?"*

*Zinner's editing of* An Officer and a Gentleman *received these critical reactions: "An Officer and a Gentleman deserves a 21-gun salute, maybe 42. Rarely does a film come along these* days *with so many finely drawn characters to care about, seemingly much shorter than its two-hour running time." Variety July 19, 1982. Of the star seen here, Debra Winger, David Ansen wrote, "Husky-throated Winger is one of those actresses who seems to open herself totally to the camera: Every moment is raw, honest, freshly discovered." Newsweek, August 7, 1982*

visual counterpart. It then becomes a matter of making the editorial best of a bad bargain. The editor often resolves the dilemma by playing the good sound-recorded voice over some alternative scene that can plausibly be cut into the dialogue—such as another person's reaction.

Interpretation is the key word to a creative director's cutting of a film. When a narrative film is photographed in master scene technique, the sheer quantity of footage from which to make a selection is enormous. The editor screens every frame of film before making a cut in order to get a feel of the story and the characters as the director perceives them, a sense of the texture of the film.

Then the editor takes script in hand and, a sequence at a time, makes a loose continuity cut to see how the narrative works in rough form. There is little fine editing at this early stage because only after the editor has seen the overall story of the film can he or she judge how each individual shot and scene should be cut in relation to the whole. Otherwise, there might be a tendency to edit a scene as if it were the only one in the film, and the interpretation may be inappropriate to the role of that sequence in relation to the film's entirety. The editor must know the script as well as do the director and actors, and the editor must have the creative instinct to sense which of the scenes will be most effective.

The editing techniques most commonly used relate to *player performance*, *rule of thirds*, *timing the cut*, *cutting on movement*, *the cutaway*, *cross-cutting*, *the jump cut*, and *sound in editing*.

### Player Performance

The player's performance quality is an important consideration in deciding whether a shot should be used and in judging how much of the take should be played out.

AN OFFICER AND A GENTLEMAN (U.S.A., 1982) DIRECTED BY TAYLOR HACKFORD.

Peter Zinner follows these procedures in arriving at what he stresses are emotional-aesthetic decisions in editing.

Zinner views film rushes several times, and individual sequences many times more, *to establish which character is carrying the scene*. The dramatic focus of a given sequence determines who will be emphasized and what shots will be used (Figure 9.7). Dramatic emphasis relates also to sound. If the character carrying the scene is reacting to what someone else is saying, then the scene will be played visually on the reactions of the important character in that sequence, rather than on the person speaking. Every cut is determined by the character who is carrying the dramatic life, the dramatic focus, at that point in the story.

Zinner suggests a number of ways in which an editor may improve a player's performance if it needs help. By pruning out the worst parts, an editor can make a mediocre performance seem creditable, a good performance seem outstanding. Little cuts here and there can make an overall difference. The tempo may be improved by tightening a pause or lengthening a reaction shot, by eliminating lines and using cutaways. Occasionally the editor may introduce a pall of silence to enhance a dramatic moment between characters—presented as a series of reactions—a moment that was not originally part of the dramatic concept. At other times the editor may decide to eliminate most or all of a character's dialogue (as happened in *Summer of '42*) and play that person entirely in reaction shots. And it has happened more than once that a player's entire performance has ended up on the cutting-room floor and the narrative told by that character eliminated.

Dramatic focus may be changed from one character to another in editing for reasons having nothing to do with the writer's screenplay or the intent of the director. In *Saving Grace*, an Embassy film in progress, the young Pope of the Catholic Church slips away from the Vatican, bearded to remain incognito, to enrich his faith among the humble peasant folk of Italy. During one sequence being edited by Zinner, there is an encounter among the Pope, a little girl, and her mother. The little girl recognizes the Pope and his true identity becomes their secret; the mother

does not recognize him, however, and her performance—originally intended to be the dramatic focus—was shifted to secondary importance when Zinner decided to emphasize the charming interplay between Pope and child.

A dramatic pause may be created in the editing of dialogue and used to emphasize a dramatic point, in what Zinner calls a "double cut." He cites this example: "The first character speaks and anticipates a response from the second character. Instead of cutting from one person speaking to the second person immediately answering, a dramatic pause is created in this way. The first person speaks in a shot held perhaps a second longer on the screen. Then there is a cut to the person about to speak, followed by a cut back to the first character, also silent, and then a cut to the second person speaking. This introduction of the *two reactions between the dialogue* of the first and the second character greatly heightens suspense. A performance is thereby created with a dimension not originally intended by writer, director, or actors, in a purely editorial form of expression."

Zinner points out that in scenes involving character development, the scene size of each shot is handled carefully. Whether a character has been photographed in full shot, medium shot, or close-up says something about the character at that point in the story, and each shot must be edited in a meaningful way in relation to the scene sizes that precede and follow it. If, during an interplay among several characters, one character begins to become fearful or suspicious, the editor may use tighter and tighter scene sizes of that person to progressively enhance the sense of growing tension.

Sometimes an editor will have the shot needed to make a dramatic point, but the length of the shot may be too short or the movement may be too fast, or it may fail on both counts. Zinner cites a case in point in *Saving Grace*, when the turn of the actor's head was needed as a transition to a flashback. The editor asked the film laboratory to double-print each frame in the shot, thereby doubling the length of the scene, and also to repeat the movement twice—printing forward, then backward, then forward again—as if the actor had turned his head twice before looking into the flashback. Thereby, a short unsuitable turn by the actor was increased in length, doubled in movement, and given the emotional quality needed for the transition. (In industry parlance, this is called *rocking the cut*.)

Zinner cautions, however, that an editor must think twice about manipulating the performance of a truly distinguished actor. The pace of the performance, the pauses, the reactions, the bits of business played with eyes and hands may be so integral a part of an artist's style that to modify it through editing would be courting problems. So solid was the presence of Spencer Tracy and so integrated his style that few editors had the temerity to do more than present his performances at the pace he chose to render them.

## Rule of Thirds

The center of interest in the outgoing and incoming scenes affects where the cut is to be made. If the center of interest is successively within the same one-third of the screen in both scenes, a smoother cut may be made than if the two are widely separated. The close proximity of the center of interest from one shot to the next presents an almost seamless transition to the audience. If, on the other hand, the center of interest is in the lower left of the outgoing scene and the upper right of the incoming scene, there may be moments of confusion as the viewers search for the new center of interest, even though the action has been matched perfectly. If the film is being projected full-size on a wide screen, the spectators may need to search across forty feet of screen if the two succeeding centers of interest are not located in the same one-third of the projected image area.

## Timing the Cut

Timing the cut is an intellectual and artistic decision. First the content should be communicated to the viewer, then an aesthetic decision should be made through the creative judgment of the editor. Much depends upon the scenes that precede and follow the content and what the mood of the scene is. A fast-action scene may require cutting as quickly as content recognition permits. A dialogue sequence may lock the images to the time required to speak the words. A mood sequence may be limited only by the editor's ability to perceive delicate shades of meaning and beauty inherent in the images. Always the editor remembers that individual shots are but a fraction of the overall atmosphere conveyed by expressive scene relationships. At the most subtle and profound levels the decisions are often made not intellectually but, as Zinner repeatedly stresses, intuitively, a process that transcends technique to become art.

Timing the cut may add as much meaning to the scene as exists in the image of the film. Given a scene of a character walking through a setting, the point at which a cut is made may determine the significance of the walk: A stroll of three or four steps will convey a different meaning from one of seven or eight steps. In a shot in which a character makes a turn, the difference of two or three frames may make all the difference in the significance of that turn. If it is a very strong move, the meaning will change according to whether the scene is cut a little short, right in the center, or a little long. "Timing the cut," Zinner emphasizes, "means knowing what dramatic effect one is seeking and then 'feeling' in one's aesthetic being when to snip the scene."

### Cutting on Movement

Cutting on movement is one of the editing uses the master scene technique allows. Because the same dramatic action may be photographed as a full shot, medium shot, and close-up, the film editor may use all three scenes to create a dramatic *single* action, cutting from one scene size to another at any point along the movement.

An important principle exists here: The film editor creates one composite movement comprising many individual shots. He or she selects only those phases of the movement from each component shot with the most graphic images in depicting the action and discards those phases that are dull or superfluous. A composite action is thereby created that is more exciting than a single shot of the same action. In *The Battleship Potemkin*, a classic use of this technique occurs when a sailor—disgusted by the maggots found in his food—seizes the dish and hurls it to the floor. The highly dramatic and symbolic movement was created by Sergei Eisenstein out of several shots photographed from many points of view into a gesture of immense power—through editing.

When making a cut during rapid dramatic action, such as a fight, an important illusionary principle comes into effect: The cut on movement is *not* made at the same phase of the movement in both scene sizes. The editor either deletes or overlaps the first few frames of the second shot according to whether the cut is made from a larger scene size to a smaller or from a smaller to a larger.

If the cut is being made from a larger scene size to a smaller one, such as a long shot to a close-up, the editor *deletes* several frames of movement at the head of the second scene. If such a cut were made without removing a few head frames from the second scene, the action would appear to jump in mid-movement.

Conversely, when a cut is made from a smaller scene size to a larger one, such as a close-up to a full shot, the editor *overlaps the tail action* of the first scene on several frames at the head of the second scene. The edited action briefly duplicates the movement because of the disorienting effect of cutting suddenly from a smaller to a larger scene size. The instant of confusion must be compensated for by briefly duplicating the action for the reorientation of the viewer. If a direct cut were made on the same phase of action in both the close-up and the full shot, there would appear to be several frames missing, even though the action matched.

Certain working principles of editing movement have emerged from the film editor's experience that can be listed here:

For an important visual action, cut to the most graphic viewpoint just before the action occurs. If the action is significant in terms of *story content*, play the entire dramatic action in full without cutting it. If, on the other hand, the action is relatively unimportant to the story, cut on irrelevant but eye-catching movement.

After each action, cut to a reaction. After each reaction, cut to an action. A unique characteristic of dramatic activity in cinema, in contrast to the stage play, is that most actions emphasize the *reactions* to dialogue or events.

In most dramatic sequences the viewer should be shown the next subject he or she expects to see or hear—but not in the *way* expected. A cut to an unusual angle, a camera movement, or a radical change in scene size will add the zest of surprise to the fulfillment of expectation. Combining surprise with fulfillment in every scene is the essence of good editing.

Directional cutting, whereby the movement of the subject in one shot is picked up in the following shot, has important continuity applications. First, it is used to maintain screen direction when creating one movement of a subject out of many shots. Second, it is used on a grander scale to reflect the sweep of mobs or armies, intercutting radically between scene sizes, so that the screen seems swollen with wildly moving images.

### The Cutaway

One might say that the cutaway is the editor's best friend, always there to help out with continuity. *Cutaways* are those shots that have no visual continuity with the previous scene, but have a *logical continuity*. A cutaway shifts the viewer's attention away from the main action to a secondary action occurring at the same time elsewhere, but it is a secondary action related in some way to the main story line. The cutaway has an immense variety of uses.

Dramatic events too expensive or dangerous to stage and photograph may be skirted by a cutaway to the reaction of a spectator. The crash of a jet airliner might be rendered by first showing the plane coming down at a steep angle, then intercutting close-ups of the pilot's desperate face, shots of the failing engines, a rush of approaching earth, and just as the airplane crashes—a cutaway to the reaction of a bystander, accompanied by sounds of screaming metal, shattering glass, and an explosion.

The emotional meaning of an event may also be created by a cutaway to the reaction of a character. An explosion may mean tragedy, humor, fear, mystery, heroism, cowardice—a broad spectrum of meanings—according to the reactions of the screen characters who witness the event. Such a cutaway cues the viewer to the intended emotional response.

Undramatic and time-consuming actions may be completed more quickly through the use of a cutaway than if portrayed in full on the screen. During a recent war movie, for example, a soldier begins to change clothes from his fatigue dress to civilian garb, talking all the while to a comrade. After showing the first soldier sitting down to unlace a boot, the film editor played the rest of the scene on the silent reactions of the second, and then cut back to the first soldier—washed, shaved, and clad in civilian garb—within fifteen seconds of screen time.

Time, suspense, and tempo may be controlled through the use of cutaways. In exciting dramatic situations, such as a chase or a pending life-or-death disaster, cutaways to more peaceful places "back at the ranch" may postpone the climax and raise the emotional temperature of the story.

Cutaways have been used for satirical commentary almost since the birth of cinema. War films that portray soldiers fighting and dying in trenches and jungles would frequently include a cutaway to reveal other men wallowing in luxury by way of comparison.

The cutaway may be used to take the onus off a director's mistake during principal cinematography. If the horseman in a western has been shown going from screen left to screen right and then suddenly is shown illogically reversing direction from right to left, the error may be masked by a cutaway to the face of a person supposedly watching the horseman change directions. The cutaway may also be used to cover up a host of other blunders: mismatched action, inconsistent lighting, jumps in the center of interest from one shot to the next, and so forth.

The *insert* is related to the cutaway. This is usually an extreme close-up of some detail, such as a light switch or a newspaper headline. The insert is often used as a cutaway to hide serious cinematic discrepancies because of its extremely disorienting qualities. An editor can renew the dramatic action in almost any way he or she chooses after using an insert.

### Cross-Cutting or Parallel Editing

Cross-cutting in dramatic film refers to the intercutting of two parallel dramatic actions occurring simultaneously and implies a plot relationship between the two events that will pay off eventually in a confrontation. Typical examples are the marching of armies against each other, a race for an objective, or the hunters and the hunted in a chase sequence. Consistent screen directions in both actions are important because the viewer must immediately know which side he or she is watching every time a cross-cut is made. The battle sequences in *The Birth of a Nation*, *The Red Badge of Courage*, *War and Peace*, and *Apocalypse Now* make clear which side is on the screen through consistent screen directions.

Cross-cutting may be used to maintain interest by switching to the action on the second side when the first side begins to lag in excitement. It may be employed to heighten suspense by showing one side

with its guard down while the other pushes forward. Cross-cutting between parallel sequences, with one placid and the other dynamic, may be cut slowly for the first and dynamically for the second in order to enhance the emotional contrast and add to the suspense (Figure 9.8).

### The Jump Cut

The term *jump cut* has two connotations, one bad and one good. The bad definition refers to mistakes: any noticeable failure to bridge a flow of action when cutting from one shot to the next. This may occur as a consequence of mismatched actions during principal cinematography, inconsistent screen directions, inconsistent lighting, jumps in the center of attention from one part of the screen to the next, and so forth. Most of these jumps are cured by the use of the cutaway, as previously discussed.

When faced with bad mismatches between shots that for reasons of continuity *must* be joined together, Peter Zinner suggests that a trick of seamless editing be used. He marks the exact center of interest of the outgoing scene on the screen of the editing machine, then runs the incoming (mismatched) scene until its center of interest comes as close as possible to that mark. There he makes his cut on outgoing and incoming scenes and splices them center of interest to center of interest, thereby holding the viewer's gaze in the same place and reducing the negative effect of the mismatched visual elements.

*Jump cut* also has positive connotations. Jump cuts are used by Zinner as a transition to move dramatic actions along quickly that might otherwise be too lengthy. In one shot of *Saving Grace*, the Pope (incognito) is walking down a long *S*-curved road toward a distant gathering of people. To play his walk out on the

**THE FRENCH LIEUTENANT'S WOMAN** (U.K., 1981) DIRECTED BY KAREL REISZ.

FIGURE 9.8 *Parallel editing made possible the filmic adaptation of John Fowles's novel. In the cinematic version, there were two parallel stories—one set in the last century and one set in the present—with the same characters played by Meryl Streep and Jeremy Irons in both stories.*

*Kenith L. Simmons wrote in* The French Lieutenant's Woman *as Metaphor: Karel Reisz's Non-Plot Centered Editing: "It is one of the novel's ironies that whereas Charles Smithson thinks he is using his superior sophistication and better means to lead a helpless woman to better her circumstances, it is in fact Charles who is led out of his conventional niche in life to face 'the unplumbed salt, estranging sea of personal freedom.' Parallel editing is responsible for expressing a similar structure in the Reisz/Pinter film."* New Orleans Review, *Summer 1984. John Fowles,* The French Lieutenant's Woman. *Boston and Toronto: Little, Brown. 1969, p. 467.*

FIGURE 9.9 *Peter Zinner uses a sound bridge in editing to pull the audience into the next scene without having any dead emotional pauses hanging on the screen. Dialogue that would normally not be heard until the second scene thereby enters during the first scene. Overlapped dialogue shortens the scenes and increases the tempo as a purely editorial function, without the writer, director, or anyone else*

screen would have seemed interminable. The editor stayed with the actor in his walk until he changed directions at the curve of the road, then he cut to a scene of the Pope fifty feet farther down the road than he really would have been. This is a functional use of the jump cut.

### Sound in Editing

Sound in editing has become a dominant creative force in cinema. The simple realistic origin of dialogue, music, and sound effects has expanded to the point that in *Heaven's Gate* one reel comprised one hundred and twenty-three separate sound tracks needing to be mixed into a single composite sound track. Zinner comments that every time he made a change in the visual editing of *Saving Grace* (after the film had been locked into music and sound effects) "forty or fifty sound tracks needed to be changed." With the advent of Dolby sound and the influence of Walter Murch in creating "total sound"—creative sound to complement the visuals, rather than imitative realistic sounds—the number of sound tracks used to edit a given scene has grown exponentially.

Dialogue scenes are difficult to edit with exciting tempo as long as the editor is enslaved by a locked in picture-and-sound relationship of someone speaking. Again, experience has evolved some editorial techniques to leaven the spoken word.

Overlaps of dialogue from one scene to the next is Peter Zinner's favored way of picking up tempo and smoothness (Figure 9.9). For example, holding the end of the outgoing scene while bringing in the dialogue of the incoming shot before the image can be seen will greatly speed up the emotional time. Zinner uses four, five, or six seconds of overlapped dialogue, but submits that even a small overlap of per-

haps a half or a whole word will create transitions smooth and swift in tempo.

A lip-synchronous sentence may also be broken visually to show a reaction shot. Then the listener would become the dramatic focus, accompanied by the voice-over sound of the speaker. This important editing technique is one way of skirting the earthbound quality of lip-synchronous dialogue. A dramatic sequence may begin with a few words of lip-synchronous dialogue, followed by reaction shots, and then conclude with a few words of lip-synchronous dialogue. The audience will be left with the impression of having viewed a completely lip-synchronous scene. Between the first few words and the last there may be a sequence of great cinematic excitement, with the dialogue presented in voice-over.

In addition, there may be delayed reactions, or cuts to details of hands, eyes, or lips rendered in subtle movements that speak eloquently in the tongues of silence. If a performer has delivered poor dialogue or the director wishes to change the meaning of a sequence, the editor may change the portrayal of a character from that of a speaking part to one that is pure action. For this approach to be viable, however, the images must be interesting. If the director is so word-oriented that the scenes consist of little more than close-ups of people talking from different points of view, the most skillful editor will have problems generating excitement.

Seldom are action and dialogue sequences intermixed. Usually the working pattern tends to be either-or. Either the narrative is told through action with cinematic time and distance, or it is rendered in dialogue in sequences staged for that purpose that accept the limitations imposed by lip-synchronous speech.

Music and sound effects may reverse their usual subordinate relationship to the changing anything. The emotional time of The Deer Hunter *may have been accelerated by half through the use of overlapped dialogue, as in this scene with Meryl Streep.*

Her comment about the role says much about Streep's professionalism. "My role is that of a stabilizing force. . . . I wouldn't call this a strong woman's part. The fact is this is a man's story, and my character is called upon to be there—strong and supportive for the men. That concept is not anywhere close to my personal values. But, don't get me wrong, working with such fine actors was just wonderful." Stephen Farber wrote in New West *magazine,* "Meryl Streep, as the woman loved by both Nick and Michael, does wonders in fleshing out what might have been a stock, sketchy role."

**THE DEER HUNTER** DIRECTED BY MICHAEL CIMINO.

**THE GODFATHER** (U.S.A., 1972) DIRECTED BY FRANCIS FORD COPPOLA.

FIGURE 9.10  *Tonal editing may be used to convey thematic meanings, as Peter Zinner achieved in his editing of* The Godfather. *The wedding sequence (Talia Shire and Marlon Brando shown here), which took place outside, was an evocation of lightness and brightness—deliberately overexposed during principal cine-* *matography at the direction of Francis Ford Coppola. This lightness contrasted with the malevolent darkness of the interior where the evil empire of crime conspired. The contrasting tonality of the scenes was an extra ingredient for commenting on good and evil in the film.*

visuals and provide the themes and emotional thrust for the images being presented (Figures 9.10 and 9.11). Zinner recounts how he conceived the baptism sequence, which concludes *The Godfather*, by rewriting the ending through editing. (He calls it "an act of creative desperation.") Director Francis Ford Coppola had yet to photograph the Sicilian sequences of the film, and he left three reels of film (one take in each reel), eight or nine minutes of the baptism itself, with 75 percent of the concluding footage as yet unphotographed. Coppola said in parting, "Why don't you try and see what you can come up with using whatever you have? I will shoot the rest when I return from Italy." There was no finished script for the concluding sequence, and with these fragments Zinner was asked to create the conclusion of a major motion picture.

The story called for the baptism of the Corleone baby, to be followed by the assassination of the family's enemies. When tentatively edited that way, however, the effect was pedestrian. One day the editor cast aside the incomplete script and decided to create a montage in which the voice of the priest was permitted to run continuously—voice-over—throughout a sequence with cross-cutting between the sacred baptism and the concurrent slaughter of the family's enemies. The priest's question to Michael Corleone, "Do you renounce the devil and all his works?" with Michael's answer "Yes," was instantly followed by the roar of gunfire and the cries of the dying, while the priest intoned his litany.

Zinner culled organ music from the public library and tentatively orchestrated it with the baptism-murders montage; it worked so well with the montage that it was included in the final score of the film. What began as a tame conclusion to an important feature film ended, through in-

**THE GODFATHER** DIRECTED BY FRANCIS FORD COPPOLA

FIGURE 9.11  *James Caan played a tragic figure as the older son of Don Corleone. Quick to fight, quick to lust, passion on a short fuse, he was slain in a vicious gang war he had brought on himself. "He was a bad Don," Brando said of his son in his role as Corleone. "God rest his soul."*

*The editing of his last fight was tight, fast, and staccato.*

spiration, as one of the truly magnificent montages of the sound film era.

Musicals are a favorite genre of Peter Zinner, who is himself a musician. His secret for editing song and dance is *never* to cut on the beat. "Cutting on the beat is 'Mickey Mousing' at best, and, at worst, analogous to pounding the sensibilities of the viewers with the obvious." His preference is to cut before the downbeat of a particular musical phrase—never in the middle or afterward. If the cut is five or six frames ahead of the downbeat, it yields a softness and smoothness analogous to that of overlapping dialogue from scene to scene.

In American editing every scene must contribute to story exposition, develop character, or get a laugh. Another dimension of content, however, seems to be growing in favor—that of savoring experiences with values known to the audience. *Testament*, for example, is a film about the aftermath of nuclear fallout in a small California town, and the viewer is given tender insightful scenes of children being children through a mother's eyes. Perhaps the most poignant scene is that of children acting in a school play, with all the serious intent they bring to it: little voices squeaking portentous dialogue, tiny figures moving clumsily in unaccustomed robes, insecure souls trying to perform well before their parents. This experiential scene savors the beauty of children who would never grow up but would die of radiation sickness. The experiential value is touching for what it is and for what it would never be.

Sound, too, may be used as a kind of cutaway to take the curse off a jump cut. A loud noise, a sudden off-screen shout, a crescendo of music or dialogue may, if dramatically plausible, momentarily distract the viewer's attention from a mismatched image. If done cleverly, the visual jump may slide by before the viewer has recovered from the shock of the distraction and the image is once again dominant.

## Atypical Editing Concepts

A number of ancillary editing concepts have evolved during the growth of cinema that often add sophisticated elements of art and communication to the finished film. These editing concepts are *the shock-attraction principle*, *the flutter cut*, *associative editing*, *metric montage*, *tonal editing*, *dialectical editing of movements*, *linkage*, and *narrative montage*.

### The Shock-Attraction Principle

The shock-attraction principle holds that when two scenes are spliced together they take on a third emotional meaning not inherent in either of the scenes—a concept related to implicit editing. This revolutionary concept was developed by Sergei Eisenstein, who was quick to realize its potential for creating filmic symbols and metaphors. In *October*, for example, when the deposed Premier Kerensky, a former head of the provisional government, is shown ascending a long ornate staircase in the Winter Palace, he is satirized using the shock-attraction principle. Cuts to porcelain peacocks reveal his alleged vanity, scenes of groveling servants, medals, and imperial statues display his love of pomp, and sequences of bowing generals and flunkies allude to his love of power.

Related to the shock-attraction principle is the *creative geography* concept developed by another Russian, Lev Kuleshov. His innovation was to use locales where the story was supposed to take place—establishing shots—and then photograph the scenes out of context at a more convenient location. This technique of fusing through editing the locale of one shot and the dramatic action of other shots is in universal use in motion pictures today.

### The Flutter Cut

The flutter cut is a subjective editing technique in which very short clips of film from different scenes are quickly intercut to staccato effect. This technique is sometimes used much like the dissolve to provide a transition from one scene to another, and sometimes it is used to reveal the subjective feelings of a character. When the flutter cut is used in lieu of a dissolve, short clips from the incoming sequence are cut into the outgoing sequence. These incoming clips are progressively increased in length until the outgoing sequence is itself reduced to short clips—and then phased out—and the incoming sequence is in full possession of the screen.

The flutter cut may be used to bring subjective memories of the past into dramatic actions with a present setting. In *The Pawnbroker*, an old Jewish man watches a gang of hoodlums beating up a boy who attempts to flee by climbing up a fence. This memory is rendered in the present tense by flutter cutting short scenes of his past in a concentration camp with close-ups of the pawnbroker. The flutter cut, if carried far enough, may be extended into a flashback to tell another story with a setting rooted in the past. The flutter cut is a powerful transition to use in creating a crescendo of thought and feeling, building tempo and emotion.

### Associative Editing

Associative editing is the splicing of two scenes in succession with similar-shaped images, such as a cut from the round mouth of a cannon to the rim of a champagne glass. Associative editing is most often used as a transitional device, in lieu of a dissolve or a wipe, to bridge a change of time or location. Sometimes this editing technique is used to connote other meanings. In *Psycho*, for example a woman is stabbed to death while taking a shower. One shot presented a slow zoom-in to an extreme close-up of the iris of her eye, then cut to a close-up of the tub drain with whorls of water running down, a symbol of her life draining away.

### Metric Montage

*Metric montage* refers to an editing technique in which scenes are cut to the beat of a metronome to create a mathematical undercurrent to the overall tempo. Metric montage does not mean, obviously, that a scene is cut on each and every beat. But when a scene is cut, at whatever length, the cut is made right on the beat of the metronome. However long or short a sequence cut to metric montage, its rhythms and progressions are given a mathematical relationship to which most viewers respond with feelings of suspense.

The classic use of metric montage in an American film is in the western *High Noon*. The sheriff of a small town is destined to face four outlaws, one arriving on the noon train, who have sworn to kill him. The tick of the clock counts the fleeting hours, minutes, and seconds even as his friends desert him. The inexorable march of time is reflected in the editing of the film—cut from beginning to end to the beat of a metronome—with the tempo gradually increasing as the story progresses to the climactic shoot-out.

### Tonal Editing

Tonal editing is actually a lighting concept in which succeeding scenes are gradually lightened or darkened to correspond to an improving or deteriorating situation in the story. In Eisenstein's film *October* the deteriorating condition of the workers under the tsarist regime is shown in the gradual darkening of the tonality of each successive shot until the fury of revolution comes. After the revolution the workers' joy is reflected in an immediate lightening of tonality.

### Dialectical Editing

Dialectical editing originated as an attempt by the Russians to fuse ideological thought with cinematic form. Dialectical editing presents a series of mass movements from scene to scene in a given direction, which is visually opposed by a major thrust of opposition, to yield a third meaning of *conflict*. This represents the Marxist-Hegelian principle of thesis, antithesis, synthesis. In Eisenstein's Odessa Steps sequence in *The Battleship Potemkin*, the relentless march of the shooting cossacks down the stairs is countervailed by a pleading woman holding up her child and other desperate flurries of panic to create an emotional third meaning of the futility of appeals to humane feeling under the tsarist regime. The principles of dialectical editing are universally used in war films to reflect the sweep, ebb, and flow of mass battle between opposing armies.

### Linkage

Linkage as an editing concept was developed by another Russian director, V. I. Pudovkin. Linkage defines the individual scene in a film as being analogous to the bricks in a building—without intrinsic meaning until assembled by the film editor. When edited, however, the scenes acquire a *cumulative meaning*, a concept related to the montage. The theory of linkage further holds that symphonies of visual beauty may be edited together regardless of the ugliness of the content in the scenes used to create that beauty. Linkage is the montage concept carried to the extreme, the antithesis of narrative editing, and is most often used in tone-poem and experimental films or in dreamy montage sequences within a narrative film.

### Narrative Montage

The function of a montage in narrative films is most frequently to fill in gaps in a story. Some characters may begin an explanation of an event that would normally require time and effort to present; then a montage presents a series of brief impressionistic scenes that recount everything within a minute or two. In *The Third Man*, a story of drugs and murder in Vienna after World War II, a British officer tells an American author about the corrupt dealings of the latter's friend, Harry Lime, in a montage that recounts the sordid evidence in a minute.

Wartime films frequently utilize a montage comprising scenes of fighting, explosions, tanks, airplanes, and advancing troops to depict a battle. Musicals often make use of a montage to show singing and dancing and exuberant good times. And, the montage is used to show the ravages of time and the change of circumstances in individual characters—as a transitional device from then until now.

A montage should be relatively brief in contemporary cinema or it may break the flow of the story, or, indeed, begin a new story within the greater narrative. Moreover, a montage should be conceived as a whole and perhaps be bound together with music and effects for thematic cohesion. According to Peter Zinner, however, bits of dialogue tend not to work in montages. A montage is a highly generalized form, whereas speech is specific—a different dimension. Speech tends to intrude upon the overview function of the montage.

The role of the film editor is crucial to the success of a motion picture. Despite all that is said and written about *auteurs* and film being a director's medium, cinema is a collaborative art, the excellence of which depends upon the talent of all major participants. Many directors now enjoy unprecedented control over their film projects; moreover, the director decides whether or not an editor may be allowed to function as a creative force in the interpretation of film content.

Some directors edit their films "in the camera" so they may be cut only one way and still make sense. Other directors stand at the editor's elbow as the film is run through the Moviola and demand that the editor be no more than a pair of scissors. The prudent and knowledgeable director will select a creative editor for the same reason he or she hires a good player or director of photography: to use his or her creative talents to evoke dimensions through editing that would not otherwise be present in the film.

Peter Zinner concludes, "Post-production may last far longer than principal photography—and should do so—because the editor is bringing all the elements together that make the final form of the film. Each frame of picture and sound should be weighed in the editor's artistic being, and the cut decided at the exact frame that will convey just the right shade of meaning and just the desired emotional impact on the audience."

WALTER MURCH

*Walter Murch is at the cutting edge of innovation in sound—as well as being a distinguished film editor—and has been recognized as follows: an Academy Award for Sound in* Apocalypse Now, *an Academy nomination for Sound for* The Conversation, *and nominations for Editing of* Julia *and* Apocalypse Now; *the British Academy Award for Editing and Sound in* The Conversation *and a nomination for Editing and Sound in* Apocalypse Now; *and Academy nominations in both Britain and America for Editing of* Julia.

# Ten

# THE SOUND DESIGNER

### *with Walter Murch*

WE CANNOT UNDERSTAND THE role of sound in contemporary cinema without transcending the notion that sound exists solely for audio realism: hearing a door slam when the door closes, hearing a voice speak when the lips move. Although this synchronous sound function is important, it is only one aspect of the role of the sound designer in creating an emotional and intellectual ambience for each sequence within a film and for the film as a whole. In order to understand this broader application of the audio track we must first comprehend the selective role of the mind in relation to hearing.

Unlike the human eye, the ear is essentially omnidirectional and perceives sounds coming from everywhere. When a new sound is added to other sounds, the new sound does not displace the others as occurs when the eyes glance first at one object and then at another. The new sound is added to a sum total of sounds that are collectively heard. The cacophony would tend to become chaotic except that the ear and the mind exercise selective awareness, much as the eyes and mind practice selective perception. Similarly, as the eye (or camera) may be brought to focus on a subject, subordinating what is before and behind it, a significant sound may be selectively perceived by the mind with all other sounds turned down or tuned out to permit concentration on what is meaningful.

For example, a person may be seated in a busy office foyer awaiting an important job interview amid the sounds typical of that environment: telephones ringing in the inner offices and people responding distantly; a typewriter clacking; a clock ticking; and a shuttle of strangers going into and out of the foyer to present requests to the receptionist. As time passes the person may become selectively aware of each of these contemporaneous sounds as they become significant at different points in time.

The person's own name may be mentioned and it will seemingly pop out of the hubbub; time may drag slowly and the tick of the clock may draw attention to the hour; a stranger may come to ask the receptionist to see the employer, triggering apprehension about competition. In each instance a given sound has meaning at that point in time, and each one is attended to selectively in the subordination or elimination—in the mind—of all others. Should an event occur having high emotional value, all sounds may be eclipsed by the mind except the one that seems important at the moment: "You're hired."

So telling is sound that an entire story may be implied through the conceptual presentation of sounds over an image on the screen that is essentially static. In a film about war, for example, a soldier lying in a foxhole may be listening for the sounds of an anticipated night attack. Without moving the viewer could sense an episode through sound effects: the false alarm of a comrade moving about in the dark, the mysterious click of metal on metal, the sudden banging of shutters on a nearby abandoned farmhouse, the hoot of an owl, the rumble of unidentified vehicles and tanks, and finally the barrage and roar of battle. The story has been told of the imagined terrors of the night entirely through sounds.

The use of sound in cinema serves this essential function: selective presentation according to significance at a given point in time. Although two dozen sound tracks may be effectively mixed into one composite track, the competent filmmaker em-

**"Underlying all I have been doing is my belief that the real power of film lies in its ability to alter our subconscious awareness of things in the same manner as dreams. Deep films have a power over our lives that is similar to deep dreams, a power that is mysterious in its sources and the paths through which it moves. Sound is particularly useful in this regard because it is rarely an overt element perceived on its own. It mostly seems hidden and subservient, and this is what makes sound so effective in speaking directly to the subconscious."**
*—Walter Murch*

289

phasizes on the screen the sound that is important—be it dialogue, music, or sound effects, or a created composite.

The possibilities of sound in film are infinitely variable because each of the component sound tracks—voices (dialogue and narration), music, and sound effects—may be recorded separately and then mixed into one track afterward. For example, the voice tracks may be recorded first under ideal circumstances in each dramatic scene, with control over sound perspective and movement. Then music tracks may be recorded to match the cinematography and editing under optimum circumstances for music. And then sound effects tracks, such as the squeal of tires or the bark of guns, may be recorded on location under the most realistic circumstances.

In those environments having high generalized noise levels, such as heavy traffic on the streets of New York, the sound designer feels no obligation to record all the individual noises present but only those that are relevant, perhaps in totality. If two players are trying to hold a conversation over the hubbub of street traffic, the recordist might transcribe no more than a loop of the background noises, which in mixing would be at first turned down and tuned out until near the end of the conversation, when it would come up again. This control of the presence of audio is directly analogous to the mind's capacity to subordinate ambient noise to permit concentration on the significant sounds.

Later, in a sound mixing studio having maximum controls for each track—with electronic filters and other devices to modify the sound quality—the voice, music, and effects tracks are combined into one sound track. The sound mixer controls the relative proportions and intensities of each track at each given point in the dramatic action to complement the image track. Although the cinema is a visually dominant medium, its emotional and communication impact is the result of an orchestration of sight and sound, with each sound element taking turns to fuse with the moving pictures and each becoming crucial at different phases of the film story. The artistic judgment of when one or the other of the sound elements will be accented is a matter of seasoning the sound stew to taste.

## Relationships

The term *sound designer* emerged from Francis Ford Coppola's decision to release *Apocalypse Now* in an expanded quadrophonic format, an innovation in dramatic film. Coppola asked Murch to utilize this format—in which sound may seem to come from anywhere in the theater—and to create sound for this film with a character unique to the experience of the Vietnam War. The almost architectural orchestration of sound in three-dimensional space seemed to combine the responsibilities of sound mixer and production designer, and so Coppola gave Murch the screen credit "sound designer." The name stuck and is now coming into general usage for those working in sound for cinema.

Walter Murch says, "The primary relationship of the sound designer is to the director because the person working in sound must create an experience in hearing that is an equivalent of what is being seen on the screen. Image and sound must fuse as one in the mind of the viewer, and for this reason one must work closely with the director who is creating that image. The screenplay is of course the sound designer's contact with the writer, and many ideas for sound come from what is indi-

FIGURE 10.1 *The sounds emanating from this air motorcycle, piloted by Mark Hamill, were created artificially and have no counterpart in reality. The creation of sounds to be the emotional equivalent of what is seen on the screen, transcending the role of enhancing realism, reflects the new responsibilities of the sound designer.*

**STAR WARS** (U.S.A., 1977) DIRECTED BY GEORGE LUCAS.

cated in the script. There is a relationship with the producer only when there are budgetary considerations in the creation of sound."

The role of the sound designer varies according to the nature of the production, and no one premise applies to all roles beyond the physical fact of recording, creating, and mixing sounds. In a small independent production for education and documentary purposes or in a low-budget feature film, the audio recordist may play a greater role in terms of designing the sound than would be the case in large studio productions. The director-sound designer relationship is similar to that of the director-cinematographer relationship in the sense that both must know the script and attempt to achieve the director's interpretations.

The working approach of the sound designer is to look at a sequence in the context of an overall film, decide what he or she wants in the forms of sounds, and then look about for devices that will provide the desired audio. Some sounds are achieved fortuitously, trying this or that, combining noises by trial and error until the one sought for effect is achieved.

Ken Miura, a sound expert, cites the example of *Return of the Jedi*. The audience heard what it thought was the sound of laser gun firing, a sound that does not exist in reality. The sound designer, searching for a sound to give this effect, found a radio transmitter tower with long support high-tension guy wires, and struck one of them with a hammer. This yielded a whining whang noise that eventually became the sound of a firing laser gun. Air motorcycles, vehicles that do not exist, were used in the same film, and the sound designer had to invent a sound for them that did not exist. This was achieved by mixing together the recorded sounds of a P-51 Mustang airplane, a P-38 Lockheed Interceptor, and a contemporary turbine engine aircraft with a slightly off synchronization. He then speeded up the mixed sounds and rerecorded them, creating the sound of an air motorcycle (Figure 10.1).

The combined and modified sound engendered in this effect is typical of the means used to create audio ambience in modern films. Among the techniques of modifying and rerecording sounds to create new sounds are these:

Speeding up and slowing down original sound to alter the pitch and then rerecording at standard speed.

Running sounds through devices such as a harmonizer to digitally expand or compress without changing the pitch.

Using dip filters to boost or reduce certain frequency bands in the sound.

Using digital reverberation devices to create electronic sounds.

Using electronic and computerized equipment to create synthetic sounds.

Recombining and synthesizing—through editing and premixing several sounds—to produce the impression of one new sound.

## Sound Characteristics

Walter Murch submits, "The term *realism* in sound requires some definition. In filmic terms one may say that *no* sound is realistic sound. Because of the differences between the ear and the microphone, a 'real' sound may record unrealistically. What we are striving for is the creation of sounds that, when put together with an image, will seem appropriate to that image and to its emotional context. In many cases the sounds one hears are not the same as the sounds one would hear if actually present at that location, but they should be in character with the subject, expand upon the image, and 'feel realistic.'"

All of the three basic sound tracks share uses and considerations that are of concern to the filmmaker. These are *fidelity, sound in character with the subject, perspective, sound movements, indistinct sound,* and *sound montages.*

### Fidelity

The term *fidelity* refers to a recording that accurately reproduces the sound and timbre of the aural source, a quality Murch refers to as a "dry recording." Fidelity is of primary importance in sound recording, particularly when recording voice and music. The average viewer may be influenced to like or dislike a screen personality according to the properties of the voice. And, as Murch indicates, the sound designer is better advised to start with an accurate recording and induce modifications later than to start with unwanted sounds and try later to delete them.

Where music is concerned, nearly everyone with normal hearing is exquisitely sensitive to tone quality; distortions of music intending to complement visuals may be almost painful to hear and may ruin an otherwise excellent film. Sound effects are less critical, in most cases, but even here fidelity of recording can only be a virtue. The sound designer may subsequently decide to depart from realism through distortions of faithfully recorded sounds, but if the original recording is itself distorted, he or she may be out of luck.

"Fidelity in sound," Murch says, "means credible sound, sound that feels real (Figure 10.2). There was a scene in *Apocalypse Now* in which a character machine-guns at close range a group of people in a sampan. The report of a machine gun is so huge that it overwhelms the electronics of the recording system. What we had to do was to disassemble the components of that sound and record them separately: back the microphone away from the source to get a clean recording, and then add in the sounds of discharging cartridges and the hiss of hot metal. This created both the emotional quality and the realism of a machine gun firing at close range, but it was not a single

**APOCALYPSE NOW** DIRECTED BY FRANCIS FORD COPPOLA.

COURTESY OF THE ACADEMY OF MOTION PICTURE ARTS AND SCIENCES.

FIGURE 10.2 *Walter Murch says, with regard to the sounds he created for* Apocalypse Now, *"The director wanted the sound to relate specifically to the Vietnam War. Every war has its own distinctive sounds according to the weaponry used, and he [Francis Ford Coppola] did not want to reprocess the sounds of earlier wars such as Korea and World War II. The weaponry of Vietnam was unique to that war and the director wanted the film to have that sound. And, importantly, that war had a psychological aspect to it quite unlike those of other wars, and we wanted to include that psychological aspect in the sound. We wanted the sound to seem to influence the state of mind of those shown fighting in Vietnam."*

direct recording of 'realistic sounds.' The sound designer must either find ways to record a sound so that it feels right, or add elements of sound to it so that the audience will subconsciously agree, 'Yes, that's how the weapon would sound if I were that close to a firing machine gun.'"

### Sound in Character with the Subject

Sounds should have audio textures in character with the subject. Rooster Cogburn of *True Grit* growls, rumbles, and spits his way through every human relationship like the rough-hewn gunfighter he is. Emma, in *Terms of Endearment*, speaks in low, soft, mellifluous tones, even when she swears, to reflect the gentle womanly being she really is (Figure 10.3). Rooster's voice never has a soft edge, and Emma's voice is never raspy. The mixer in a sound studio can manipulate the audio textures of each person to reflect his or her role in the film, through the use of electronic filters and other devices.

### Perspective

Perspective is as much an element of sound as of picture. A full shot of a man speaking ten feet from the camera must not have the sound quality of a voice speaking ten inches from the camera or it may lose its credibility. Whether the scene records a subject in extreme close-up or from the distance of an establishing shot, the perspective of the sound should be proportionate to the distance of the subject from the camera.

"Perspective in sound," recounts Murch, "is a surprisingly powerful tool that enhances realism and conducts emotions. I like to think that I not only record a sound, but the space between me and the sound: The subject that generates the sound is merely what causes the surround-

ing space to resonate, like the string and the body of a violin."

Perspective can either be captured at the time of recording or synthesized later in post-production. Creating perspective at the time of recording dialogue is a matter of controlling the proportions of direct sound and reflective sound. Direct sound is what is spoken directly into the microphone, reflective sound is what comes off the walls. When a person stands close to a microphone, the proportions may be 90 percent direct, 10 percent reflective, and that person will sound close. If the person stands at the far end of the room, or turns away to speak, the proportions may be 10 percent direct and 90 percent reflective. The greater the proportion of reflective sound, the greater the sense of perspective.

"Until two or three years ago," Murch continues, "I used to record at the actual distance because nuances and validity are best obtained, whenever possible, under direct conditions. Sound with overtones of perspective can be created in post-production, however, given a dry recording to begin with. Perspective may be induced by either an echo chamber or a digital reverberation device. The echo chamber is the traditional means of rerecording sound with a feeling of depth. Within the past two or three years digital reverberation machines have enabled sound designers to control sound in perspective in a very precise way."

### Sound Movements

Sounds move with their subjects. As a screen character moves toward or away from the camera, or laterally across the screen, the sounds of his or her voice must seem to progressively move in relation to the camera. Moreover, the sound movements should reflect the environment

FIGURE 10.3 *Debra Winger and Shane Serwin, in their roles as Emma and son, share a playful moment before departing for a new life in another state. The sound designer must be exquisitely sensitive to the proper recording of dialogue in order to render voices reflective of* the person's character in the film. A viewer may be influenced to like or dislike a character by the textures and timbre of the voice. This is a subtle matter, but important in fusing sound with image for a single emotional impact.

**TERMS OF ENDEARMENT** (U.S.A., 1983) DIRECTED BY JAMES BROOKS.

through which the subject is moving. If two persons are trying to talk while walking through a crowd at a football game as the quarterback is passing for a touchdown, the two must be seen and heard as trying to speak over the shouts of the spectators. If they are talking in normal conversational tones while the background shouts are merely turned down in volume, the effect will be patently false to the viewer. The addition in recent years of stereophonic and Dolby stereo sound, especially when used in conjunction with the wide-screen formats, has notably enhanced the emphasis on perspective and movements.

"Making sound seem to come forward or move back is not only a matter of turning the volume up or down," Murch explains. "Movement to control audience awareness is created by changing the *textures* of the sounds. In *American Graffiti*, for example, George Lucas wanted to have forty-five hit songs of the early 1960s playing continuously in the sound track for the length of the film. To play music continu-

FIGURE 10.4 *American Graffiti is one of those rare films that has a continuous music track from beginning to end.* "This much use of music," *comments Walter Murch,* "made it often spill over into the domain of sound effects and, occasionally, into the realm of dialogue." *Murch recounts how audience awareness of the music was controlled by manipulating its texture.*

**AMERICAN GRAFFITI** (U.S.A., 1973) DIRECTED BY GEORGE LUCAS.

ously at a full level of awareness for the length of a feature film would have exhausted the audience (Figure 10.4).

"The problem was resolved by switching between two continuous tracks, one crisp and one soft. We took a dry recording of the forty-five songs out into a backyard and played it on one tape recorder while rerecording it on another in the open air. I placed the microphone and manipulated the alignment so they were never exactly in phase. This gave us an atmospheric track of the songs that had all the rough edges removed, a track of the same length as the original. Then, in mixing, we switched from the dry to the atmospheric recording whenever the music was intended to recede as, for example, behind dialogue. Conversely, we switched to the dry recording with all its edges whenever the audience was intended to be conscious of the music as a thematic element."

Murch emphasizes this point: "An important principle exists here in sound that is analogous to selective focus in photography, depth of field in a lens. If both foreground and background are in focus, the eye has a hard time separating them and finding the center of interest. Selective focus creates the separation. Fundamental to selective focus of sound is controlling the proportions of reflective sounds in order to soften the edges of sounds. Turning the volume of the sound up and down will not do the job because the edges of the music are still 'in focus.' An atmospheric track may be played at closer to full volume without drawing the conscious attention of the viewer . . . [whereas] a dry recording played at the same or a lower level will draw the viewer's attention because of the sharpness of its elements. The sound designer can manipulate the attention of the audience by changes of texture alone.

"Horizontal movements in sound," Murch adds, "is an effect achieved by apparently placing the sound source in its relationship to the microphone. There are subtle shifts of proportion in direct and reflective sound that make the apparent movements convincing. There is also a complex phase interaction between direct and indirect sound in what we hear. Getting these nuances is better done at the time of recording than later during the mix."

### Indistinct Sound

Indistinct sound is intended to reflect the realism of life itself. Indistinct sound is acceptable when presenting unimportant dialogue in distant perspective, evocative music, or atmospheric sound effects. Dialogue or narration that carries important content, however, should be distinct enough to be clearly understood without straining. Any time viewers have to consciously work at trying to perceive some aspect of the presentation, their reservoir of patience begins to drain away. Indistinct sound plays a functional role in supportive sound, but in communicative dialogue and narration the words should ring out clearly.

### Sound Montages

The sound montage is the audio counterpart of the visual montage: A sound montage consists of snatches of dialogue, narration, music, and sound effects to total a meaning that is different from its component elements. In *The Magnificent Ambersons*, for example, the confusion of the great family upon the death of the grandfather is reflected in a sound montage containing snatches of worried phrases, weeping, shouting, recriminations, slamming doors, running footsteps, and so forth; none of these sounds has intrinsic meaning, yet the third meaning of the sound montage is understandable—pandemonium (Figure 10.5). The sound montage is most often used for a stream-of-consciousness effect.

The sound montage was used to brilliant effect by Walter Murch in *Apocalypse Now*. In an opening scene the character played by Martin Sheen (Captain Willard) is shown seated in a room alone listening to the cacophany of the Saigon streets. To indicate the character's yearning to be out in the jungle, Murch successively phased over each of the city sounds with a jungle sound: The policeman's whistle became the cry of a tropical bird, the whirring of motorscooters became the buzzing of insects, the car horns were transmuted into the howls of monkeys.

City progressively became jungle, one sound at a time, over a period of thirty seconds. First there were seven city sounds and one jungle sound. Then there were six city noises and two jungle sounds. And so forth, until all eight tracks had been phased over to apprise the viewer of what was happening in this man's mind. He was physically still in the room, but he was mentally and spiritually gone to the primal land. Within thirty seconds these effects had been achieved: The mood had changed from jangling city to forest primeval; his character was revealed as a loner who loved to roam the back country; and the emotional state of the protagonist was clearly at the point where he was prepared to undertake a dramatic action that would trigger the story of *Apocalypse Now*. And this transition was achieved entirely by Murch's sound montage.

Each of the major sound elements—*dialogue, music, sound effects,* and *narration*—has acquired certain usages in the language of film. Walter Murch puts it this way: "If I were to place dialogue, music, and effects on a polar spectrum of light, I would place dialogue at the ultraviolet (denotative) end, music at the infrared (connotative) end, with sound effects somewhere in the middle. Dialogue is usually dominant and intellectual, music is usually supportive and emotional, sound effects are usually information. Their uses, however, are not inflexible. Sometimes dialogue is nonintellectual and aesthetic, sometimes music is symbolic, and on occasion sound effects may serve any of those functions. Any of these elements may be dominant or recessive according to the sharpness or softness of the sound and the relationship of the sound to the image."

## Dialogue

Dialogue is lip-synchronous, simultaneously seen and heard, and intended to be credible as realistic conversation between the characters living out a dramatic story. In screen dialogue the viewer usually remains a third party to the story, eavesdropping into other lives, and is seldom addressed directly on a one-to-one basis as in television narration.

Dialogue is intended to be acceptable to the viewer as true to real life. Real-life conversations, however, seldom have dramatic quality or content. They are filled with superfluous comments, jokes, complaints and are peppered with incomplete phrases and sentences, many of which would not make sense in a dramatic film. *Realism* in screen terms means reducing dialogue to the absolute minimum by saying as much as possible with visuals. Only those concepts that are intrinsically verbal and cannot readily be said with images are expressed as dialogue in most American films.

Murch comments, "Some films today

FIGURE 10.5 *This scene with Tim Holt (and Agnes Moorehead overhead) depicts one of the great sound montages, and great acting performances, of the sound film era. The death of the father in the film reveals that the once-wealthy* *family is now destitute, and the sound montage reflects the panic and anxiety through snippets of cries, weeping, slamming doors, running feet, and snatches of dialogue to a cumulative effect of pandemonium.*

**THE MAGNIFICENT AMBERSONS** DIRECTED BY ORSON WELLES.

are silent films with sound in the sense that the image carries almost all the exposition, with most of the sound—dialogue, music, and effects—used for emotional enrichment." An example of this would be *Days of Heaven*, a story of wheat harvesters, in which virtually the entire story is carried in the images with the emotional support given by the three dimensions of sound and the occasional chirping voice of a little girl supposedly recounting the story. After her friend murders another man she sighs, "Nobody's perfect," which released a ripple of laughter from the audience.

Screen dialogue has three important functions, which are the same as those given in Augustus Thomas's dictum about stage dialogue: A line must *advance the story*, *develop character*, or *get a laugh*. One additional function of film dialogue is to enhance *continuity*.

### Story Advancement

Advancing the story means using dialogue as exposition. In *The Andromeda Strain* a deadly virus accidentally brought to earth from outer space suddenly begins to mutate—a process of change that would make no sense visually to a lay viewer unless explained in dialogue, as it is, by one of the scientists in the story. The daily soap operas on television are drenched with exposition carried in dialogue so that audiences may go about their daily tasks while listening to them, rather than watching them. (Soaps are really radio with pictures.)

Dialogue exposition is usually heaviest at the beginning of a drama in order to present the theme of the story, to explain the events that lead up to joining of the conflict, and to give a brief history of the protagonist. In *Lust for Life*, Norman Corwin summed up in expository dialogue the history of failures by Vincent van Gogh when that creative soul tried to become a missionary, his last attempted career before becoming an artist. The opening sequence depicts his rejection by the missionary board in two minutes of dialogue that reveal ten years of failures:

*Dull gray yellow manila folder*

LAY-MISSIONARY COMMITTEE
Application of:
VINCENT VAN GOGH
October 1878

*Camera starts to pull back, as we hear—*
Bokma
This is the case I mentioned to you. . . .

*Pietersen's Voice*
He's been waiting all day. . . . In fairness to him, I don't think we should put it off any longer.

*By now, Camera has pulled back to disclose a conference table, around which sit four lay members of the Belgian Committee of Evangelization: De Jong and Van Den Brink: Dr. Bokma, a small wiry man sitting opposite them; and Pietersen, obviously chairman of the group.*

*Pietersen (to Bokma, indicating the folder)*
Dr. Bokma, are you going to stand by this report?

*Bokma (with conscientious care)*
I'm afraid I must. His classwork is wholly unsatisfactory. His speech is poor; his dress is careless. He is arrogant and headstrong; he resents criticism.

*Van den Brink*
What's his history?

*De Jong (consulting the folder)*
Discharged from a clerkship in Paris . . . failed at teaching in England . . . left a job in a bookstore.

*Bokma (summing it up)*
A wanderer . . .

Dialogue exposition may serve a number of other purposes. It may be used to explain the movements of characters not present in a given scene, to describe other locales, other times, other places, and other events—although these expository functions are often served by the cutaway or the flashback.

## Character Development

The development of character is a second function of dialogue. Until a person speaks, the viewer does not really know what to make of the character in terms of personality, attitudes, occupation, educational background, and socioeconomic milieu. What a screen character says in his or her interrelationships with other screen characters reveals what kind of person he or she is at the beginning, and what kind of person he or she becomes at the end.

Moreover, dialogue reveals the emotional condition of a character at any point in the drama. A simple "yes" or "no" may be spoken with a range of expression that renders the gamut of human emotions and explains the relationship of one character to all other characters.

## Getting a Laugh

Getting a laugh in dialogue is a third function of drama. Humorous dialogue, which is difficult to write because humorists are born and not made, is needed in a dramatic film to relieve sustained tension. If a long suspense film is produced without occasional comic relief, inner tension may build in the viewers to the point that they may laugh uncontrollably when a character is skewered with a stiletto or a man and woman tenderly make love.

## Continuity

Continuity may be enhanced through the use of the *dialogue hook*. A dialogue hook consists of repeating a key word or phrase in character-to-character exchanges to subtly impress an important clue upon the viewer. These verbal echoes may be as long as a sentence or as short as a single word:

"I will never sell this place."

"Never sell?"

"Never."

The use of repeated questions is a variant of the dialogue hook used to enhance interest, a technique that plays upon the curiosity of the viewer:

"Where have you been until two in the morning?"

"Out."

"Out where?"

"Out visiting a friend."

"What friend?"

"An old friend."

"A male friend or a female friend?"

If the question is answered with a question, it adds the element of confrontation:

"Where have you been until two in the morning?"

"What business is that of yours?"

"Don't you think I have a right to know?"

"What makes you think you have the right to know?"

"Aren't you playing word games to be evasive?"

The *soliloquy*—a long delivery of solitary dialogue—was attempted early in dramatic sound films, usually in close-up, but was generally discarded as pretentious and destructive of cinematic time; it was considered an attempt to impose theatrical conventions.

The television soliloquy, however, seems to have a slightly different impact on the viewer. A filmed soliloquy that aroused impatience when seen in the movie theater becomes acceptable on its television rerun. The difference in acceptability may be simply a matter of screen size. A face in close-up on a forty-foot theatrical screen is gigantic, often repelling, whereas on a television screen it nearly approximates life-size. It appears that dramatic films and videotapes made solely for television release may sustain far more dialogue, including soliloquies, than may their theatrical forms.

The function of dialogue in most American films is primarily to reveal dramatic facts that cannot be rendered visually. If it wanders from its lean and functional role to become an end in itself, or to become truly realistic—a mishmash of mumbles and verbiage—it may stop the flow of cinema. Dialogue should contain only the words and phrases needed to implement the story and all else should be ruthlessly blue-penciled. Edited screen dialogue should be weightless and move as lightly and swiftly as all other elements of cinema.

## Music

"Music is almost always used for itself, and not for some other purpose," says Walter Murch. "Music exists primarily for emotional dimensions and aesthetic enrichment in a supportive sense. On occasion music may serve the intellectual function of dialogue, or the expositional uses of sound effects, but for the most part music is added for the pleasures that only music can give."

Original music for films is unique in the sense that it is conceived and composed to complement the cinematography, editing, and story content and is not intended to stand alone as music. This does not prevent many film themes and scores from becoming widely popular and from being recognized as fine music on their intrinsic merits, but this is seldom the intent at the time of genesis. Music is composed for film to make such dramatic contributions as development of *character themes, locale themes, mood, tempo, continuity, dramatic emphasis, premonition, commentary,* and *satire, humor, transitions, and information.*

### Character Themes

Character themes are widely used to identify a certain person in a film, such as "Lara's Theme" in the historical film *Dr. Zhivago.* Once the strains of a theme have been identified with a given character, it may be played in almost any setting and circumstance in the film to arouse a haunting memory. Whenever Dr. Zhivago rides to meet his mistress, remembers her, writes about her, wins her, loses her, suffers a heart attack at a glimpse of her in the crowd, the music track swells with "Lara's Theme." The same principle applies to less-savory characters: Komarovsky, in the same film, has a minor-key theme with a harshly grating quality to echo his existence, visually present or not. The use of a minor chord to imply a menacing presence is, of course, universal.

### Locale Themes

Locale themes orient the viewer and evoke memories of things past in a certain setting. The Texas western has its harmonica rendition of "Red River Valley," and the New York eastern has its rollicking strains of "Lullaby of Broadway." Once music has been introduced as relating to a given locale, it may be played again later in the film to echo the memories of other times, other places, other people.

## Mood

The mood of a scene or an entire film may be created by its music. The coronation of a king may be rendered as a farce or an event of majesty by its musical accompaniment. Laughter and joy on the screen may be chilled by an undercurrent of implied musical menace. The death of a man may be made hilarious if accompanied by jolly music, as in Alfred Hitchcock's macabre jest *The Trouble with Harry*. An exquisite use of mood music was Burt Bacharach's "Raindrops Keep Fallin' on My Head" in *Butch Cassidy and the Sundance Kid*, in which the essentially childlike and charming character of Butch was dramatized in mood music as he clowned around on that symbol of the encroachment of civilization: the bicycle.

The moods of music sometimes go far afield and exist almost independently of the image track, yet affect it, if only through counterpoint. Some European directors, such as Ingmar Bergman, frequently use classical music to accompany the major sequences of their films. The dignity of the music enhances the dignity of the film and transfers a degree of its prestige, regardless of the intrinsic cinematic merit of that film. Socialist filmmakers in general, and the East Germans in particular, often use classical music to dignify ideological concepts.

## Tempo

The tempo function, an extension of mood music, is intended to complement rapidly moving dramatic actions on the screen. The confused sequences of desperate aerial combat in war films, the hot pursuits of a thousand and one westerns, the pratfalls of comedians from Mack Sennett to the present have been accompanied by fast-moving music. Climactic sequences seem to be those in which dynamic music can contribute most of the dramatic impact without the music drawing attention to itself. And the editing of these scenes is frequently done in close conjunction with the sound track in order to carefully play picture against sound for heightened tempo.

## Continuity

Continuity music may tie together a series of unrelated scenes, such as a montage depicting travel, a search, or a long period of time. The music then reflects the spirit of the dramatic action and proceeds continuously and more or less independently of the subjects' movements. In *Butch Cassidy and the Sundance Kid* the relentless pressures of the law and the tightening grip of civilization drive the two main characters to a decision to take their girl and flee to Bolivia, which is still primitive enough for them to live the old outlaw life. Bacharach's continuity music ties together the travel sequence as they flee the West to New York, through the boat trip to South America, to Bolivia—eight thousand miles covered in a few minutes—tied together with music of immense charm.

## Dramatic Emphasis

Dramatic emphasis is the most pervasive use of music in a theatrical film. A single word or phrase in the story, or even a noise, may be loaded with content significance that could be missed by some viewers if not underscored with an orchestral crescendo. This was once done to excess in Hollywood films. The heavy-handed use of music to complement each and every crisis, typical of many tear-jerker movies made around World War II, is far less common today. Recently the trend has been away from the slathering of music over an entire film in favor of musical emphasis primarily at moments of intense crisis.

Music for dramatic emphasis may also be used in documentary films. In *Thursday's Children*, an exquisite British film about the education of deaf children, a moment of achievement occurs when a deaf-mute boy manages to speak a word he has never heard: *bath*. As he deserves, the victory is commemorated by a triumphant trill on the flute.

### Premonition

Premonition music warns of things to come. The doomed sweethearts of *The Diary of Anne Frank* talk happily about their prospects for a postwar future while heavy Teutonic premonition music promises only the gas chambers of an extermination camp. Virtually all war and western films signal impending battle with the enemy by premonition music that the viewer commonly identifies with a national or racial entity. And virtually all films in which doomed characters make plans for the future seem to have a menacing chord to punctuate their dreams, pluck the heartstrings of the viewer, and announce that their hopes can never be.

### Commentary

Commentative music is a ballad whose words give expression to feelings and ideas having no visual counterpart. It is most often used to introduce the theme of a film, to express the inner thoughts of a character, or to make a satirical comment on one of the characters. In *I Walk the Line*, in which a middle-aged sheriff is torn between his passion for a nubile woman and his duty to his dowdy wife, his inner thoughts are crooned softly in a ballad sung to accompany his pensive face. Commentative music is increasingly used in lieu of stream-of-consciousness dialogue spoken over a silent close-up.

### Satire, Humor, Transitions, and Information

Music may be used in several other ways: for *satire*—the helicopters of *Apocalypse Now* swoop to attack accompanied by the strains of "The Ride of the Valkyrie"; for *humor*—Mickey Mousing and thereby the walk of a screen character; for *transitions*—from one related sequence to another; for information—using authentic Navajo music in an educational film about an aspect of that Indian culture. No description can encompass all the nuances and ramifications that a skilled film composer's or sound designer's contributions can make to a motion picture. Except for the musical, however, or sequences in which music becomes an end in itself, this element of the cinema carries only one stricture: Music should be felt rather than consciously heard.

Realism is better served in some documentary and dramatic films with minimal use of music, and what music is used reserved for emotional crescendos. In *Murphy's War*, a story of one man's revenge on a German submarine, virtually the entire film story is told in the cold realism of dialogue and sound effects. Only the two emotional high points in the film—the machine-gunning of a helpless British crew in the water (the first conflict) and Murphy's sinking of the submarine, while killing himself (the climax)—had musical accompaniment to reinforce their dramatic magnitude. The absence of music in other parts of the film gave it magnified impact at those two points.

FIGURE 10.6   The Conversation *is an example of a film in which sound effects served important functions in exposition. In the first half of the film, dialogue was dominant. But in the second half—which had little dialogue—sound* *effects came forward to reveal insights and information, and the audience listened carefully, as in this episode of violence featuring Gene Hackman.*

**305**
SOUND EFFECTS

**THE CONVERSATION** (U.S.A., 1974) DIRECTED BY FRANCIS FORD COPPOLA.

## Sound Effects

Walter Murch observes, "The absence of dialogue activates the mind to listen to other sounds. Those background sounds normally pushed back by the conscious mind come forward and are listened to when there are no spoken words. *The Conversation* is a film about sound (Figure 10.6). After the first half of the film the characters virtually stopped talking and the audience started to listen to the effects for insights and information. Foreground dialogue receded into the background and background effects moved into the foreground."

Sound effects are the fourth sound mode and serve the primary function of enhancing realism: complementing and enhancing the viewer's understanding of what he or she sees on the screen. The sight of a door slamming shut is fused with the sound of a door slamming shut. The sight of a dog barking is synchronized with the sounds of a dog barking. Audio effects can serve many other functions, however, that transcend realism. Some of these are *to extend the limits of what is seen, to create mood, to imply nonexistent locations,* and *to create sound effects montages.*

### Extending Visual Limits

Sound effects may be used to imply all kinds of activities happening just beyond the periphery of the screen. A scene of a housewife working in a small kitchen may be expanded through the sounds of children running and toys banging in an unseen playroom, a television set droning in the family room, the clang of pipes as a plumber repairs a leak in the basement, and the distant roar of a lawnmower, certifying that the man of the house is implementing his wife's orders—all extensions of reality created by sound effects. The viewer is led by sound to believe that what he or she sees on the screen is only a small part of a big world beyond.

### Creating Mood

The mood function of sound effects is important in suspense films: the maniacal cry of a loon streaking over a mist-shrouded lake, the quiet tread of footsteps and the creak of an opening door in a supposedly empty house, unexplained noises and objects rattling, wind shrieking like a calliope as it plays over the rusted metal screen runners of an abandoned factory, the bark of a distant fox heard from the warm fringe of a campfire. The unexplained sounds of the unseen seem to touch some atavistic fear of the unknown; an unidentified sound must be seen and certified as harmless before we can relax. This human survival instinct can be manipulated by the clever filmmaker to create mood and suspense.

### Implying Nonexistent Locations

Nonexistent locations may be implied by the clever use of sound effects—a common practice in dramatic film to obviate the need for expensive filming with a crew and cast on distant locations. For example, there is a small pond on the MGM production lot that is fringed by rushes and surrounded by trees, with a small sand beach. That pond has been the tropical location for productions ranging from the Tarzan movies of the Thirties to the jungle warfare films of the Seventies, with the locale implied by the sound effects of exotic birds and howler monkeys, machine gunfire and the curses of the enemy shouted in foreign tongues. That pond, conveniently located in Los Angeles, has seen more marine assaults than any beachhead of any war in the world.

This use applies also to interiors. A factory sequence, for example, may be set up in one corner of a sound stage and equipped with a workbench, tools, blueprints, and so on. By adding a sound track with the throb and rattle of punch presses, drill presses, lathes—all conveniently recorded at a real factory with a light portable tape recorder—that sequence will appear to be authentically produced at a factory without incurring the high costs of location filming.

### Creating Sound Effects Montages

The sound effects montage is tied to memories, fears, emotions. In *I Never Sang for*

*My Father*, a middle-aged man ruminates over the political career of his near-great father, now old and forgotten by the city of which he had been mayor. As the son talks with the young woman who is his current playmate, the effects track carries the faraway sounds of parades, shouts, unintelligible speeches, and applause—the cacophany of a last hurrah expressed through a sound effects montage saturated with ineluctable nostalgia.

## Narration

Narration is a voice-over visuals concept in which an unseen speaker discusses and explains what the viewer sees on the screen. Narration is most often used in documentary and educational films because it is a straightforward informational technique that is inexpensive, easy to do, and may be added after the visuals have been edited. Narration is most often used at the beginning of dramatic films.

Walter Murch notes, "The problem with narration in a dramatic film is identifying it immediately as being different from dialogue, as well as conveying the interior quality of the words themselves. The quality is that of subjectivity. The microphone must become a person to whom the narrator speaks, and the force of that personality must come through the microphone. By treating the speaker as the head of a person to whom one is speaking intimately, a much more personal and subjective tone is induced into the narration.

"Voice tonality may be modified," Murch continues, "by the way the dialogue or narration is recorded. In *Moby Dick*, for example, there was a narrator who gave exposition (Figure 10.7) The director John Huston wanted a distinctive dimension to the narrator's voice that would be qualitatively different in a textural sense from the dialogue used by the characters. Changing the volume would not achieve this because the audience might think it was an off-screen character. Then the narrator inadvertently stood too close to the microphone and this voice flooded through the room that seemed to have an 'other world' dimension, and it was adopted. . . . The head of the studio sound department protested, but the decision was Huston's and the narration for *Moby Dick* had that unique tonality that separated it from the dialogue. Les Hodgson, the sound editor on *Moby Dick*, worked subsequently with me to achieve a similar narration tonality in *Julia* and *Apocalypse Now*."

Narration is most frequently used in nonfiction films to serve the following functions:

To add relevant verbal information to the visual information seen on the screen. A documentary film about refugees from Pakistan being fed in India might include such verbal information, for example, that the food was contributed by the United Nations.

To clarify some visual relationship that requires verbal interpretation. A sequence showing an oceanography vessel with a drilling rig, sonar equipment, and computers—all three operating in split-screen unison—would require narration to explain that they are not drilling for oil, but are core-drilling the surface of the sea bed to measure its age.

To relate what the viewer is looking at to what he or she has already seen. A how-to-do-it film on the assembly of a jet engine might near the conclusion of the film refer back to a technique introduced earlier to explain the rela-

FIGURE 10.7 *This classic tale recounts the story of a sea captain maddened by his mutilation by a whale's flukes and his obsession to harpoon and slay the beast. This scene of Gregory Peck shows Captain Ahab at the moment of* revenge. *To preserve the sense of personal narrative in the sound design of the film, the director had the narrator stand close to the microphone to create an internalized dimension apart from typical dialogue.*

**MOBY DICK** (U.S.A., 1956) DIRECTED BY JOHN HUSTON.

tionship between past and present visual processes.

When one of these three functions is not being served, the sound track is better given over to music or sound effects. Garrulous narration tracks often permeate documentary film and television presentations, primarily because the producers cannot stand to let the visuals speak for themselves. The result is that many viewers turn off the programs; or, if trapped in a classroom, their minds depart for happier places and leave an unoccupied body to stare with glazed corneas at the babbling screen.

Visual presentation of a documentary subject should precede the narration unless the words are being used for transitional effects. The viewer should see what the subject is before he or she hears any explanations, or the words may slide in one ear and out the other with scarcely a pause. Viewers tend to forget what they hear unless they can relate it to something they see or already know. Some filmmakers feel that they will pique the interest of the viewers by feeding them information before presenting the content visually. If the intent is only to provide transitional entertainment to arouse their interest and the content of the introductory information is unimportant, fine. But if the content is to be remembered, the picture should precede the narration.

Narration should be written to be heard, not read. It is the ear, not the eye, that counts, and narration should be tried aloud and revised until it flows trippingly on the tongue and is easily understood when heard. The active voice is preferable to the passive, and simple declarative sentences make the best sense. Certain forms common in written prose ought to be scrupulously avoided: convoluted sentence structure; highly involved clauses;

exotic words and obscure phrases; and language style that is out of character with the film, such as iambic pentameter in a film about welding. Simplicity, lucidity, and euphony are the hallmarks of good narration. The words and sentences should be revised until they are easy to speak, pleasant to hear, and simple to understand.

Labeling what the viewer can already see is a bane of narration that seems to haunt educational film and television programs. One film about Mexico, currently being distributed to elementary schools, includes the following gem: The opening scene reveals a little Mexican boy leading his donkey through an adobe village. The narrator says, "This is a little Mexican boy leading his donkey through an adobe village."

Other vices to avoid in writing narration are these: bleeding copy, in which content belonging exclusively to a given sequence is allowed to slop over into a following sequence that introduces something new; statistical information, in which facts and figures are shot into the air to ricochet off the viewer's eardrums and be remembered by virtually no one; verbal descriptions of subjects that never appear visually on the screen; purple prose, in which a humble subject is treated with verbal majesty; humorous remarks made by someone who is not a humorist; extravagant claims and statements unsupported by corroborating visual evidence; the trumpeted finale, a summary repeated ad nauseum after the film has reached its logical conclusion; and the loaded sound track, saturated with more information than a viewer can absorb at a sitting because the sponsors or educators are determined to get their money's worth.

Narration can take any of several stylistic forms to complement the subject and the intended purpose of the film. The major kinds of narrative styles that have evolved include *lyric free verse*, *personal narrative*, *subjective microphone*, *direct appeal*, *descriptive*, and *instructional forms*.

### Lyric Free Verse

The lyric free verse style is best suited to subjects with an epic or poetic quality. But it must be used only when the viewers are in the right emotional state to receive it. If used during a period when the mood of the audience is coldly pragmatic, lyric free verse is likely to evoke laughter. A good example of lyric free verse narration used in the right kind of film at the right time in history is *The River*, the classic documentary produced during the pit of the Depression in the Thirties. This film tells the history of the erosive rape of the soil in the Mississippi Valley and makes a passionate appeal to save the land and the people living on it with ringing lyric free verse. It begins:

> From as far West as Idaho,
>     Down from the glacier peaks of the
>     Rockies—
> From as far East as New York,
>     Down from the turkey ridges of the
>     Alleghenies—
> Down from Minnesota, twenty-five
> hundred miles,
>     The Mississippi River runs to the
>     Gulf.
> Carrying every drop of water that flows
> down two-thirds the continent,
>     Carrying every brook and rill, rivu-
>     let and creek,
> Carrying all the rivers that run down
> two-thirds the continent,
>     The Mississippi runs to the Gulf of
>     Mexico.

### Personal Narrative

The personal narrative form harkens back to the minnesinger and storyteller. The narrator speaks as if the story on the screen were a projection of his or her own memories of things past. Some dramatic films begin with a voice-over narrative to fill in background on the story to follow and then change to dialogue.

*The Summer of '42* recounts a boy's introduction to adult love in the arms of a suddenly widowed woman; it begins with the voice of the boy, now grown to manhood, reminiscing about those bygone summer holidays in the buttery sun of the island. The personal narrative form is also used in documentary and educational films to give history the feeling and intimacy of personal experience.

### Subjective Microphone

The subjective microphone technique is a kind of voice-over sound montage in which several points-of-view are expressed by different people who chime in, one after another, to present a cross section of opinion. This technique originated during the great days of radio and carried over into the sound tracks of documentary films produced during World War II. *The True Glory*, an epic historical film that recounts the Allied assault on Hitler's Fortress Europe, uses the subjective microphone technique throughout to allow soldiers, sailors, marines, pilots, officers, and enlisted men—those who did the fighting—to express their feelings about the invasion and the war. They joke, laugh, and swear in words and phrases, snips of sentences, which add up to a montage of courage, humor, and high resolution.

### Direct Appeal

The direct appeal is essentially a call for action directed at the viewer. This narrative form is a one-to-one message from the narrator to the viewer asking that he or she do something immediately. Anyone who has ever watched a television commercial and listened to fear appeals ("Don't risk the lives of your loved ones by driving with worn-out wiper blades") or reassurance appeals ("You can trust your car to the man who wears the star") will not fail to recognize the direct appeal. During wartime the direct appeal may be used in documentary films as a clarion call to arms. This is the most commonly used narration form when trying to evoke a simple behavioral response: Join the Army.

### Descriptive Narration

The descriptive narrative style is used to add ancillary verbal information to the visual statement on the screen. A documentary film about the business of heroin may show a scene of an "ounce man" walking down the street while describing his relationship to the smuggling syndicate and explaining how he cuts the drugs to smaller proportions, seals them in their typical plastic packets, and wholesales them to the street pusher.

### Instructional Narration

Instructional narration consists of unabashedly nuts-and-bolts directions on how to implement a process: weld stainless steel, conduct a chemistry experiment, assemble a jet engine, light a television studio. This form of narration is the purview of those filmmakers who have a student audience willing to sit through anything to learn the skill or process being taught by the film or television presentation. The desired virtue here is clarity.

## The Right Sound

Walter Murch articulates a vital principle for the sound designer. "The ultimate goal is to find the one sound in a situation that will release all the other related sounds already in people's minds. They tend to exist in groups in the mind, and each syndrome of sound has one key element that will, when played, trigger all the others. If the designer can find that one triggering note, all the other sounds will be heard in the minds of the viewers even though only one component is played. Although the track may seem simple and not much to listen to, the sound track would be complete because it was internalized within the brain."

Murch cites *The Rain People*, directed by Francis Ford Coppola, in providing such an example. A character in the film goes to make a telephone call at a booth beside the New Jersey Turnpike, and Murch needed to make a background track of the traffic noises. The first track was a composite of all the noises present and it was overwhelming, although realistic in a literal sense. Murch then searched his component tracks until he found one with a low traffic rumble and the distant clang of a wrench being dropped on concrete. That one track released all the related sounds and implicitly said it all.

Silence, too, is sound and sometimes is a blessing. If a dramatic film has been orchestrated throughout, as was the romantic film *Dr. Zhivago*, high points of drama are sometimes prefaced by a moment of silence. The contrast of dead quiet alerts the viewer to the imminence of important dramatic action. Silence finds similar expressive use in documentary films. In *Thursday's Children*, the disability of the deaf is given cinematic form by presenting a close-up of a teacher's lips as she speaks to her class, while gradually turning down the volume of her voice to nothingness as her lips continue to speak. After a moment of silence the narrator says, "But the children do not hear."

Walter Murch concludes with these generalizations about the role of the sound

FIGURE 10.8 *Walter Murch is shown here mixing the sound for* Apocalypse Now. *Notice that the sound designer is viewing the film at its theatrical release size in order to feel all dimensions of the visuals while synthesizing elements of sound that will fuse with the image to create a single emotional impact upon the viewer.*

WALTER MURCH

designer. "Basically," he says, "it is a person who has the same relationship to the sound track as the director of photography has to the overall look of the picture. The sound designer is the one person that the director can turn to—not only to help develop what the director has in mind—but to come up with his or her ideas of a good approach to use in the sound of a given film (Figure 10.8). It is the sound designer who will ultimately take responsibility for the overall effect of the sound, as the director of photography is responsible for the overall look of the film" (Figure 10.9).

FIGURE 10.9 *Return to Oz was Murch's debut as a film director, but he took a keen interest in the creation of the sound track, which had the same release format as* Apocalypse Now. *A complete fantasy world had to be created in sound, as well as in the visuals, and the thematic development of certain realistic sounds heard in the beginning—the Kansas section—was continued and expanded in the sounds Dorothy hears when she returns to Oz.*

*Director Walter Murch picked Fairuza Balk to play Dorothy in part because she has "a look of innocence with no hard edges . . . and the widest set of blue eyes any of us had ever seen." Murch goes on to say that his relationship with the young star was that of mutual professional respect. "Looking back, it was a rare relationship, one of the most beautiful and poignant I have ever known." A fine tribute.*

**RETURN TO OZ** (U.S.A., 1985) DIRECTED BY WALTER MURCH.

*George Lucas, shown here with the death ma-chine from* Star Wars, *and his cinematic wiz-ards at Industrial Light and Magic have raised the verisimilitude of visual effects to unprece-dented levels in his* Star Wars *series (only to sur-pass themselves in* Who Framed Roger Rabbit).

*As extraordinary as the cinematic achieve-ments of George Lucas have been —*Star Wars *won seven Academy Awards—his pervasive concerns have been moral: the themes of good versus evil in personal accountability that are the essence of* Star Wars.

# Eleven

# VISUAL EFFECTS

*with Artists
of Lucasfilm*

WHAT WALT DISNEY CALLED the plausible impossible and the Germans called *Der Trickfilm* has been with us since the earliest days of cinema. The first cinematic legerdemain was created in 1900 by a professional magician named Georges Méliès who discovered that more than one image could be photographed on the same length of film. He astounded viewers by having people appear and disappear before their boggled eyes with the first dissolves. The spirit of magic and the traditions of the experimental filmmaker have ever since provided the impetus for the visual effect.

The term *visual effect* is an umbrella category that originally referred to the combining of the visual elements of two or more scenes into one single scene, as in the humble dissolve. When more tricks began to come out of the cinematic bag, they were classified, for want of a better term, as visual effects: superimposures; small models photographed and printed to seem huge; animation combined with live-action footage; monsters and extraterrestrial beings; explosions of battlefield bombs, crashing airplanes, and demolition of bridges; foreground disasters and background earthquakes painted on glass; live-action subjects photographed in a studio combined with live-action backgrounds photographed at distant locations. Every kind of incongruous and surrealistic relationship was eventually lumped under the term, *visual effect*.

What most of these effects have in common is that they require composite photography of two or more elements that could not otherwise be achieved in conventional live-action work and that they must be photographed in such a way as to pass for reality within the premise of the film—no matter how fantastic the story (Figure 11.1). Once the viewer is emotionally absorbed into the life on the screen, he or she must believe that everything seen is really happening.

The vast number of conceptual and technical means for achieving visual effects are beyond the scope of a single chapter. What we will attempt is to define the roles of the major figures associated with creating visual effects and then to survey the conceptual and technical forms most used (Figure 11.2).

## Relationships

Creating visual effects falls within the bailiwicks of four specialists: the *storyboard artist*, the *art director*, the *director of effects cinematography*, and the *effects artisan and animator*. The first three are common to nearly all forms of feature filmmaking, but their work assumes paramount importance in films that rely for their verisimilitude upon imaginative but convincing effects. The latter professional, the effects artisan and animator, is unique to specific kinds of visual effects and will be treated later in the survey of major forms of effects.

### Storyboard Artist

The work of a storyboard artist, such as Dave Carson of Industrial Light and Magic (ILM), literally touches every aspect of the production of a feature film because the film takes form pretty much the way it is drawn (Figure 11.3). A storyboard is a visual statement of a verbal script consisting of a series of drawings

"The underlying issues, the psychological motives, in all my movies have been the same: personal responsibility and friendship, the importance of a compassionate life as opposed to a passionate life. . . . [The success of *Star Wars* and the other films in the series was a result of] classic themes told in an innovative way."
—*George Lucas*

315

**STAR WARS** DIRECTED BY GEORGE LUCAS.

FIGURE 11.1  Star Wars (Darth Vader is shown here) was a cinematic phenomenon of such magnitude that the term itself became a household word and part of the language of diplomacy. Daniel Henninger wrote, "Star Wars is the first entertainment in recent memory to put the filmgoer back where he belongs—on that tipsy, giddy, well-worn edge of his seat." The National Observer, *June 14, 1977*

Ten years later, when most films have been consigned to oblivion, Jim Harwood wrote with regard to Star Wars, "Nobody was more surprised than George Lucas himself, who always thought he was creating an excellent popular entertainment which would turn a pleasant profit, but had no idea he was birthing a worldwide phenomenon whose traces would eventually extend into serious international concerns such as nuclear disarmament." Variety, *June 3, 1987*

FIGURE 11.2  *Dennis Muren has four times received the Academy Award for special visual effects*—Return of the Jedi, The Empire Strikes Back, Indiana Jones and the Temple of Doom, *and* E. T.—The Extra-Terrestrial; *he contributes his insight and expertise to this chapter. In this scene he is "lighting live-action subjects [Carrie Fisher and Mark Hamill] for composite printing." The visual effect of an exciting air motorcycle chase through the redwoods for* Return of the Jedi *begins with Muren illuminating and photographing the subjects to match perfectly the atmospheric light of the forest.*

*A modest Muren insists, however, "The really creative aspects of visual effects are actually done by directors like George Lucas and Steven Spielberg. My job is to give convincing visual forms to their dramatic ideas."*

FIGURE 11.3 *This storyboard indicates the care with which the Lucasfilm artists visualize the action of a film. Most of the feature films produced in the United States are rendered as drawings, scene by scene, for the entire length of the film before principal cinematography begins.*

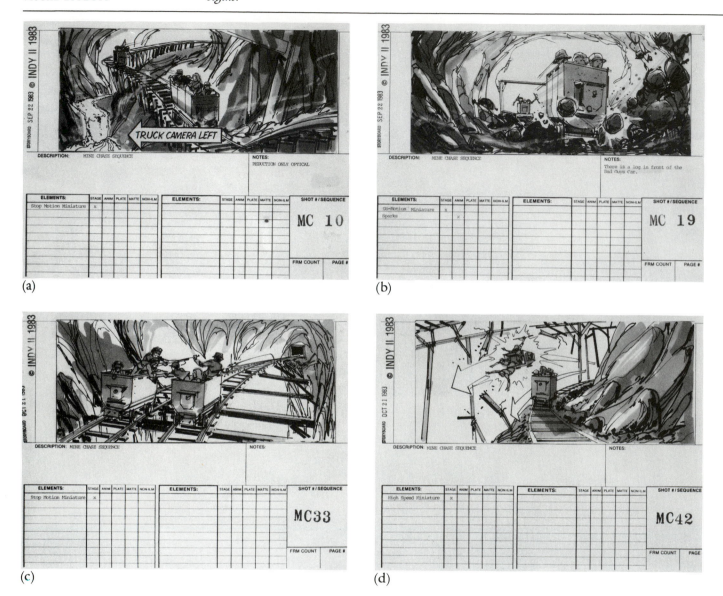

INDIANA JONES AND THE TEMPLE OF DOOM (U.S.A., 1984) DIRECTED BY STEVEN SPIELBERG.

that depict every scene and visual effect planned for a movie. Dialogue, narration, music, and sound effects are indicated below the scene panels in which they are to occur in the film. Synchronous presentation is important because sometimes a visual may be keyed to a single word. Each major change of scene, sequence, or visual concept in a film is indicated with a storyboard sketch. All movements—zooms, pans, tilts, and so on—are rendered in black and white rather than in color because the intent is to see the elements of the story visualized. Monochrome is also preferable because it allows for subsequent photocopying for the various people involved in production.

Storyboards are rendered in pencil and pen and ink. Realism is important in storyboards for visual effects because miniatures, models, and puppets are sometimes literally copied from them, and visual and mechanical effects are structured to meet the requirements of the storyboards. If a shadow has to be there for story or exposition reasons, the artist draws the shadow. The cameraperson may shape the shadow, but the shadow must be there. In the profoundest sense, the storyboard artist is the first to give a film its visual form. Changes do, however, take place later, and often the effects director or cameraperson will redesign the shot based on technical or creative ideas.

The storyboard artist usually begins work with a cursory reading of the script to get an idea of what the story is all about—concentrating on main actions, characters, settings, moods. First the artist tries to get it down all at once, crudely and immediately. When artist and director are working together, the enthusiasm sometimes becomes contagious and the sketches are dashed out with x's, o's, and arrows—unintelligible to anyone but the creators. This first storyboard is virtually cryptic. Then the artist sits down to draw the second set of storyboards very carefully so that all of the elements agreed upon by the director will be clear to everyone else. Storyboarding is therefore a two-stage process: Sketch it quickly while creative fires are hot, then render it finely into a comprehensive form. Storyboard development is almost always done with the director or producer, seldom with the writer. The rendered panels come close to being finished illustrations because of their importance as production guides.

The storyboard becomes the reference point for everyone concerned with production. The producer can estimate the actual production costs by the number of scenes stated and the number and characteristics of the visual elements therein. A major studio will not begin a feature film unless it has an estimate of costs based upon a comprehensive storyboard.

For the director of players, director of cinematography, director of effects, sound recordist, and everyone else immediately associated with location and studio production, the storyboard becomes the reference point for problem solving. Every element stated in the storyboard—sets, miniatures, models, animation, visual and mechanical effects—is listed, counted, and produced essentially as drawn.

Deviation from the storyboard depends on whether the production is being done in-house, as when Lucasfilm created *Star Wars*, or whether it is being done by a special effects house for another studio, as when Industrial Light and Magic produced the effects for *Star Trek III: The Search for Spock*. When the effects are being storyboarded for another production company, they are rendered in fine detail to be specific.

### Art Director

The film's art director is the one who gives the movie its overall look, its color and mood. According to Nilo Rodis-Jamero of ILM, the art director may sometimes be approached more than a year in advance of anyone else to come up with a series of paintings to interest investors in films such as *Star Wars*. Projective art renderings are intended to be evocative of the spirit and action to be seen in the incipient film, rich in color and redolent in emotional qualities. If the paintings are effective, funds will be allocated to write a script and draw a storyboard, and then authority will be given to "art design the film."

Such art designs include the overall color design of the film to ensure chromatic and tonal consistency, color coding of individual sequences to ensure that they reflect the mood of the dramatic action, design of costumes and sets to ensure harmony between subjects and backgrounds, and art direction of visual effects to be studied by the effects directors and other members of the production crew.

"Anticipation," says Rodis-Jamero, "is half the art director's battle. Often the director wants one thing and the producer another, with both having valid points of view but differing interpretations. The art director is often an art negotiator who must come up with results acceptably pleasing and producible to everyone."

The film art director functions *not* as a solo artist, soul searching and singularly motivated, but as part of a creative group whose end artistic product is a motion picture. Rodis-Jamero submits that everyone associated with this collaborative venture must subordinate artistic ego to the synthesized quality of an entertainment film. And the art director must be simultaneously creative and artistic, yet keep a steady eye on budgets, production schedules, deadlines, and the date the film is scheduled for release. The mark of the professional is one who can start work knowing how and when the film is to end,

and structure all his or her efforts toward that conclusion. Rodis-Jamero comments wryly, "You have to fight for every penny. If you plan for a dime, you must expect to produce it for a nickel because the chances are that your budget will be cut in half during production—or the expectation doubled."

Paradoxically, he considers the spirit of play to be vital to art direction in filmmaking. "If you are not playing, you are not entertaining people. We are serious about budgets, deadlines, good stories, convincing characters, and producing films as inexpensively as possible commensurate with quality. It's a business, ultimately, but we are talking about taking people away for two hours to have a good time, and we can do that only if we enjoy our work."

### Effects Director

Making the impossible believable is the work of the director of effects cinematography. Dennis Muren of ILM insists, however, that the real creative work is done by directors like George Lucas and Steven Spielberg, and that it is his job to translate their ideas into cinematic reality. Muren submits that the primary responsibilities of an effects specialist are to worry about such things as execution, the emotional impact of each scene, the dramatic point to be made with each scene, and controlling the center of interest from one scene to the next. His concern is that the viewer should not merely be watching the film, but experiencing it. Muren's working methods in using miniatures for visual effects are as follows:

Action sequences, once outlined on a storyboard, should then be tested on videotape. Effects are so expensive and time-consuming to render on film that using videotape is necessary to find out what works visually and thereby to cut down on

FIGURE 11.4 *Miniature models of Luke and Leia were used for the chase-through-the-redwoods scenes of* Return of the Jedi *in which the movements were so swift that the use of small models in lieu of people was undetectable.*

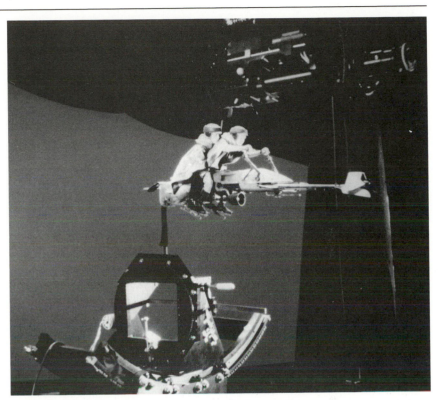

**RETURN OF THE JEDI** DIRECTED BY RICHARD MARQUAND.

production expenses. The mine chase sequence in *Indiana Jones and the Temple of Doom*, for example, was first drawn as a storyboard and then rendered in action with hand-held models to see how the continuity worked dramatically on videotape. While working, they improvised gags with small models to test their dramatic effects. Once into the spirit of a story it is easy to try various effects and see immediately their dramatic possibilities. The videotape need not be sophisticated; a hand entered the scene to lift and carry the mining car from one track to another simply to get an idea of what might work. This tape was transferred to film and given to the film's director and editor to cut in as a guide, and they pre-edited the film to see what would be required in the final effects cinematography.

Similarly, in *Return of the Jedi*, an air motorcycle chase sequence through a redwood forest was tested with hand-held models on videotape (Figure 11.4). When the characters Luke Skywalker and Princess Leia see two enemies leap onto air motorcycles and speed away, they leap onto their own air motorcycles in hot pursuit and two-and-one-half minutes later catch up with them. Every maneuver of the two-and-one-half minute pursuit was planned to the second on videotape. The models used were static versions, but this did not matter. Movement was the subject, and the path of the movements, and this is what was worked out on videotape in real time.

Once the final actions have been decided on videotape, the effects director decides how to render the effects on film. At this point new storyboards will be drawn and breakdowns will be rewritten where shots are changed. The issue of what is best for the film is the primary consideration, followed by factors of cost and availability of qualified personnel. Dennis Muren submits that once the storyboard and its videotape equivalent are rendered, the effects director should think entirely in terms of film footage that will pass for the real thing, and should ask these questions:

What is the best way to make this effect seem life-size and convincing on film?

How would the director, if this were live action, depict this scene?

Where would the live-action cinematographer put the camera? How would he or she light the scene? What lenses and filters would he or she use if it were life-size and realistic?

How would the sequence be edited if it were realistic?

If film footage of puppets and miniature sets are intended to be intercut with live-action cinematography—and pass for the real thing—then the effects, directorial style, lens, filter, and film stock use, image quality, atmospheric effects, and model and puppet movements must simulate those of real life.

The effects director should be present when live-action cinematography is in progress. He or she can study whether the live-action director prefers scenes with a lot of camera movements, the cameraperson's selection of lenses and filters, and whether scene sizes are primarily close-ups, medium, or long shots. The effects director can then plan and photograph their equivalents in miniatures with a clear idea of what he or she should emulate. Muren discounts the old trick of shooting models with wide-angle lenses so the models would look bigger, then tilting the camera angle strongly up or down. He stresses that this alerts the viewer to deception: If everything else is photographed with normal and long focal length lenses, and the images of every scene size are suddenly rendered with a wide-angle lens, the viewer will sense the change before anything else happens and will know the miniature to be a miniature.

The effects footage must correspond in style and feeling to the live-action footage into which it is intended to fit. Effects footage may look good when seen by itself, and yet not fit in believably when edited with the live-action footage. Muren has his effects footage cut into the live-action footage almost as soon as it is back from the laboratory to be sure that it has the look and the feel of the live-action footage. The effects cameraperson must share the sensibilities of the live-action director in terms of style and feeling. He or she must also compare all the other aspects of the shot—the design and details of the miniatures, any movements of models within the shot, the quality of any animation or optical compositing that may be used, and the image quality in terms of film grain, contrast, and resolution.

## Major Visual Effects

The nature of visual effects requires that we consider them first on an individual basis, and then that we examine how they are combined through optical printing. The subject is technically difficult at best but rewarding and fascinating. We will begin with the simplest of visual effects and progress to the most complex combinations. The major effects to be surveyed here include *glass shots, matte shots, and background painting*; *mechanical effects*; *puppets and miniatures*; *rear screen and front screen projection*; *optical printer and traveling mattes*; *hands-on animation and rotoscoping*; and *chroma-key*.

### Glass Shots, Matte Shots, and Background Painting

Glass shots, the related matte shot, and background painting are necessary when circumstances fail to provide the visual elements required for cinematography. If a lovely location is found somewhere needing only a village to complete the setting called for by the script, and the village does not exist, then a skilled artist may be commissioned to complete the setting with the appropriate images of houses, fences, hedgerows, and whatever else may be desired. These three techniques are often used in historical and space-future films to create the illusion of authentic settings, interior and exterior, by presenting cornices, parapets, cornerstones, entire castles, and even cities—past, present, and future—possibly devastated by catastrophe.

Glass shots and matte shots, both rendered on glass, combine techniques of painting and cinematography; they are frequently done in tandem by a matte artist and a matte cameraperson, such as painter Michael Pangrazio and cinematographer Craig Barron of ILM. Their synthesized comments recount, as follows, the evolution from primitive glass shots to the contemporary technique of what Pangrazio calls matte shots and Barron describes as the latent image technique, each speaking from the perspective of his own expertise (see Plate 11).

The principle of both the glass and the matte shot is that the desired visual elements for a scene are added to location cinematography by painting them on glass and combining them on film. The basic difference between them is that the glass shot of bygone days was actually painted on location, while cast and crew waited, and the scene was then photographed. The contemporary matte painting and latent image cinematography method reverses this sequence by shooting the location footage first, with the visual elements painted and added later in composite cinematography.

The methodology of the glass shot is as follows (Figure 11.5). A pane of glass is set up and interposed between the lens and the area to be photographed, and the needed elements are then painted on the surface by an artist in advance of cinematography. The camera then photographs the interposed elements of painting and the distant scene perceived through the glass at the same time, combining the two elements into one scene.

The glass shot has some limitations on stage or on location. For an interior scene the sets must remain illuminated while the painting is being made in order to ensure a match; and, on location, the cast and crew must wait while the artist paints as quickly as possible: The sun moves, the shadow patterns change, and the director often votes for the light patterns of 2 P.M. so that he or she can get by with a couple of hours of cinematography before the real shadows are too different from the painted shadows. This limits the cast and crew and is expensive for the producer. A glass shot painting made today for cinematography tomorrow was often unsatisfactory when weather conditions would change, sometimes bringing rain for a week. Glass paintings were the infant stage of matte painting. They were the easy answer to a lot of problems in black and white during the early stages of cinema, before technology became truly complex, viewers became sophisticated, and the advent of color demanded a higher degree of naturalism for credibility. The glass shot has generally fallen into disuse, having been superseded by matte painting and latent image cinematography.

The methodology of matte painting and latent image cinematography is as follows, keeping in mind the premise that the location photography will be completed first and the matte painting completed later to match the photographic image:

The matte artist begins by going out on location with the storyboards and with a clear pane of glass measuring 2½ feet by 6 feet. The pane of glass and the camera are set up facing the setting in which the dramatic action is to occur. The artist must

FIGURE 11.5 *This drawing illustrates how a traditional glass painting, rendered on location, may be photographed to combine the glass image with a location background in a single roll of the camera.*

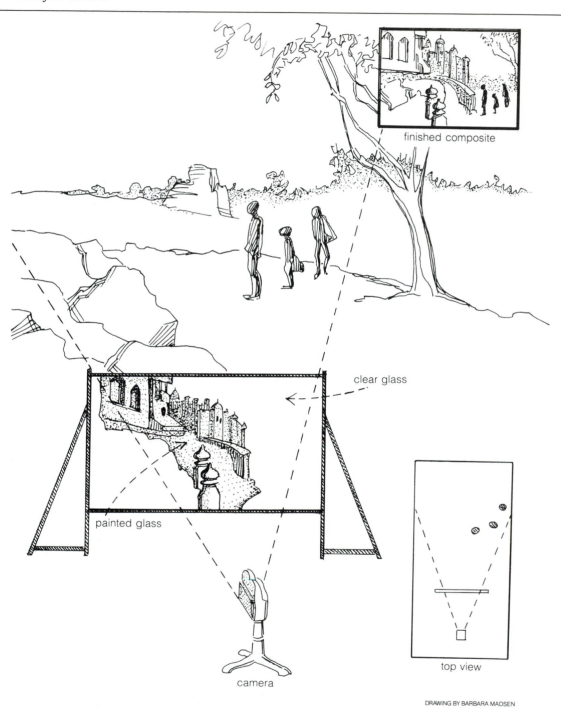

finished composite

clear glass

painted glass

camera

top view

DRAWING BY BARBARA MADSEN

be on location long enough, with the camera in a fixed position, for him or her to see through the camera viewfinder to determine where the edges of the matte painting should be and to get a feel of what will be required to make the painting convincing as an integral part of that location film footage. Instead of painting the desired elements on glass, however, the artist paints only a black matte on the glass onto which he or she will later paint the visual elements appropriate to the scene. This flat black area on the glass, when photographed in conjunction with the dramatic action on location, will remain in the camera as a latent area of unexposed film (see Plate 12).

While on location, certain aspects of cinematography and dramaturgy must be considered. The lens must be selected, focus determined, shutter speed noted, and aperture setting established so that these technical considerations may later be duplicated in the studio. An artist paints the matte line on the pane of glass, and a rehearsal is held to be sure that no heads bob into the matte area before the matte area is painted solidly in black. The scene is then photographed on location and will eventually be combined with the scenic elements painted in the studio—*within the camera*—in a second roll of the camera.

When the rehearsal is good and there is going to be a take, the cinematographer first runs off fifty to two hundred feet of test footage on location to obtain the images for the artist to match. The rest of the actual scene, with the dramatic action, *remains in camera*—unprocessed.

A short segment of the test footage, perhaps five feet, is taken out and sent to the laboratory for development of the negative and printing of a positive. A frame of positive print is projected up on a screen to be studied for color, exposure, and so forth. If possible, the shots that precede and follow the matte shot are similarly projected and studied in a kind of sequence sandwich to work out what needs to be painted convincingly in the center shot. When the matte shot is painted and photographed, all three shots should blend together perfectly without any shift in color, jump in action, or flaw in content. The intent is to hide the painting so the viewer is unaware that any part of what has been seen is other than the true location cinematography.

A pane of glass is now set up in the studio, painted flat black in its entirety, and a camera is set up with the same relationship as existed on location. A frame of negative footage will be put into a camera with a light inside, called a *rotoscope unit*, and the image will be projected up onto the pane of black glass.

When the negative is projected on the pane of glass, the matte area painted black on location will show up as white on the negative, and the matte line will be sharp against the now all-black glass. A white grease pencil is then used to trace the edge of the black matte, above which all the visual elements are now to be painted. Everything above the white line must be painted as naturalistically as possible to match the location footage in whatever forms of content are appropriate to the scene.

When the artist has carried the artwork as far as he or she can without seeing the combined results, about five feet of the painting is photographed with the camera and film (still in the camera) used on location. This footage is called a *shutter wedge*. It combines location footage with newly painted content, and because the glass below the matte painting has been painted a flat black, there is no second exposure of the footage photographed on location.

Composite footage is projected on a

screen, and everyone associated with visual effects critiques the quality of the painting and the credibility of its match to the location footage. There may be such comments as, "I don't like that cloud," or "Let's move the castle over an inch," or "It needs more haze to look farther away." Once a consensus has been reached as to what requires change, the artist returns to the matte painting and further develops the work. Another twenty frames will be exposed, combining painting and location footage, processed, and similarly projected to see how convincing the composite image has become. After three to six shutter wedge critique sessions the painting will have reached the stage of extreme refinement. Then the director or producer may be called in and asked for an opinion. Aside from a minor change or two, the matte painting is completed and is turned over to a matte cinematographer for composite photography of the two scenes within the camera.

When the film is sent to the laboratory for processing, both the scene shot on location and the matte painting now included within each frame represent camera original footage. This means optimum quality, with none of the slight degradation of grain that accompanies an effects shot in which the elements of two scenes are photographed separately and then printed together.

The limitation inherent in matte painting and latent image cinematography, conclude Craig Barron and Michael Pangrazio, is that the camera must, under most circumstances, be kept in a fixed position; any attempt to pan or tilt the camera would displace the matte position in relation to its background within the frames of film. This limitation may be offset somewhat by photographing the matte scenes on a larger film format than is used in the rest of the film, for instance, photo-graphing the matte scenes on Vistavision rather than on the 35 mm used throughout the remainder of the film. This way, when the larger format is printed, moves may be optically printed into the larger format and the resulting footage printed down into 35 mm to integrate it into the film. Despite these restrictions, the image quality resulting from matte painting and latent image cinematography is the best obtainable because all visual elements are rendered as camera originals.

Background paintings have been used almost since the beginning of cinema. The object of a background painting is to convince the viewer that he or she is watching a dramatic action happening somewhere other than the studio in which it was filmed. Verisimilitude in sets has come a long way, however, since Méliès presented a stage background roll drop painting depicting the surface of our lunar companion in *A Trip to the Moon*. Film artists today can make convincing portrayals of entire cities—past, present, or future—intact or in ruins, day or night, which virtually defy detection as not being the real thing. And some artists are able to paint the backgrounds behind miniatures so realistically that even when enlarged on the screen, the setting remains credible. Both matte painting and background painting are dependent upon artists of extraordinary virtuosity.

### Mechanical Effects

A mechanical effect is a machine or mechanical device filled with hinges and wires and covered with hair to become *King Kong* grabbing at airplanes or a (big) life-size model of a great white shark designed to masticate its way through hapless bathers in *Jaws*. Several models of a 25-foot shark were made for *Jaws* and *Jaws 2*, one designed to be pulled through the

FIGURE 11.6 *The jolly pig guard, in clay (Figure 11.6(a)) and finished with costume (Figure 11.6(b)), reveals the development of a mechanical effect intended to be credible as a living creature on the screen. The man creating the walk of another model (beneath the scenes) is Dennis Muren, visual effects director (Figure 11.6(c)).*

**327**

MAJOR VISUAL EFFECTS

water while guided by scuba divers who manipulated the tail and fins, the others constructed as lengthwise half-sharks, and filled with rams, pulleys, and motors to open and close the jaws, wave the fins, lash the tail, and roll the eyes toward the next tasty victim. To judge from the screams of the audience, the mechanical shark was truly convincing.

Mechanical effects are dependent not only on skilled and innovative mechanics, but on expert sculptors who can model convincing life forms, cast them into foam rubber and polyurethane forms, and finish them with colors and textures that will withstand the scrutiny of a close-up on a wide screen (Figures 11.6(a), 11.6(b), 11.6(c), 11.7, 11.8).

Related to mechanical effects are certain visual effects: detonation of small charges in smoke pots that billow clouds of smoke to create the illusion of bombs exploding on a battlefield; suspension of actors with belts wired to overhead tracks so they will appear to be flying over a city projected on a screen behind them, or optically printed around them; fires raging on a stage in controlled settings of backgrounds, and glass shots that create the illusion of a city aflame; blowing up of full-size bridges with people-size dummies and real trains; gentle wafting of plastic snowflakes from a rolling drum, and the roar of a tropical monsoon rain from overhead sprinklers. Anything that works mechanically and is visually believable is used, including fog from spray cans (Figure 11.9).

*Puppets and Miniatures*

Puppets and miniatures fall into two categories in cinema. The first type has no pretensions of being other than a puppet; this form is treated in Chapter 12, "Animation." The second form of puppet is in-

FIGURE 11.6(a)

FIGURE 11.6(b)

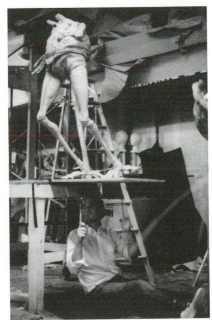

FIGURE 11.6(c)

**RETURN OF THE JEDI** DIRECTED BY RICHARD MARQUAND.

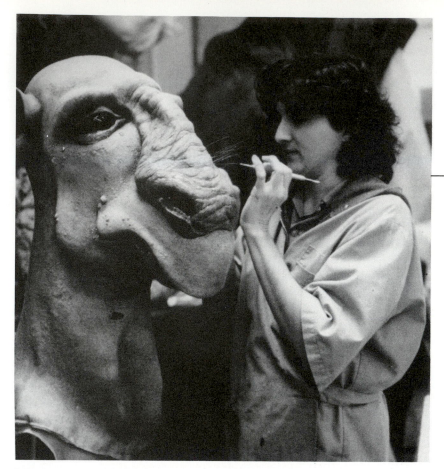

FIGURE 11.7 *Large-scale models are sometimes intended to be worn as costumes, as in
this example created for use in* Return of the
Jedi.

**RETURN OF THE JEDI** DIRECTED BY RICHARD MARQUAND.

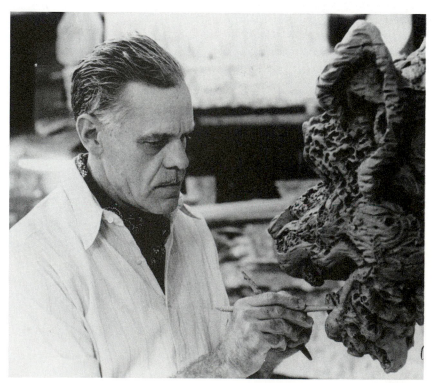

HELEN MUELLER

FIGURE 11.8 *Architectural sculpture, for sets
and artifacts must be skillfully done to achieve
historical accuracy and must be rendered boldly
for effect in photography. Chris Mueller, for
decades the preeminent film sculptor in Hollywood, here models a griffin head for an open
beamed ceiling in* Camelot. *Mueller's work has
been seen in* An American in Paris, Hello,
Dolly!, Creature from the Black Lagoon, Jungle
Book, 20,000 Leagues under the Sea, *and
countless others. He was a designer and sculptor
for the original Disneyland and for Disney
World in Florida.*

FIGURE 11.9 *A cinematic downpour, be it mist or deluge, is released by overhead sprinklers, an effect created here by Vilmos Zsigmond.*

VILMOS ZSIGMOND

tended to pass for being live players in situations too difficult, too dangerous, or too expensive to dramatize with living people (Figure 11.10). The latter form is our primary concern in this chapter on visual effects.

Televised replays of the original *King Kong* and *The 7th Voyage of Sinbad* brought Tom St. Amand into the world of puppets and miniatures; his work for Industrial Light and Magic sums up in many ways the uses of puppets in live-action cinematography.

The construction of models, miniatures, and puppets usually begins first as sketches, which when approved are then sculpted into clay. Hydro-cal molds are made of the clay models; the clay is removed, and an armature is made for insertion into the hollow model. The armature is constructed of wire, with ball-and-socket joints, hinges, and swivels located where one would normally find them in a skeleton of the subject. The artist draws a schematic indicating the location of joints and then takes a photograph to illustrate where the screws are found for loosening and tightening joints; weight-bearing joints, such as the ankles, are tighter than those of the arms and neck. Once the armature has been thus documented, the artist fixes it within the mold and injects rubber latex under pressure so that it pours around the armature and fills the mold. The rubber mold, once hardened, is then cured in an oven until ready for clothing.

The sets for puppet animation offer problems similar to those used in theatrical productions, but at far less cost. The mine chase sequence in *Indiana Jones and the Temple of Doom* was partially done with models and puppets because it was less expensive than building a set a half-mile long and, needless to say, it was far safer for the talent (see Plate 15). All of the par-

aphernalia appropriate to the story—in this instance tracks, trestles, mine cars, tunnels with uprights, and so forth—were constructed in three dimensions. These are most easily made of balsa wood, which can be readily carved and joined. Exterior landscapes or the interior of a mine may be constructed of papier-mâché spread over a wire or cardboard structure and painted. Redwood trees, shrubs, and other growth may be made of balsa, too.

In addition to the three-dimensional pieces for the foreground and middle ground, a distant background is usually needed as well. For interiors, it can be the open-top, three-sided square of the conventional theater, painted and decorated according to the mood of the story. For exteriors, a diorama may be more effective in creating the sweep of an outside landscape. For authenticity and realism, animated models, puppets, and miniatures may be combined with a live-action background through front screen or rear screen projections and the blue screen methods—techniques covered later in this chapter.

After the puppets are made and the sets are completed, the stage must be lighted with small floods and spotlights. The play of light over the puppets should be tested as they are put through their paces on the set, with care taken to eliminate unexpected dark *holes* or *hot spots*.

Action should be blocked for puppets as if they were living talent. In this instance a line is drawn on the floor of the set indicating where the subject is to move. Sometimes this *flow line* is divided into increments in order to have the puppets move from one point to another in a given time, computed at twenty-four frames per second, one exposure per frame. More often, according to St. Amand, a machinist's surface gauge is used, a device with a little pointer at

FIGURE 11.10 *Miniature puppets are created for those sequences in which the subjects are so small or the movement so rapid as to make their detection as puppets difficult, as in this model being made by David Carson.*

**RETURN OF THE JEDI** DIRECTED BY RICHARD MARQUAND.

the top. The point is put to a reference area on the puppet—say the back of the head—and the puppet will be moved a small increment away from the point, perhaps a sixteenth of an inch, between each exposure.

Where really fast or wild action is involved, such as the mine chase sequence in *Indiana Jones,* such precise control is not only unnecessary but actually impossible: unnecessary because the movements are so fast as to make minor errors undetectable; impossible because the irregular structure of the mine interior precludes having a surface smooth enough for a gauge and pointer. In this instance St. Amand drew on experience to animate the mine cars and puppets so skillfully that they passed unquestioned on the screen as being live-action subjects involved in a hair-raising chase. Movement itself became the subject and the errors, if any, were undetectable.

Once the puppets, models, and sets have been made and all the moves plotted, it is time for the effects cinematographer to take over to be sure everything is photographed believably. Photography of miniatures more closely resembles live-action cinematography than it does conventional animation. The subjects are three-dimensional, upright, and throw shadows. The cameras used for their cinematography must be able to pan, tilt, track, and zoom, with tripod heads geared for remote control with a joystick.

Cinematography of this miniature magical world has certain unique prob-lems, among which are the *illusion of real distance,* and *the real forces of natural phenomena.*

Atmosphere, the illusion of real distance, is a major problem when using puppets, models, and sets in film footage intended to be intercut with and accepted as live-action footage. In *Return of the Jedi,* for example, the actual distance of the artificial redwoods of a tabletop forest from the camera—two to twelve feet—was not sufficient to create the illusion of one hundred and two hundred feet of actual distance. Dennis Muren created an illusion of depth in the redwood forest sequence of *Return of the Jedi* in the following way. He draped twenty feet of diaphanous scrim material horizontally across the sets and photographed the forest through the scrim to give the effect of

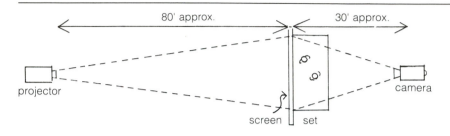

REAR SCREEN PROJECTION

FIGURE 11.11 *Rear screen projection is a useful and inexpensive studio technique for combining a background projected on a translucent screen from the rear with performers standing in front, as shown in this diagram.*

distance. Another method suggested by Muren consists of placing two sheets of fine glass horizontally through the sets, at appropriate distances, and giving each a slight dusting of dulling spray.

Other means of photographically enhancing the effect of distance on a miniature set include progressively reducing the levels of illumination, shifting the color balance toward the blue for atmospheric effects, lightening shadowed areas, and darkening highlights in the distance.

The viewers' experiences with the forces of natural phenomena are another critical factor when using miniatures. A filmmaker can get away with almost any effect when dealing with spaceships or monsters in situations of which the audience has no reference experience. Once committed to dramatic situations that people recognize, however, the laws of physics, motion, behavior, and gravity apply. Small puppets, automobiles, projectiles, and other light objects do not have the same mass and weight as their life-size equivalents, and the viewers will recognize the simulation if the objects fail to move according to the laws of nature. A miniature automobile run off the edge of a small cliff will look like a falling toy if photographed at a normal speed of twenty-four frames per second, and some perceptive child in the back row will yell "Fake!"

The cinematic solution is to photograph the movements of a miniature at speeds faster than normal film speed and then play the scenes back at normal projection speed. This slow-motion technique creates the illusion that the miniatures move as slowly as their life-size equivalents; the car would fall from the miniature cliff with the apparent mass, weight, and speed of the real thing, with a cutaway at the last instant and the sound of a loud crash.

*Rear Screen and Front Screen Projection*

Rear screen projection is a means of combining studio subjects with unrelated backgrounds photographed at a distant location (Figure 11.11). The technique requires that actors stand before a translucent screen on which the slide or motion picture background is projected from the rear, and the subjects and their backgrounds are then photographed together from the front. Scenes of lovers whispering sweet nothings before Niagara Falls are often photographed this way, as are close-ups of the hero walking a tightrope over the Grand Canyon, or standing alone with one cartridge in a jammed revolver against a herd of thundering buffalo or the whooping braves of an Indian tribe on the warpath. More commonly, rear and front screen projection are used in conversations that take place in automobiles to show a city whizzing by outside the car windows.

Rear screen projection of backgrounds offers some important creative advantages: The filmmaker can see both the actors and their background at the time of studio cinematography, enabling him or her to compose their visual relationships carefully. The actor can see the background projected and can react appropriately to it. And the cinematographer can freely pan, tilt, and truck the camera, within the limits of the screen, while the actor performs.

The rear screen projection system also offers other, broader advantages. Difficult or dangerous scenes can be produced in the studio in comfort and safety; an actor can apparently dangle from a ledge on the fiftieth floor of the Empire State Building although actually hanging five inches off the studio floor. Background scenes of distant locales may be photographed separately and integrated visually with foreground action staged in a studio. Finally, exterior and interior photography may be executed separately, enabling the filmmaker to pay careful attention to each visual component.

Disadvantages exist, too: There is often a *hot spot* in the center of the screen from the projector bulb and a tendency of the projected scene to soften into a vignette around its periphery. The film grain quality of the subject and the background may differ because the background image is actually being photographed a second time and is further diffused in passing through the translucent screen. All subject lighting must be kept off the screen. Despite the drawbacks, rear screen projection is probably the most practical low-cost means of combining studio actors and scenes of a distant location, particularly when televi-

sion reruns will obscure the degraded grain of the background.

A famous example of rear screen projection occurs in Alfred Hitchcock's *North by Northwest* when the actor is shown fleeing toward the camera and away from a low-flying airplane that is attempting to murder him (Figure 11.12). The actor, Cary Grant, was actually fleeing in a studio, with the airplane and the cornfield projected on a screen behind him. The movements of man and airplane distracted from the differences in film grain.

Front screen projection simply reverses the position of the camera, the actors, and the projector in relation to the screen: All now function in front (Figure 11.13). The screen is coated with high reflectance material that in fact returns over 95 percent of any image projected at a right angle to the screen. This results in a background image of bright, sharp resolution. The projected image also splashes on the players who are acting before the screen, but this is not apparent to the camera or to the viewers for two reasons.

First, the projected image must be at almost a perfect right angle to the screen in order to be projected back at all for the perception of the camera—a peculiarity of the 3M material coating the screen; this is only a remote possibility when photographing the varying surfaces of the players. Second, the players are positioned far enough in advance of the screen to be independently lighted, and the key and fill lights overpower any flicker that may reflect from the projected image on some hard surface at an inadvertent right angle, such as a button. Front screen projection offers the advantages of being easy to use, requiring a short throw for the projector, and extremely low cost.

A classic use of front screen projection occurs in *2001: A Space Odyssey* when the

**NORTH BY NORTHWEST** (U.S.A., 1959) DIRECTED BY ALFRED HITCHCOCK.

primordial ape first realizes that a bone can be used as a weapon. The prehistoric landscape projected as a background was actually a front screen image, and it passed scrutiny on a wide screen as being photographed on location.

Certain problems restrict the use of front screen projection, despite the clear advantage of offering a bright, sharp image. The required right angle of the projector to the surface of the screen precludes camera tilts or pans to follow the movements of players, which in a practical sense prevents players from moving in any direction that would unbalance the composition. Therefore, both rear and front screen projection offer similar restrictions of movement: rear screen because of the hot spot in the center and vignetting of images around the periphery; and front screen because of the fixed right-angle relationship between projector and screen. Both work best when the actors are logically in a fixed position, as when seated in conversation in an automobile or an airplane, with a projected background streaking past outside. Both tend to be perceived by the viewer as visual effects if held too long because of the sharp edges around the subjects and the differences in film grain.

### Optical Printer and Traveling Mattes

The optical printer and traveling mattes are herein lumped together because the former is the means of implementing visual effects achieved with traveling mattes. The optical printer, however, is the laboratory machine used to print all feature films; we will briefly describe how it works before explaining its use with traveling mattes.

The optical printer is essentially a precise camera interlocked with a projector, used for rephotographing a previously ex-

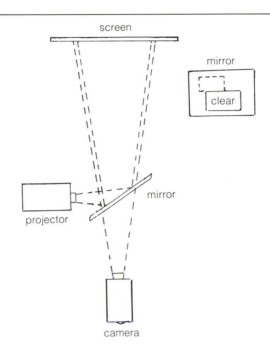

FRONT SCREEN PROJECTION

DRAWING BY BARBARA MADSEN

FIGURE 11.13 *In front screen projection, projected image and camera perception must both be at nearly a right angle to the screen or the image will not be projected back to the camera for photography.*

FIGURE 11.14 *The optical printer is the device that makes possible so many of the visual effects we see on the screen. It is essentially a camera that rephotographs the displayed images of original film, with effects created by interposition of filters and lenses to modify the original image.*

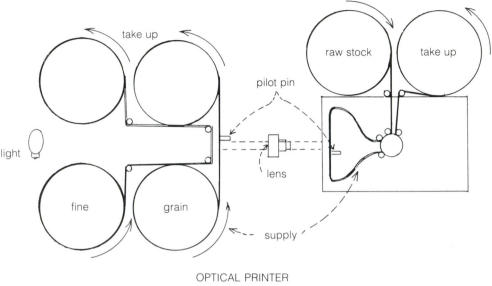

OPTICAL PRINTER

DRAWING BY BARBARA MADSEN

posed scene (Figure 11.14). The projector of the optical printer moves a length of film frame by frame through its aperture, with a focused beam of light behind the film in the projector's aperture. The camera lens of the optical printer is synchronously focused on each frame of film as it appears in the projector's aperture, thus rephotographing it on the fine-grain film stock in the camera's magazine.

During the process of rephotographing the scene the images of the original footage may be modified within the optical printer: A prism lens may multiply the single image of a subject into dozens of images of that subject within the reprinted scene, all performing the identical actions. A ripple lens may distort the normal view of a subject into one seen through the warped perceptions of a person drunk or on drugs. Or, colored filters may be used to raise or lower the emotional temperature of a dramatic sequence.

The optical printer is the most common means of combining the visual ele-

ments of two or more shots into one scene. An animated cartoon figure printed with a live-action figure and background would be one example; a live-action actor photographed in a studio and printed with footage of a faraway location would be another. This is accomplished with multiple exposures in the optical printer with the desired visual elements of each occupying distinct and separate areas in the optically printed scene. The underlying principle is multiple exposure of the fine-grain film stock in the camera magazine of the optical printer with the scenes placed before it in the projector. The execution of multiple-runs effects derives from the same re-run principle used in making the dissolve: The images of one scene are exposed first, then the film is run in reverse with the shutter closed to the starting point of the first scene, and the succeeding scene is photographed. The dissolve thereby executed is a simple optical effect combining the images of two scenes.

Photographic traveling mattes—

FIGURE 11.15 *This illustration of black and clear mattes reveals how a reversed match of opaque black and transparent image areas permits the combining of multiple subjects—photographed at different times and places—by using the mattes to control the exposure of image areas (in the film composite of images) during each successive run through the optical printer.*

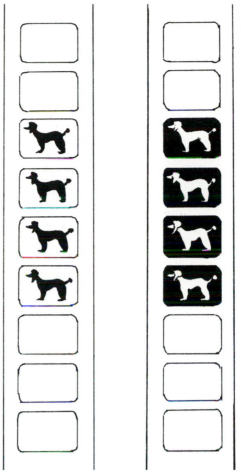

DRAWING BY BARBARA MADSEN

opaque black in interdicting areas and transparently clear in print-through areas—must be used in succeeding runs through the projector and camera (Figure 11.15). The photographic black and clear mattes are used to conceal unexposed portions of the fine-grain raw film so those areas may be rephotographed later with the visual elements of the second scene.

This was the means used by Dennis Muren to create the air motorcycle chase through the redwood forest by Luke Skywalker and Princess Leia in *Return of the Jedi* (see Plate 13). The final composite sequence of the chase was originally photographed as two scenes: puppets and miniatures photographed in a studio before a blue screen background; and the location background photographed of the redwood forest through which the chase took place.

The blue screen background in the studio shots is the means of creating photographic traveling mattes (see Plate 14). The background against which the subjects are photographed—the blue screen—is printed as clear and black. The blue screen background is a color blue from so narrow a segment of the color spectrum in its illumination that it will *not* register on the color film stock. The technical means of achieving photographic mattes are outside the scope of this book, but they should be remembered as result-

ing in two lengths of film: one with a clear core and surrounding black area, the other with a black core and a clear surrounding area. The procedure for combining the studio subject with a location background, in two passes through the optical printer, is as follows.

The studio shot of Leia and her motorcycle is printed first in conjunction with the matte that is clear in the center and black all around: The black matte here protects the background to be printed later during the second pass. The back-

FIGURE 11.16 *Real people and animated cartoons may be combined in the optical printer using photographic mattes, as indicated in this diagram.*

**338**
VISUAL EFFECTS

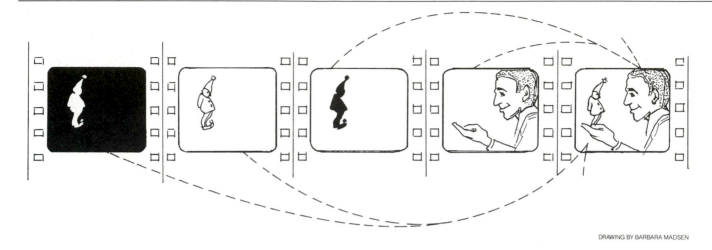

ground forest scene is then printed around Leia with a matte that is black in the center and clear all around; the black center matte protects the image of Leia already printed, and the clear area of the matte permits the background to be printed around Leia. In the composite print of studio Leia and location background—presto!—Leia is flying through the redwood forest, courtesy of the optical printer.

Combining live-action footage with animated images in the optical printer is similarly achieved by the photographic matte process just described, with some variations (Figure 11.16). The first step is to photograph both live-action footage and animation footage to obtain the lengths of film for which the visual elements are to be combined. The photographic black and clear mattes are then created on the animation stand: Each animation cel, with its inked and painted subject, is photographed in silhouette by lighting it from the back and then photographing it from the front with high contrast film stock. The photographic matte thus obtained has opaque black areas and transparently clear areas. A reverse print is made of this silhouette matte to obtain a negative version, which has a reverse rela-

tionship of transparently clear areas and opaque black areas. The two photographic mattes have a male-female relationship, matching each other perfectly, and matching the animation areas and live-action areas of the films to be printed together.

The live-action footage and the animation footage are then run separately through the optical printer, each accompanied by a photographic matte. When live-action $A$ and matte $A$ are run together through the projector of the optical printer, the opaque portion of the matte prevents the exposure of the corresponding area of the raw film stock, whereas the clear area of the matte permits the desired images to be printed through to the raw film stock. When animation $B$ and print $B$ are run together through the optical printer, the already exposed areas of the previous run are protected by the black portions of matte $B$, and the formerly masked areas are now exposed with the images of print $B$. The desired images of live-action $A$ are thus combined with the images of animation $B$, uniting the two images in print $C$.

Through the use of the optical printer, subjects photographed in the studio may

PLATE 11  This glass painting and composite reveals how the painting of the castle from *Indiana Jones and the Temple of Doom* is rendered on a jet black background (top)—remaining an unexposed area—to be imprinted later with the scene of the live-action background (bottom). The visual effect is that of a nonexistent castle appearing at a genuine cinematic location.

PLATE 12  In these illustrations of matte elements and composite, the painting (left) is photographically combined with the location cinematography (right) to create the illusion of an Indian village (bottom) in *Indiana Jones and the Temple of Doom*.

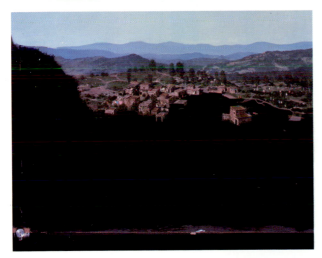

a

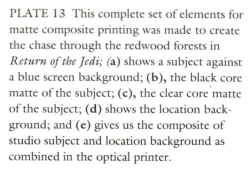

b

PLATE 13 This complete set of elements for matte composite printing was made to create the chase through the redwood forests in *Return of the Jedi;* (**a**) shows a subject against a blue screen background; (**b**), the black core matte of the subject; (**c**), the clear core matte of the subject; (**d**) shows the location background; and (**e**) gives us the composite of studio subject and location background as combined in the optical printer.

c

d

e

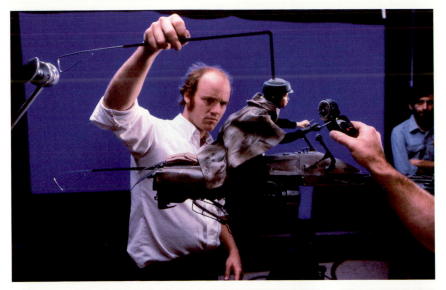

PLATE 14 (left) The use of a special blue color on a screen, which is not perceived by ordinary negative color-film stock, makes photographic mattes possible. Here, Dennis Muren sets up a blue screen shot for *Return of the Jedi.*

PLATE 15 (below) Miniature animation is often done when the cost or the safety risk of using live players is prohibitive. Here, Tom St. Amand is animating miniatures for the exciting mine chase sequence in *Indiana Jones and the Temple of Doom.*

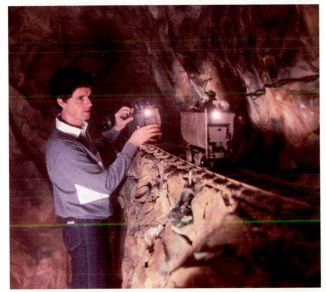

PLATE 16 (top) The integration of live action with animation in *Who Framed Roger Rabbit* was achieved in part by adding lights and shadows to each scene in the optical printer to make them fully interactive. By layering tones according to the apparent distance between the subjects, and tracking focus between them, a strong sense of three dimensions was achieved.

PLATE 17 (middle) Ken Ralston of ILM is shown here overseeing an effect with Bob Hoskins in a Toontown sequence from *Who Framed Roger Rabbit*. In this blue-screen shot, Hoskins is intended to seem as if he is falling away from the camera, on the way down grabbing at a flagpole where Tweety is perched. Actually, a Vista Vision camera rolled away on a track 100 feet long to create the illusion. When printed with the animation, under Ralston's supervision, Hoskins apparently hurtled toward the ground printed around him. For his skill in fusing live action with animation in the optical printer, Ken Ralston shared the 1988 Academy Award for Visual Effects.

PLATE 18 (left and right) Tone passes in the optical printer were crucial to giving animated cartoons the roundness and form that would make them credible as being interactive with live action characters, as in these scenes from *Who Framed Roger Rabbit* of cartoons relating to Bob Hoskins.

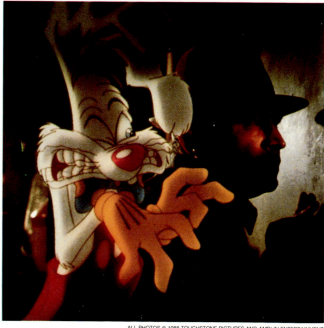

FIGURE 11.17 *This delightful whimsy of a boy (Sean Marshall) —very much alive—and his pet dragon—animated, probably—was made possible by the technique diagrammed in Figure 11.16.*

**PETE'S DRAGON** (U.S.A., 1977) DIRECTED BY DON CHAFFEY.

© 1977 THE WALT DISNEY COMPANY.

be combined with a background photographed anywhere in the world by using the same technique of printing $A$ image to $A$ matte, and $B$ image to $B$ matte, to obtain a $C$ print that unites subjects and backgrounds in the same scene (Figure 11.17).

Combining images on the optical printer offers many advantages: Either the studio subject or the background scene can be photographed first, depending upon which is more convenient. Once the foreground subjects have been photographed in the studio, the background scene can be changed as many times as desired—and errors corrected—during composite printing without ever having to rephotograph expensive talent in the studio to make a correction. The photographic quality of the studio scene and its background can be produced separately at optimum levels and printed together for the best color balance. If necessary to change the sharpness of either the foreground subjects or the background images or to modify the depth of field, it can easily be done through manipulation of the separate images in the optical printer.

The optical printer is to a creative filmmaker what paint, brushes, and a gigantic canvas are to a painter: infinite in its possible rendering of themes, concepts, subjects, and interpretations. It provides the filmmaker with a canvas broad enough to encompass any idea he or she can conceive and photographically render—manipulating the images in any sequence, relationship, or time continuity—to the limits of the viewers' comprehension.

The optical printer's disadvantages are conceptual. Because the studio subjects and the background scenes are photographed at different times, it is impossible for the filmmaker to view the actors against their backgrounds while they perform in order to be sure that the composition and perspective elements are correct. The actors, in turn, find it difficult to react to a background they cannot see and that may not yet exist. Panning and tilting movements are virtually precluded because they would require corresponding movements across a background that cannot be seen. And, there are sometimes perceptible differences in lighting between subject and background.

### Hands-On Animation

Hands-on animation is a way of clarifying or supplementing live-action footage with artwork, usually in the form of artist-drawn animation. It differs from conventional animation in the sense that it is supportive and most often used as a visual effect intended to pass for live-action footage.

Perhaps typical of hands-on technique

was the laser swordfight between the villain Darth Vader and the Jedi hero Ben Kenobi in *Star Wars* (Figure 11.18). In the original live-action cinematography the fiberglass swords were covered with a high-reflectance material that shimmered so much light that they glittered—but did not quite glow. George Lucas, the director, wanted them to glow. They were made to glow by hands-on animation as follows:

> The processed film of the swordfight was put *inside the camera* of an animation stand, and with the aid of a *rotoscope unit* the images were projected down through the lens to the surface of an animation table. (In this case, the camera, normally the receiver of images, becomes a *projector.*)
>
> Animators then traced on paper the exact positions of the two laser swords in each frame of live-action film.
>
> The animators took their tracings and rendered them in paint on sheets of cellophane (cels) and then returned to the animation stand to photograph them in the exact positions of the original projected images of the swords.
>
> The animated images of the laser swords were then printed with the live-action images of the swordfight in the optical printer. By soft-focusing the painted swords in the printing process, they made the swords seem to glow, as Lucas wanted.

Hands-on animation is frequently used to sharpen bolts of lightning or electricity or to add cartoon figures, birds, or even fish, as in *Mr. Limpet*. Animation concepts and techniques are treated in Chapter 12.

### Chroma-Key

Chroma-key is a video electronic system that offers another means of combining

FIGURE 11.18 *The swords of Darth Vader (Dave Prowse and voice of James Earl Jones) and Ben Kenobi (played by Alec Guinness) were supposed to glow instead of glitter, according to George Lucas; the glow was created frame by frame by combining the live-action footage with hands-on animation: swords painted on animation cels by artists.*

**STAR WARS** DIRECTED BY GEORGE LUCAS.

live action with animation, or live action with live action, for use in film or videotape programs for television. Color separation is the basis for combining the visual elements of two different scenes into one. In this respect, its concept is similar to that of the blue screen color-key lighting technique described earlier except that its technology is not chemical but electronic.

Chroma-key is a color matrix system based upon the capability of a color spectrum unit to electronically suppress all luminance information of selected portions of the spectrum. It is the electronic equivalent of the blue screen technique. For example, if a live-action subject is photographed against a blue screen background—when blue is the color suppressed by the color-key unit—the background of the subject will remain an undeveloped area, prepared to receive the images of the animation footage and its background. The images of the live-action subject (with blue screen background) and the images of the animation or visual effects are channeled through the chroma-key unit and the visual effects amplifier to a videotape recorder; there the animated images or visual effects are elecronically imprinted upon the blue screen background of the live-action background, thereby becoming an integrated composite on videotape. Editing is done electronically by the filmmaker while watching each visual element over videotape monitors, and then the composite videotape program is ready for broadcast over television.

The chroma-key system has two obvious advantages in its immediacy and low production costs. Its disadvantages are threefold: First, the lack of an accurate registration system makes it difficult to achieve eye-to-eye relationships between the combined subjects. Second, because the images are combined by electronically cutting a hole in the background to receive the subjects in the foreground, the contours between the two are delineated by a hard-edged halo, which is easy to see. Third, any blue in the foreground figures—a blue dress or a blue necktie, for example—may bleed through and appear transparent.

## Minor Visual Effects

A number of minor visual effects have been developed for esoteric purposes, some of which are achieved in cinematography and some in the printing process. These are *slow motion, time lapse, distortion, the spin, the freze-frame, reverse movements, skip-framing*, and *the multiple-image effect*.

### Slow Motion

Slow motion, the portrayal of a dramatic action in a far longer span of time than it would really take to occur, is a cinematography visual effect used to connote several meanings depending upon the circumstances of the story. This effect is achieved by photographing the action at faster than sound speed, and then projecting the film at a slower rate of speed. The use of slow motion to expand the important instant of death, first used by Japanese filmmakers, is now widely adopted in American films. In *They Shoot Horses, Don't They?* the mercy killing of a horse at the beginning of the film and the slaying of a woman at its end were rendered in slow motion as the slain creatures floated rather than fell to the ground. Other uses of the slow-motion technique are to simulate the perspective of someone who is fantasizing, drunk, or on drugs.

## Time Lapse

Time-lapse photography is a means of recording movements in subjects whose changes are so slow as to be imperceptible to the unaided eye. The technique consists essentially of exposing one frame of film at widely separated intervals of time; the professional method is to use a device called the *intervalometer*, which can be preset to trip the camera shutter at specific intervals of time. A common application of time-lapse photography is the photographic recording of growth in plants. A frame of film exposed at one-minute intervals could render the growth, budding, and flowering of a plant that would present, when projected at sound speed, a graphic portrayal of growth patterns. Time lapse is used in narrative film for aesthetic effects, such as accelerating the rising and setting of the sun, which is frequently found in science fiction films.

## Distortion

Distortions in the perception of a subject are often used to create subjective connotations that the person is drunk, on drugs, or having hallucinations. A distortion may be created with a special lens designed specifically to achieve that effect. An ordinary automobile, for example, can be smeared by a distortion lens until it looks like a caterpillar humping along the road—a visual effect created by optical distortion. Other forms of distortion, such as ripple dissolves and ripple effects, can be achieved by lenses designed for that purpose or by ripple glass inserted between camera and subject to achieve surrealistic effects.

## The Spin

The spin consists of revolving a scene or a title around its own center point. The spinning movement is seldom more than an eye-catcher used to hold the gaze of the viewers until the whirling scene slows down and stops, enabling them to read the name of the commercial product or whatever is intended to be the center of the viewers' attracted attention. The spin may be executed by a rotating lens on an optical printer or a rotation device on an animation stand.

## The Freeze-Frame

The freeze-frame is a single frame within a motion picture that is held still on the screen for the viewer's perusal before starting to move. The effect is used when the content of a single frame is intrinsically so meaningful or poignant that the filmmakers feel it should not be lost in movement, but held for the attention of the viewer. In *Tom Jones*, for example, in scenes of unabashed lechery, freeze-frames were used at magic moments for the amusement of all.

## Reverse Movements

Reverse movements present a subject moving backward instead of forward, seeming to defy normal directions of locomotion, the law of gravity, and the continuity of time. The reverse movement of a subject is achieved by loading the unexposed film stock on the take-up reel of the camera magazine instead of the supply reel, and then exposing the film in reverse. When the film is processed and projected in the normal forward motion, the subjects will move backward. This technique was used in *Indiana Jones and the Temple of Doom* to create the illusion of a heart being torn out of a man's chest.

## Skip-Framing

Skip-framing is an optical printing technique in which frames of the original

FIGURE 11.19 *Three aspects were involved in the creation of this extraordinary film: The first phase concerned the staging and cinematography of the live-action scenes at Amblin Entertainment in Los Angeles under the direction of Robert Zemeckis. The second part was the rendering of the animation (to be combined with the live-action portion) at Elstree Studios in London under the artistic supervision of Richard Williams.*

scene are periodically omitted in printing. The effect is to introduce a slight jitter in the subject's movements and to apparently speed up the subject's actions. The effect is achieved by setting the optical printer to skip every fifth or sixth frame, depending on how jittery an effect is desired. The skipping may be done at any preselected interval of frames, but the practical maximum distance of the effect is about every twelve frames, at half-second projection intervals. Beyond the half-second perception time, skipping tends to be interpreted as an error or a jump cut. Skip-framing finds its greatest uses in comic effects and television commercials.

### The Multiple-Image Effect

The multiple-image effect, in which several events are occurring simultaneously in several panels within a single scene, is in current vogue giving vigorous exercise to the film literacy of the viewer. The separate images are supposed to add up to a third meaning not inherent in any of the events occurring on the screen—the meaning being inferred by the viewer.

In the dramatic film *Grand Prix*, for example, multiple-image panels were used to show each of the racing cars being started, the determined frenzy of the mechanics, and the intensity of the drivers. Later, during the most competitive moments of the race, multiple-image panels were presented to show the simultaneous anxiety and excitement of the bystanders and the determined faces of the drivers. And when tragedy struck, the viewer saw the instantaneous reactions of widely separated viewers.

Another dramatic application of the multiple-image concept appeared in *The Andromeda Strain*. A woman scientist began to think about various aspects of a scientific problem. Her image was then re-duced to a small square in one corner of the screen while her ideas were visualized one panel at a time on the screen, leading the viewer visually through her thought process.

Multiple images may be used to present several different subjects having only an implied content relationship, with that relationship to be inferred by the viewer. A scene might contain, for example, separate images of a snowy forest, a mechanized lumbering operation, deer browsing on spruce twigs, children tobogganing down a slope, and a Canada jay scolding a man shoveling his front walk—the sum meaning revealing the lifestyle of Ontario in *A Place to Stand*.

The one great advantage of the multiple-image technique is flexibility. Thanks to the optical printer's capacity to play images of any size anywhere on the printing film stock—in separate passes—each image may be printed at any desired size, time, and place in any given scene, with a perfect relationship to all other images similarly printed. Moreover, because the separate images are printed in separate runs through the optical printer, each image may be modified in printing with filters and special lenses, independently of any other image. The multiple-image concept promises insights not formerly possible in the cinema.

The major and minor forms of effects surveyed here barely skim the surface of the world of visual effects, but we may now be sensitized to how the impossible is indeed made plausible. As the sophistication of the audience grows, so will the imagination and skills of the creative effects people (Figure 11.19).

The making of *Who Framed Roger Rabbit*, discussed in Chapter 1, required the use of virtually every known technique of visual effects, with innumerable new methods created for this brilliant combi-

"And the third part was Industrial Light and Magic, who had to put Bob Hoskins and Roger Rabbit together," says Robert Watts, line co-producer of the film. "That," he says, "was the most difficult part of the film. The live-action part was extremely difficult because it was like making a huge 'invisible man' movie. All the props had to move and there was nobody there. It was difficult, particularly for Bob Hoskins and Christopher Lloyd, because they were doing a lot of one-to-one scenes with two characters and they were actually performing to thin air. Then, subsequently, live action and animation had to develop new methods in order to match together. Then, all this had to be amalgamated into one film—and make it believable—which is where ILM came in. . . . They did a wonderful job of sticking two movies together to make one film: Who Framed Roger Rabbit."

**WHO FRAMED ROGER RABBIT** DIRECTED BY ROBERT ZEMECKIS.

nation of live action and animated cinema.

Robert Watts said, "The film's director Robert Zemeckis was determined to photograph the live-action portion with in-depth lighting and mobile camera, rather than the flat lighting and locked-down camera used in previous interactive films. The animation director Richard Williams was equally determined to make the animated cartoons fully modeled, rather than flat, and fully interactive with the live-action portion. We were essentially making two films—one live action and one animated—to be fused together into one film by the optical department of Industrial Light and Magic."

Frank Marshall explained, "Early on, it was decided that instead of incorporating the light and shadows on a single cel of animation and simply compositing these cels with the live-action portion (as was done in the past with interactive films), each frame of film would be composed of a multitude of independent film and animation elements to be combined by use of the optical printer. Not only did each frame include the live-action background and the cels of character animation, but all of the tones were layered onto each character and its background. By adding lights and shadows to each scene, printing them into both live-action and animated portions, the optical department of Industrial Light and Magic was able to combine the animated cartoons with the living characters convincingly and make them fully interactive." (See Plate 16.)

Ken Ralston, working at ILM, was responsible for creating the optical effects that would, when the cartoons were printed with the live-action portion, enable Roger Rabbit to apparently blow his nose into a real handkerchief with one hand while holding a real glass of liquor in the other. Ralston was present during

FIGURE 11.20 *Mechanical effects were crucial to the success of visual effects in this film. Here we see Hoskins interacting with a pipe and spigot that are spewing water with the fixtures eventually covered by a cartoon of Roger Rabbit spitting out dishwater. For his creativity in making these mechanical effects, George Gibbs shared the 1988 Academy Award for Visual Effects with Ken Ralston.*

cinematography to assure that the effects being choreographed could indeed be combined convincingly as visual effects in the optical printer (see Plate 17).

Ralston said, "We ran tests with every effect to see how they would work. Bob Zemeckis blocked the action with the actor Bob Hoskins so that the robotic effects occurred where they could later be integrated with the cartoons. It was the job of George Gibbs to place the mechanical arms and fixtures and work them so the visual effects would be convincing and yet be done with hardware that would later be covered up by the cartoons.

"One example of this," Ralston continued, "was the scene in which Hoskins submerged Roger Rabbit in the dishwater while the weasels ransacked the apartment. When Hoskins let Roger come up for air, the rabbit was supposed to squirt out a mouthful of dishwater. Gibbs created the mechanical aspect of this effect by having a spigot mounted at the height of Roger's mouth when he came up, with a thin nozzle to spew out the water. The animators later drew the cartoon over the spigot and nozzle and puckered his mouth around the point that would emit the water (Figure 11.20). All of the mechanical devices were essentially constructed in this way to achieve their effects—photo-

**WHO FRAMED ROGER RABBIT** DIRECTED BY ROBERT ZEMECKIS

graphed as part of the live-action cinematography, with the animated cartoons rendered later to cover up the devices and reveal only the effects."

The realistic quality of the lighting on the cartoons in *Roger Rabbit* has been widely noted. Ralston explained, "The animators achieved credibility in this way. Rubber puppets in the scale of Roger Rabbit (or other cartoon characters) were photographed so the animators could see how lighting played on their surfaces when they were three-dimensional. Frames of film from the puppet footage were photostatically enlarged to the size of an animation field guide (the size at which most animators work), and the animators drew and painted the lighting on the cartoons that was indicated by the fall of light on the puppets.

"When the puppets had been photographed in each scene, they were removed, and George Gibbs rigged mechanical devices in their places at the correct angles and heights appropriate to the intended effects, so that Bob Hoskins could interact with an imaginary character that would eventually become Baby Herman smoking a real cigar, Roger Rabbit spitting out real water, Weasels shooting real firearms."

Frank Marshall added, "Articulate mattes were drawn for every frame in the movie where an animated character went behind or interacted with props on the set. In all cases, including Toontown, the live action was photographed first, then the Toon characters were drawn to interact with what already existed. Of course, what 'already exists' had to be a 'live set,' a set that was in motion because of what the invisible Toons were doing. That was the most difficult aspect of set and prop design. When the live action shooting was finished, we basically had an invisible man movie starring Bob Hoskins."

Ken Ralston described how the optical printer at ILM was used to combine the invisible man live-action movie with the cartoon animation movie so that Roger Rabbit and the other characters would interact with Bob Hoskins in the real world. "What helps us blend a cartoon effect into the live-action world is to break up its elements into component pieces so that each of them can be modified by the optical department. For example, the cel drawings of Roger Rabbit are flat and two-dimensional cartoons. To add a three-dimensional quality, we would superimpose effects on the cel of Roger. If a light was coming through the live-action window, we would print rim light on his ears, cheeks and shoulder—high contrast elements that had color added to them. If there were shadows from Roger in this scene, these would be printed into the live-action portions, again in color. To give a sense of modeling of the form (as a real person would be shaded by light and dark), we did tone passes which essentially gave shading and form to the features and clothing of the cartoon characters (see Plate 18).

"Moreover," Ralston concluded, "each element of light, shadow, and tone passes for form were further controlled by selective focus: sharp focus for the foreground, softer focus for the middle ground, softest focus on the background. Through selective control of focus, the animation elements were given the appearance of depth of field found in the live-action elements. And this was further emphasized by a series of dissolves going to different focus levels according to the apparent distance of the cartoons within the scene. We actually rack focused on cartoon characters, something that had never been done before. By changing the sharpness of focus on the elements and dissolving between them, the optical printer enabled us to give the sense that everything was happening at once in full interaction between Roger Rabbit and Bob Hoskins."

*Who Framed Roger Rabbit* was visual effects filmmaking at its most difficult.

This challenging synthesis of live action with animation required the creation of new techniques to conjure new effects never before seen on the screen. The result was a *tour de force* of cinema, a fantasy film unsurpassed in its riot of imagination.

*Art Scott has had a distinguished career in animation: a director and writer at Walt Disney Productions, John Sutherland Productions, Charles Mintz Studio, his own Art Scott Productions, and for over two decades a writer, director, and producer for Hanna-Barbera Productions.*

# Twelve

# ANIMATION
## *with Art Scott of Hanna-Barbera*

THE ANIMATED FILM IS an extraordinary creative opportunity for the filmmaker to give full rein to his or her imagination in defiance of the laws of gravity and reality. Whatever may be thought of and given graphic visual form may be expressed in the animated film. That potential has been exploited primarily for entertainment, in forms that range from the exquisite beauty of *Snow White and the Seven Dwarfs* (Figure 12.1) to the extravagant fantasy of *Who Framed Roger Rabbit* (Figure 12.2), and includes zany television shows such as "Scooby-Doo" and "The Flintstones" (Figure 12.3).

The television advertising industry seized upon animation to make their cereals go snap, crackle, pop and filled the tube with caricatured potato chips and aerosol cans. The animated film has also spread steadily through the artistic coteries of experimental film and has permeated educational film and television programs to express visually nonrealistic ideas that could not otherwise be given graphic perceptual form. The use of animated film to give visual form to ideas is the substance of this chapter.

## Live-Action Film and Animation

Live-action film and animation represent radically different approaches to film, such as *subject matter*, *photography concepts*, *production techniques*, *interpretative values*, *selection of content*, and *imaginative freedom*.

### Subject Matter

The subjects of live action and animation are dissimilar. The live-action subject is usually alive and in motion at the time of cinematography, and the filmmaker's concern is to photograph scenes of the subject's actions suitable for editing. In animation, however, the subjects are traditionally still artwork, objects, or puppets, which are seldom alive or in motion at the time of photography.

### Photography Concepts

Photography concepts of the two forms are reversed. Live-action cinematography is photographed with long sustained runs of the camera, often recording shots that may number thousands of exposed frames. Animated film, on the other hand, is single-frame photography on motion picture film. The film is exposed one frame at a time. Only when it is projected does it become cinema. Because the essence of the animation technique is the single-frame exposure, each move of the subject before the camera, between exposures, must be planned incrementally.

### Production Techniques

Production techniques of the two forms are totally different. Live-action cinematography is extremely mobile, with the camera capable of being turned in any direction and moved to any location—on land, sea, or air—to achieve a desired effect. Live-action dramatic scenes are customarily photographed from several different camera positions in order to obtain a variety of scene sizes and movements with an infinite variety of lenses and lighting. Traditional animation cinematography is just the opposite: The camera is mounted rigidly on a column, pointed toward the animated artwork, and can only

> "Animation at its best may be considered an extension and compilation of many of the classic arts, and displays the kind of graphic magic and fantasy found in no other art form. This twentieth century medium carries on the kind of whimsical creativity of Aesop, Grimm, Andersen, Carroll, Twain, and others. Animation provides entertainment and information to millions of people around the world in what might be called the ultimate graphic art form."
> —*Art Scott*

FIGURE 12.1   Snow White and the Seven Dwarfs *was Walt Disney's first feature-length animated film. This innovative motion picture contained many inspired sequences with choreography that has seldom been equaled since, such as the dish-washing episode with the small animals and the uproarious party with Snow White and the seven dwarfs.*

**SNOW WHITE AND THE SEVEN DWARFS** DIRECTED BY WALT DISNEY.

FIGURE 12.2    *Actor Bob Hoskins says with regard to his role in* Who Framed Roger Rabbit, *"I realized that if I was actually going to make a relationship with Roger, I had to see him, and there was nothing there for me to see. . . . Unless there was a strong relationship between Roger and Eddie, it was going to be a technical achievement, not a movie. I spent hours with my three-year-old daughter, playing games with her imaginary friends. As an adult, your imagination is pushed to the back of your head. I forced my imagination to the front. By the end of the film, I started to lose control. I would be talking to a friend and see a weasel." Aljean Harmetz, "Arts and Leisure,"* The New York Times, *June 19, 1988*

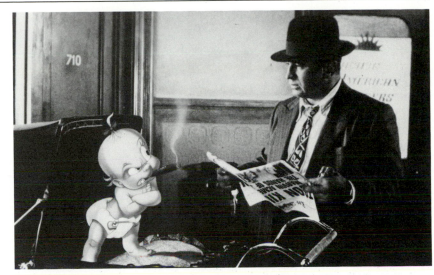

**WHO FRAMED ROGER RABBIT** DIRECTED BY ROBERT ZEMECKIS.

© 1988 TOUCHSTONE PICTURES AND AMBLIN ENTERTAINMENT AND COURTESY OF THE AMPAS.

FIGURE 12.3    *Fred Flintstone is one of an extended family of characters created by Art Scott and Hanna-Barbera for television viewing entertainment.*

© 1983 HANNA-BARBERA PRODUCTIONS

move toward or away from the subject. The traditional animation camera can view the subject only from a right angle; it cannot pan or tilt or change its angle of view. The illusion of a pan or tilt is created by moving the compound on which the artwork is mounted in the desired direction, but apparent lateral moves are no more than cinematic illusion.

### Interpretive Values

Interpretive values of live action and animation are different. Live-action cinematography, because of the great flexibility afforded by changes of lenses and lighting and camera mobility, can provide an infinitely variable range of interpretations of a single subject engaged in almost any action. Moreover, the resulting scenes may then be edited narratively and implicitly to provide meanings and evoke emotions that transcend the content of the scenes. The broad, flexible methods of live dramatic actions, with the possibilities of much improvisation and free interpretation, are at the opposite pole of cinema from the tight, precise methods of the animated film.

Animated film can offer only the interpretive values of the subjects presented to the one lens and one angle of the camera, with the subject lighted with a fixed relationship. Moreover, the resulting footage is not edited unless a mistake has been made, and the visual images of an animated film are photographed at one time, in one location, and in exactly the order in which the animated sequence will appear on the screen. Every move of an animated (actually static) subject before the camera is plotted almost microscopically and implemented by small shifts of minutely calibrated controls.

### Selection of Visual Content

Selection of content is an important contrast between live-action and animated film. The live-action director must to some degree photograph things as he or she finds them and accept the limitations of reality. The director can stage props and block performers' actions, but his or her creativity is nevertheless constricted by the forms of things as they are. The animator, on the other hand, may select any visual element from life that he or she wishes to use, without regard to the limitations of reality (Figure 12.4).

### Imaginative Freedom

If live-action cinematography is so flexible and animation generally so rigid and difficult, why then make animated films at all? The reason lies in their final, fundamental difference. The live-action camera, like the human eye, can only see (and therefore photograph) what already exists in physical reality: You cannot photograph a thought. The animated film is an extension of the human imagination and can give graphic form to anything the mind can imagine through the artwork presented before the camera. Live action can reproduce anything that physically exists. Animation can reproduce any idea that can be visually conceived. The animation filmmaker has total freedom and flexibility to express any idea he or she may have on film—be it totally nonobjective in form, a combination of live-action cinematography, animation, and visual effects, or realism itself. Paradoxically, the animated film, the most inflexible of film techniques, is the most infinitely variable in its film forms and concepts (Figure 12.5).

## Relationships

Art Scott says, "The creation of animated films, and the talents required to produce animated films, are quite different from those that make live-action films. Most of

FIGURE 12.4   *Michael Corleone tries to concentrate on his artwork while his Italian father Angelo yells at him for wasting his time and his Jewish mother brings him a "little breakfast."*

*Ralph Bakshi, the brilliant animator, says about his film* Heavy Traffic: *"A cast of thousands: cabbies, drunks, barflies, muggers, rapists, suicidal maniacs, hipsters, gangsters, and just ordinary people—all the things I love about New York!"*

**HEAVY TRAFFIC** (U.S.A., 1973) DIRECTED BY RALPH BAKSHI.

FIGURE 12.5   *This adult fantasy film anthropomorphized rabbits into a cast of characters having a full spectrum of human characteristics in a way that was as far as one could image from the idylls of Bambi and Thumper.*

*Producer/director Martin Rosen adapted Richard Adams's best-selling book for the screen. "I spent five years on it for just one reason: I wanted to see it myself."*

**WATERSHIP DOWN** (U.S.A., 1978) DIRECTED BY MARTIN ROSEN.

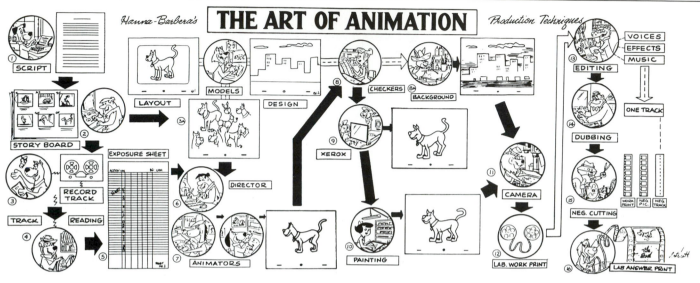

© 1982 HANNA-BARBERA PRODUCTIONS

those who create traditional animated films are trained in drawing and painting, the classic skills of the artist. Indeed, most of the process of making animated films consists of specialized forms of artwork. The art director or layout person is responsible for supervising all aspects of production, making sure that all the animation is suitable for the backgrounds, color keying the entire production, and coordinating all the personnel to ensure effective cooperation in rendering this art on film. Perhaps the best way to indicate who does what is to survey the basic steps in producing an animated film" (Figure 12.6).

### Script-Storyboard

The script-storyboard phase of a film determines its forms and content (Figure 12.7). For narrative animation the story is usually written in pictorial form because of its emphasis upon mood, characters, and entertaining situations. Often the storyboard drawings are themselves pho-

tographed on the animation stand and projected to give a feel of how the film will ultimately look.

### Sound Recording and Bar Sheets

It is easier to synchronize drawn pictures with sound in animation, than sound with pictures, as in live-action cinematography. The voice track, music track, and effects track are usually recorded on magnetic tape and later mixed and transferred to magnetic film. The magnetic film is locked into a sound reader and a synchronizer, or the sound head of an editing machine, and the sounds of words and music are then measured in frames. These bar sheets are the reference points for animators and background artists who determine from them how much time the cartoon characters have to make their moves on the screen.

### Layout

The layout artist is the designer of the whole film. Working from the storyboard,

FIGURE 12.7 *A storyboard is a series of drawings of every major scene in the film; the storyboard visualizes the characters, movements, colors, and design of the production. The storyboard then becomes a reference point for everyone associated with the creation of the motion picture.*

he or she scales the small drawings up to workable size for animation and designs the background composition, architecture, props, mood color and perspective, and the basic moves of the animated cartoons. The layout artist then works with the animators to decide the scene sizes of the images, the dynamism of the animated moves, and the scenes that are to be animated by zooms and pans on the animation stand. The final effect of the animated film in terms of mood, rhythms, tempo, and color key is largely in the hands of the layout artist.

### Backgrounds

The background artists work closely with layout artists in planning and painting their backgrounds (Figure 12.8). The background artist creates the backgrounds to meet the specifications of the layout and the animation moves; the artist follows a color key to build the emotional components of the individual scenes, yet keep them harmonious with the overall tenor of the film. Sometimes the layout and background artist are one and the same person, but functioning in separate and clearly defined fields.

### Animation

After the general movements of the animation across the background have been worked out between the layout artist and the animator, the animator makes the extreme drawings and spacing charts for each action (Figure 12.9). The *in-betweener* then draws the in-between pictures of the action and tests its smoothness by flipping the drawings. The animation drawings are usually photographed on the animation stand and projected for a final critique of the flow of animation. If there are flaws in the flow of the animation, the drawings are redone and rephotographed until an acceptable degree of animation continuity is achieved.

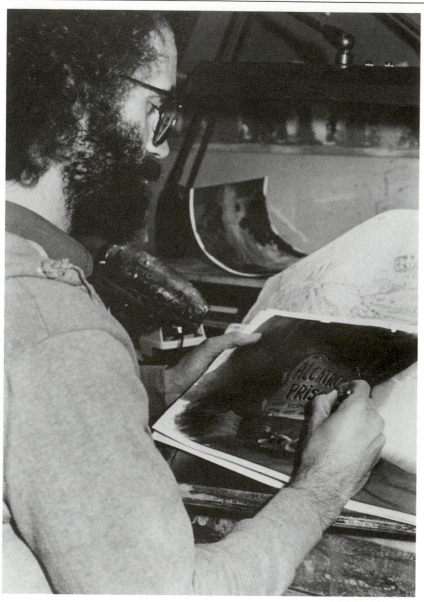

**FIGURE 12.8** *A background artist paints color backgrounds of landscape scenery and interiors from pencil layout drawings and the storyboard.*

### Inking and Painting

Traditionally, animation drawings are then sent to the inkers and painters, who trace the drawings in ink on the front of cels and then paint them on the reverse side with opaque colors (Figure 12.10). Recent technological developments have resulted in pencilled drawings being photocopied instead of inked, with computer-generated color used in animation intended for television broadcast; we survey these new technologies after completing this review of traditional techniques.

### Exposure Sheets

Exposure sheets account for every frame of film for the entire length of the production and for every animation cel, background, and move on the animation stand (Figure 12.11). They are the reference point for everyone involved in the production, and they follow the film's development to the directors, layout artists, animators, in-betweeners, inkers and painters, and background artists. It is now a common practice in many studios to combine the bar sheets and exposure sheets into one-page units in order to reduce the errors that creep in when frame counts are transferred from bar sheets to exposure sheets. When the production is ready for photography, the exposure sheets are handed to the cameraperson with the appropriate cels and backgrounds.

FIGURE 12.9  *The animator makes cartoon characters come to life by following the story board, director's exposure sheets, layouts, and voice recordings.*

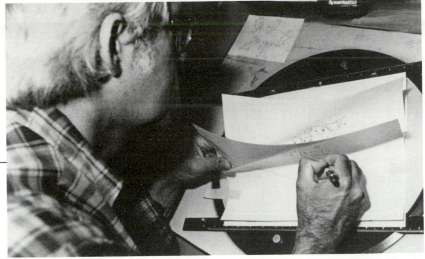

FIGURE 12.10  *Paint is brushed on the reverse side of a cellulose sheet containing an inked outline of animation characters. Here we see a cel being painted for "The Smurfs."*

FIGURE 12.11  *The animation director is responsible for planning and timing the actions of the cartoon, making out exposure sheets, and directing the animators as to what the attitude and personality of the characters should be.*

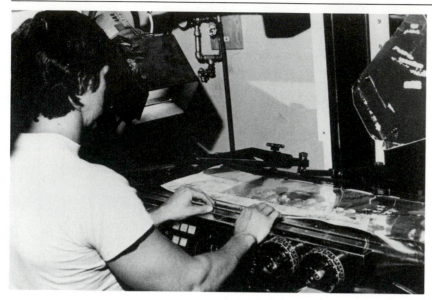

FIGURE 12.12 *The camera operator of the animation stand photographs the completed animation cels and backgrounds—one scene at a time—by following the director's instructions on the exposure sheets.*

the exact length of the sound track and perfectly synchronized (Figure 12.13).

## Computer-Assisted Animation

Hanna-Barbera Studios has developed a computer system for electronically inking, painting, and photographing drawings, and then combining the animated images with the conventionally painted backgrounds.

Art Scott, innovator in the integration of computer systems into traditional animation production methods, describes it this way. "The early stages of animation are done as they have always been done. But, at the point where the pencil drawings have been cleared by the checker, they are *not* sent on to inkers and painters. Instead, the pencil drawings are sent to an animation stand to be photographed with a videotape camera and to have their images converted to digital information. The animation pencil drawings need to be a little darker than usual, and the lines must be unbroken to permit coloring later without electronic spillover.

"The video camera," Scott continues, "copies the animator's drawings frame by frame as digital information in the computers. The video camera has single-frame control, and the images may be rendered in whatever numbers the exposure sheets call for. No zooming, panning, or compound moves are rendered at full size and

### Animation Photography

A person is assigned to check everything to be photographed to ensure every item is in the correct order according to the exposure sheets (Figure 12.12). All the finished cels, backgrounds, and titles are then sent to the animation cameraperson together with the exposure sheets. The exposure sheets advise the camera operator of the correct sequence of cels and backgrounds to use for each frame of film, including complete instructions regarding zooms, pans, compound moves, and any matte or optical effects to be done in the camera, including titles. The exposed film is then sent to the laboratory.

### The Composite Print

The exposed film is processed and printed with an optical sound track, which—if produced exactly as the bar sheets indicated in terms of frame count—should be

FIGURE 12.13 *Yogi Bear, the preeminent citizen of Jellystone National Park, is a proud and lovable woodland creature who tries to preserve the spirit and substance of the wilderness. Hanna-Barbera's famous character has a commendable code of ethics—he is always gentle and friendly.*

**YOGI BEAR** (U.S.A., 1983) DIRECTED BY ART SCOTT.

© 1982 HANNA-BARBERA PRODUCTIONS

FIGURE 12.14 *The traditional phase of inking cels is herein bypassed when a scanner feeds a pencil drawing directly into the computer by means of a video camera. The drawings will later be displayed on a cathode-ray tube for electronic coloring.*

then digitally stored and stacked. Such moves are delayed until after the linear drawings have been called up for display on an electronic light box for coloring" (Figure 12.14).

The backgrounds are painted the traditional way and are similarly photographed on the video animation stand; then the information is stored in the form of digital signals. Long pans across backgrounds are photographed (unlike the animation drawings) panel by panel by panel, and stored digitally as sections *A*, *B*, and *C* of a single pan. These will be combined later with the animation drawings by chroma-key video technology.

Color is electronically painted into the cartoon character as follows. A television monitor displays the outline of the cartoon and a spectrum of colors along the lower edge of the monitor (Figure 12.15). Beneath the television monitor is a black

horizontal tablet that is the same size as the television screen and is wired to correspond electronically to the screen. Attached to the tablet is an electronic stylus, which functions as a coloring brush. A dot of light (cursor) appears on the television screen that moves to correspond to the position of the electronic stylus over the wired tablet. Wherever the electronic stylus moves over the tablet, the cursor moves across the screen. (The system is a variant of what is technically called an interactive vector graphic display mode.)

To color a cartoon figure, the colorist first touches the electronic stylus to one of the colors displayed across the bottom of the screen, say, a blue to be applied to the coat of a cartoon character. Having touched the blue color, the colorist then moves the electric brush across the horizontal tablet until the cursor on the screen arrives at the coat to be colored. When the stylus is touched to the tablet, the blue color selected will electronically spread of its own volition on the television screen until it has filled all areas of the coat as defined by the outline. Because the color will spread until it is stopped, there must be continuous unbroken lines in the drawing to prevent electronic spillover, as if it were spilled paint, into adjacent areas.

As each cartoon figure is colored, it is individually stored as digital information in the computer bank, along with the background: colored animation and colored backgrounds waiting to be combined.

When the cartoon is ready to be com-

FIGURE 12.15 *The colorist touches her stylus—the electronic paint brush—to one of the colors displayed under the television monitor, then touches the area to be colored on the electronically wired tablet. The color will spread of its own accord until it fills the area defined by the lines. If the line has a break in it anywhere, the color will electronically leak through the break and fill the screen with unwanted color.*

bined with its background, a computer programmer sits down with the exposure sheets and types instructions to the master computer—frame by frame, level by level—indicating how they are to be merged on the screen (Figure 12.16). These instructions may include scene size (called *field size*), animation moves, position called for, which colored drawings are to be superimposed over which other drawings, the speed of panning backgrounds, and so forth.

Every possible animation effect—panning moves, compound moves, scene sizes and positions, and relative positions of characters—have all been preprogrammed into the computer, and whatever artwork appears on the screen may be activated by keying it into the desired preprogrammed effects. Zoom-in effects are limited because they require video enlargement of details and consequent softening of lines and areas. Whenever a zoom-in is mandatory, it may be implemented twice, with a half-step difference in the second zoom in order to sharpen images.

Once all the elements of a sequence have been combined through programming, it then becomes a matter of waiting overnight for the computer to do the work. In the morning, the computer good fairy will have left a videotape for viewing in which cartoon figures have been col-

ored and animated, combined with their backgrounds, infused with apparent camera moves and optical effects, and rendered with a broad spectrum of scene sizes. And, because every image on the videotape comes with a digital number along the edge of the tape, there is an easy reference point for locating whatever may need changes or corrections.

Art Scott concludes by indicating how changes are made at Hanna-Barbera: The videotape is transferred to film, the film is edited to achieve the desired changes, and the changes are then reprogrammed into the computer—which again delivers a revised videotape for viewing in the morning. Editing the corrections on film and then reprogramming the elements for the computer has been found to be quicker and less expensive than editing corrections on videotape editing consoles.

For the final form of the program, an-

FIGURE 12.16 *Computer programming is the means of electronically combining animation and backgrounds. Here the computer programmer enters data in Hanna-Barbera's main computer room, housing its three computers— named Azarel, Astro, and Gazoom.*

other videotape-to-film transfer is made for the purposes of mixing dialogue, music, and sound effects into a track that is the exact length of the program. Image and sound are then synthesized on videotape and transferred to one-inch videotape for broadcast.

This computer-assisted technology applies primarily to animation or graphics used for television where image quality is much less critical. If such an image were enlarged for projection in a theater, the grain of the television raster would become painfully apparent. Lines would blur and break up and colors would spread in a kind of chromatic mush. Traditional inking and painting techniques are required wherever high quality is needed for a projected image (Figure 12.17).

## Animation Styles

Animated film styles have evolved into a variety of formats to suit the intended uses of the films and the characteristics of the target audiences. Stylistically, these film styles constitute a continuous spectrum, but for practical purposes we may consider them in terms of *realism, caricature, decorative form, schematics, symbols,* and *nonobjective animation.*

### Realism

Realism, or a related style, is the most effective form for communicating ideas to

FIGURE 12.17 *This schematic drawing reveals how computer-assisted animation differs from traditional animation in the production sequence. Conventional techniques are used until the pencil drawings are completed, then electronic techniques and digital computer programming supercede the traditional methods of inking, painting, and cinematography.*

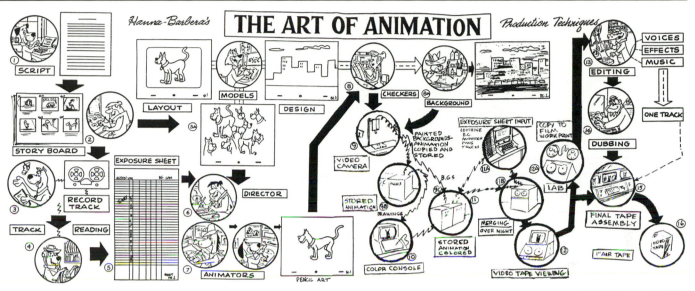

the greatest number of people. Recognizable forms are meaningful even to those with low levels of film literacy and formal education; therefore realism is the most widely used style in educational, industrial, and sales films. The realistic style, however, does not preclude the use of strongly designed shapes and distortions when dramatically appropriate to the visual concept.

On the other hand, any attempt to invade live action's facsimile naturalism with animation is a misapplication of the medium: Naturalistic animation usually fails to approximate what live-action cinematography can do better; naturalistic animation costs far more and results in losing both the charm of animation and the naturalism of live-action cinema. The rightful world of the animated film is that of the imagination; a realm wide enough to wander, without attempting the probable failure of fool-the-eye naturalism. Nevertheless, every step away from recognizable forms narrows the communication effectiveness with the target audience of the animated film. Recognition of content is mandatory in any form of universal communication.

### Caricature

Caricature animation presents recognizable forms but is a step toward formal art values. This decorative approach emphasizes the basic shapes of objects in nature but rejects irrelevancies of detail in favor of stylized, simplified forms. The caricature is very popular in creating zany cartoon figures for theatrical short subjects and television commercials and is responsible for the popular stereotype of animated film as a cartoon medium for children. Figures and backgrounds are drawn and distorted into simple shapes—circles, squares, triangles, free forms—that caroom around the screen with lives of their own, unencumbered by any visual inhibitions except those relating to a sponsor's product, presented with realism.

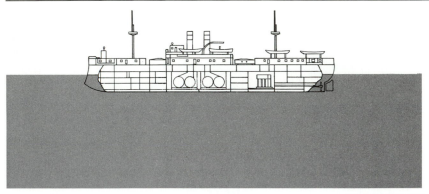

FIGURE 12.18 *Animation techniques offer a means of communicating concepts not otherwise explainable by conventional live-action or video media. Shown here is a technical schematic of a vessel.*

### Decorative Form

Decorative animation is a style common in Eastern Europe, particularly in Czechoslovakia and Yugoslavia and derives from the techniques used in book illustration. Although animated film styles in most nations developed in slavish imitation of the Disney productions, the Czechs adopted his technology but ignored his style. They turned instead to their own folk culture and animated their legends in the charming style of children's book illustrations. Many of their films resemble engravings, watercolor and pencil drawings, gouache paintings—subjects rendered in the round instead of in a flat pattern—and leave the viewer with the delightful sensation of having seen a story.

### Schematics

Schematic interpretation is another step away from realism toward symbolism (Figure 12.18). Schematic forms usually present a two-dimensional cutaway of a three-dimensional object already known to the viewer. The target audience at this point must bring some knowledge of the subject and a degree of film literacy to the viewing in order to properly interpret the sche-

matic forms. Schematic animation is widely used in instructional films and videotapes to reveal hidden layers or the functioning of internal parts.

### Symbols

Symbols such as the cross, the swastika, and the sickle and hammer embody emotional associations, both positive and negative; such symbols may be animated in propaganda films. Similarly, the use of graphic symbols having universal meaning—the arrow, the circle, the self-animated (scratch-off) line—may be used to emphasize special subjects or give special meaning to areas within a scene.

### Nonobjective Animation

Nonobjective animation is at the opposite end of the communication spectrum from naturalism. This style is based upon the premise that abstract forms and colors should themselves be the subjects of art without relation to recognizable shapes for aesthetic values or identification and that they should be produced without regard to any target audience. Nonobjective animation has often been orchestrated with music in symphonies of the eye and ear to the effect of having no counterpart in any other media form. The advent of digital and analogue computers, combined with special effects in the optical printer, now offer new possibilities of creating nonobjective forms in motion.

# Animation as Communication

The animated film has enormous potential for teaching purposes in film, television, and instructional technology because it enables the filmmaker to present ideas and otherwise abstract concepts in their true and understandable relationships. Educational film and television libraries are heavily stocked with films about the objective world that reveal a great deal of *what*, a certain amount of *how*, but very little *why*. The *what* and the *how* are, of course, live-action films and videotapes that present facsimiles of things as they are or pictures of lecturers pointing earnestly to visual aids and talking about things as they are.

The *why* is the educational realm of the animated film; it reveals rather than explains the invisible principles that underlie surface realities. The functions that animation may serve are the *revelation of invisible forces, depiction of processes, simplification of processes, desensitization of subject matter, creation of visual generalizations and projections, recreation of the past, progressive presentation of related elements, offering of visual cues, animation of visual analogies,* and *giving character to ideas*.

## Revelation of Invisible Forces

Tangible but invisible forces can be revealed in graphic forms expressive of their true natures: stresses, chemical reactions, light waves, sound waves, gases, and such progressive changes as the continental drift.

## Depiction of Processes

Animated film can depict processes and abstract relationships that cannot otherwise be portrayed. Mathematical forms and quantitative relationships that exist in a conceptual sense but have no realistic shapes to render in living form can be graphically presented in animated form, with color codes used to separate parts or emphasize elements. Such unseen biological processes as changing genetic chromosome patterns, the neurological response modes between brain and limbs, the cause-and-effect relationships between medication and internal organs of the body, and the forms and functions of the DNA molecule can easily be portrayed in animated film. The unseen processes awaiting rendition in animated form may number in the hundreds of thousands in chemistry, physics, electronics, oceanography, medicine, aerospace, mechanical engineering, and technological areas.

## Simplification of Processes

Through animation the filmmaker can simplify processes, ideas, organisms, and technical structures so complex in reality as to defy visual presentation by any other means: the essential functions and subfunctions of the digital and analogue computer, with each aspect selected in turn for a graphic presentation of relationships; the orbital and gravitational relationships among astral bodies; the electrochemical processes of the nervous system; the spread of a primary carcinoma of the lungs to neighboring lymph nodes and further extension through the body; the effects of pollution on the ecological processes of the sea, or the effects of thermal change on the transmission of sound waves in the ocean; the processes of conception, development, and parturition in every form of life; the basic structural relationship of the space rocket. All of these complex processes may be simplified and presented in their essences—one selective phase at a time—through the infinitely variable visual capabilities of the animated film.

### Desensitization of Subject Matter

Certain human functions may become embarrassing or gross when presented in educational films that portray living people. Subjects in dealing with menstruation, defecation, menopause, various sexual activities, and so forth may be more tastefully presented in animation than in live-action film. By transmuting them from a specific to a more generalized form, animation gives these subjects universality.

### Creation of Visual Generalizations and Projections

Animation can make visual generalizations and projections from specific examples and broadcast them to all those people who might be interested. A small scientific experiment with limited immediate use but with incalculable future possibilities may have its true potential visualized for the influential viewer who may not be a reader of obscure journals. Moreover, the once broad public support for research that has shriveled in recent years might be renewed if people could be made to understand the benefits that may ensue from their funding of certain research and development projects; animation can project those favorable consequences as in the glory days of space flight research.

### Recreation of the Past

Animation may be used to recreate the past as well as project the future. The formation of mountain ranges, the rising and sinking of the ocean floor, the shifting relationships between changing land masses and the migrations of ancient peoples, the religious and cultural rituals of long-dead nations, the evolution of various forms of extinct life over millennia, and the recreation of paleontological patterns that stretch back as far as the genesis of life may be given graphic contemporary form. The past and the future may be animated in the present.

### Progressive Presentation of Related Elements

A progressive accumulation of related elements is a teaching technique that finds unique application through animation. A base element may be introduced and other animated elements then added to it. To the presentation of a skeleton, for example, may be progressively added the forms and functions of gross muscle structure, the cardiovascular system, the nervous system, the major glands and their functions, and so forth to the final epidermal skin. With each new accumulation of elements, the functional relationship of the new parts to what was presented earlier may be shown in phase-by-phase animation. The teaching principle of starting with a base element and adding new elements to it through animation has vast applications to the physical and biological sciences and to the teaching of such ideographic written languages as Chinese. Conversely, progressive subtraction of related elements may be used to trace effects to their cause, such as following genetic consequences back to their evolutionary origins.

### Offering Visual Cues

Visual cues may be animated to point out what is important and to subdue or eliminate what is unimportant in any phase of the film. Color changes may draw the attention of the viewer to a selected part, such as the location of the pituitary gland, and through selective animation relate its functions to blood vessel tone, water metabolism, and uterine contractions.

Changes of values—shades of light and dark—can shift in and out when introducing each part in relation to the whole, as when describing cell collaboration with the nervous system in adjusting the body to changes in the environment.

Arrows, circles, dotted lines, and scratch-off lines (apparently self-animated lines moving across the screen) may appear and act independently to point out important parts and functions and then relate those elements to other parts and functions within the same scene.

Movement of one part may be presented at normal speed whereas the movements of all other parts are accelerated, decelerated, or held in limbo to express precisely those ideas the filmmaker wishes to communicate.

Animation may reveal not only how things work, but what they mean. Although concepts such as prejudice, tolerance, and freedom are intangible, they can nevertheless be given credible, visible form through animation. Creativity, that most intangible of human capabilities, is explored in the film *Why Man Creates*, which expresses each primary circumstance and condition under which people are stimulated to innovative thought.

### Animation of Visual Analogies

Animated analogies may be drawn for young viewers to introduce the unfamiliar in terms of the familiar and expand the viewers' inventory of understanding. An infection may be portrayed as an invasion by an army of bacteria and its treatment and defeat by the body's defensive white blood cells, assisted by administered medication. The functions of the human eye may be revealed as an analogy to the lens of a camera. Although analogy may

be misleading if improperly used and is sometimes educationally suspect, it permits the placing of accents and emphasis exactly where they should be for maximum teaching effectiveness. Animated analogies have been used with exceptional success to teach abstract ideas to mentally disabled children.

### Giving Character to Ideas

The animated cartoon figure can give character to ideas in teaching films for children by recounting historical trends and abstract forces in symbolic form and by sparking viewer interest in subjects that otherwise lack intrinsic interest. The animated film can illustrate the essence and spirit of great events in the shapes of cartoon figures, armies, cities, industries, and civilizations, all rendered in the liveliest form of the liveliest art.

Through animation, all the elements of line, form, color, value, and movement are at the filmmaker's command to communicate ideas exactly, uninhibited by the strictures of naturalism.

## Combining Live Action with Animation

Live-action stories that include cartoon characters and animated films that include live-action characters have been with us since the great days of the Disney animation studios. *The Three Caballeros* and *Mary Poppins* contain both forms in charming vignettes. In most entertainment films, however, there is something jarring about seeing live action combined with animation on the screen at the same time. All one form or all the other does not challenge credibility, but seeing them together somehow does. The viewer tends to approach live-action and animated films with different frames of reference, prepared to accept either on its own terms. When the two have been combined, however, they have seemed dramatically to be neither fish nor fowl.

The apparent incompatibility ended with the Amblin-Disney production of *Who Framed Roger Rabbit*, the live-action portion of which was directed by Robert Zemeckis and the animated portion of which was supervised by Roger Williams. The amazing verisimilitude achieved in combining these two forms began with a break in tradition. Instead of flat lighting the live-action portion to accommodate the limitations of flat-painted cartoons, the director insisted on full modeling for the live-action scenes and asked that the cartoon characters be similarly modeled in three dimensions. By enlarging each frame of live-action footage and having the animators work over these enlargements, a close match was achieved in values, chiaroscuro, and eye-to-eye contact between living actors and their cartoon counterparts. Their success opens up a new realm of possibilities for the narrative cinema.

In education, the more common practice in combining live action with animation is to use completely animated sequences within a live-action film. From an intellectual and learning point of view, it provides the best of both worlds in relating inner to outer reality.

## Related Animation Forms

We can scarcely encompass all the multivarious forms taken by the infinitely variable animated film in one chapter. The following genres comprise some of those forms developed to meet specialized needs or unique aesthetic goals.

### Animation of Objects

Animation of objects is an easy, inexpensive form of animation frequently used to depict processes in teaching, business, and industrial films and to sell products in television commercials. The method, stated simplistically, is as follows: First, the filmmaker must decide how long it will take the object, such as a frankfurter, to leap to the embrace of a bun. This time is multiplied by twenty-four frames per second (sound speed) to determine how many increments the hot dog will have to be moved to reach the object of its passion. Then, the actual distance of its move is marked off in the total number of time increments. Finally, the object is moved one increment for each exposure until it has been moved and photographed for the full distance. When projected on the screen—presto—the hot dog has raced to the arms of the bun. If mustard or relish are to be added to create a ménage à trois, they would be animated similarly.

### Puppet and Clay Animation

Puppet and clay animation are more closely related to live-action cinematography in their concepts than they are to animation (Figure 12.19). Puppets and clay models are staged on a lighted set and photographed by a tripod-mounted camera, with varying lenses and scene sizes, mobile camera and shifting lens movements, and other production characteristics more typically found in conventional cinematography. What places puppet and clay films within the realm of animation is that the subject is always static at the time of photography and is photographed after each increment of a move. It remains still photography on motion picture film. Puppets may be delightful if they are fanciful caricatures, as is true of the puppet forms of Czechoslovakia, whose filmmakers are

FIGURE 12.19 *Movements and the spirit of life are created in clay animation (claymation) by squeezing the shapes a small increment at a time between each single exposure by the camera. These shapes modeled here are created by Will Vinton and Susan Shadburne.*

the masters of this animation form. And clay animation has whimsical charm. Naturalistic puppets, however, invite comparison with reality, and in this comparison may sometimes become macabre. Puppetry properly belongs to the world of unabashed make-believe.

### Cutout Animation

Cutout animation or collage animation is found mostly within art education and the coterie of the experimental film. Cutout animation usually takes three forms: the painted cutout with jointed limbs, which is lighted from the top of the animation stand in the conventional way; painted cutouts, which are mounted on unphotographed sticks; and the black cutout with jointed limbs, which is lighted from beneath to throw the animation into silhouette. The esoteric genre of black cutout animation has been raised to the level of an art form by Lotte Reinegger of Germany. Her animated figures are cut from black paper with the delicacy of filigree work; they are assembled with fine joints and photographed in silhouette to exquisite effect.

### Filmograph

A filmograph, sometimes called kinestasis, is an animation technique that utilizes still photographs or artwork and infuses them with implied movement by means of optical effects, zooms, and pans. If the filmmaker keeps the still photographs in almost continuous motion, the viewer will tend to accept the film as a genre of motion picture. Historical filmographs have been made that had so much spirit of life and illusion of motion they defy detection as deriving from still illustrations. The filmograph is most widely used in art, documentary, and historical films and as sequences within those live-action films in which the needed representation of events has no other visual form.

### Visual Squeeze

Visual squeeze is a form of filmograph in which related still photographs are presented so rapidly that the viewer can scarcely perceive one image before it is replaced by another. The entire history of the United States was presented in four minutes with hundreds of pictures in *American Time Capsule* by the visual squeeze technique, and it managed to include most of the major events.

### Pixilation

Pixilation, the technique of photographing live actors with still-frame photography, yields a flickering, tricky effect as the actors move from point to point and pause en route to be photographed a frame at a time. Pixilation began in experimental film and found its way into the humorous television commercial.

### Ultraviolet Animation

Ultraviolet animation is a form of object animation in which the animated subjects are coated with a fluorescent surface and everything else is painted a flat black. The subject is lighted with black light and moved by an assistant wearing black gloves to the effect that only the images of the animated model appear on film. This technique is used by institutes of technology for specialized purposes.

### Painted Animation

Painting animation directly on clear film stock—picture and sound—was developed by Norman McLaren at the National

FIGURE 12.20 *Norman McLaren creates one of his famous paint-on-film (or scratch-off-film) motion pictures, rendering directly on film stock without the intermediate phases of photography and processing.*

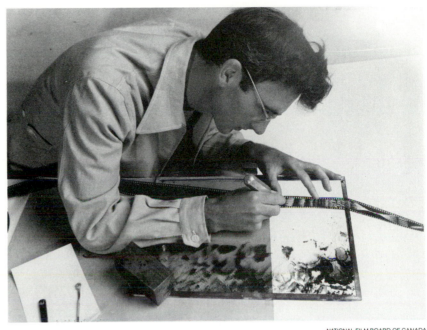

NATIONAL FILM BOARD OF CANADA

Film Board of Canada. This eye-straining technique involves special magnifying devices and the patience of Job but yields an experimental effect that is nothing less than sensational (Figure 12.20).

### Pinhead Shadow Animation

Pinhead shadow animation is a unique form in which rows of pins pressed into a board are raised and lowered, with strong cross lighting; the changes of shadow patterns are rendered by stop-motion photography.

### Pastel Animation

Pastel animation substitutes changes in a chalk drawing, between exposures, for changes of cels (Figure 12.21). This technique spreads the focal point of making a pastel drawing from the end product to the process itself. A frame of film is exposed between each stroke, smudge, and smear.

FIGURE 12.21 *In pastel animation the artist photographs the process of making a pastel drawing—exposing a frame of film between each stroke and smudge—and when the picture is done there is also a completed motion picture.*

NATIONAL FILM BOARD OF CANADA USED BY PERMISSION.

## Restricted Use of Animation

We have seen that animation can make immense contributions to education. Why, then, is it not more widely used?

Cost is the first factor. Traditional cel animation requires that 1,440 cels be drawn, inked, and painted for each *minute* of screen time, a labor-cost factor that precludes the use of animated film in education in all but the most vitally needed areas. The educational communication society has heretofore not been able to afford the needed animation capability.

Image is the second factor. Funny cartoons for the kids that go wham, bang, pow and animated cereals that go snap, crackle, pop have unfortunately created an image that seems incompatible with the goals of education. The mention of animation in education tends to evoke smiles among teachers and elicit academic humor about our "Mickey Mouse course." This image is wearing thin as more and more content experts become aware that animation is an effective way to communicate ideas.

## Computer-Animated Film

A revolutionary technique has been developed that is transforming animated film from the status of being the most difficult, laborious, and time-consuming of the media to one of the simplest, quickest, and least expensive. Through the use of analogue and digital computers, it is now possible to produce animated films in a third of the time and at a tenth of the cost of standard animated films. Had these new techniques been available to Walt Disney, he might have produced *Snow White and the Seven Dwarfs* in a matter of months instead of the years required with standard animation techniques. The future impact of the computer-animated image upon educational film and television programs can scarcely be exaggerated.

The principle of computer animation is that the subject to be animated is displayed upon a 525-line cathode-ray tube for external photography in real time by a 16-mm or 35-mm camera or for recording on videotape. This relationship of displaying images to be photographed is common to both analogue and digital animation.

### Analogue Computer Animation

The analogue computer works on the basis of variable levels of electronic voltage, and therefore has a *continuous nature* enabling it to render images quickly, in real time. It has the capacity to receive and translate images from real artwork—prepared especially for this use and viewed by a vidicon camera—onto the surface of a cathode-ray tube. The images can then be animated in real time, through special image controls, under the direct artistic direction of the operator-animator.

The analogue computer is quick, infinitely variable, low cost, and permits aesthetic decisions to be made on a trial-and-error basis. The analogue computer is—in a very real sense—a new artistic tool that permits creative endeavor as it eliminates the labor of in-between drawings and much of the other drudgery of traditional animation. The moves planned and executed on the analogue computer are remembered in an interlocked digital computer memory bank. Standard animated movements, such as running or walking, can be stored in the memory bank and called up to animate different cartoon figures.

Any energy output can be used to

modulate the image or any of its components as the animator watches the rendering of the animation on the monitor. The animator can produce animation by drawing with a joystick or by manipulating knobs (the joystick lends itself better to the free-form drawing habits of an artist). In the Scanimate system, a videosonic circuit system performs lip-animation directly through a special circuit, without sound reading or bar sheets, and music animates the image in perfect synchrony with a sound track.

### Digital Computer Animation

The digital computer is a quantitative system based on a vastly extended capability of following the simple instructions of yes or no, add or subtract, multiply or divide; it has the advantages of reliability, speed, precision, a wide range of applications, and a large memory bank capacity. The digital computer is ideal for business data processing and reduction of statistical data, where a large number of simple calculations are performed and repeated over and over again. Its application to computer-animated graphics is one of the most dynamic aspects of computer-based technology today.

The application of the digital computer to the creation of computer-animated images requires a machine language designed to control the image on the cathode tube, programming of immense quantities of information, and little flexibility or tolerance of trial and error. Digital computer animation has the advantage of precision in rendering images, which makes the system invaluable in scientific and technical work. An electronic microfilm recorder can plot points and draw lines a million times faster and far more accurately than a human draftsperson. The digital computer animated film therefore becomes important when precision of rendering becomes important, as in mathematical and scientific treatments. From this simple repertoire programmed on tapes and discs, it can draw ten thousand to one hundred thousand points, lines, or characters per second.

A special machine languge is used on those animation forms in which the digital computer system itself generates the images, and the language is unique to that system. The three main programming languages used in computer-animated graphics are FORTRAN, PASCAL, and LIST, with others being developed.

To use this system, instructions are keyed into the computer, and a record is documented containing spot-by-spot picture descriptions, later to be read by a microfilm printer. These are intended to activate a 252 by 184 mosaic of spots numbered 0 to 7. The computer keeps a complete visual record of the image presented to it, packed in the high-speed memory bank, three bits per spot.

The programmer uses two levels of language. After the first and most detailed level of control, the computer programmer directs scanners to peruse the two-dimensional mosaic array, reading numbers and optionally writing new numbers into these positions. At the second level of control, the programmer instructs the system to draw lines, arcs, letters, and other curves, using its own scanners for doing most of the work. The operator can also program instructions for copying, shifting, transliterating, zooming, dissolving, and filling in areas bounded by previously drawn lines.

Perhaps the most dynamic area of computer-assisted animation involves the interfacing of artist and computer in a system called the interactive vector graphic

FIGURE 12.22 *In an image that interfaces live-action footage, the artist, and the computer, the visual possibilities are virtually unlimited when electronic media become an extension of the artist's creativity. In this scene, Sark, played by David Warner, has decreed that peaceful computer programs be put to death on the video game grid.*

**TRON** (U.S.A., 1982) DIRECTED BY STEVEN LISBERGER.

mode, with the artist drawing and coloring on a tablet that electronically displays the images on the television screen (Figure 12.22). (We mentioned this system in relation to the computer-assisted technologies used by Hanna-Barbera.) This technology permits creative spontaneity by the artist working with the system and lends itself to graphics of all kinds and to simplified forms of animation.

The problem inherent in doing conventional animation with this system, however, lies in controlling the in-between drawings to provide smoothness of subject movement from one drawing to the next, in controlling the relationships of multiple moving subjects within the frame, and in controlling the relationship of subject to background. Nevertheless, the system provides the closest interaction between artist and computer developed so far, with immediacy and images rendered in real time and no need to learn a machine language or programming.

The computer has revolutionized the field of animated films. We now see that computer-controlled animation stands to expedite photography of conventional cel animation, computer-based in-betweening of extreme drawings, computer coloring of images intended for television only, computer-generated visual effects, and computer synthesis of live-action cinematography, conventional animation, and computer-generated visual effects. One thing the computer has not been able to do, and will never be able to do, is to create an appealing cartoon character with whom the viewer can identify. The computer has vastly expanded the potential for visual effects, but the purview of the human image and soul belongs, as it always has, to the artist (Figure 12.23).

FIGURE 12.23 *Huckleberry Hound finds the pot of gold for Hanna-Barbera Productions.*

# GLOSSARY OF FILM TERMS

**abstract film**   A film that shows only the essential visual elements of the original forms. Loosely, any non-representational film.

**Academy standards**   Standards established by the Academy of Motion Picture Arts and Sciences for film leaders, projectors, and camera apertures.

**acoustics**   The science concerned with the attributes of sound, as it is heard. Also, loosely, the characteristics of an enclosure—such as a room—as they affect sound. (UFVA)*

**action cutting**   The cutting of film from one shot to another to yield the impression to the audience that the action as seen on the screen is continuous and uninterrupted, even though changes of camera position have taken place. This is usually achieved by overlapping the action on successive shots so that the beginning of shot *B* includes action appearing at the close of shot *A*, but can also be achieved by running two or more cameras simultaneously. Thus a transfer from shot *A* to shot *B* can be made to appear to be continuing action. The principle is also applied in editing shots in which actors enter or leave the action field and in shots in which an action starts or stops within the field. (UFVA)

**actor**   Any person serving as a performer in a play or film.

**actuality**   Activities or events that occur in the real world and not as contrived or fictional performances.

*Entries with UFVA listed are courtesy of the University Film and Video Association.

**aerial perspective, atmospheric perspective**   The phenomenon in which successively distant objects and parts of the landscape appear to have lighter tones and to be smaller. The illusion is created in part by distance, backlight, or sidelight and haze.

**agent**   A person who for a fee or percentage negotiates sales or contracts between writers, directors, and other talent and film producing organizations.

**ambient light**   Light that is scattered about by various sources and reflecting surfaces.

**angle shot**   A shot continuing the action of a preceding shot, but from a different camera angle. (UFVA) See also, *shot*.

**animation**   The art or process of synthesizing apparent mobility of inanimate objects or drawings through the medium of cinematography. This is usually achieved by exposing films in units of one, two, or three frames followed by slight progressive changes of the materials or objects being photographed.

**animator**   The person who determines the amount of progressive change in objects or drawings used for animation.

**answer print, trial print, first trial composite, trial composite**   The first combined picture and sound print, in release form, of a finished film. It is usually studied carefully to determine whether further changes are required prior to release printing. (UFVA)

**antagonist**   According to the theory of opposing forces in conventional or traditional technique, the audience must be able to identify with the forces of virtue in a struggle for dominance over the forces of evil. The protagonist or hero represents the forces of virtue, with which the audience is sympathetic; the antagonist is the villain, the threat, the force of evil, without which the story would not be worth telling. (UFVA)

**art director**   The person who assesses the staging requirements for a production and arranges for and supervises the work of set design and preparation.

**aspect ratio**   The width-to-height ratio of a motion picture frame, usually expressed as $1 \times 1{:}33$ in 16 mm cinematography. (UFVA) Also, the ratio of the frame dimensions as projected on a screen.

**available light filming**   Filming with whatever interior light is in use with no additional lighting, often with fast film, fast lenses, and forced processing.

**backlight**   A luminaire positioned behind and in line with subject and camera, used to create highlights on the subject as a means of separating the subject from the background and increasing the subject's appearance of three dimensionality. In studio lighting, the backlight is usually a spotlight positioned above and behind the subject. For outdoor cinematography the sun is often used as a backlight. Also, the term refers to the illumination created by a backlight.

**backlot**   The outdoor work area of a studio complex where exterior sets are maintained and where inactive sets and properties are stored. See also, *lot*.

**bar sheets, lead sheets** A chart showing words of dialogue that have been recorded and the number of motion picture frames of duration for each syllable and pause in the dialogue, used chiefly in animation.

**bipack camera, bipack contact matte printing, bipack printing** Any camera or printer arrangement or setup in which two pieces of film are run through together for purposes of matting or double exposure. (UFVA)

**blocking, blocking the action, blocking the scene** Planning and schematizing the movement and positions of performers, especially in relation to the delivery of their lines of dialogue and to the camera.

**blue screen process** Photography action in front of a blue background in order to make a matte. See also *traveling matte*.

**boom, camera boom** A sturdy vehicular support providing vertical, horizontal, pivotal, and translational movement for camera and operator, enabling them to assume, rapidly and conveniently, almost any desired angle or movement in relation to the scene to be photographed. (UFVA) See also, *crane*.

**bounce lighting, bounce light** Light coming from conventional lighting instruments that are aimed not at the subject but at ceilings and walls with the result that the illumination for cinematography is very diffuse and general.

**box office** The small room from which theater tickets are sold. Also, income from film showings or an indication of the popularity or success of a film or star.

**bridge, bridge music** A short piece of music used in the sound track to cover a transition in a film.

**business** Action introduced for the purpose of building up to or reinforcing an idea or trend in the plot of a play or film. (UFVA) Also, the economic activity involved in the financing, production, distribution, and exhibition of films.

**camera right, camera left, screen right, screen left** An east-west orientation useful to directors, directors of photography, and camera operators concerned with translating scripted or unscripted scenes into images that can be edited into consistent movement patterns.

**casting director** The person responsible for the selection of film actors other than the principal actors.

**cel** A transparent sheet of cellulose acetate or similar plastic serving as a support for drawings, lettering, and other figures in animation and title work. Usually it is punched, outside the limits of the camera field, with holes that fit pegs similarly arranged to facilitate registration of successive cels during preparation and photography.

**chroma** The amount of saturation of a color.

**cinéma vérité** A style of filmmaking begun in Europe in the Fifties involving the use of portable sound cameras, recorders, and lights and the cinematography of interviews and events on location. Commentary, sometimes obtained from interviews and hidden recorders, was used as well as lip-synchronous sound. *Cinéma vérité* films usually sought strong, sometimes radical, opinion. Often one of the filmmakers asked questions.

**cinematic** Referring to the large matrix of factors that go into the makeup of films, including the technological, economic, and sociological as well as the artistic. Thus, the methods of financing and distributing a film (and the forces these factors exert upon the film) are a part of *the cinematic*. The factors relating distinctly and exclusively to film modes then are called *the filmic*. See *filmic* for a differing definition of *cinematic*.

**cinematographer** A motion picture director of photography, cameraperson, or assistant cameraperson. (UFVA)

**comedy of manners** Frequently humorous treatment of dramatic characters that satirizes or cynically examines their social aspirations and adherence to class values.

**composition** The distribution, balance, and general relationship of masses and degrees of light and shade, line, and color within a picture area. (UFVA)

**computer animation, computer-generated animation** Animation made by various techniques involving the formation or control of images by means of computers and associated rasters or other pattern-formation devices, with the resulting images recorded on motion picture film. In some cases, videotape is used with continuous image formation, and the stored images are later transferred to film.

**continuity** (1) The cinematic portrayal of a logical flow of events. (2) A shooting script, ready for production, containing all visual and audio specifications, subject only to the decisions of the director. (UFVA) (3) The consistency of action, props, decor, and costumes in the forward movement of a motion picture.

**continuity cutting** Conventional systematic editing of film to present story action in logical, smooth-flowing sequence and in a manner that will best preserve the illusion of reality for the audience. (UFVA)

**contrapuntal sound** Sound, especially music, that contrasts or conflicts with the action in a motion picture, and in so doing creates tension, conflict, or contrary feelings or ideas.

**contrast** A preponderance of dark and light tones in an image, with little in the way of intermediate tones.

**costume designer** One who conceives or invents the costumes that are worn by characters and that help to establish the screen personalities and characterizations of actors.

**crab dolly, crab** A vehicular camera support equipped with special steering controls that permit movement in any direction. (UFVA)

**crane, camera crane** A movable vehicle that has a long boom on which a camera can be mounted and moved up much higher than on a small dolly.

**crop** To limit the area shown in an image through arbitrary or accidental framing.

**cross cut** A cut from one line of action to another that occurs at the same time. Also applies as an adjective to sequences that use such cuts. Also used as a verb.

**cross fade, cross dissolve** In sound mixing, fading out one track while simultaneously fading in another track. See also, *segue*.

**cutting in the camera** Making shots in such a way that acceptable continuity results with little or no editing. (UFVA)

**cutting on action, invisible editing** Cutting from one camera position to another on actor movement, made possible by overlapping shots made with a single camera or by using two or more cameras operating simultaneously. Also, cutting on action just as the subject enters or leaves a frame, goes around a corner, starts movements, and so on. In general, it is the practice of cutting during movement rather than when the action is static. Cutting on action is used to achieve a smooth, continuous flow of images. See also, *matching action*.

**dailies, rushes** Pictures and sound workprints of a day's shooting, usually synchronized for interlock showing before the next day's shooting begins.

**day for night, day-for-night filming, D/N, la nuit américaine** Indicates shooting that is to be done in daylight, but with exposure, filtration, and processing that will render the action as taking place at night.

**deep-field cinematography, deep-focus cinematography, deep focus** Cinematography that renders objects in focus at both near and far distances through the use of small f-stops, short focal length lenses, or both.

**denouement** The closing action of a film, following the climax, in which loose ends may be brought together, explanations may be made, and the story may be generally tidied up before the end title appears. (UFVA)

**depth of field** The distance in front of a camera and its lens in which objects are in apparent sharp focus. Depth of field is determined through the arbitrary selection of a minimum circle of confusion and the use of depth-of-field formulas.

**director of photography (D.P.), cinematographer, cameraperson** The person responsible for designing the lighting and camera operation for a film, working either alone or with the assistants making up the camera crew. In large studios the director of photography usually does not operate cameras.

**dissolve lapse** Short shots made at intervals and connected by dissolves, used to record processes in much the same way as time-lapse photography.

**dolly** (1) A small, sturdy wheeled platform built to carry camera and cameraperson to facilitate movement of the camera during shooting. (2) To move the camera by means of a dolly while shooting. (UFVA)

**dolly tracks, camera tracks** Usually channel rails, often shimmed level, to control and smooth out the movement of a dolly during a shot.

**double exposure, multiple exposure** The photographic recording of two (or more) images on a single strip of film. The images may be either superimposed or side by side in any relationship, sometimes individually vignetted. (UFVA) Two such images are called *split screen*, whereas many blocks or images are called *mosaic*.

**dub** To transfer sound from one medium to another, from units that are for playback only. Also, to put dialogue (sometimes foreign) into a film after it has been shot.

**dutch tilt angle, dutch angle** A camera angle achieved by tilting the camera from its normal vertical and horizontal axes. Also called a *canted shot* or *canted angle*.

**dynamic cutting, dynamic editing** Systematic editing of film by joining shots not part of a single continuous line of action. The contextual relation of shots can be used to achieve both contrast and analogy, and the use of frequent reestablishing shots creates the impression of continuity. (UFVA) See *montage*.

**editing, cutting** The process of assembling, arranging, and trimming film, both picture and sound, to the best advantage for the purpose at hand. (UFVA)

**editor** One who edits film. Also a machine that is used to cut and edit film.

**establishing shot** Usually, a long shot that shows the location of ensuing action and that also shows time and place. May also be a close-up or even a medium shot that has some sign or other cue identifying the location. Sometimes called a *cover shot*. It may also set tone and ambience.

**executive producer** A studio administrator who does not directly produce films but supervises the work of producers. Sometimes the executive producer will have no involvement in the film other than having arranged for financing its production.

**expanded cinema** Motion pictures that make use of recent technological developments, such as computer-generated visuals, videographics, and holograms. A term originated by Gene Youngblood in his book *Expanded Cinema*.

**experimental film** An independent, usually noncommercial film that is the product of the personal vision of the filmmaker.

**expressionism** Fantasy and distortion in sets, lighting, acting style, and costumes used as a means of expressing the inner feelings of both filmmaker and characters.

**fade-in** (1) An optical effect in which the screen gradually changes from black to image or sometimes to another color. (2) A gradual change from silence to audible sound.

**fade-out** (1) An optical effect during which the screen gradually goes from image to black or another color. (2) A gradual change from audible sound to silence.

**fast film** A film that has relatively high sensitivity to light, usually an exposure index of 100 or higher.

**feature film, feature** A fictional narrative film lasting more than an hour, made for showing in commercial theaters.

**filmic** A term used to refer to those elements that are film-specific, that is, that only occur in films. This term is narrower than *cinematic* because *cinematic* includes all aspects of films and *filmic* only includes those elements that are film-specific. For example, business contracts are drawn in the making of films and in other aspects of life, but the juxtaposition of a view of downtown San Diego and of the Mississippi (joined by a cut, projected onto a cinema screen) is specific to film: the first is cinematic; the latter is filmic.

**final shooting script** The draft of a script that is approved for cinematography. As opposed to the author's version, the shooting script is usually broken down into separate shots or scenes.

**fine cut** Film workprints that have been so edited that the film is close to its final form.

**first answer print, first trial print, first trial composite** The first print of a film that is projected with an optical (or magnetic) sound track and examined by the producer to determine whether the timing, color corrections, and sound are satisfactory.

**flip-over, flip-over wipe, flip wipe, turnover** An optical effect yielding the impression that the picture as seen on the screen is turned over rapidly on its vertical axis to reveal a second picture on what appears to be the reverse side of the original picture.

**flashback** A shot or sequence that shows action that occured before the film's present time.

**flashforward, flashahead** A shot or sequence that shows future action or action that will occur later in the film, or following the film's later time.

**flashing** (1) Exposing film to a weak light before or after exposure in the camera, but before processing, to reduce contrast. (2) The process of reexposing reversal positive film after it has been partially processed.

**focal length** The distance from the optical center of a lens to the film plane when the lens is focused at infinity.

**force process, force develop, push** To develop film longer than the normal period in order to compensate for underexposure.

**frame** (1) One individual picture, as defined by the limits of the camera aperture, on a piece of motion picture film. (2) To bring the limits of an individual picture on a piece of motion picture into coincidence with the limits of the projector aperture in projection. On projectors this is achieved through manipulation of a special framing mechanism. (3) To compose a shot. (UFVA)

**freeze-frame, stop-frame, hold-frame** A frame that is printed repetitively so that the image in the print can be seen without movement for a desired length of time.

**front projection process, front projection** Any of several methods of projecting a background image along the axis of a camera lens on actors and a screen behind the action. The image projected on the actors is eliminated by supplemental lighting.

**f-stop, stop, lens stop, lens aperture, aperture** The relationship between the focal length of a lens and the effective diameter of its aperture. An adjustable iris diaphragm permits any ordinary photographic lens to be used at any stop within its range. The numerical series 1.0, 1.4, 2.0, 2.8, 4.0, 5.6, 8, 11, 16, 22, 32, 45, 64 constitutes a range of *full stops* in that closing the diaphragm from any one of these f-numbers to the next higher number reduces exposure by one-half; or, opening the diaphragm from any number in the series to the next lower number doubles the exposure.

**full shot, full-figure shot** A shot that is framed just above the head and just below the feet of an actor or actors.

**gaffer** In production units, the electrician in charge of lighting circuits and equipment. (UFVA)

**genre** A film type, such as a western or science fiction movie, that usually has a formula plot structure and characters and that uses expected conventions and icons.

**glass painting** A painting of scenery on a portion of a glass sheet, used in making a glass shot.

**glass shot** A shot taken through a sheet of glass bearing titles or other artwork in order to superimpose the titles or artwork on the moving background. (UFVA)

**grip, production assistant** In large production units, the general handy person available on the set for odd jobs, such as moving or adjusting sets or repairing props. A stagehand. (UFVA)

**head-on shot** A shot of action coming directly toward the camera.

**high-angle shot, high shot, down shot** A shot made with the camera in a position above the action. A downward-angle shot. See also, *overhead shot*.

**high contrast** The appearance of an image in which tones grade quickly from white to black with few intermediate values.

**high-key** A visual quality of any picture in which the emphasis is distinctly on the lighter tones. Also, in lighting, a relatively high level of illumination of subject with relatively short-scale tonal rendition. (UFVA)

**high-speed film** (1) Film that has extra perforations for use in high-speed cameras. (2) Film that is more than normally sensitive to light.

(3) A film made using mostly high-speed cinematography.

**imaginary line** An assumed line passing through two or more performers. In shooting over-the-shoulder shots and reverse angles, crossing the imaginary line with the camera will result in a *false reverse* that will not edit properly. (UFVA) See also, *line of action*.

**in-camera matte shot** A shot made with part of the action field blocked off by a black mask placed in front of the camera or at the focal plane. The film is then wound backward in the camera and other action is photographed using a complementary mask.

**independent filmmaking** Film production initiated by a person or persons not under contract to a commercial studio. Some independents may produce without making use of union personnel or commercial facilities, other than a laboratory. Others may subcontract the production to a union personnel and commercial facilities.

**inker** An artist who applies acetate ink to the top surface of animation cels, rendering outlines and details.

**interior monologue** A type of action in which the performer is seen and the actor's voice, indicating thoughts, is heard although the actor's lips do not move.

**interlock** Any arrangement permitting the synchronous presentation of picture and matching double-system sound. The simplest consists of a mechanical link connecting picture viewer and sound reproducer, both being driven by a common synchronous drive.

**in-the-camera effects, in-camera effects** Visual effects made in the camera by the use of mattes, variations in speed, upside-down shooting, and rewinding the film for double or multiple exposure, as when creating dissolves, fade-ins, and fade-outs.

**invisible cut** A cut made during the movement of a performer, achieved either by overlapping the action or by using two cameras, then matching the action during editing. Such cuts make shifts of camera position less noticeable. See also, *matching action*.

**iris** (*in* or *out*) A wipe optical effect in which the wipe line is a circle. It may either start in the center of the frame and go out or start at the edge of the frame and go in. (UFVA) An iris wipe may go from image to image or to or from black, or to another color.

**jump cut** An instantaneous advance in the action within a shot or between two shots due to removal of a portion of film, due to inconsistent pictorial continuity, or due to intent.

**key light** The luminaire that creates the main, brightest light falling on a subject.

**Kuleshov effect** Imputation by audiences of various places, actions, or emotions from the context of juxtaposed shots as determined through editing; based on experiments conducted by Lev Kuleshov in Russia during the 1920s.

**lens** (1) In optics any transparent system by which images may be formed through the light-refracting properties of curved surfaces. Photographic objectives usually are made up of a number of individual units, each having a combination of positive and/or negative spherical section surfaces. In some instances the unit combination includes a neutral or plane surface. The several units are mounted in a specific relationship to each other in a cylindrical mounting, or barrel, that usually also includes an iris diaphragm with its calibrated external scale and a mechanical device to permit focusing. Glass of appropriate index of refraction is used for each of the unit elements, some combinations of which may be affixed together with an optical cement. Other combinations may be related by an air space, as dictated by the demands of the specific lens design. (2) Commonly, any optical system complete with barrel, focusing ring, and other elements. (UFVA)

**lighting balance** Correct levels of light in various parts of a set ensuring that actors and objects at various locations will have the desired exposure.

**lighting ratio** The difference in the intensity of the key and fill light, usually expressed in ratios such as 2:1, 3:1, 4:1, and so forth. The ratios are derived from two formulas: K to F, where the key light and fill light do not overlap, and K + F, where the key light and fill light overlap.

**limited animation** A type of animation in which main figures remain still while small parts, such as mouths and eyes, are animated. Used to reduce costs.

**line of action** See *imaginary line*.

**linkage** An editing principle, formulated and used by Vsevolod I. Pudovkin, that emphasizes smooth continuity and contextual dynamics as opposed to the collision-type montage created by Sergei Eisenstein.

**live action** The photographed action of living things, as distinguished from action created by animation.

**long shot, LS** A shot that shows all or most of a subject and usually some of the surroundings. Also, a sequence shot, that is, a shot that is temporally long. See also, *full shot*.

**looping** The technique of recording speech to fit the movement of the lips of performers in films already shot. The language may be the same as that used at the time of shooting or it may be different. Sections of the film are made up into loops and as each loop is projected repetitively, the performer speaks the lines until a take with good synchronization is achieved.

**lot**   The general area around a studio and associated with the studio where outdoor sets are erected and scenery and props are stored. See also, *backlot*.

**low-angle shot, low shot**   A shot that shows action occurring above the position of the camera and with the camera pointing upward. Low-angle shots make the action seem to come toward (or go away from) the camera more quickly, to emphasize the size of the object photographed, and to place the audience in a psychologically inferior position. It can also serve effectively as a subjective shot of a character looking upward.

**low key**   (1) Pictures in which the majority of tones lie toward the darker end of the scale. (2) In lighting, a generally low level of illumination of subject, with relatively short-scale tonal rendition. (UFVA)

**makeup artist**   A member of a production crew responsible for the application of facial and body cosmetics for performers, both for purposes of lighting and for visual characterization.

**master shot technique, master scene technique**   A practice used by directors in which action is covered in long shot, then repeated for medium shots and close-ups, to permit match-action cutting and hence to achieve smooth continuity. Sometimes, instead of using repetitions, several cameras are used simultaneously. See also *multicam* or *multiple camera technique*.

**matching action**   The process of aligning overlapped-action film in order to achieve a smooth action cut. See also, *overlap*. (UFVA)

**matte**   A device designed to modify or obstruct light. In camera work, an obstruction to all or part of the field or view, usually fixed, and supported in front of the lens during photography. In printing, a similar device at some point in the light path, serving to modify or obstruct light used for exposure. Called *traveling mattes* or *matte rolls* when set up as film rolls

synchronized with the film being duplicated. (UFVA)

**matte shot**   Any of various types of shots in which a portion of the action field is masked off with the action put in later either in the original camera, in a bipack camera, or in an optical printer. See *bipack camera*. See also, *traveling matte*.

**medium shot, MS**   A shot that shows part of a person or object. A medium shot of a person is usually one that includes head, shoulders, chest, and enough additional space for hand gestures to be seen.

**method acting**   Interpretation of a role by an actor that follows the introspective approach developed by Konstantin Stanislavski; the actor tries to derive characterization from his or her personal experience in circumstances the same or similar to the character's.

**Mickey Mouse, Mickey Mousing** To make music and sound effects noticeably copy the action, for example, musical instruments going up a scale when a cartoon figure runs up a flight of steps.

**miniature, model**   A small-scale set or object used in motion picture photography in a way that makes it appear to be of normal size. (UFVA)

**mise-en-scène**   The way in which the elements in the action field—such as settings, costumes, action, and lighting—are combined to produce the total visual impact of the image.

**mix**   To combine sound from two or more sources into a single recording, usually with adjustment of tonal quality and/or relative volume level. (UFVA) Also, the completed recording itself.

**mixer**   The person who supervises the rerecording and mixing of sound.

**montage**   The assembly of shots, hence, editing, and especially the portrayal of action and creation of ideas and emotions through the use of many short shots. In the 1920s, the Russians formulated several kinds of montage styles. Later, in the United States, montage came to mean a se-

ries of related shots, often with superimpositions and optical effects, showing a condensed sequence of events, for example, a crime wave in a city.

**motif**   A repeated musical passage or theme. Also, generally in the U.S. motion picture industry, *rapid cutting*.

**multiplane**   In animation photography, the use of artwork at more than one plane in the camera field.

**multiple camera technique, multi-cam technique**   Simultaneous cinematography with more than one camera, usually with a choice of camera angles and selection of lenses that will permit acceptable variations of shots when the film from the several cameras is intercut.

**multiple exposure**   The addition of images to a strip of film after the initial exposure, done by rewinding and reexposing the film in the camera more than twice, or by synthesizing images in printing.

**multiple image**   Having several images, not superimposed, within the frame. See also, *split-screen effect*.

**narration**   Commentary spoken by an off-screen voice. In informational films, the voice is usually that of an anonymous expert. In dramatic films, it may be the voice of one of the characters. See also, *voice-over*.

**negative film, negative**   Film designed specifically to produce a good-quality negative image when exposed and processed.

**objective camera angle, objective camera**   Camera coverage that places the audience in the position of an observer of the action.

**obligatory scene**   Action that must occur as the logical result of plot events that lead up to it.

**optical printer**   A printer consisting essentially of a projector and a camera. Light passing through the film, which is to be printed subsequently, passes through a lens system before striking the print stock. The lens system and associated devices permit reduction and enlargement and the making of various kinds of visual effects.

**outtake, out**   In general, any shot that is removed from a film. More specifically, shots that are not work-printed.

**overhead shot**   A shot made from a position directly above the action.

**overlap**   (1) The repetition of some of the action at the end of one shot in the beginning of the next shot in order to make possible a match-action cut. (2) To shoot action in such a way as to achieve the above. (3) To carry sound from one shot over into another shot.

**over-the-shoulder shot, OSS**   A shot made from behind and to the side of an actor, often including part of the shoulder and head, and with the camera aimed in the direction in which the actor is looking.

**painted matte**   A matte that has images on it, for example, a roof, forest, or ceiling used to fill out an action field that in the set is incomplete, and also to save money.

**pan, pan shot**   The effect achieved by moving the camera in azimuth while shooting. To move the camera in azimuth. Loosely applied to any pivotal movement of the camera. (UFVA) In a pan shot, the camera does not follow any particular action, although *pan* is sometimes used to mean follow.

**parallel action and cross-cutting, parallel editing**   The intercutting of shots of two or more simultaneously occurring lines of action.

**pencil test**   A technique used to check speed and smoothness of movement in cartoon animation before cels are painted. Rough drawings on white paper are filmed, usually rear-lighted, and projected at normal speed.

**perspective**   The appearance of depth in objects receding from one's point of view.

**pin screen animation**   A method of animation, developed by Alex Alexeieff in 1932, that uses thousands of pins in holes in a metal sheet. The height of the pins is varied to form images.

**pixilation animation, pixilation**   Animation of people, achieved by having performers move slightly between exposures, then hold position while one or two frames are exposed.

**plot**   Interrelated incidents, situations, actions, and events forming the dramatic texture and shape of a screen story. (UFVA) Aristotle: "The arrangement of incidents" in the story.

**point-of-view shot, p.o.v. shot, POV**   A shot made from a camera position close to the line of sight of a performer who is to be watching the action shown in the point-of-view shot. See also, *subjective camera shot.*

**pop-in or pop-on**   Animation technique in which indicators (lines, arrows, and so on) are placed in position on the copy between single-frame exposures, which leads to their sudden appearance at that point in the frame sequence. (UFVA)

**prime lens**   A lens of fixed focal length.

**principal photography**   Filming that involves performers.

**process projector**   A projector that projects moving backgrounds on a translucent screen in front of which actors perform and are photographed. Process projectors are interlocked with the cameras so that their shutters are open and closed at the same time.

**producer**   The entrepreneur who initiates and/or manages film production activities. (UFVA) Also, the administrator who is assigned to manage the production of a contract film.

**production book**   A collation of work sheets relating to every aspect of production for every day of principal cinematography, together with performers, lighting charts, production personnel, waivers, and equipment to be used. The complete book of references for a given film production.

**production schedule**   A schedule of the shot sequence for a film, together with locations, crews, performers, equipment, transportation, and in some instances alternate plans in case of bad weather.

**props, properties**   Articles used to furnish a set or for use in business. Sometimes differentiated as hand props, action props, and set props. (UFVA)

**puppet animation**   Animation of puppet figures that often have numerous heads and body parts with slightly different expressions and positions.

**rack-focus shot, shift-focus shot**   A shot during which the point of focus and depth of field are changed for emphasis on the action at a different plane.

**reaction shot**   Any shot, usually a cutaway, in which an actor reacts to or notices action that has just occurred.

**rear projection, RP, rear screen projection, back projection**   The projection of still or moving backgrounds on a translucent screen in front of which actors are lighted and filmed. Used to achieve easier scheduling of actors and better sound and lighting but primarily to reduce expenses.

**recordist**   A person who operates sound recording equipment. (UFVA)

**reversal film**   A film that is normally processed in such a way as to produce a positive image after exposure to a subject. A reversal print of a negative would have a negative image, however.

**reverse action, reverse motion**   Action that goes backward on the screen, achieved either by shooting with the camera upside down and then turning the processed film end over end, by shooting with camera right side up and action reversed, or by reverse printing in an optical printer.

**rough cut**   A trial stage in the process of editing a film. Shots and sequences are laid out in approximate relationship, without detailed attention to the individual cutting points. (UFVA)

**rushes**   See *dailies*.

**scene, SC**   (1) A setting. (2) A shot. (3) A continuously developed unit of action. (4) Loosely and commonly used for *sequence*.

**scratch-off animation, wipe-off animation, rub-off animation**   Animation of completed artwork that is made with water-soluble paints and shot upside down. Small amounts of the artwork are removed between exposures, and the processed film is turned end over end to erect the image. The artwork then appears to move and lay itself out on the screen. Scratch-off animation must ordinarily be done with double-perforation film, but it can sometimes be done satisfactorily with 8-mm film by shooting into a mirror.

**screen direction**   Movement within the frame. It is often oriented to compass points, for example east-west being right-to-left movement, north-south, top-to-bottom, and so forth. In *constant screen direction* the direction of movement does not change from shot to shot. In *contrasting screen direction* the direction of movement changes from shot to shot. In *neutral screen direction* the movement is toward or away from the camera.

**screenplay**   A written plan for a film; a script.

**screenwriter**   One who prepares stories, treatments, and scripts for motion pictures.

**script**   A set of written specifications for the production of a motion picture. (UFVA) See also, *screenplay*. Different kinds of scripts contain specifications for settings, action, camera coverage, dialogue, narration, music, and sound effects, in varying degrees of explicitness.

**segue**   (1) The termination of a piece of music, followed immediately by the start of a new piece. (2) An audio cross fade.

**selective focus**   Rendering only part of the action field in sharp focus through the use of shallow depth of field.

**sequence**   A series of shots characterized by inherent units of theme and purpose.

**shooting schedule, production**   A form sheet that lists the shots to be made on a given day, together with performers, production personnel, and equipment to be used.

**shot**   (1) A single run of the camera. (2) Footage that results from such a run. Systematically joined together in the process of editing, shots are synthesized into scenes and sequences that in turn are joined to form the film as a whole. The specific meaning of designations for shots varies with the application; in general, *close-up* suggests that the frame area is well filled by the image of the subject, whether it is a mountain or a molehill. In a similar way, long shot suggests that the image of the subject occupies a relatively small portion of the frame area and that the central subject is in this way visually related to its immediate environment. Thus, the camera-to-subject distance, the focal length of the lens, and the absolute size of the subject all influence the arbitrary designation for a specific shot. In view of these variable factors, the exact meaning of shot designations should be interpreted in relation to specific applications. (UFVA)

**sneak preview**   A showing of a film prior to its general release for the purpose of gauging audience reaction or stimulating business by means of word of mouth. Sometimes changes are made in the film as a result of information gathered from the audience.

**sound track, track**   The physical portion of the length of film reserved for the sound record. Also, any length of film bearing sound only. (UFVA)

**split-screen effect, split screen, split-screen shot**   The division of the film frame into two or more separate nonoverlapping images, done either in the camera or in an optical printer.

**stand-in, double**   A person who resembles a lead actor in size and facial tones, and who stands in the place of the lead actor while lights and equipment are being adjusted.

**star system**   The marketing strategy of developing audience appeal through publicity that stresses a leading performer rather than other elements of a film. Begun in the second decade of this century with such stars as Mary Pickford and Charlie Chaplin, the star system allows highly visible actors to command huge salaries.

**stop-motion cinematography, stop motion, stop action**   A trick effect achieved by having performers stop their motion during a shot while something is removed or added to the action field, and then continuing the action to the end of the shot. The camera may or may not stop, but if it does not stop, a portion of film is cut out later. In this way, objects or performers can be made to appear or disappear suddenly. This term is sometimes used to refer to fast-motion cinematography, time-lapse cinematography, and single-frame cinematography. Originally called the *pop-on* or *pop-off*.

**storyboard**   A pictorial outline of a film's continuity, with sketches or photographs representing shots and usually including in writing the speech, music, and sound effects that are to go with each shot.

**stunt man, stunt woman**   One who performs dangerous action. In some cases, the stunt man or woman actually plays the part of a character in the film, whereas in other cases he or she doubles for a lead actor.

**subjective camera shot**   (1) Generally used to refer to a p.o.v. shot. (2) Use of the camera to show such mental action as dreams, memories, and fantasies. (3) In screenwriting, any shot seen through the eyes of a person or being who has not yet appeared on camera.

**subtitle**   A title superimposed over action, usually at the bottom of the frame, used to translate foreign language or to identify the scene (UFVA)

**swish-pan, blur-pan, zip-pan, flick-pan, flash-pan, whip-pan**   An effect arising from rapid camera movement in azimuth as a shot proceeds. Occasionally used successfully as a transitional device. (UFVA)

**synopsis**   A summary of the events in a story, play, novel, or script.

**take**   A shot. Also, a term used to indicate the number of times a given shot has been made. Takes are usually numbered sequentially and identified in picture by slate and in track by voice. (UFVA)

**target audience**   The audience for whom a film is intended. The group for whom a film would have a special appeal. (UFVA)

**telephoto lens**   Any photographic objective lens designed to yield a compact combination of short back focal length (rear vertex of last lens to focal plane) and long focal length for the lens as a whole. This is commonly achieved by the use of the rear lens element of negative power. Also, loosely, any lens of greater than normal focal length. (UFVA)

**theatrical film**   A film, usually a feature, made for commercial exhibition in theaters.

**theme**   The story subject matter from which the general value or idea forming the intellectual background for a film is evolved. (UFVA)

**tight shot**   A shot in which the frame lines are close to the subject.

**tilt**   Any vertical movement of the camera while it is on a pivotal base.

**time-lapse cinematography, time lapse**   A motion picture technique used for visualizing normally invisible slow processes. In the original photography, a greater-than-normal time interval elapses between exposures of successive frames. Projection at normal projection speed results in an apparent speed-up effect that depends on the time interval between successive exposures when the original is made. (UFVA)

**track, tracks**   (1) A sound track. (2) The rails sometimes used to support a moving dolly. (3) To make a tracking shot.

**tracking shot, traveling shot, trucking shot**   A shot made while the camera and its entire support are moving.

**traveling matte, matte roll**   A matte film that travels through a printer with the printing film to create a certain effect. See also, *blue screen process*.

**unit manager**   A film production crew manager who is responsible for housing, transportation, meals, payroll, and supplies.

**upstage**   (1) The rear of a stage. (2) Action by one actor that causes another to face upstage or that draws audience attention away from other actors.

**vignette**   (1) To reduce the boundary portions of a picture, while the image at the center is left unaffected. (2) Any picture so treated.

**visual effects**   Any shot unobtainable by straightforward motion picture techniques. In this category fall shots requiring contour matting, multiple-image montages, split screens, vignetting, models, and the like. Term also applies to explosions, ballistic effects, and mechanical effects.

**voice-over, V.O.**   (1) A sound and picture relationship in which a narrator's voice accompanies picture action. (2) Any off-screen voice. (3) A narration job.

**walk-through**   A rehearsal, usually without dialogue, in which performers proceed through the action for a shot.

**wide-angle distortion, wide-angle effect**   Exaggerated foreshortening and roundness of objects photographed by a wide-angle lens from a close position. Also, vertical lines may tend to diverge unnaturally, and objects near the edge of the frame may be stretched out of shape in shots made with a wide-angle lens.

**wild recording**   A recording that is made without synchrony with a camera.

**wipe**   An optical effect used to join one shot to another. In its most common form, scene *A* appears to be wiped off the screen by the progressive revelation of scene *B* as a vertical dividing line separating the two advances across the screen from left to right. Many modifications of this basic form have been used, such as vertical, diagonal, iris, spiral, and even atomic bomb wipes. (UFVA) Some wipes go to black.

**workprint**   Any positive duplicate picture, sound track print, or magnetic duplicate intended for use in the editing process to establish through a series of trial cuttings the finished version of a film. The purpose is to preserve the original intact and undamaged until the cutting points have been established.

**zoom lens, varifocal lens, variable focal length lens**   A lens with effective focal length continuously variable within a limited range. Changing the focal length of such a lens as a shot progresses simulates the effect of camera movement toward or away from the subject. (UFVA)

# BIBLIOGRAPHY

## 1 / THE PRODUCER

Adams, William B. *Handbook of Motion Picture Production*. New York: John Wiley, 1977.

Bach, Steven. *Final Cut: Dreams and Disaster in the Making of Heaven's Gate*. New York: William Morrow, 1985.

Balio, Tino, ed. *The American Film Industry* (rev. ed.). Madison: University of Wisconsin Press, 1985.

Baumgarten, Paul A., and Donald C. Farber. *Producing, Financing and Distributing Film*. New York: Drama Book Specialists, 1973.

Curran, Trisha. *Financing Your Film: A Guide for Independent Filmmakers & Producers*. New York: Praeger, 1986.

Glimcher, Sumner. *Moviemaking: A Guide to Film Production*. New York: Washington Square Press, 1975.

Goodell, Gregory. *Independent Feature Film Production*. New York: St. Martin's Press, 1982.

Gregory, Mollie. *Making Films Your Business*. New York: Schocken Books, 1979.

Kindem, Gorham, ed. *The American Movie Industry: The Business of Motion Pictures*. Carbondale: Southern Illinois University Press, 1982.

Lees, Davis, and Stan Berkowitz. *The Movie Business: A Primer*. New York: Random House, 1981.

MacCann, Richard Dyer. *Hollywood in Transition*. Boston: Houghton Mifflin, 1962.

Manvell, Roger. *The Living Screen: Background to the Film and Television*. London: Harrap, 1961.

McClintick, David. *Indecent Exposure*. New York: Dell, 1983.

Monaco, James. *American Film Now: The People, the Power, the Money, the Movies* (rev. ed.). New York: New American Library, 1984.

Singleton, Ralph S. *Film Scheduling*. Beverly Hills: Lone Eagle, 1984.

Tromberg, Sheldon. *Making Money Making Movies: The Independent Moviemaker's Handbook*. New York: New View Points/Vision Books, 1980.

Wiese, Michael. *The Independent Film and Videomakers Guide*. Westport, Conn.: Michael Wiese Film Productions, 1986.

## 2 / THE SCREENWRITER

Armer, Alan. *Writing the Screenplay: TV and Film*. Belmont, Calif.: Wadsworth, 1988.

Bronfeld, Stewart. *Writing for Film and Television*. Englewood Cliffs, N.J.: Prentice-Hall, 1981.

Dmytryk, Edward. *On Screen Writing*. New York: Focal Press, 1985.

Egri, Lajos. *The Art of Dramatic Writing*. New York: Simon & Schuster, 1960.

Field, Syd. *Screenplay: The Basics of Film Writing*. New York: Dell, 1979. Expanded in 1982.

Gessner, Robert. *The Moving Image*. New York: Dutton, 1968.

Giustini, Rolando. *The Filmscript: A Writer's Guide*. Englewood Cliffs, N.J.: Prentice-Hall, 1980.

Goldman, William. *Adventures in the Screen Trade*. New York: Warner Books, 1983.

Halas, John, and Stan Hayward. *Visual Scripting*. New York: Hastings House, 1976.

Lawson, John Howard. *Theory and Technique of Playwriting and Screenwriting*. New York: Hill & Wang, 1961.

Lee, Robert, and Robert Misiorowski. *Script Models: A Handbook for the Media Writer*. New York: Hastings House, 1978.

Nash, Constance. *The Screenwriter's Handbook: What to Write, How to Write It, Where to Sell It*. New York: Holt, Rinehart & Winston, 1980.

Rilla, W. P. *The Writer and the Screen*. New York: Morrow, 1974.

Root, Wells. *Writing the Script: A Practical Guide for Film and Television*. New York: Holt, Rinehart & Winston, 1980.

Salachas, Gilbert. *Federico Fellini: An Investigation into His Films and Philosophy*. New York: Crown, 1969.

Straczynski, J. Michael. *The Complete Book of Scriptwriting*. Cincinnati: Writer's Digest Books, 1982.

Swain, Dwight V. *Film Script Writing: A Practical Manual*. New York: Hastings House, 1976.

Vale, Eugene. *The Technique of Screen and Television Writing*. New York: Simon & Schuster, 1982.

Walter, Richard. *Screenwriting*. New York: New American Library, 1988.

## 3 / ADAPTATION

Bazin, André. "Theatre and Cinema," in *What Is Cinema?* Vols. I and II. Hugh Gray, ed. and transl. Berkeley: University of California Press, 1967.

Beja, Morris. *Film and Literature: An Introduction*. New York: Longman, 1979.

Bluestone, George. *Novels into Film*. Baltimore: Johns Hopkins Press, 1957.

Bryan, Margaret B., and Boyd H. Davis. *Writing about Literature and Film*. New York: Harcourt Brace Jovanovich, 1975.

Eckert, Charles W., ed. *Focus on Shakespearean Films*. Englewood Cliffs, N.J.: Prentice-Hall, 1972.

Gedlevd, Harry M., ed. *Authors on Film*. Bloomington: Indiana University Press, 1972.

Jinks, William. *The Celluloid Literature: Film in the Humanities*, 2nd ed. Beverly Hills: Glencoe Press, 1974.

Jorgens, Jack J. *Shakespeare on Film*. Bloomington: Indiana University Press, 1977.

Kernodle, George R. *An Invitation to the Theatre*, 3rd ed. New York: Harcourt Brace Jovanovich, 1985.

Kittredge, William, and Steven M. Krauzer, eds. *Stories into Film*. New York: Harper & Row, 1979.

Manvell, Roger. *The Theatre and Film: A Comparative Study of the Two Forms of Dramatic Art, and the Problems of Adaptation of Stage Plays into Films*. Rutherford, N.J.: Fairleigh Dickenson University Press, 1979.

Marcus, Fred Harold, ed. *Film and Literature: Contrasts in Media*. Scranton, Penn.: Chandler, 1971.

Nicoll, Allardyce. *Film and Theatre*. London: Harrap; New York: Crowell, 1936.

Wagner, Geoffrey Atheling. *The Novel and the Cinema*. Rutherford, N.J.: Fairleigh Dickenson University Press, 1975.

Zambrano, A. L. *Dickens and Film*. New York: Gordon Press, 1977.


## 4 / THE PRODUCTION DESIGNER

Barry, Jonathan. "The Art of the Art Director." *Film* 59 (Summer 1970): 15.

Barsacq, Léon. *Caligari's Cabinet and Other Grand Illusions: A History of Film Design*. Boston: New York Graphic Society, 1976.

Bay, Howard, *Stage Design*. New York: Drama Book Specialists, 1974.

Bordwell, David, and Kristin Thompson. *Film Art: An Introduction*, 2nd ed. New York: Alfred A. Knopf, 1986.

Carrick, Edward. *Art and Design in the British Film: A Pictorial Directory of British Art Directors and Their Work*. New York: Arno Press, 1972.

—————. *Designing For Films*. London and New York: Studio Publications, 1949.

Clarnes, C., and M. Corliss. "Designed for Film: The Hollywood Art Director." *Film Comment* 14 (May/June 1978): 25–35ff.

"Designing Hollywood." *Image* 22 (1979): 31, n. 2.

Dillon, Carmen. "The Art Director." *Films and Filming* 3 (May 1957): 12–13, n. 8.

Durgnat, R. "Art for Art's Sake." *American Film* 8 (May 1983): 41–45, n. 7.

Durgnat, Raymond. "Movie Eye." *Architectural Review* 137 (March 1965): 186–193.

Field, Alice Evans. "The Art Director's Art." *Films in Review* 3 (February 1952): 60–66.

Firmature, M. J. "The Art Director." *American Premiere* 2 (December 1981/January 1982): 26–27.

Gray, Martin. "The Shape of Things Past." *Films and Filming* 5, (February 1959): 11ff, n. 5.

Harper, S. "Gainsborough: What's in a Costume?" *Monthly Film Bulletin* 52 (October 1985): 324–327.

Issacs, J. "The Visual Impact." *Sight and Sound* 19 (April 1950): 81–82.

Kuter, Leo K. "Art Direction." *Films in Review* 8 (June–July 1957): 248–258.

Laine, R. E. "The Heyday of Studio Art Departments." *American Premiere* 3 (December 1982/January 1983): 21ff.

Lee, N. "Effects Art Director for *Star Wars and Return of the Jedi*." *American Cinematographer* 64 (June 1983): 78–80.

Locker, L. "Film Stylist Reveals Backstage Lore." *Making Films in New York* 8 (December 1974): 24–25.

Luft, Herbert G. "Production Designer Horner." *Films in Review* 10 (June–July 1959): 328–335.

Markle, W. "The Development and Application of Colorization." *SMPTE Journal* 93 (July 1984): 632–635.

Marner, Terrance St. John. *Film Design*. New York: Barnes, 1974.

Meistuch, I. J. "The Production Designer and His Vision." *Print* 32 (July/August 1978): 52–59.

Rickey, C. "Art Directors: Theatrical Realism." *Film Comment* 18 (January/February 1982): 32–33.

Stein, E. "The Art of Art Direction." *Film Comment* 11 (May–June 1975): 32–34.

"The Art of Art Direction." *Focus on Film* 34 (1979): 19–20.

Thomson, D. "The Art of the Art Director." *American Film* 2 (February 1977): 12–20.


## 5 / THE DIRECTOR

Armer, Alan A. *Directing Television and Film*, 2nd ed. Belmont, Calif.: Wadsworth, 1990.

Arnheim, Rudolf. *Art and Visual Perception*. Berkeley: University of California Press, 1974.

—————. *Visual Thinking*. Berkeley: University of California Press, 1969.

Bálazs, Béla. "The Face of Man," in *Theory of the Film*. New York: Dover, 1970.

Bare, Richard L. *The Film Director*. New York: Macmillan, 1971.

Gelmis, Joseph. *The Film Director as Superstar*. New York: Doubleday, 1970.

Hall, Edward T. *The Hidden Dimension*. Garden City, N.Y.: Doubleday, 1966.

Henderson, Ron. *The Image Maker*. Richmond, Va.: John Knox Press, 1971.

Higham, Charles. *The Celluloid Muse*. London: Angus and Robertson, 1969.

Jacobs, Diane. *Hollywood Renaissance*. New York: Dell, 1980.

Jacobs, Lewis. *The Movies as Medium*. New York: Farrar, Straus and Giroux, 1970.

Jacobs, Lewis, ed. *Introduction to the Art of the Movies*. New York: The Noonday Press, 1960.

Jacobs, Lewis, et al. "Movement" in *The Movies as Medium*, Lewis Jacobs, ed.

New York: Farrar, Straus and Giroux, 1970.

Kolker, Robert Phillip. *A Cinema of Loneliness: Penn, Kubrick, Coppola, Scorsese, Altman*. New York: Oxford University Press, 1980.

Lawson, John Howard. *Film: The Creative Process*. New York: Hill & Wang, 1967.

Lindgren, Ernest. *The Art of the Film*. New York: Macmillan, 1963.

Lutz, Bacher. *The Mobile Mise en Scène*. New York: Arno Press, 1978.

Madsen, Roy P. *The Impact of Film: How Ideas Are Communicated Through Cinema and Television*. New York: Macmillan; London: Collier Macmillan, 1973.

Marner, Terence St. John, ed. *Directing Motion Pictures*. New York: Barnes, 1972.

Phillips, Gene D. *The Movie Makers: Artists in an Industry*. Chicago: Nelson-Hall Co., 1973.

Reynertson, A. J. *The Work of the Film Director*. New York: Hastings House, 1970.

Ruesch, Jurgen, and Weldon Kees. *Nonverbal Communication*, 2nd ed. Berkeley: University of California Press, 1972.

Samuels, Charles Thomas. *Encountering Directors*. New York: G. P. Putnam's, 1972.

Sarris, Andrew. *Interviews with Film Directors*. New York: Avon Books, 1967.

——————. *The American Cinema: Directors and Direction, 1929–1968*. Chicago: University of Chicago Press, 1968.

Sherman, Eric. *Directing the Film: Film Directors and Their Art*. Boston: Little, Brown, 1976.

——————. *The Director's Event*. New York: Atheneum, 1977.

Sommer, Robert. *Personal Space*. Englewood Cliffs, N. J.: Prentice-Hall, 1969.

Taylor, John Russell. *Directors and Directions: Cinema for the Seventies*. New York: Hill & Wang, 1975.

Thomas, Bob. *Directors in Action*. Indianapolis: Bobbs-Merrill, 1973.

Zettl, Herbert. *Sight-Sound-Motion: Applied Media Aesthetics*, 2nd ed. Belmont, Calif.: Wadsworth, 1990.

## 6 / THE PLAYERS

Barr, Tony. *Acting for the Camera*. Boston: Allyn & Bacon, 1982.

Blum, Richard. *Working Actors: The Craft of Television, Film, and Stage Performance*. New York: Focal Press, 1989.

Braudy, Leo. "Acting and Characterization," in *The World in a Frame*. Garden City, N.Y.: Doubleday, 1976.

Fast, Julius. *Body Language*. New York: M. Evans and Company, 1970; Pocket Books, 1971.

Godfrey, Lionel. *Paul Newman: Superstar*. New York: St. Martin's Press, 1978.

Griffith, Richard. *The Movie Stars*. Garden City, N.Y.: Doubleday, 1970.

Harmon, Renee. *The Actor's Survival Guide for Today's Film Industry*. Englewood Cliffs, N.J.: Prentice-Hall, 1984.

Haskell, Molly. *From Reverence to Rape*, 2nd ed. Chicago: University of Chicago Press, 1987.

Hull, S. Loraine. *Strasberg's Method, A Practical Guide for Actors, Teachers and Directors*. Woodbridge, Conn.: Ox Bow Press, 1985.

Karshner, Roger. *Film Scenes They Haven't Seen*. Toluca Lake, Calif.: Dramaline Publications, 1983.

Karton, Joshua A., ed. *Film Scenes for Actors*. Toronto and New York: Bantam Books, 1983.

Lewis, M. K., and Rosemary Lewis. *Your Film Acting Career: How to Break into the Movies and T.V. and Survive in Hollywood*. New York: Crown, 1983.

Matson, Katinka. *The Working Actor: A Guide to the Profession*. New York: Viking Press, 1976.

Morris, Eric, and Joan Hotchkis. *No Acting Please*. Burbank, Calif.: Whitehouse Speiling Publication, 1977.

Munk, Erica, ed. *Stanislavsky in America*. New York: Hill & Wang, 1966.

Noose, Theodore. *Hollywood Film Acting*. South Brunswick, N.J.: Barnes, 1979.

Pate, Michael. *The Film Actor: Acting for Motion Pictures and Television*. New York: Barnes, 1970.

Pudovkin, V. I. *Film Technique and Film Acting*. New York: Grove, 1970.

Sandler, Bernard, and Steve Posner. *In Front of the Camera: How to Make It and Survive in Movies and Television*. New York: Elsevier-Dutton, 1981.

Schickel, Richard. *The Stars*. New York: Bonanza Books, Dial Press, 1962.

Stanislavski, Konstantin Sergeivich. *An Actor Prepares*. New York: Theatre Arts Books, 1936.

Walker, Alexander. *Stardom: The Hollywood Phenomenon*. New York: Stein and Day, 1970; London: Penguin, 1974.

## 7 / COMEDY AND HUMOR

Burr, Lonnie. *Two for the Show: Great Comedy Teams*. New York: J. Messner, 1979.

Byron, Stuart, and Elizabeth Weis, eds. *The National Society of Film Critics on Movie Comedy*. New York: Grossman Publishers, 1977.

Cavell, Stanley. *Pursuits of Happiness: The Hollywood Comedy of Remarriage*. Cambridge, Mass.: Harvard University Press, 1981.

Crafton, Donald. *Before Mickey*. Cambridge, Mass.: MIT Press, 1982.

Doaque, Leland H. *The Cinema of Frank Capra: An Approach to Film Comedy*. South Brunswick, N.J.: Barnes, 1975.

Gehring, Wes D. *Charlie Chaplin's World of Comedy*. Muncie, Ind.: Ball State University, 1980.

——————. *Leo McCarey and the Comic Anti-Hero in American Film*. New York: Arno Press, 1980.

Grote, David G. *The End of Comedy: The Sit-Com and the Comedic Tradition*. Hamden, Conn.: Shoe String Press, 1983.

Jacobs, Diane. *. . . But We Need the Eggs: The Magic of Woody Allen*. New York: St. Martin's Press, 1982.

Jordan, T. H. *The Anatomy of Cinematic*

*Humor*. Brooklyn: Revisionist Press, 1975.

Kerr, Walter. *The Silent Clowns*. New York: Alfred A. Knopf, 1975.

Lax, Eric. *On Being Funny: Woody Allen and Comedy*. New York: Manor Books, 1977.

Maltin, Leonard. *The Great Movie Comedians: From Charlie Chaplin to Woody Allen*. New York: Crown, 1978.

Manchel, Frank. *The Box-Office Clowns: Bob Hope, Jerry Lewis, Mel Brooks, Woody Allen*. New York: Watts, 1979.

——————. *The Talking Clowns: From Laurel and Hardy to the Marx Brothers*. New York: Watts, 1976.

Mast, Gerald. *The Comic Mind*. Chicago: University of Chicago Press, 1979.

McCabe, John. *Mr. Laurel and Mr. Hardy* (rev. ed.). New York: New American Library, 1985.

McCaffrey, Donald. *Focus on Chaplin*. Englewood Cliffs, N.J.: Prentice-Hall, 1971.

Reilly, Adam, et al. *Harold Lloyd: The King of Daredevil Comedy*. New York: Collier Books, 1977.

Rheuban, J. *Harry Langdon*. Princeton: Farleigh Dickenson University Press, 1983.

Seidman, Steve. *Comedian Comedy: A Tradition in Hollywood Film*. Ann Arbor: UMI Research Press, 1981.

Smurthwaite, Nick, and Paul Gelder. *Mel Brooks and the Spoof Movie*. London and New York: Proteus Books, 1982.

Wead, George. *Buster Keaton and the Dynamics of Visual Wit*. New York: Arno Press, 1976.

Wilde, Larry. *How the Great Comedy Writers Create Laughter*. Chicago: Nelson-Hall, 1976.

Wood, Tom. *The Bright Side of Billy Wilder, Primarily*. New York: Doubleday, 1970.

Yacower, Maurice. *Loser Take All: The Comic Art of Woody Allen*. New York: Ungar, 1979.

## 8 / THE CINEMATOGRAPHER

Adrian, Werner. *Speed: Cinema of Motion*. New York: Bounty Books, 1975.

Alton, John. *Painting with Light*. New York: Macmillan, 1949.

Bacher, L. *The Mobile Mise en Scène: A Critical Analysis of the Theory and Practice of Long-Take Camera Movement in the Narrative Film*. New York: Arno Press, 1978.

Barr, Charles. "Cinemascope: Before and After," in *Film Theory and Criticism*, Gerald Mast and Marshall Cohen, eds. New York: Oxford University Press, 1979.

Birren, Faber. *Color, Form and Space*. New York: Reinhold Publishing, 1961.

Bresson, Robert. *Notes on Cinematography*. New York: Urizen Books, 1977.

Campbell, Russell, ed. *Photographic Theory for the Motion Picture Cameraman*. New York: Barnes, 1970.

Clark, Charles G. *Professional Cinematography*. Hollywood: American Society of Cinematographers, 1964.

Englander, A. Arthur, and Paul Petzold. *Filming for Television*. New York: Hastings House, 1976.

Hacker, Leonard. *Cinematic Design*. New York: Arno Press, 1979.

Harpole, Charles Henry. *Gradients of Depth in the Cinema Image*. New York: Arno Press, 1978.

Higham, Charles. *Hollywood Cameramen*. Bloomington: Indiana University Press, 1970.

Johnson, Lincoln F. *Film: Space, Time, Light and Sound*. New York: Holt, Rinehart & Winston, 1974.

Maltin, Leonard. *The Art of the Cinematographer: A Survey and Interviews with Five Masters*. New York: Dover Publications, 1978.

Maltin, Leonard, ed. *Behind the Camera: The Cinematographer's Art*. New York: New American Library, 1971.

Marner, Terence St. John. *Film Design*. South Brunswick, N.J.: Barnes, 1974.

Mascelli, Joseph V. *The Five C's of Cinematography: Motion Picture Filming Techniques Simplified*. Hollywood: Cine/Grafic Publications, 1965.

Mathias, Harry, and Richard Patterson. *Electronic Cinematography: Achieving Control over the Video Image*. Belmont, Calif.: Wadsworth, 1985.

Mercer, John. *An Introduction to Cinematography*. Champaign, Ill.: Stipes, 1971.

Nilson, Vladimir. *The Cinema as Graphic Art*. New York: Hill & Wang, 1959.

Rainsberger, Todd. *James Wong Howe: Cinematographer*. New York: Barnes, 1981.

Samuelson, David W. *Motion Picture Camera Techniques*, 2nd ed. London and Boston: Focal Press, 1984.

Souto, H. R. M. *The Technique of the Motion Picture Camera*. New York: Hastings House, 1977.

Stromgren, Richard L., and Martin F. Norden. *Movies: A Language in Light*. Englewood Cliffs, N.J.: Prentice-Hall, 1984.

## 9 / THE EDITOR

Ash, Rene L. *The Motion Picture Film Editor*. Metuchen, N.J.: Scarecrow Press, 1974.

Barry, Iris. *D. W. Griffith: American Film Master*. Garden City, N.Y.: New York Museum of Art; distributed by Doubleday, 1965.

Crittenden, Roger. *The Thames and Hudson Manual of Film Editing*. London: Thames and Hudson, 1981.

Dmytryk, Edward. *On Film Editing*. Stoneham, Me.: Focal Press, 1984.

Eisenstein, Sergei. *Film Form and Film Sense*. New York: Harcourt, Brace, 1949.

Hollyn, Norman, *The Film Editing Room Handbook*. New York: Arco Publishing, 1984.

Jacobs, Lewis, "Art: Edwin S. Porter and the Editing Principle," "D. W. Griffith: *The Birth of a Nation* and *Intolerance*," in *The Rise of the American Film*. New York: Teachers College Press, 1968.

Kuleshov, Lev Vladimirovich. *Kuleshov on Film*. Berkeley: University of California Press, 1974.

Lustig, Milton. *Music Editing for Motion Pictures* (new ed.). New York: Hastings House, 1980.

Mayer, David. *Eisenstein's Potemkin: A Shot-by-Shot Presentation*. New York: Grossman Publishers, 1972.

Nizhny, Vladimir. *Lessons with Eisenstein*. New York: Da Capo, 1979.

Reisz, Karel, and Gavin Millar. *The Technique of Film Editing*, 2nd ed. London and New York: British Film Academy; Hastings House, 1970.

Robertson, J. F. *The Magic of Film Editing*. Blue Ridge Summit, Penn.: TAB Books, 1984.

Rosenblum, Ralph. *When the Shooting Stops . . . The Cutting Begins: A Film Editor's Story*. New York: Viking Press, 1979.

Walter, Ernest. *The Technique of the Film Cutting Room*. New York: Hastings House, 1969.


10 / THE SOUND DESIGNER

Alten, Stanley R. *Audio in Media*, 3rd ed. Belmont, Calif.: Wadsworth, 1990.

Bernstein, Leonard. *The Joy of Music*. New York: Simon & Schuster, 1959.

Blake, Larry. *Film Sound Today*. Hollywood: Hollywood Reveille Press, 1984.

Cameron, Evan William, ed. *Sound and the Cinema: The Coming of Sound to the American Film*. Pleasantville, N.Y.: Redgrave, 1980.

Clair, Rene. "The Art of Sound," in *Film: A Montage of Theories*. Richard Dyer MacCann, ed. New York: Dutton, 1966.

Frater, Charles. *Sound Recording for Motion Pictures*. New York and London: Barnes, 1979.

Hagen, Earle H. *Scoring For Films*. New York: Wehman, 1972.

Huntley, John, and Richard Manvell. *The Technique of Film Music*. London and New York: Focal Press, 1957.

Knight, Arthur. "The Movies Learn to Talk," in *The Liveliest Art*. New York: Mentor, 1979.

Kracauer, Siegfried. "Dialogue and Sound," in *Theory of Film*. New York: Oxford University Press, 1960.

Lang, Edith, and George West. *Musical Accompaniment of Moving Pictures*. New York: Arno Press, 1970.

Lustig, Milton. *Music Editing for Motion Pictures*. New York: Hastings House, 1980.

Manvell, Roger, and John Huntley. *The Technique of Film Music*. London and New York: Focal Press, 1957.

McCarthy, Clifford. *Film Composers in America*. New York: Da Capo, 1972.

Nisbett, Alec. *The Technique of the Sound Studio for Radio, Recording Studio, Television and Film*. London: Focal Press; New York: Focal/Hastings House, 1979.

Overman, Michael. *Understanding Sound, Video and Film Recording*. Blue Ridge Summit, Penn.: TAB Books, 1978.

*Photographic Sound Recording and Reproduction*. London: British Kinematograph Sound and Television Society, Education and Training Committee, 1975.

Prendergast, Roy M. *Film Music*. New York: W. W. Norton, 1977.

Thomas, Tony. *Music for the Movies*. New York: Barnes, 1973.

Weis, Elizabeth, and John Belton, eds. *Film Sound: Theory and Practice*. New York: Columbia University Press, 1985.

Whitney, John H. *Digital Harmony: On the Complementarity of Music and Visual Art*. Peterborough, N. H.: Byte Books, 1980.


11 / VISUAL EFFECTS

Agel, Jerome, ed. *The Making of Kubrick's 2001*. New York: Signet, 1970.

Barnouw, Erik. *The Magician and the Cinema*. New York: Oxford University Press, 1981.

Baxter, John. *Science Fiction in the Cinema*. New York: Barnes, 1970.

Broadbeck, Emil E. *Movie and Videotape Special Effects*. Philadelphia, New York, and London: Chilton Book Company,

Brosnan, John. *Movie Magic: The Story of Special Effects in the Cinema*. New York: St. Martin's Press, 1974; London: Abacus, 1977.

Bullock, Vic. *The Art of the Empire Strikes Back*. New York: Ballantine Books, 1980.

Clark, Frank P. *Special Effects in Motion Pictures: Some Methods for Producing Mechanical Special Effects*. New York: Society of Motion Picture and Television Engineers, Inc., 1966.

Culhane, John. *Special Effects in the Movies: How They Do It*. New York:

Ballantine Books, Hilltown Press, Inc., 1981.

Fielding, Raymond. *The Technique of Special Effects Cinematography*, 4th ed. Markham, Mass.: Focal Press, 1985.

Finch, Christopher. *Special Effects: Creating Movie Magic*. New York: Abbeville Press, 1984.

Fry, Ron. *The Saga of Special Effects*. Englewood Cliffs, N.J.: Prentice-Hall, 1977.

Harryhausen, R. *Film Fantasy Scrapbook*. South Brunswick, N.J.: Barnes, 1978.

Imes, Jack. *Special Visual Effects: A Guide to Special Effects*. New York: Van Nostrand Reinhold, 1984.

Johnson, William, ed. *Focus on the Science Fiction Film*. Englewood Cliffs, N.J.: Prentice-Hall, 1972.

Perisic, Zoran. *Special Optical Effects in Film*. London and New York: Focal Press, 1980.

Rovin, Jeff. *From the Land Beyond*. New York: Berkley Publishing Corp., 1977.

_____. *Movie Special Effects*. South Brunswick, N.J.: Barnes, 1977.

Schechter, Harold, and David Everitt. *Film Tricks: Special Effects in the Movies*. New York: A Harlin Quist Book, 1980.

Wilkie, Bernard. *Creating Special Effects for Television and Film*. New York: Focal Press, 1977.


12 / ANIMATION

Canemaker, John. *The Animated Raggedy Ann and Andy: An Intimate Look at the Art of Animation, Its History, Techniques, and Artists*. Indianapolis: Bobbs-Merrill, 1977.

Disney Productions. *Animated Features and Silly Symphonies*. New York: Abbeville Press, 1980.

Edera, Bruno. *Full Length Animated Feature Films*. New York: Hastings House, 1977.

Finch, Christopher. *The Art of Walt Disney*. New York: Abrams, 1973.

_____. *Walt Disney's America*. New York: Abbeville Press, 1978.

Halas, John. *Computer Animation*. New York: Hastings House, 1974.

_____. *Film Animation: A Simplified Approach*. Paris: UNESCO, 1976.

_____. *The Techniques of Film Animation*. London and New York: Focal Press, 1976.

Halas, John, ed. *Graphics in Motion: From the Special Effects Film to Holographics*. New York: Van Nostrand Reinhold, 1984.

Halas, John, and Roger Manvell. *Design in Motion*. New York: Focal Press, 1962.

Hayward, Stan. *Computers for Animation*. London and Boston: Focal Press, 1984.

_____. *Scriptwriting for Animation*. London and New York: Focal Press, 1977.

Hoffer, Thomas W. *Animation: A Reference Guide*. Westport, Conn.: Greenwood Press, 1981.

Holloway, Ronald. *Z is for Zagreb*. New York: Barnes, 1972.

Holman, Bruce L. *Puppet Animation in the Cinema*. New York: Barnes, 1976.

Lenburg, Jeff. *The Encyclopedia of Animated Cartoon Series*. Westport, Conn.: Arlington House, 1981.

_____. *The Great Cartoon Directors*. Jefferson, N.C.: McFarland and Co., 1983.

Levitan, Eli L. *Electronic Imaging Techniques: A Handbook of Conventional and Computer-Controlled Animation, Optical, and Editing Processes*. New York: Van Nostrand Reinhold, 1977.

Levitan, Eli L. *Handbook of Animation Techniques*. New York: Van Nostrand Reinhold, 1979.

Madsen, Roy P. *Animated Film: Concepts, Methods, Uses*. New York: Interland Publishing, Inc. dist. by Pitman Publishing Corp., 1969.

Ohmer, Susan. "Who Framed Roger Rabbit: The Presence of the Past," in John Canemaker, ed. *Storytelling in Animation, Vol. 2: The Art of the Animated Image*. Los Angeles: American Film Institute, 1988.

Peary, Danny and Gerald Peary, eds. *The American Animated Cartoon: A Critical Perspective*. New York: Dutton, 1980.

Perisic, Zoran. *The Animation Stand*. New York: Hastings House, 1976.

_____. *The Focalguide to Shooting Animation*. London and New York: Focal Press, 1978.

Rider, David, ed. *The Great Movie Cartoon Parade*. New York: Bounty Books, 1976.

Rubin, Susan. *Animation: The Art and the Industry*. Englewood Cliffs, N.J.: Prentice-Hall, 1984.

Russett, Robert, and Cecile Starr, eds. *Experimental Animation: An Illustrated Anthology*. New York: Van Nostrand Reinhold, 1976.

Salt, Brian. *Movements in Animation*. Oxford and New York: Pergamon, 1976.

Schickel, Richard. *The Disney Version*. New York: Simon & Schuster, 1969.

Solomon, Charles. *The Complete Kodak Animation Book*. Rochester, N.Y.: Eastman Kodak Co., 1983.

Stephenson, Ralph. *The Animated Film*. New York: Barnes, 1973.

Whitaker, Harold and John Halas. *Timing for Animation*. New York: Focal Press, 1981.

Wilson, Steven S. *Puppets and People: Dimensional Animation Combined with Live Action in the Cinema*. San Diego: Barnes, 1980.

# INDEX